WOMEN AND THE JET AGE

WOMEN AND THE JET AGE

A GLOBAL HISTORY OF AVIATION AND FLIGHT ATTENDANTS

PHIL TIEMEYER

CORNELL UNIVERSITY PRESS
Ithaca and London

Copyright © 2025 by Phil Tiemeyer

All rights reserved. Except for brief quotations in a review, this book, or parts thereof, must not be reproduced in any form without permission in writing from the publisher. For information, address Cornell University Press, Sage House, 512 East State Street, Ithaca, New York 14850. Visit our website at cornellpress.cornell.edu.

First published 2025 by Cornell University Press

Library of Congress Cataloging-in-Publication Data

Names: Tiemeyer, Philip James, 1970- author.
Title: Women and the jet age : a global history of aviation and flight attendants / Phil Tiemeyer.
Description: Ithaca : Cornell University Press, 2025. | Includes bibliographical references and index.
Identifiers: LCCN 2024045100 (print) | LCCN 2024045101 (ebook) | ISBN 9781501781773 (hardcover) | ISBN 9781501781780 (paperback) | ISBN 9781501781803 (epub) | ISBN 9781501781797 (pdf)
Subjects: LCSH: Jugoslovenski aerotransport—Employees—History—20th century. | Air Jamaica—Employees—History—20th century. | Flight attendants—Yugoslavia—History—20th century. | Flight attendants—Jamaica—History—20th century.
Classification: LCC HD8039.A432 T54 2025 (print) | LCC HD8039.A432 (ebook) | DDC 387.7/4209497—dc23/eng/20250130
LC record available at https://lccn.loc.gov/2024045100
LC ebook record available at https://lccn.loc.gov/2024045101

Contents

Acknowledgments vii
List of Abbreviations xi

Introduction: The Confines of Cosmopolitanism … 1

Part I: Combating the West's Cartography of Colonialism

1. Clare Boothe Luce: The West's Postwar Cartography of Colonialism … 23

2. The Nonaligned Airline: JAT Airways and Yugoslavia's East-West-South Axis … 40

3. G. Arthur Brown: Air Jamaica's Precarious Founding … 68

Part II: Forging Cosmopolitan Working Women

4. Alix d'Unienville: The West's Strict Confines on Cosmopolitan Working Women … 95

5. Dragica Pavlović: JAT Stewardesses at the Crossroads of East, West, and South … 107

6. Marguerite LeWars Kirkpatrick: Making Jamaican Women Racially Eligible for Jet Age Labor … 129

PART III: EMBRACING AND COMBATING JET AGE FEMINISM

7. Mary Wells Lawrence: The Launch of America's Jet Age Feminism — 143

8. Love, Fashion, and the *Stjuardesa*: Yugoslavia's Jet Age Feminism — 166

9. "Rare Tropical Birds": Postcolonial and Neo-imperialist Legacies of Jet Age Feminism — 197

10. Jet Age Feminist Subversives: Firsthand Accounts from Air Jamaica and JAT Stewardesses — 223

Conclusion — 250

Notes 257
Bibliography 293
Index 303

Acknowledgments

Composing this book has been a labor of love. It traces an intellectual path through people and places that have captivated me. As an often-bored kid growing up in the American Midwest, I always wondered where airplanes flying over my backyard might take me. The wanderlust in me spurred my desire to journey far away, especially overseas. It still does. Thus, aviation for me, like for the various historical personalities I chronicle in this book, has always signaled freedom, adventure, and discovery. The kid in me has been overindulged while working on this book, especially by opening me up to faraway places that have brought me so much intellectual and personal satisfaction. I have plenty of people to thank for their companionship while writing this book, especially those in Kingston and in Belgrade.

At my home bases in Kansas and Washington, DC, I owe my gratitude to a scholarly community that has nurtured this book into existence. Kansas State University's History Department has provided me with a wonderful academic home. My colleagues have supported me and my work, and my students have kept me passionate about teaching and learning, laughing with me at key points along the way. This book owes its existence to the Smithsonian National Air and Space Museum (NASM) and its Verville Fellowship program, which supported me for a year as I struggled to get it off the ground. I am particularly grateful for the support and friendship of Dominick Pisano in this process. And I'm also grateful for the laughs and love that Collette Williams shared with me at NASM. Rest in peace, Collette.

My work in Kingston has been nurtured by both fellow scholars and by archivists who have made my research on Air Jamaica possible. I owe a special thanks to Kathleen Monteith, who took an interest in my book from the moment we met at the Association of Caribbean Historians conference long ago. She also opened doors to the Air Jamaica papers at the Jamaican Ministry of Finance and Public Service, where I owe Helen

Rumbolt and her team much gratitude for their assistance. I am also grateful for the help provided by archivists at the University of the West Indies and the Jamaica National Library.

I am deeply indebted to the Fulbright Fellowship Program, which sponsored my semester-long stay in Belgrade in 2018. Without this financial support, completing this book would have been impossible. The fellowship gave me a teaching home at the Faculty of Political Sciences, where Dragan Živojinović was a generous host, and the students in my weekly seminar taught me much about life in Serbia, and even a few things about aviation. The fellowship also opened doors to the Archives of Yugoslavia, Serbia's Diplomatic Archives, and the National Library of Serbia's holdings. I am grateful to the archivists at these places who facilitated my research, all the while tolerating my weak spoken Serbian with a smile, and never a laugh. At the US embassy in Belgrade, Vukica Stanković and Tanja Bakraclić not only supported my work but became friends as well. They also alerted me to the reality that many Belgrade families have links with JAT and aviation. Tanja even gets credit for setting me up with my first interview with a JAT flight attendant, her husband, whose words sparked the realization that a fascinating history lay ahead to discover, and that former flight attendants held the key to unlocking it.

A project this intellectually vast needs so much support to take shape. I am therefore exceptionally grateful to colleagues who helped me in crucial moments with poignant conversations and, quite often, by reading early drafts of this work. I am especially indebted to Vladimir Petrović for his critique of several early chapters, not to mention for his personal kindness—as landlord, as friend, as fellow fan of smoky Negronis. I also am thankful for provocative and laughter-filled conversations with Velimir and Sandra Isaković, both of whom share my affection for aviation and for Judith Butler. My conversations with ex-Yugoslavia's most knowledgeable aviation aficionado, Luka Popović, have also been wonderfully enriching and always fun. The other scholars and friends who so generously critiqued my work through the years include Jane Ferguson, Kelsey Gilbert, Michael Krysko, Eva-Maria Muschik, Anke Ortlepp, Ale Pålsson, and Kaori Takada. I'm also grateful to my late colleague at KSU and fellow Philadelphia Eagles fan, Al Hamscher, who reviewed an early draft of this document with a fine-toothed comb, as he's done for so many of our K-State history graduates through the decades. Thanks also to anonymous readers who offered exceptionally helpful feedback to my book editor, Sarah Grossman. Their work, and Sarah's, have made this book vastly better.

What nurtured me the most through this very long research and writing process have been the people at its heart: the former flight attendants who worked at Air Jamaica and JAT Airways. Their stories were personally captivating for me, and I hope the tidbits included in this book captivate others as well. These women and men exhibit how flight attendant skills never age: they remain charming, intelligent, witty, curious, humorous, and so much fun to talk with. And their love for flying is still as alive as during the glory days of JAT or Air Jamaica. It was a pleasure to meet them one-on-one, and it was an even bigger joy to share in their fellowship when they met as a group. As such I am particularly grateful to the JAT alumnae and alumni who welcomed me into their circle at Belgrade's Aeroklub. I always left these gatherings with a full heart and a head full of new ideas to add to this book. I also want to thank my friend Gavrilo Burković for helping with my conversations with flight attendants that took place in Serbian. He served as more than a top-notch translator, he's also a charming conversationalist who primed our interviews for success. Gavrilo is also personally responsible for my forever-to-remain fondness for the city of Belgrade and its nightlife. Hvala ti, Gašo! A huge thanks also to my friend Srđan Krivošić in Belgrade for helping with the very last work before this book launched: securing copyright permissions for the various photos that came from Serbian sources.

Last but not least, I have to mention Shaun, who had no idea what he was getting into when we first met. A man without a passport with an amazing life grounded in DC meets a man with a chronic case of wanderlust who finds the vastness of the United States too confining. And yet, from DC to Kansas to Belgrade and points beyond, Shaun continues to follow me with open eyes and open heart, leading me in new directions and loving me throughout. No lie, we've both also benefited from the best emotional support dog of all times. Sisi has learned to cope with jet lag and speak foreign languages as well as her dads, a gift that has made our travels together all the richer. Shaun, in my life that operates on a route network as large as any medium-sized airline's, you are my hub.

Abbreviations

AFŽ	Women's Anti-fascist Front (Antifašistička fronta žena)
BCS	Bosnian, Croatian, Serbian
BOAC	British Overseas Airways Corporation
BWIA	British West Indies Airways
CAB	United States' Civil Aeronautics Board
CDC	Colonial Development Corporation
ČSA	Czechoslovak State Airlines (Československa Statni Aerolinie)
ECJ	European Court of Justice
GUCVS	Main Authority for Civil Air Transport (Glavna uprava civilnog vazdušnog saobraćaja)
GUVS	Main Authority for Aviation Transport (Glavna uprava vazduhoplovstvog saobraćaja)
IATA	International Air Transport Association
ICAO	International Civil Aviation Organization
IDT	Industrial Disputes Tribunal
JAT	JAT Airways, also JAT Yugoslav Airways (Jugoslovenski Aerotransport)
JLP	Jamaica Labour Party
JTB	Jamaica Tourist Board
JUSTA	Yugoslav-Soviet Joint Stock Company for Civil Aviation (Jugoslovensko-sovjetsko akcionarsko društvo za civilno vazduhoplovstvo)
KLM	Royal Dutch Airlines (Koninklijke Luchtvaart Maatschappij voor Nederland en Koloniën)
LOT	Polish Airlines (Polskie Linie Lotnicze)
NAM	Non-Aligned Movement
NASM	Smithsonian National Air and Space Museum
NIEO	New International Economic Order
NOW	National Organization for Women

ABBREVIATIONS

PanAm Pan American Airways
PNP   People's National Party
SAS   Scandinavian Airlines System
SFWR   Stewardesses for Women's Rights
SIV   Federal Executive Council (Savezno izvršno veće)
TWA   Trans World Airlines
UDC   Urban Development Corporation

WOMEN AND THE JET AGE

Introduction
The Confines of Cosmopolitanism

In the heady days of early 1943, as Soviet troops drove Nazi forces from Stalingrad and a string of Allied victories in North Africa brought invasions of Italy and France closer, a decisive change of tone was evident in Washington, DC. While more than two years of agony lay ahead, some politicians began the more optimistic work of crafting a postwar world order. One of the freshest voices in such discussions came from the Republican congresswoman from Fairfield County, Connecticut, who was newly elected in November 1942. Despite running during a moment of resurgent masculinity due to the war, Clare Boothe Luce found a way to neutralize the supposed deficiencies of her gender, won a close election in her swing district, and proceeded to muscle her way into the Capitol's national security debates.

When she did so, she balanced hard-nosed, nationalist sentiments with a loftier idealistic globalism that, she hoped, would together shape the postwar international order. While nationalism and globalism are often perceived as contrasting impulses, Boothe Luce cast them as inseparable partners. For her, the postwar moment should be both more cosmopolitan—a better connected world with more opportunity for cooperation and prosperity—and simultaneously more

American-dominated, since, in her opinion, the United States alone could provide global security and foster economic prosperity. Thus, her cosmopolitanism, while far-reaching in its geographic aspirations, existed within distinct ideological confines.

She included such sentiments in her first speech from the podium of the House of Representatives, which addressed a central focus of her political career: the future of commercial air travel. In her view, the airplane and air travel would return to being promising heralds of cosmopolitanism after the war, and they would be newly primed for expansion due to impressive wartime innovations. There were going to be more airplanes flying more people to more places than ever before. However, she was also resolved that these developments should transpire under American tutelage. "Our [wartime] pilots returning from all the continents of the world will yearn to keep America out of another world war," she proclaimed, "and they know how: by keeping America on wings all over the world."[1]

These pilots were the product of one of aviation history's greatest accomplishments: the American military's establishment of aerial dominance over both its wartime rivals and allies. Putting "America on wings all over the world" was an impressive achievement that played out thanks to numerous technological innovations, an incessant commitment to aircraft production, and a massive expansion of air supply routes on every continent. As Boothe Luce looked ahead to the peace, she saw an inevitable path from military air superiority to postwar commercial predominance. Her thinking thereby embodies the same one-two punch of American global power that the historian Daniel Immerwahr chronicles in his work *How to Hide an Empire*. He begins exactly where Boothe Luce's speech does, with the many innovations that made the US military an imposing presence in every world region during World War II. Aviation's growth was just one of many advances forged by America's military-industrial juggernaut. These also included improved radio technology, the introduction of plastics and other synthetics, and the deployment of powerful new pesticides.

The connectivity begotten by radio and aviation were vital. With these improvements, as Immerwahr claims, "Dramatically, and in just a few years, the military built a world-spanning logistical network that was startling in how little it depended on colonies." Then, after the war, following the will of pro-business politicians like Boothe Luce, industrialists employed this "startling" infrastructure to expand their own footprint. Thus, this network "was also startling in how much it centered the world's trade, transport, and communication on one country, the United States."[2] As war gave way to peace in the few years after Boothe Luce's speech, the military's aviation successes fostered a postwar reality in which American companies were now the primary carriers of "America on wings all over the world." The result was what the historian Victoria DeGrazia calls an American "Market Empire," which she describes as "a great imperium with the outlook of a great emporium."[3] Boothe Luce's speech helped tilt the scales in Washington toward using postwar aviation to forge this global capitalist empire.

Yet, Boothe Luce's speech also matters for the globalist idealism that peppered her America-first rhetoric. Especially compelling was her rendering of America's youth, whose attitudes toward not only aviation, but also engagement with the world were different from that of older Americans. She assumed a motherly air and praised the virtue of America's next generation. She cited their fascination with model airplanes, their awe at how quickly assembly lines churned out new machines, and their avid tracking of new aerial supply routes. In these ways, young people were "talking the language of tomorrow, the language of the air" in a way older Americans could not.[4] Boothe Luce marveled that airplanes had instilled a novel yearning: "The post-war air policy of these hundreds of thousands of young air-minded Americans is quite simple. It is: 'We want to fly everywhere. Period.'"[5] Here, she could have added how young people growing up elsewhere were infected by this same cosmopolitan desire.

Instead, Boothe Luce merged the idealism of "fly everywhere, period," with aspirations of expanding American military and economic power. She applauded the notion that America's youth, unlike their isolationist forebears, would see the entire world as their rightful proving ground. And yet, as they moved beyond their national borders, these youth would first find preexisting outposts of America's "Market Empire" and then expand on them. Thus, the fruits of the freedom to fly everywhere would accrue mainly to Americans and, to a lesser extent, to their political and economic partners in the North Atlantic region. For Boothe Luce these were the acceptable class-based, racial, political, and economic confines of cosmopolitanism that should persist after the war.

Alternative Takeoffs for the Jet Age

One of the goals of this book, like all works in the field of global history, is to correct the Americentrism and Eurocentrism found in historians' accounts of global events.⁶ Thus, while including the American vision for postwar aviation forged by Clare Boothe Luce and likeminded others, I also look at perspectives from Yugoslavia and Jamaica when chronicling aviation's growth in the Cold War era and its impact on societies. By expanding the confines of the congresswoman's cosmopolitan-yet-still-Americentric vision, these examples also serve as a corrective to previous histories of aviation's postwar growth with their nearly exclusive focus on developments in the North Atlantic realm.⁷

Without necessarily sharing Boothe Luce's political and economic aspirations for postwar aviation, young men and young women in Europe's socialist East and in the Global South were also transfixed by the wonder of aviation. They too dreamt of using airplanes to traverse oceans in a matter of hours; to surmount borders, which were sadly more numerous and less penetrable during the Cold War; and to expand their limited exposure to other societies through travel. Thus, yearnings to "fly everywhere, period," permeated the Iron Curtain and spread beyond the North-South divide that splintered the Cold War cosmos into three supposedly distinct "worlds."⁸

In these less prosperous regions, aviation's spread stimulated more than just certain individuals' wanderlust. It also promoted two kinds of hope that serve as the dual focus of this book. First was a state-level aspiration: that aviation's spread could spur economic development, allowing these poorer, often newly independent states to compete more credibly against the United States' economic interests. Because of this, the American hegemony via aviation that Boothe Luce promoted and that Immerwahr chronicles would not go unchallenged. Second came personal aspirations that transpired on the social level once aviation was implanted in these regions and offered citizens of non-Western countries new opportunities to traverse the globe. Particularly important for this book are the ways aviation enabled women to undertake new forms of work and new types of travel. I examine these evolving women's roles—and the hopes and anxieties that came with them—via the stewardesses who worked for new national airlines founded in Europe's East and the Global South.

In 1943, the same year as Boothe Luce's inaugural speech in Congress, a young boy growing up in the hills of what was then Nazi-occupied Serbia was mesmerized by what he saw in the sky. Kosta Bojović, a child of mixed Serbian and Montenegrin heritage, was born in a small mountain village to an illiterate mother and a handyman father, and his life prospects initially seemed confined to herding sheep in the pastures surrounding his native home. The first chance he had to see airplanes was when Allied bombers flew overhead on their way to attack Nazi oil fields in Romania, part of Operation Tidal Wave, initiated in August 1943. Even though these planes were playing out the gruesome rivalries of Europe's great powers, young Kosta was starstruck. "I've always had a vast imagination," he told me in 2018. "I started thinking only about flying. It became something guiding me; I saw people's progress as bound to the sky, that it was there that a man could achieve bigger things."[9]

Bojović's childhood dream to escape into the skies eventually became reality. He benefited from the Communist Party's ambitious plans for modernizing the newly reassembled Yugoslavia, which included founding a new national airline, JAT Airways (Jugoslovenski Aerotransport), in 1947. After finishing his schooling, Bojović was able to become a pilot, first for the Yugoslav military and then for JAT. This upward vector of national and personal development allowed Bojović to move from his boyhood home in the rural south to Yugoslavia's more cosmopolitan capital city, Belgrade, where he raised a family of his own. There, he flourished in a thirty-year career that culminated in piloting JAT's DC-10 jumbo jets, connecting the far-flung locales of New York, Belgrade, Singapore, and Sydney. Captain Bojović stands as a testament to the fact that cosmopolitan yearnings for freedom via aviation knew no ideological divides. Thanks to the Yugoslav government's investment in its own airline, young men and women growing up there could aspire, like their peers in the West, to fly to distant places as pilots or flight attendants.

Similar yearnings took hold in the world's vast colonized yet soon-to-be independent regions in the Global South. However, the persistence of colonialism into the postwar era delayed the attainment of such dreams by another generation. Sharon Brandt was not even ten years old when Jamaica finally secured independence from its British overlords on August 6, 1962. She still was in high school when the first Jamaican pilots and stewardesses began flying for the new national carrier, Air Jamaica, in 1969. "Growing up, I always wanted to be a flight attendant—or an actress," recalled Brandt. Even though there was no Jamaican airline when she was a girl, she said, "I knew about flight attendants because British Overseas Airways [BOAC] was flying out of here. That was my dream, because I just thought it was fabulous, and I'm a people person, definitely a people person. So I thought that would be the right thing."[10]

Great Britain's flag carrier at the time, BOAC (since renamed British Airways) did not hire Jamaicans or other Caribbean colonial subjects to be pilots or flight attendants.[11] The other long-serving airline in Kingston was Pan American Airways (Pan Am), which, as an American carrier, also hired locals only for their ground operations. Thus, befitting Jamaica's history of colonial domination and racialized subjugation, the only opportunity open to women like Brandt—non-white and lacking British or US citizenship—was the Caribbean offshoot of BOAC, British West Indies Airways (BWIA). This small carrier based in Trinidad linked British-held Caribbean colonies with each other and to the nearest cosmopolitan metropoles of Miami and New York.

The fulfillment of Brandt's dream came only when the newly sovereign government of Jamaica established its own airline. When Air Jamaica hired its first stewardesses, Brandt's interest grew more intense. She applied for the position in 1972, soon after completing high school, as part of the carrier's fourth overall stewardess class. She thereby joined a very small and select group: these were, with few exceptions, the only Jamaican women granted careers flying on airplanes. Her training at the airline's flight attendant academy instilled in Brandt the patriotic dimensions of her work: "I remember Mrs. Marguerite Kirkpatrick, our trainer, always telling us that once you go out of here, you are an ambassador for your country, you're representing your country. So, that was instilled in me... that when I go out there, fingers will be pointing that, 'She is from Jamaica. She is an Air Jamaica flight attendant.'"[12]

Brandt realized for herself what had been an out-of-reach childhood fantasy as part of her new nation's postcolonial aspirations for equal footing on the world stage. The ability to fly—for the country, and for the woman herself—meant ascendance into the rarified air of full citizenship in the global community, replete with full admission into the heavily policed confines of cosmopolitanism, which had been closed to all previous generations of non-white, colonial-era Jamaicans. By the time she retired at the beginning of the twenty-first century, Brandt held Air Jamaica's coveted number one flight attendant position, marking her as the most senior stewardess—and possibly as Jamaica's most-traveled woman in history.

Brandt's chosen career of in-flight service quickly became female identified in the Cold War decades. For this study, it therefore matters more than the piloting career that Kosta Bojović chose, which remained a male-only domain for far longer. Indeed, stewardessing also matters for examining how women's roles were evolving more broadly. After all, while its limited educational demands placed it on the border between a working-class and middle-class profession, the work was coded as ultramodern and enticingly cosmopolitan. Stewardesses thereby were harbingers of a future womanhood that was more tech savvy and mobile. They were an avant garde of sorts for women back on the ground.

The Global Jet Age

While there was a lag of a decade or more between 1945 and its onset, the Jet Age was still a by-product of World War II. The first promising prototypes of jet planes debuted during the war, resulting from engine and rocket programs that both the Allied and Axis powers pursued in the hopes of gaining air superiority. Jet technology was barely used in the war itself, but soon thereafter both Soviet and American design teams crafted more effective jet fighters and bombers for the military. Commercial jets still lagged, however, especially since the first British commercial jet, the de Havilland Comet, which debuted in 1952, was mothballed until late 1958 when structural defects begot fatal accidents. Thus, the Jet Age started in earnest for the world's flying public only in the late 1950s. Vastly more powerful engines cut flying times in half and extended the range that planes could fly, while also supporting considerably larger cabins that at least doubled passenger capacity. Aviation's mass transportation age had begun.

For some, jet technology rekindled a sense of wonder that paralleled the excitement of aviation's earliest years a half century in the past, when the very sight of a machine flying in the air elicited awe. The most impressive feat, at least in the West, came with the debut of Pan Am's first Boeing 707 route between New York and Paris on October 26, 1958. Replicating Charles Lindbergh's famed 1927 nonstop solo flight, Pan Am's jet aircraft now traced Lindbergh's course with an impressive payload of 111 passengers and another 11 crew members, completing the flight in just 8 hours 41 minutes. Running almost at crosscurrents with the excitement of the pioneering Lindbergh moment, but exciting in its own way, the Jet Age promised a more democratic future. Thanks to their vast increase in seat capacity, Jet Age planes needed more customers, meaning more than just elites would be flying. Like Clare Boothe Luce's promise that America's youth could "fly everywhere, period," the Jet Age seemingly delivered on the highest ideal for modernization projects in the Cold War: that more of the world's peoples would benefit profoundly from the proliferation of new technologies.

The Jet Age was also more democratic, or at least more universal, in another way. These planes appeared at roughly the same time in all three Cold War worlds, despite Boothe Luce's interest in keeping aviation under American control. After the grounding of Britain's Comet in the early 1950s, the Soviet airline Aeroflot was the first to successfully introduce safer (though still accident-prone) jets in 1956, with the Tupolev-104. A year later, the USSR's most important collaborator in civil aviation among its satellite states, Czechoslovak Airlines (ČSA), took possession of its first Tu-104s. This earlier inauguration of the Jet Age east of the Iron Curtain marked a Soviet propaganda victory in the Cold War, resulting in a sense of euphoria that would be amplified when Yuri Gagarin orbited the earth in 1961. Just as the Soviets beat the Americans to the Space Age, they also pioneered the civilian Jet Age.

The Global South was not left out of the Jet Age for long. In 1960 a handful of airlines in Asia and Africa joined their peers in Europe's East and the North Atlantic states by securing jets, even though these countries did not produce such machinery domestically. Instead, they purchased aircraft from American, British, French, or Soviet manufacturers. Air India became Asia's first jet airline, introducing the Boeing 707 in early 1960. To keep pace, its rival Pakistan International Airways began leasing a 707 from Pan Am later in 1960. In Africa, the airline now known as Egyptair, then called United Arab Airlines, inaugurated a fleet of three Comet jets in July 1960, while in the sub-Saharan region, Ghana Airways began flying Boeing 707s in 1961. Meanwhile, in the Caribbean, BWIA, which was now Trinidad and Tobago's national airline, began flying Boeing 727 jets in 1964, while Cubana de Aviacion saw its jets delayed due to upheavals in the Cold War. The airline, privately held before Fidel Castro's revolution, became one of the first Latin American carriers to order jets from Boeing in 1958. However, the Castro government nationalized Cubana in 1959 and terminated this order. Instead, Cubana waited until the late 1960s to receive its first jets, Ilyushin-62s from the Soviet Union.

Yugoslavia and Jamaica, the focus of my case studies, were by no means leaders in the Jet Age, but each kept pace with this transition. JAT Airways purchased its first jets, Caravelles, from the French manufacturer Sud Aviation in 1963, while Air Jamaica purchased jets from the US-based Douglas Corporation for its 1969 debut as a self-sufficient airline. While these countries, both relatively poor and relatively small, were not the fastest to enter the Jet Age in terms of machinery, their people were indeed early adopters of Jet Age travel. The fervor of Yugoslav citizens for jet travel was perhaps unexpected, given the country's status as a communist-run dictatorship in Europe's East. It was in fact the only one of these societies whose citizens were free to travel without politically motivated limitations. Moreover, thanks to Josip Broz Tito's politics of nonalignment, which kept the country out of both the Eastern and Western blocs while also nurturing close ties to the Global South, the country's passport in the 1960s offered visa-free entry into the largest number of countries of any in the world.[13]

With only poverty holding back Yugoslav and Jamaican citizens, both countries saw significant domestic growth for air travel in the Jet Age. These states each possessed not only their own small elite class of frequent-flying jet-setters (celebrities, business managers, and politicians whose clout rivaled Western elites), but also a growing middle class who flew occasionally for work or leisure. Far more numerous was a group of less frequent fliers: the countries' working-class citizens. Their work and family lives had transpired in transoceanic settings for decades. Jamaicans were canal builders in Panama and migrants to Harlem and London, while members of Yugoslavia's constituent nations worked in the steel mills of Pennsylvania and the mines of Australia. Such migrations continued unabated during the Cold War, though now aided by jets that helped retain ties to the faraway homeland.[14]

This social adaption to the Jet Age meshed neatly with another development that allowed aviation to grow quickly in these regions: Europe's East and much of the Global South experienced strong economic growth in the 1950s and 1960s. Rosy predictions of continued growth led some smaller and poorer countries like Yugoslavia to expand their airlines even before the Jet Age took hold. Most impressively, JAT expanded to Paris, London, Cairo, and Beirut by 1954, at the dawn of the country's commitment to nonalignment. These new routes were more than political, however. They reflected Yugoslavia's economic progress, with its industrial goods and raw materials now finding growing export markets. By 1963, JAT had upgraded these routes to the West and South again, making them its first jet destinations.

Similarly, many still-colonized entities in the Global South, including Jamaica, benefited from rapid economic growth and increasingly earnest promises from their European colonizers to grant them independence throughout the 1950s. From the moment Jamaicans voted for independence as their own state (rather than part of a West Indies Federation) in 1961, plans for Air Jamaica quickly took shape.[15] This planning occurred in years of speedy development for the island's tourism sector and high growth rates for the overall economy. Once the airline finally launched, it was able to press Pan Am and BOAC for market share on crucial routes to New York and Miami, while also engaging in impressive expansion to other cities across North America and Europe.

Such promising political and economic developments enabled the Jet Age to become a bit less Western dominated, as the Yugoslavias and Jamaicas of the world exploited modest openings in America's and Western Europe's aerial hegemony. These airlines saw their most promising moments at the dawn of the Jet Age, in the 1960s and early 1970s. Unfortunately, the oil shocks of 1973-74, which plunged the world into recession and exacerbated the debt crisis for countries like Yugoslavia and Jamaica, caused these airlines to become less competitive. Consequently, this book mainly covers events up through the 1970s and focuses more on the growth years of the 1950s and 1960s. These decades offer intriguing, even if short-lived and incomplete, visions of what a more democratic Jet Age might have become, one that certainly was not part of Clare Boothe Luce's calculus in 1943.

Glocalizing Aviation and the Stewardess

Even in the years of greatest promise in Yugoslavia and Jamaica, power brokers in the West's metropoles like Clare Boothe Luce determined far more of the Jet Age's contours than actors like the Yugoslav or Jamaican governments, much less their common citizens like Kosta Bojović and Sharon Brandt. In conformity with Boothe Luce's nationalist-globalist vision, the fleets of jet aircraft assembled by airlines in the United States dwarfed those of the rest of the world put together. Additionally, on the world's most lucrative international routes, it was mainly other airlines from the North Atlantic region that competed with American carriers, though as rivals with far fewer advantages. Thus, even as the Jet Age democratized air travel, Western nations and their airlines predominated. These Western states, with America in the lead, also were the most prolific centers of aviation-related social innovations, including changes to stewardesses' roles through the years.

Much of this American predominance came about via standard-setting. As Immerwahr notes, the United States frequently exercised power in the Cold War era by establishing universal standards, including in aviation, where "air traffic controllers and pilots must speak the same language, plane parts must be similar enough that repairs can be made in any country, and the world's radio frequencies must be [synchronized]."[16] That US aviation officials succeeded in standardizing global aviation by 1950 shows how "the United States took advantage of its position—as the undisputed economic and political superpower, with its wartime logistical network installed in more than a hundred countries—to push its standards beyond its borders. . . . This was standardization on the scale of the planet."[17]

Confronted with this predominance, administrators in both Yugoslavia and Jamaica opted to integrate into this American aviation system. They adopted American tools and technologies, American-developed management practices, and American-derived safety protocols. Each airline also purchased only Western aircraft for the entirety of their existence—though JAT had one ill-fated exception in 1957, when it purchased Soviet aircraft that quickly had to be replaced.[18] In this way, these airlines were always seeking to "walk in step" with Western aviation, in the words of a prominent Yugoslav planner.[19] They wanted to rival Western competitors with both their hard product (the aircraft they flew) and their soft product (passengers' on-board experiences). A core component of the airlines' soft product was their stewardesses, whose grooming, comportment, and efficiency were often used by customers as criteria to judge the overall quality of the airline, and even the entire nation for which her airline flew. While domestic customers were vital, these airlines actively lured Western businesspeople who might invest in the local economy and Western tourists who would spend much-needed hard currency at each country's beaches. Stewardesses were thereby trained to present as cosmopolitan (read: Western) when at work.

Of course, this adherence to the American system did not beget total subservience to American aviation goals, nor to its gender roles. Instead, just as JAT and Air Jamaica forged unique route networks and wrested market share from their Western rivals, so too did their stewardesses diverge from the American mold. Always, however, these airlines and their stewardesses operated from within the American system. Thus, Yugoslav and Jamaican officials simultaneously attended to two foci in their aviation choices: the realties and needs of their home country and, at the same time, developments in aviation arising out of the United States and Western Europe. In his study of the origins of reggae music, the Jamaican sociologist Orlando Patterson offers helpful language for the process of syncing global with local needs and norms: glocalization. He stresses the creative power of glocalization: "Far from homogenizing the local musics of the world, the diffusion of musical traditions from one part of the world to others has generated a vast amount of musical creativity, in which indigenous traditions are hybridized with foreign elements to produce wholly new and exciting creations."[20] Patterson's consideration of reggae—which Jamaican artists created by fusing local musical styles with global influences, before reexporting their new synthesis back around the globe—allows him to speak of glocalization with optimism, as a process that renders "exciting creations" and empowers smaller societies like Jamaica to exert a creative impact on the larger world.

When shifting from the realm of music to that of aviation I do retain some of this enthusiasm about the potential for smaller and poorer regions to forge "exciting creations" via glocalization. I therefore comment positively on some of the unique innovations that both JAT and Air Jamaica introduced in the Jet Age. Nonetheless, I am also more sanguine about the outcomes of glocalized aviation. Building out aviation infrastructure in Yugoslavia and in Jamaica was an extremely expensive investment that drew resources away from other pressing priorities. Moreover, running an airline is, even in the best of conditions, a fickle enterprise. Even Western carriers possessing far more resources struggle to make a profit over a sustained number of years. Thus, when these states sought to forge greater political and economic sovereignty via their airlines, they ran a sizable risk. If new routes or new airplane investments were not reliably profitable, these investments became something far different from an "exciting creation." They led instead to further indebtedness that accrued on the state's balance sheets and thereby further limited the potential for future investment in other new and exciting creations.

Similarly, my second area of interest in Jet Age aviation—the impact of the flight attendant position on women's roles—is also not an unambiguously positive account of glocalization. I detail how societies in all three of the so-called "worlds" during the Cold War struggled to adapt to an exciting novelty: women now worked as flight attendants, which was wage-earning work in the modern space of airplanes that flew thousands of meters off the ground and took them thousands of kilometers from home, without a male chaperone. As such, stewardessing could have become an impressively liberating career for women all over the world. Instead, this liberatory potential was circumscribed everywhere with sexist strictures that kept these women nearly as subordinated as they were on the ground.

The United States' iteration of this heavily compromised version of women's liberation is something I call "Jet Age feminism." This pastiche rendition of empowerment defused the liberatory potential of this job by keeping these women subjected to low wages, almost no potential for advancement, and what feminist Betty Friedan called the "feminine mystique": an obsessive-compulsive regimen of grooming and style choices, since women acquired value only via their looks and their charming-but-passive demeanor.[21] The Jet Age ultimately gave these women a fashionable makeover to make them look and feel even more in sync with modern life. Yet, the age-old tradition of women's subordination remained.

As American stewardesses' Jet Age feminist ethos circulated around the globe in the late 1960s, stewardesses at JAT and Air Jamaica confronted it as well. Their negotiation of glocalization was also more somber than Patterson articulates. These stewardesses needed to be both creative and subtly assertive, so that their hybrid fashioning of new stewardess norms—their glocalizing—might respect their local cultural values and stand as even remotely pro-woman. Like stewardesses in the North Atlantic region, they only partially succeeded in making their Jet Age workplace more responsive to their aspirations for greater dignity. Moreover, most of these struggles to make Jet Age feminist expectations less damaging were waged outside the public sphere, in women's private lives.[22]

Ultimately, then, this book provides a more cautionary history of glocalization. Whether regarding the proliferation of non-Western airlines or the entrenchment of stewardesses aboard them, the Jet Age certainly saw a creative mixing of Western technologies and Western norms with local needs and norms. In both cases, these glocalized results were more inspiring and equitable at some times than at others, when they were woefully inadequate in helping smaller and poorer states—and their women—attain greater sovereignty. Even as these airlines and their flight attendants stood as beacons of modernity taking root in Yugoslav and Jamaican societies, they were compromised standard-bearers.

Not-So-Idiosyncratic Case Studies

Readers may find my decision to research aviation and stewardesses in Yugoslavia and Jamaica unusual. Both states have fascinating Cold War-era histories, but neither boasts much historiography, at least not by historians from the North Atlantic region. I nonetheless profile them for several reasons: while one is simple practicality, the others are intertwined with the preceding discussion of glocalization. Indeed, Yugoslavia and Jamaica both matter in similar ways to the global history of aviation because, firstly, they opted to conform to the American-constructed aviation system that Clare Boothe Luce advocated for in 1943. Despite the immense costs, both countries updated their airports, radio communications, and ground systems to American-established standards, and their airlines competed for customers based on Western expectations of aircraft quality, safety, and customer service.

Yet, secondly, both countries chafed against the neo-imperialist outcomes that this American-established global aviation system imposed. Both Yugoslav and Jamaican officials thereby resisted what I call the "cartography of colonialism" implicit in Boothe Luce's vision. Her market-imperialist views would have consigned both Yugoslavia and Jamaica to the status of minor players in Cold War–era aviation—as simple fly-over states, refueling points, or, at best, short-haul destinations for Western airlines linking them to the nearest economically important metropoles. Under this "cartography of colonialism" Western airlines were to be the active crafters of the world's aerial connectedness, with smaller and poorer states consigned to passive roles, awaiting their exploitation in whatever way these actors deemed expedient.

By embodying the tension of both conforming to the American system and resisting it, both Yugoslavia and Jamaica engaged in the process of glocalization. And herein lies a third point of importance for these case studies, as both states' aviation systems and their stewardess cultures thereby became "in-between" hybrids of Western and local norms and priorities. Neither Yugoslavia nor Jamaica are pristine representatives of their respective Cold War worlds. Rather than being an unadulterated prototype of Second World communism, Yugoslavia instead was an "in-between" hybrid of Western and Eastern Europe, politically and culturally, as well as in the aviation sphere.[23] And rather than being a pristine example of a Third World state, the Jamaican government styled itself as both proudly postcolonial—and therefore similar to other states of the Global South—and, almost always, as a reliable partner of the United States in the Cold War. Culturally, too, even as more Jamaicans embraced Pan-Africanism in the 1960s and 1970s, the population also felt persistent pulls to Britain and the United States. Thus, Jamaica also was a political, cultural, and aviational "in-between" hybrid, though here as a mix of the West and the Global South.[24]

"In-between" states from the Cold War era are important historical precedents for what came thereafter. Historical developments in the first couple of decades after 1990 resulted in the rise of a unipolar world—the era of globalization—in which states, companies, and cultural forces based in the United States and the West typically predominated in all areas: political, economic, and social. After 1990 there was no Soviet bloc (Second World) that could hope to cordon itself off from and rival the West. Likewise, by 1990, there were no Third World–inspired alternatives to Western predominance—no Non-Aligned Movement, no New International Economic Order—that might have allowed states in the Global South to inoculate themselves from Western hegemony. Thus, under globalization the entire non-Western world increasingly resembled the in-betweenness of Cold War–era Yugoslavia and Jamaica.

The final factor leading me to choose Yugoslavia and Jamaica is sheer practicality. It was essential that this book employ non-Western archives and oral histories as a counterbalance to the traditional overemphasis on the West in aviation history. Faced with this necessity, these two states became attractive candidates. I have lived in both places, and I have learned enough of the main language(s) of ex-Yugoslavia—Bosnian, Croatian, Serbian (BCS)—to know how to access and interpret materials from aviation archives there as efficiently as from the English-language holdings in Jamaica. I also knew that interviews with former JAT and Air Jamaica stewardesses would be possible, given the still-vibrant esprit de corps that exists among veteran flight attendants from these now-defunct airlines.

Although such sources were theoretically available, I still required significant help unlocking them. To this end, I am particularly grateful for the myriad archivists in Kingston, Belgrade, and points beyond who assisted me. I am especially indebted to the dozens of women in Kingston and Belgrade who sat with me to share their fascinating accounts of stewardessing in the Jet Age. Without their generosity, this global history of aviation and feminism would have gone unwritten. I should also note that, in exchange for their candor on sensitive issues, I promised each of them anonymity. Thus, although their charm and candor come across in this book, their names remain hidden behind nondescript titles like "Anonymous A." Their contributions were important: these women deserve to be named. My hope is that having this chronicle of their accomplishments and struggles recorded for posterity's sake is an acceptable tribute.

Flight Plan

Even while chronicling a brisk global exchange between West, East, and South regarding the political, economic, and social developments tied to aviation, this book follows a rather predictable structure. There are three parts, each of which are organized into three chapters that consistently follow the same geographic rotation. The first chronicles a seminal moment from Western aviation that established a new precedent with tremendous global appeal. The second covers developments in Yugoslavia, while the third covers Jamaican realities.

Part I continues the discussion that this introduction began by concentrating on the political and economic issues tied to aviation. Special emphasis is placed on the rival visions for postwar aviation that arose from the United States and from Yugoslavia and Jamaica. Chapter 1 returns to Clare Boothe Luce, examining in further detail how Western architects of postwar aviation sought to keep aerial resources in the West's hands by resuscitating its prewar predominance in global aviation. It also continues to stress Boothe Luce's gender comportment, found both in her political and personal biographies, as a cosmopolitan novelty arising out of the United States.

Chapter 2 turns to the founding and expansion of JAT Airways in socialist Yugoslavia. JAT found a unique and productive niche within the global aviation system by building routes based on Yugoslavia's commitment to nonalignment, which entailed cordial relations (both political and economic) with Eastern and Western Europe and especially close ties with certain countries in the Global South. JAT thereby differed from its Western competitors in its polydirectionalism. Its route expansion followed Tito's diplomatic work and Yugoslavia's growing trade flows from its hub in Belgrade to points in all three Cold War worlds.

Chapter 3 turns to Air Jamaica, chronicling the work of its founder and longtime chairman, Sir G. Arthur Brown. Brown created an intriguing financial model for this postcolonial airline that would have insulated it from significant economic risk if his plan had not been foiled by American aviation authorities. When finally allowed to fly, Air Jamaica, like its American and British rivals, was dependent on Western customers, especially North American vacationers. However, unlike in the preindependence landscape, Air Jamaica competed effectively against Pan Am and BOAC in the early 1970s on existing routes, while also pressing to open new routes and run fuller schedules than its competitors. These moves converted Jamaica from an afterthought, a way station on Western airlines' long-range routes into South America or Mexico, into an aviation hub of its own—a model of what the cartography of postcolonialism could look like.

Parts II and III turn to women's issues and how they were reflected in stewardesses' experiences from the 1950s to the 1970s. Both parts trace the glocalization occurring among stewardesses, particularly emphasizing Yugoslav and Jamaican women who balanced American or Western European stewardess standards with local norms and aspirations. Part II examines stewardesses in the pre-jet era from 1945 to the early 1960s. These women were the first generation of women to take this job, at least outside the United States. Even though the job was indeed cosmopolitan (permitting travel far and wide while interacting with the world's elites) and it involved its share of arduous work, its designation as women's work enabled supervisors to treat these employees in profoundly discriminatory ways. There were, however, differing aspects of this gender-based discrimination depending on where women were located, and part II reflects this, making it the most diverse, and perhaps the least cohesive, section of the book.

Chapter 4 introduces the most famous woman among Air France's first stewardess class of 1946, Alix d'Unienville. When she composed a best-selling memoir of her work in 1949, d'Unienville drew even more young women across Western Europe into this new profession. Meanwhile, left unstated in her book, *En vol: Journal d'une hôtesse d'aire*, was how stewardesses at Air France and across the Western world endured extreme discrimination. Their employers prohibited stewardesses from marrying or getting pregnant, enforced rigorous weight limits, and often fired women in their mid-thirties. D'Unienville herself grew disillusioned and bored by her work, so she resigned after a few years, even as her book continued to draw Western European women into the job.

Chapter 5 covers Yugoslavia's first flight attendant, Dragica Pavlović, and her colleagues in JAT's first generation of stewardesses. Working women in socialist Yugoslavia enjoyed greater legal protections than in the West, meaning JAT's stewardesses were free from most of the harsh restrictions that d'Unienville encountered. Nonetheless, Pavlović's generation still faced rampant sexism. Most troublingly, they endured a growing emphasis on elevating their physical appearance and maintaining a demeanor of servile docility through the 1950s, as JAT began to attract Western European customers for their flights between London, Paris, and the Middle East. Pavlović herself publicly likened her work to that of a housewife, even though she experienced far more personal freedom than domestic caregivers. Stewardesses in Yugoslavia saw their employer increasingly prioritize their beauty and servility, while providing few promotion opportunities—typical features of "women's work" in the West as well.

Chapter 6 has the peculiar task of chronicling Jamaican stewardesses in the pre-jet age, when neither Air Jamaica nor Jamaican stewardesses existed. Instead, it covers the island's popular beauty pageant culture, which served as an important precedent for Air Jamaica's stewardesses corps. A key figure linking these two entities was Marguerite LeWars Kirkpatrick, who in her youth won the title of Miss Jamaica 1961 and then proceeded to become Air Jamaica's first director of stewardesses in 1969. In this role, she educated her trainees—the first cohort of Air Jamaica flight attendants—in the same techniques of dress, cosmetic application, bodily comportment, and behavioral charm that she learned from the pageants. Importantly, in LeWars' pageant-competing years of the late 1950s and early 1960s, beauty queens, like so many Jamaican women, chafed against society's harsh racial barriers. In the earliest postwar years, non-white African-descended women were rarely seen as beautiful, especially by society's elites. Thus, only with the expansion of racial equality in these decades did notions of beauty begin to broaden, first to include women with light brown skin like LeWars, then later those with darker brown complexions. As such, racial prejudice was another confine of cosmopolitanism confronting prospective Jamaican stewardesses before the Jet Age. Ironically, these non-white women had to wait for anti-racist progress before they could become stewardesses, though their job's conflation of workplace roles with beauty pageant roles—which women like Marguerite LeWars Kirkpatrick helped to instill—exposed them to a variety of sexism that was no less harsh.

Part III examines stewardesses in the Jet Age, especially starting in 1965, when the United States' Braniff Airways became the first airline in the world to reconceptualize the image of stewardesses. This transition embodied the ethos of "Jet Age feminism," which arose when profound changes to women's social roles were in the air. Both feminism and the sexual revolution were at this time prominent issues, not only in the West, but also in Yugoslavia and Jamaica. Thus, the ways that Braniff, JAT, and Air Jamaica molded their stewardesses for the Jet Age offers a complex mixture of women's liberation and regression, including updated ways to trap these women in the beauty-based rigors of the "feminine mystique." Even as each society was on the cusp of

THE CONFINES OF COSMOPOLITANISM   19

feminist progress, stewardesses in the Jet Age were more eroticized, with hemlines hiking upward, dresses hugging more tightly, and stewardess-based advertising becoming bawdier.

Chapter 7 focuses on the mastermind behind Braniff Airways' embrace of Jet Age feminism, the Madison Avenue advertising executive Mary Wells Lawrence. I trace how she borrowed heavily from other social voices who were promoting an ethos for modern, supposedly liberated women that encouraged them to work and assert greater autonomy over their sexual choices, while also pressing them to dress and groom themselves in sexualized ways. *Cosmopolitan* magazine's Helen Gurley Brown was a leading proponent of this ethos through her best-selling 1962 book *Sex and the Single Girl*. Even the fashion designer who Wells Lawrence chose to design Braniff's new stewardess uniforms, the Florentine designer to the stars Emilio Pucci, was an advocate for keeping women exceptionally stylish, and unequal, as they negotiated their newfound freedom to move around urban landscapes as aspiring jet-setters.

Chapter 8 examines developments among JAT stewardesses as the Jet Age also coincided with the sexual revolution in Yugoslavia. While these women were not as eroticized as their peers at Braniff or Air Jamaica, their roles in popular culture as sex objects grew, the sexual suggestiveness of JAT ads featuring stewardesses increased, and their fashion makeover from a top Yugoslav designer, Aleksandar Joksimović, made them increasingly bold style icons. Joksimović's work was as modern and trendsetting as Pucci's creations for Braniff, though less colorful. In these ways, Jet Age feminism came to JAT, albeit in more muted tones.

Chapter 9 turns to Air Jamaica's first stewardesses from 1969, a group whose employers completely bought into Braniff's sexualized aesthetic. These women debuted to the world wearing exceptionally tight and high-cut minis in bold tropical colors, with Air Jamaica's advertisers lustily christening them "rare tropical birds." To complete the orgiastic fantasy for the local Jamaicans and, especially, the North American tourists aboard, the airline served a boozy cocktail named the "rum bamboozle." It also instituted fashion shows that involved stewardesses changing clothes in flight to complete all phases of a beauty pageant, right down to the swimwear. The danger these stewardesses faced was acute, as passengers and coworkers frequently objectified them to the point of sexual harassment and abuse.

Chapter 10, the fourth chapter on Jet Age stewardesses, blends interview materials from former JAT and Air Jamaica employees. It focuses primarily on their efforts, usually through private subversive acts, to resist the most demeaning threats of Jet Age feminism. It also offers the closest side-by-side analysis of these two non-Western case studies. When viewing JAT and Air Jamaica stewardesses together—despite the vast geographical, cultural, and racial differences between them—the overall perception is that their commonalities, especially their struggles against the increasingly bald sexism of the Jet Age, were much more numerous than their differences.

The main actors in this aviation history are more than white men from the North Atlantic region and more than airline CEOs, engineers, or pilot-heroes—the most common subjects of traditional aviation histories. Here, the actors that matter most are American women in politics like Clare Boothe Luce; socialist aviation planners in Belgrade; non-white Jamaican aviation planners like G. Arthur Brown; the first generation of stewardesses in France, Yugoslavia, and Jamaica; American women creating iterations of Jet Age feminism on Madison Avenue; socialist-era Yugoslav fashion designers; and Jamaican beauty pageant queens. Such actors matter because aviation's history during the Cold War is about more than planes, companies, and route networks. It is ultimately about whether postwar aviation and its cultural heritage would "[keep] America on wings all over the world" or whether an aviation industry—and an aviation-supported culture of feminism—that was more cosmopolitan and more diverse would find a way to flourish.

PART I

Combating the West's Cartography of Colonialism

CHAPTER 1

Clare Boothe Luce

The West's Postwar Cartography of Colonialism

The historian Jenifer Van Vleck describes Clare Boothe Luce's 1943 speech as the "quintessential expression of air-age nationalism," one that heavily influenced American aviation policy thereafter.[1] Of course, it was immaterial to the value of her ideas that Boothe Luce was a woman. After all, her views were echoed by plenty of men—on Capitol Hill, among airline executives, at the Pentagon, and ultimately in the Roosevelt White House—establishing that there was nothing uniquely feminine about them. But the fact that Clare Boothe Luce had such an impact on the future of aviation as a woman does indeed matter.

After all, aviation and feminism were contemporaneous travel companions, if you will, in the twentieth century. When what we now call the first wave of feminism crested in the United States with suffragists winning the right to vote in 1920, aviation was in its infancy. This was the decade that the world's first airlines began to fly, including America's most storied carrier, Pan Am, in 1927. Then came another moment of synchronicity in World War II, when women entered the labor market en masse as the country's factories were producing the aviational juggernaut that Boothe Luce celebrated in her 1943 speech. Indeed, women worked these very assembly lines, providing the labor that undergirded America's aerial predominance. Two decades later, the onset of the Jet Age coincided with a new wave of feminism in the United States and around the world.

The yearning Boothe Luce articulated in her 1943 speech—the freedom to "fly everywhere, period"—is also an impulse at the core of feminism: the freedom as a woman to be anything and do anything. Period. Both of these boundary-transgressing impulses are built on a deeper yearning for personal enrichment that comes from being allowed to sample a diversity of experiences and positionalities. Indeed, Boothe Luce penned her first articulation of the freedom to fly everywhere not for the US Congress in 1943, but rather for a feminist character in a wildly successful Broadway play that she wrote in 1936. Thus, for Boothe Luce, the freedom to fly was something primordially connected with women's liberation. This chapter thus focuses both on Clare Boothe Luce's feminism (an admittedly conservative version thereof) and on the aviation policy she helped bring to life starting in 1943 (also admittedly quite conservative): the resuscitation of the prewar cartography of colonialism and its retrofitting for novel postwar realities.

A New Kind of Woman in Politics

Clare Boothe Luce did not become famous through politics; rather, it was thanks in part to her preexisting fame that she won her seat in Congress in 1942. As a ten-year-old, she performed as a child actor on Broadway, thereby stimulating a passion that later became her first chosen career. Then, around 1919, in her late adolescence, another pathway opened. Her first political job was with the National Women's Party working for the final passage of women's suffrage. These mutual passions only began to merge in 1936, when Boothe Luce was at the peak of her first career as a Broadway playwright. Her play *The Women* debuted that year, offering audiences what seemed to be a light-hearted comedy in which a female cast shared their various infatuations with men. It became a massive hit, garnering her a handsome sum of $200,000. The play boasted not only a successful Broadway run, but also a second life as Hollywood's second-highest grossing film in 1939.

Yet, part of the story's power was its ability to deliver subtly political feminist sentiments, even if they were always delivered with light-hearted wit. This included Boothe Luce's first articulation of the freedom to fly everywhere, though here with a more discernably feminist bent. At one point, the character Mary, played by Oscar-winning actress Norma Shearer in the film, pointedly quips, "These days, darling, ladies do all the things men do." Then, in detailing examples, she provides a virtual resume of Boothe Luce's life: "They fly aeroplanes across the ocean, they go into politics and business." Herein lay the first merging of Boothe Luce's various life commitments: to Broadway and politics, and to feminism and aviation. The freedom to fly everywhere in this iteration was part of a deeper aspiration for "ladies [to] do all the things men do."[2]

While her aspiration may have been to equal men, Boothe Luce's realist reflexes expressed themselves as she built a path from Broadway to politics. Indeed, she relied on a traditional patriarchal tool, marriage, to forge such opportunities for herself. Her 1929 divorce from her first millionaire husband provided her the seed money to move to Manhattan and set herself up as a career woman, where she served as managing editor at *Vanity Fair* magazine before making it big as a playwright. Her second marriage was even more lucrative and moved her even closer to politics. A mutual friend, Juan Trippe, the chairman of Pan Am, played matchmaker in 1935, when he introduced her to New York's wealthiest and most eligible bachelor, Henry Luce. As the owner of two of America's largest magazines, *Time* and *Life*, as well as other media holdings, Luce was exceptionally well connected in both political and economic circles. The two married just months later. They thereby became one of the United States' first power couples, a husband and wife duo, both independently successful, who set aside family commitments in favor of mutually benefiting each other's careers.

As World War II approached American shores, the Luces opted to turn their mutual gaze to politics. Henry delivered an even more famous political treatise than Clare's 1943 speech on postwar aviation, at an equally momentous political moment. His famous open letter to the American people from early 1941—months before Pearl Harbor—pressed for the United States to enter the war on the Allied side and thereby to promote American values and ensure a century of American-led prosperity and peace. As Henry Luce urged then, "we can make isolationism as dead an issue as slavery, and we can make a truly American internationalism something as natural to us in our time as the airplane or the radio."[3] This was the opening foray in Clare's political career as well, with the two thereafter strategizing on how she should effectively campaign for Congress to promote the views they held in common. His "American century" essay was effectively the opening statement in her electoral campaign; her February 1943 speech, which echoed her husband's call for an American internationalism and fleshed out his enthusiasm for the airplane, was its culmination.

In between came the hotly contested 1942 election campaign, the first since Pearl Harbor forced the United States into the war. This was a time of acute crisis for the nation. It was also, however, a time of crisis for feminist politicians, and Clare Boothe Luce resolved to forge an entirely new model for women in politics, even though she shared the same Republican Party affiliation as the woman who set the original mold as the nation's first Congresswoman back in 1916. She even shared a similar class standing as the famous Jeannette Rankin of Montana: both were economically privileged, though Rankin was part of a prosperous ranching family out West, while Boothe Luce married into wealth in the Northeast.

The main realm in which Clare Boothe Luce resolved to rewrite Rankin's script for women politicians was national security. She strongly disagreed with Rankin's pacifist views, which Rankin had fastidiously maintained since her vote in 1917 against America's involvement World War I. Rankin based that decision on the idea that women by nature were inclined toward nonviolence, claiming, "I felt the first time the first woman had a chance to say no to war, she should say it."[4] Her vote garnered fervent allies in the women's movement, of which both Rankin and Boothe Luce were committed members. Many such activists concurred with Rankin's adherence to the philosophy of separate spheres, which held that women should use their public and political roles to promote the traditionally feminine tasks of caring for the needy, looking after the upbringing of children, and maintaining the peace. Men, in this worldview, would continue to wield society's tools of national security and state-sanctioned violence.[5] Rather than embrace the notion of separate spheres, Boothe Luce promoted an alternative feminist vision, one cheekily summarized in her blockbuster play: "These days, darling, ladies do all the things men do."

The national mood had changed drastically between Rankin's vote in 1917 and her second war vote on December 8, 1941, the day after the Japanese attacked Pearl Harbor. This vote was calamitous for her political career, as she was the lone member of Congress to abstain from declaring war on Japan. The public threats of violence against Rankin and characterizations of her in the press as traitorous and naïve convinced her to never again stand for election. Yet, these same attacks only emboldened Clare Boothe Luce, a generation younger than her predecessor, to insist on forging a more hard-knuckled vision of women's power on Capitol Hill. Boothe Luce wanted to win the open Congressional seat in Fairfield County, Connecticut, to break the male monopoly on making war and peace, and to acquire a seat for herself at the tables of power where military, economic, and technological policies were being crafted.

To counteract the public's association of women with pacifism, Boothe Luce and her husband developed a strategy to bolster her national security credentials before the election. In early 1942 they flew aboard a Pan Am Clipper plane that had been requisitioned by the US military across the Caribbean to South America before crossing the Atlantic to the Allied front lines in North Africa. From there they flew along the front lines of the Middle East and Asia, ultimately crossing the Himalayas into Allied China. Henry hired his wife to write dispatches from the front—interviews with generals, updates of troop deployments, profiles of the various politicians keeping the Allied effort together—which were then published in *Life* magazine. Her national security bona fides were thereby impressively polished, allowing Boothe Luce, in extreme contrast to Rankin, to come to Congress as a hawk. She promised to be an aggressive voice against the New Deal at home and fully engaged on national security issues abroad. She even used her and her husband's extensive connections to secure a position on the House Committee on Military Affairs, becoming the first woman to serve in any sort of national security policymaking position in Congress.[6]

Boothe Luce's Embrace of the Cartography of Colonialism

For her first speech in Congress, it is not surprising that Boothe Luce selected a tone that established her differences with previous congresswomen and her ability to equal or surpass her male peers in both articulating national security concerns and pressing aggressive ad hominem political attacks. Her expertise with managing media also primed her well to draw headlines in hundreds of the following day's newspapers. While the title of her address was cerebral, "America in the Post-War Air World," her Broadway-honed rhetorical style enraptured the assembled crowd. This included a fellow anti–New Dealer, the Southern Democrat Edward Cox of Georgia, who followed her to the House podium and gleefully remarked, "I desire to make the observation that the very brilliant and statesmanlike address just delivered by the gentlewoman from

Connecticut has been well worth the day that many in the gallery and on the floor have spent waiting to hear it."[7]

In terms of content, Boothe Luce conveyed an awareness that the eventual conclusion of World War II would result in a massive expansion of civil aviation, one which, in her assessment, must be harnessed to an American internationalist economic and foreign policy. She began by articulating her topic's importance for the future of the United States: "This I know[:] that the airplane has been the most dynamic instrument of this war and that the airplane will surely be the most dynamic instrument of the peace." She then shifted to the Roosevelt administration's postwar planning, already revving up in early 1943, and her concern that New Dealers were steering postwar civil aviation strategy in a direction in which "America can lose the peace."[8] For her, American predominance in postwar aviation was not only good for the United States, but it was also the surest guarantor of worldwide peace: "Make no mistake; I believe that we should maintain our position of international civil air supremacy for the greatest and best of all reasons: Our responsibility to the whole world and to ourselves, to assume democratic political leadership in this hemisphere and cooperate elsewhere with the United Nations in leadership, requires and demands a commensurate civilian air position."[9] With this as a preamble, she then proceeded to advocate for "keeping America on wings all over the world."

The real reason for Clare Boothe Luce's high-profile intervention was to thwart a rival postwar vision for aviation that risked undermining the Market Empire–supporting aviation system that she favored and jeopardizing American airlines' global predominance. She and the corporate interests that had her ear were particularly worried about ideas voiced by Roosevelt's then–vice president, Henry Wallace. The more progressive and more globalist Wallace had raised the possibility of opening all the world's skies and airports to any nation's airlines, matching the shipping world's freedom of the seas, which allowed ships from any country to use any port.[10]

Thus, after opening her speech by praising aviation's ability to counter American isolationism and voicing her embrace of the youthful freedom to fly everywhere, Boothe Luce then shifted gears from idealistic to acerbic and called out the vice president by name. Wallace and others in the Roosevelt administration, whom she labeled as "all-out post-war cooperationists," were seeking to forge a postwar order for aviation that overlooked the vast differences between the United States, Britain, and the USSR: "In a noble effort to formulate some master plan and some master economy which will cozily embrace not only our own capitalistic democracy but the British Empire and its colonial system, and Russia and its totalitarian system, the all-out post-war cooperationists have begun to shoot the works, at least verbally, for a bigger and redder and more royal New Deal for the whole world."[11] In her most memorable rhetorical flourish, Boothe Luce added: "But much of what Mr. Wallace calls his global thinking is, no matter how you slice it, still 'globaloney.'"[12] Her phrasing elicited raucous laughter in the House chamber and became rich fodder for newspaper headlines around the country the next day, most of which belittled Wallace's views and lionized Boothe Luce's muscular appeal to American strength.

To rally broad-based support for her more nationalist and protectionist vision of aviation, Boothe Luce also stressed how Wallace's views would effectively surrender American sovereignty over its own airspace. At one point she turned to an unnamed colleague from Kansas and evoked a menacing prospect under Roosevelt and Wallace. She described a future airport in Wichita, or perhaps greater Kansas City, dominated by foreign aircraft:

> And yet, . . . shall I stand on a plain in the heart of the gentleman from Kansas' fair land, in the year 1949, and see at the great central terminus that may be there the air liner Queen Elizabeth put in, the Stalin Iron Cruiser, the Wilhelmina Flying Dutchman, the Flying de Gaulle, the airships of all the nations on earth—perhaps even those of the German and Jap. But shall I scan, like Sister Anne, the skies in vain, searching for the shape of an American Clipper against the clouds?[13]

Deploying a casual racism that undercut her own larger commitments to globalism, Boothe Luce reassured the nation's instinctive isolationists that her brand of American internationalism would safeguard national security, while also validating jingoistic notions of national supremacy. She then concluded her speech by paraphrasing Winston Churchill and his prioritizing of national self-interest: "We, gentlemen, were not elected by our constituents, on either side of this aisle, to preside over the liquidization of America's best interests, either at home or abroad."[14] For Boothe Luce, it was clear that "America's best interests" were not found in Wallace's views. Instead, America's crafting of postwar aviation must "only be determined from the standpoint of what the American people believe is their real, their practical, self-interest" and not "based upon emotional altruism nor sentimental aspiration."[15]

For Boothe Luce, the choice was clear: postwar aviation should primarily transpire on American aircraft, with American pilots, and with ticket revenue going to American airlines. She framed this vision while looking forward to the novel security exigencies that would predominate after the war. Nonetheless, this forward-looking stance justified her advocacy for turning global aviation backward to the status quo ante of the 1930s. Then, too, most air traffic utilized American aircraft, with almost all the rest on Western European carriers. The United States' advantage before the war was indeed substantial, as she makes clear: "For the record, let us note that in October 1941 our American system's Pan American Airways route-miles were roughly two and one-half times greater than B.O.A.C.—British Overseas Airways Corporation. We had 99,000 miles of route as against the British system's 39,000.... In early 1939, before the outbreak of the war, Pan American was flying more air miles than all the major European countries put together."[16] If Boothe Luce's views were to prevail, which they ultimately did, this same cartography of colonialism would return and expand after World War II.

There was, however, one major difference from America's prewar dominance under the cartography of colonialism and its postwar dominance under a similar, resuscitated cartography. Before the war, air routes established by the West's great legacy airlines were very much embedded in the reality of imperialism. Through the 1930s they replicated earlier shipping routes and had the same purpose: to link far-flung colonies to their imperial metropoles. After the war, as Immerwahr's work establishes, the Clare Boothe Luces of the United States had no desire to retain an empire in the traditional sense. Instead, they aspired to forge what he calls a "pointillist empire"—a network of control that built out important nodes from colonialism's transportation infrastructure, while simultaneously ceding political and military control of the hinterlands to local authorities.

The postwar pointillist empire enabled the United States to become the first Western power to both decolonize, when it gave up the Philippines in 1946, and simultaneously to grow in global clout thanks to its increasing control over important points in the global trade system. These points that the United States nurtured around the globe were always cities containing ports and/or airports, from which American political representatives, companies, and banks could administer American expansion more widely. While some were bolstered with an American military presence (Honolulu, Panama, Manila, Seoul), others were exclusively economic "emporia," as Victoria DeGrazia calls them.

Cities like Hong Kong, Singapore, and Beirut (except during brief military occupations in the 1950s and 1980s) fit this economic model.[17]

In short order, America's leading airlines bolstered their fleets and expanded their route networks to serve as the sinews holding together these various points of influence. Of course, there was competition from Europe's imperial states to provide this connectivity. After the damaging experience of war, these countries were much more invested than the United States in restoring their imperial grandeur. In their efforts to reassert control over their Asian colonies after Japanese occupation, they quickly restored their airlines' prewar routes to Hong Kong (served by Britain's BOAC, the successor to its original—and aptly named—flag carrier, Imperial Airways), Hanoi (Air France), and Batavia/Jakarta (KLM [Koninklijke Luchtvaart Maatschappij voor Nederland en Koloniën]). Yet, despite the competitive advantage Europe's airlines enjoyed due to prewar know-how on these routes, they were quickly overtaken by Pan Am and newcomer Trans World Airlines (TWA).

Thanks to the massive wartime enlargement of America's aerial resources, both these airlines expanded across the Atlantic, through the Mediterranean, and onward to Asia. Pan Am's footprint was the biggest, as it became the first airline to initiate a round-the-world route in 1947. The route began with a New York–London flight, then puddle jumped through Western Europe before making it to Istanbul and the Middle East. At this stage, Pan Am's route mimicked those of the Western European airlines noted above, following BOAC's route to Hong Kong most closely. Beyond Hong Kong, Pan Am's planes continued along the transpacific route first forged in 1936, ending in San Francisco.

In the aftermath of her well-received speech, Clare Boothe Luce's vision of a confined cosmopolitanism—of a globalism built upon the freedom to fly everywhere, but always forging an American sphere of influence—became orthodoxy in Washington. It particularly shaped the United States' maneuverings at the International Civil Aviation Conference that took place in Chicago in 1944, resulting in an agreement for international air travel still in effect today that locked in American airlines' preexisting advantages from before and during the war.[18]

American Internationalism Takes Flight

Boothe Luce's speech in February 1943, replete with its warm reception from the press and a broad anti–New Deal coalition of Republicans and conservative Democrats, galvanized opposition to Wallace's views on aviation. For a variety of reasons not pertaining directly to aviation policy, President Roosevelt marginalized his vice president after February 1943, to the point that Wallace was dropped from the ticket in 1944 and replaced by the more conservative Harry Truman. Meanwhile, the administration's point people for aviation endured similar turnover. Most importantly, Adolf Berle, a longtime trusted adviser to Roosevelt, was placed in charge of civil aviation matters in 1944, and he hewed closely to Boothe Luce's American internationalist views.

Berle's new responsibilities for US civil aviation policy placed him in command of the US diplomats who assembled representatives from fifty-four nations in Chicago in November 1944 for the International Civil Aviation Conference, which set the ground rules for the global postwar aviation industry. By this time, Berle and other key members of the Roosevelt administration were strongly committed to reviving the prewar International Civil Aviation Organization (ICAO) along lines that were favorable to US carriers. Most importantly, any notions of freedom of the skies were sidelined at the Chicago Conference.

Rather than cooperative models that would have managed global aviation either as an internationally regulated public utility or, analogous to seafaring, as a democratized competitive market with all the world's airlines flying wherever they chose, the prewar system was restored. As the historian Alan Dobson chronicles, the Chicago conference reestablished the prewar principle that the sky over a nation's land was proprietary territory of that nation. As a result, protectionism predominated in all domestic aviation markets: these routes were left to national governments to distribute as they saw fit, meaning that they almost always remained the exclusive purview of a state's own airline(s). Importantly, the largest domestic aviation market in the world, the United States, thereby remained exclusively in American hands. On international routes, like before World War II, there would also be no freedom of the skies. These routes would be established in state-to-state bilateral treaties, with further permissions required from states over whose territory aircraft flew. Once established by such treaties, these routes were also the proprietary possession of each state, not an international system.

A system of bilateral treaties suited the United States government and its airlines, since these two entities worked together to exercise their sizable advantages over the states they negotiated with. In its prewar dealings with Latin American and Asian governments, the tandem of State Department diplomats and Pan Am executives effectively deployed the United States' economic and political clout and Pan Am's technological superiority to strike deals that established American aerial dominance. This disproportionate leverage was also evident during the first postwar bilateral negotiations under the Chicago system, at the Bermuda Conference in 1946 between the United States and United Kingdom. Even though BOAC was the largest non-American airline, it could not match Pan Am's capacity to service the myriad potential routes up for negotiation between American airports and either mainland Britain or Britain's various colonies in the Caribbean, Asia, and Africa. BOAC simply did not have the aircraft or personnel to match Pan Am's arsenal. Moreover, the British government was also still financially dependent on American money, both for its wartime borrowing and its postwar reconstruction needs. Thus, negotiations at Bermuda took place on an unlevel playing field that heavily favored the Americans.

The resulting compromise saw both American gains and modest British success at maintaining at least formal parity between the two aviation rivals. On the one hand, the final terms of the Bermuda Agreement did reconfirm the prewar era's core principle that instilled a de jure equality into bilateral aviation agreements. This was the principle of reciprocity, under which each country typically designated the same number of national airlines (usually just one per country) to fly each route, generally with the same number of weekly flights per airline.[19] Yet, on the other hand, the British were forced to accept a massive expansion of Pan Am's routes in British-administered territory, including a push into parts of the British Empire where Pan Am had never flown before. Most importantly, the American airline now gained access to routes in British-held parts of the Middle East and South Asia so that it could initiate its 1947 round-the-world flights. Because British negotiators acquiesced on this count in the face of determined American pressure, the smaller and weaker BOAC had to compete with Pam Am for passengers all the way from London to Hong Kong.

The Bermuda Agreement became the postwar era's precedent for future bilateral air agreements. First, it enshrined the principle of reciprocity as sacrosanct, but second, it also confirmed that the United States would negotiate aggressively to ensure that its airlines gained the advantages they needed to predominate. Thereafter, even when negotiations rendered an equal distribution of flights on a particular route, American carriers typically enjoyed an advantage. When customers were given the choice between a successful and deep-pocketed American airline and a smaller national start-up, they tended to opt for the

American airline. In marketing campaigns through the 1950s, Pan Am wisely promoted itself as "The World's Most Experienced Airline," highlighting its edge in safety, reliability, and in-flight service.[20]

Clare Boothe Luce was a bit disingenuous in her speech regarding international competition. She claimed to both envision and desire stiff competition, singling out BOAC in particular: "I have every desire to see the British Overseas Airways Corporation shoving us so closely in many regions of the world." She also accepted the need for some sort of niche for other nations' airlines, saying, "I have every hope that the air commerce of all the United Nations will expand constantly." However, she failed to envision how this would occur, whether under American suzerainty or in competition with its airlines.[21]

As an ardent anti-communist, Boothe Luce envisioned no role in global aviation for the USSR or the other socialist states like Yugoslavia that would soon be established in Europe's East. On this topic, she claimed only: "I can muster that there is a vast area of specific war and peace aims which can never be clarified, stated or proposed, and certainly not enjoined upon the world, until we know what goes on in the mind of Joseph Stalin." Various aspects of postwar planning, she added, "all await the ukase of the master of Moscow and the gallant conqueror of Stalingrad."[22] As though living up to their characterization as unpredictable, the Soviets were last-minute no-shows to the Chicago conference in November 1944, and they refused to sign the final treaty. As such, the Soviets exiled themselves from the Chicago aviation system, having determined that this scheme would too blatantly serve American economic and political interests. They also forced all but two of their soon-to-be satellite states, Poland and Czechoslovakia, to disconnect from the international aviation system.[23]

As a result of the Chicago system, the postwar aviation world reinscribed the prewar political and economic inequalities between the North Atlantic region—with the United States predominant—and the rest of the world. In one of the Cold War's worlds, the West, aviation expanded at a dizzying clip, fueled mainly by domestic expansion in the United States and increased frequencies between Europe and New York City. New York–London quickly became, as it is today, the world's most lucrative international route, but it was soon complemented by routes between New York and almost every other Western European capital. Thanks to the principle of reciprocity, Western European airlines added their own transatlantic routes, complementing service from Pan Am and TWA. By the late 1950s, the tarmacs of New York City's Idlewild

Airport, renamed after 1963 to honor John F. Kennedy, contained a colorful cornucopia of airplane liveries from across Western Europe and the United States.

Yet, except for a smattering of South American airlines (Varig of Brazil or Avianca of Colombia, for example), the pre-jet aviation years saw no carriers from Europe's East or the Global South enter the United States.[24] Given that fact, the primary subjects of this book—Yugoslavia and Jamaica—were consigned to positions of aerial inferiority. Neither place was destined to become a vital node in the United States' growing pointillist empire—nor did the United States necessarily desire that they should. Nonetheless, both states saw a sizable uptick in American economic trade and political influence during the Cold War. Jamaica had already been part of America's banana empire for decades, with the Boston-based United Fruit Company playing an outsized role in land ownership in and shipping to Jamaica. The British colony became even more vital to the United States in the 1950s when bauxite, the raw material required for aluminum, began to be mined there. Yugoslavia, meanwhile, became an American partner only after Stalin's decision to disown Tito in 1948, at which point the United States agreed to bankroll the country in the hopes that other communist satellites would follow its example and break with the Soviet Union.[25]

Thereafter, at least from an American perspective, these two states held similar places in the pointillist-imperial landscape: the United States could best administer its growing economic and political ties with these states from other more important nearby regional hubs. For Jamaica, this meant that American interests handled their affairs, largely from Havana (before 1959), Miami, or Panama. For Yugoslavia, Frankfurt or Munich would suffice—with an assist from Switzerland's Zurich. If Clare Boothe Luce were running aviation policy in these regions, she would have recommended running Pan Am routes from these more vital hub cities to the countries in question and let that be that. Never would these states have hosted economic and aviation hubs of their own, especially not with air routes that connected them to alternative points on the globe that did not align with American or Western European capital flows.

Under Boothe Luce's ideal scenario, these regions would have seen a return to conditions from the 1930s. In Jamaica's case Pan Am initiated service to Kingston early in the decade with great fanfare, as Charles Lindbergh piloted the first "flying boat" to land in Kingston Harbor. Yet, once these festivities passed, a more mundane reality took hold, in which Kingston served as little more than a refueling point and an overnight port of call. A few nights a week, Pan Am's passengers deplaned and spent the night in the stylish Myrtle Bank Hotel, while a team of technicians serviced and refueled the plane and a steward replenished provisions for the onward journey. For the crew and almost all passengers, Jamaica was not the ultimate destination; the voyage continued further south to the strategically valuable American-administered Canal Zone in Panama or the lucrative commercial centers of Barranquilla, Rio de Janeiro, and Buenos Aires.[26]

Meanwhile, Yugoslavia in the prewar years did have a veneer of aerial independence. A Belgrade-based airline named Aeroput initiated flights in 1928, mostly with a domestic net to link larger cities like Zagreb and Sarajevo to Belgrade. Additionally, a precursor of Air France was stopping in Belgrade on its route, which mimicked the tracks of the Orient Express from Paris to Istanbul, as early as 1923. Especially because Aeroput also flew a few international routes to nearby commercial centers—Venice, Thessaloniki, and Prague were its furthest destinations—Belgrade was a crossroads of sorts for early aviation, even as its overall connectivity lagged behind cities further west. Nonetheless, getting from Belgrade to points further afield was better managed on Europe's great colonial-era airlines: Britain's Imperial Airways (which later rebranded as BOAC) stopped there occasionally on its route between London and Delhi, as did KLM on its flights between Amsterdam and Batavia (Jakarta). Deutsche Luft Hansa's flights also stopped there on routes between Germany and Athens or Istanbul. Thus, as with Jamaica, Yugoslavia was barely a destination in itself under the cartography of colonialism.

Befitting their status as overlooked aviation societies, these case studies were largely absent at the Chicago conference, though there is a caveat: a Yugoslav delegation was present, but it consisted of low-level officials headed by the Chicago-based consul general. The delegates' assignment came from the royal Yugoslav government-in-exile in London, not from Tito's communist-led Partisans, who were gaining ground in Yugoslavia and growing quite effective at governing the territory outside the king's purview. The lack of clarity regarding which entity was Yugoslavia's rightful government led to the erratic decision to send delegates to Chicago but not to sign the final treaty. When Tito's communists won elections in late 1945 and became Yugoslavia's sole governing authority, the choice not to sign the treaty was reaffirmed.[27]

Jamaica, meanwhile, had no representation, either at the Chicago conference or at the 1946 Bermuda Conference. As a colony, it lacked legal standing at international conferences. While home rule developed during and after the war, these London-approved experiments extended only to domestic policies. Thus, even though the Chicago conference set the parameters for air travel in Jamaica and the Bermuda Conference determined which American and British airlines would fly there, diplomats reached these decisions based on the needs and interests of London, not Kingston. In this respect, Jamaica's plight was no different than all the other soon-to-decolonize areas of the Global South. The Chicago system made no provision for them until independence, meaning that the 1944 meeting saw only limited participation from Africa, Asia, and the Caribbean. From Africa came just a handful of independent states (Egypt, Ethiopia, Liberia, and South Africa); South and Southeast Asia were similarly overlooked (only Nationalist China, Thailand, colonial India, and the still-colonized Philippines participated); and the Caribbean was sparsely represented as well (with only Haiti, the Dominican Republic, and Cuba present).[28]

For Boothe Luce and America's airline boosters, excluding communist states and subjugating colonies' interests were acceptable aspects of the Chicago system. Eastern Europe showed little economic promise for routes stretching beyond what soon became the Iron Curtain. Meanwhile, America's success in bargaining for more routes with the British at the Bermuda Conference established London as a pliant partner, akin, at least in this limited way, to small postcolonial states. Thus, for the time being, the realities of the resuscitated cartography of colonialism meshed with the new realities of the Cold War. Only one of the Cold War worlds—the West—had airlines that were robust enough to expand broadly, which they did, at least to other destinations in the West and Global South. Europe's East was left outside this international system. Meanwhile, as long as it lasted, colonialism assured that aviation growth in the Global South was left for American airlines to dominate, with lesser-funded Western European carriers competing as they could.

No matter how much her speech elicited cosmopolitan yearnings—especially the aspiration to fly everywhere—Clare Boothe Luce's actual recipe for postwar aviation was decidedly parochial. In fact, her speech was effective in preventing postwar aviation and its passengers from achieving this lofty aspiration. Stressing what she saw as irreconcilable differences between the Allied powers, she accepted that the postwar world would be divided. Thus, instead of enabling a globally connected world via aviation, these divisions, as Boothe Luce already perceived in 1943, was likely to leave Europe's East excluded from this aviation system and the Global South's aviation resources built up only around certain points of American interest. Rival visions that might have enabled truly universal connectivity, whether through managing aviation as a collective global utility or opening all the world's airports to global competition, were dismissed in Boothe Luce's rendering as "globaloney."

As small states with little potential to become hubs of American interest, both post-1948 Yugoslavia and postindependence Jamaica had strong incentives to fight back against the return of the West's cartography of colonialism. Their opposition had slightly different ideological roots, with Yugoslavia driven by nonalignment and Jamaica by postcolonialism. After being disowned by Stalin, the Yugoslav government fought fiercely to forge an independent position between the rival blocs in the Cold War. It ultimately found common cause with certain countries in the Global South who felt similarly compromised when forced to choose between the Americans' or Soviets' cumbersome conditions for support. Meanwhile, Jamaica's government was driven less by Cold War frustrations and more by its push to nurture its economic and political sovereignty after three centuries of British imperialism.

Whatever their motivations, each government ultimately shared common desires in their aviation policies. They perceived the West's attempts to resuscitate and expand the cartography of colonialism as inimical to their own economic progress and their political independence. After all, returning to the prewar status quo would have meant retaining the deficiencies in these countries' transportation connectedness to the larger world; enriching Western airlines and stockholders whenever their own citizens flew; and keeping the highly skilled and well-paying jobs of piloting, in-flight service, and aircraft maintenance in Western hands.

To wage this fight, the governments of both Yugoslavia and Jamaica used the only good tool offered in the Chicago system. Even smaller and poorer states that possessed airlines of their own had the power to insist on reciprocity rights when negotiating bilateral air agreements. This limited right to be treated equally, if used creatively, could then allow even a small airline belonging to a small country to design its own aerial cartography—to help move their home countries from the periphery of the cosmopolitan world closer to its center. In the process, these airlines could also foster much-needed economic growth, either as a booster of exports or as a vehicle to deliver foreign tourists. As such, both postwar governments created airlines of their own, with Yugoslavia's JAT Airways founded in 1947 and Air Jamaica established in the half decade after independence in 1962. These were expressions of opposition from Europe's East and the Global South to Clare Boothe Luce's too-parochial vision for postwar aviation.

Chapter 2

The Nonaligned Airline

JAT Airways and Yugoslavia's East-West-South Axis

Historic challenges faced the Yugoslav state at the conclusion of World War II. The war devastated the country in a multitude of ways: in addition to the profound loss of life and destruction caused by the invading fascist powers, the country also lost its political integrity. In a way that eerily foreshadowed the breakup of the country in the 1990s, the state of Yugoslavia was dissolved. Armies from Germany, Italy, Hungary, and Bulgaria divided the country into distinct entities with precariously drawn borders that exacerbated the region's already profound ethnic animosities.[1] A civil war transpired within the larger context of a war of liberation against foreign occupiers, replete with acts of genocide akin to those a half century later. When the war ended, these nationalist rivalries persisted, though a fragile stability finally took root in late 1945, once both foreign and domestic fascists had been driven out and elections had installed a unified leadership under Josip Broz Tito and Yugoslavia's Communist Party. The former king, Petar II, who led a wartime government-in-exile in London, at this point begrudgingly abandoned efforts to restore a capitalist-oriented, democratic-inflected monarchy, though he left behind large numbers of royalist and nationalist dissidents in the newly socialist state.

The chaos of the postwar moment was profound: deep social distrust from the internecine bloodshed was coupled with economic devastation, creating unstable political ground for Tito's new and controversial revolutionary regime. Of course, just as before the war, Yugoslavia faced the daunting challenge of overcoming its economic underdevelopment. Demographic markers from 1946, just as from 1936, reflected a country that had only begun to transform into an industrial economy: per capita wealth was well below West European levels and the populace was still heavily agricultural, tied to labor-intensive farming that failed to create the surpluses needed to finance industrialization.[2] The profound progress in aviation this chapter chronicles, which prepared Yugoslavia and the newly founded JAT Airways to compete admirably when the Jet Age began, arose from the ashes of this deprivation. The invading Germans destroyed the entire fleet of Yugoslavia's prewar airline, Aeroput. By 1946, with no remaining planes and a government antagonistic to private enterprise, Aeroput was liquidated, leaving the Defense Ministry to operate the country's only civilian flights on a haphazard basis.

Yet, even before the war, profound infrastructural shortcomings placed the country well behind states further west and even behind Central and Eastern European states like Poland, Czechoslovakia, and Romania. No civilian airport had a concrete runway until the Nazis paved Belgrade's, meaning that all Aeroput's takeoffs and landings had taken place on grass fields that were unusable in wet or snowy weather. Radio, radar, and lighting installations were also deficient, further limiting the reliability of flights and effectively restricting them to daylight hours. Thus, when US diplomat Melvin Turner reported on Yugoslavia's aviation industry, he glumly concluded that, as of 1948, "Jugoslav civil aviation was in the stone-age."[3]

Walking in Step with Europe—Both East and West

The first step in restarting the aviation industry came in August 1945, when the country's transitional government commissioned an esteemed aviation expert, Milenko Mitrović, to assess the state of aviation infrastructure. Mitrović not only knew the prerequisites for running an airline, since he served as Aeroput's chief technology officer, but he also was well acquainted with aircraft production and design, given his work as the designer of the Yugoslav-produced MMS-3 lightweight airplane. His assessment in 1945 pointed out various challenges for the aviation sector. Yet, Mitrović also emphasized one crucial advantage: postwar Yugoslavia retained a good amount of aviation know-how. Several pilots—some of whom started the war in exile flying for the United Kingdom's Royal Air Force, others for the Nazi-allied Croatian Air Force—had eventually joined Tito's Partisans and were now ready to work for the new regime. Meanwhile, many of Aeroput's engineers and technicians, including Mitrović, were also eager to return.

This fact gave Mitrović enough optimism to conclude his report with an urgent but hopeful imperative for restarting civil aviation. Noting that the war had already fostered a well-developed aviation industry among "the great powers and the industrially advanced and strong countries," he warned that a "small countr[y] like ours—if it does not want not fall behind the great powers in its development—will have to give all available resources so that aviation is reinforced in full measure."[4] Here, Mitrović was articulating a desire to keep Yugoslavia in sync with the United States and Western Europe (the "great powers" who were "industrially advanced and strong"). However, he was less specific about where in Europe—east or west—Yugoslavia might land. Instead, he noted that Yugoslavia's overall desire to modernize was dependent on a retooled aviation sector: "Only in this way can the nation, at least to some extent, walk in step with the general development of social life in Europe."[5] In August 1945 this aspiration to "walk in step" with Europe did not yet beg the obvious Cold War–era follow-up question: which Europe—East or West—would Yugoslavia's aviation system link up with?

When governmental authorities approved Mitrović's calls to recalibrate factories and revitalize civil aviation, there were two competing visions that would be reconciled only after the Soviet premier Joseph Stalin's decisive split with Tito in June 1948. In 1947 national security conditions were finally settled enough to transfer civil air operations from the Defense Ministry to the civilian-run Ministry of Transportation and its newly established Main Authority for Civil Air Transport (Glavna uprava civilnog vazdušnog saobraćaja, or GUCVS).[6] This is when the Yugoslav government made a choice that was unique among the Soviet Union's Eastern European satellites: it established two airlines at once. While the moribund Aeroput was dissolved, JAT was incorporated in 1947 as a wholly owned entity of the Yugoslav federal government and managed directly by the GUCVS. Meanwhile, a second airline called JUSTA (Yugoslav-Soviet Joint Stock Company for Civil

Aviation) was founded as a joint venture between Yugoslavia and the Soviet Union.[7] This airline technically reported to the GUCVS as well, but it was managed by its own board of directors, with a Soviet official in the position of general director and several other Soviets, including pilots, conducting day-to-day operations. JUSTA also held a three-year contract to administer the country's major airports, including air traffic control. This arrangement gave Soviet technicians oversight over arrivals and departures at the country's two largest airports, in Belgrade and Zagreb. Clearly, Tito's government in 1947 had no misgivings about working closely with the Soviets, even to the extent of ceding control of certain national security assets. Yet, at the same time, he resisted keeping all aviation assets under the Soviets' purview.

This Yugoslav-Soviet collaboration through JUSTA is just one of the Eastern-leaning (if you will) facets of Yugoslavia's efforts to "walk in step" with Europe.[8] The Tito government's choice to follow Stalin's example and not sign onto the Chicago convention was also a definitive move eastwards. Without signing the convention, Yugoslavia could not become a member of the ICAO (the International Civil Aviation Organization) nor could its airlines join IATA (the International Air Transport Association), both of which established norms of international air transport and eased access to treaty members' airports. Without these memberships, neither of Yugoslavia's new airlines would be able to fly to Western states who were convention members, at least not without considerable difficulty.[9]

Stalin's USSR heavily influenced this decision, one that was also imposed on the other communist regimes in Eastern Europe, save for two exceptions: Poland (a Chicago signatory since 1945) and Czechoslovakia (which signed in 1947, before the country's communist-led coup). In key ways, this eastward drift aligned with Tito's stated goals for Yugoslav aviation. In a discussion with Foreign Minister Leo Mates in April 1947, Tito shared a more modest vision that prioritized links to other communist-run states: "we will certainly establish routes to Moscow, Albania, Poland, Bulgaria, and the ČSR [Czechoslovakia]." In terms of routes to the West, he was far more equivocal, "maybe [there will be routes to] Italy and Austria and westwards, to Paris. But all of this is a question for the Leadership." By leadership he meant the country's federal presidency, with him at the head, not the direct overseers of aviation in the GUCVS.

Importantly, while Tito's advocacy of an aviation system that linked Yugoslavia only to other socialist states replicated Stalin's vision, this eastern orientation reflected something other than Stalin's desire to economically isolate Europe's East from the West. Instead, Tito was primarily motivated by anti-capitalism and anti-imperialism as he took aim at the goals promoted by Clare Boothe Luce in 1943 and realized in the Chicago system, which was a cornerstone of America's Market Empire. In additional remarks to Mates, Tito expanded on how routes to the West would have to work: "our Leadership agrees to establish international routes between Yugoslavia and other countries in which reciprocity is possible, taking into account our technical abilities." On any route to the West, he concluded, "we must be assured that reciprocity be not only on paper, but in the air. . . . Our aircraft [must] fly and not just foreigners'."[10]

While brief, this statement recognized crucial concerns pertinent not just to Yugoslavia as it arose out of its so-called "stone-age" of aviation, but also to all states whose economic and technological development lagged behind the West's. It recognized Yugoslavia's limited "technical abilities" and insisted on parity in how routes were divided between Yugoslavia's airlines and the Pan Ams and BOACs of the West; Yugoslavia had to defend itself against being overtaken by these wealthier and more accomplished rivals that did not have local interests at heart.

Of course, to implement an eastern-oriented vision, one airline—JUSTA—would have sufficed, just as similar joint ventures with the Soviets adequately served neighboring Hungary, Romania, and Bulgaria.[11] The JUSTA agreement also offered a further advantage of quickly addressing the country's critical lack of infrastructure: Moscow agreed to send ten Lisunov-2 aircraft (the Soviet-built wartime version of the United States' exceptionally reliable DC-3 passenger planes that debuted in 1936). These planes would be more than adequate for the routes Tito prioritized to the east. Importantly, the Soviets also agreed to subsidize JUSTA financially, making the Soviet government responsible for half of the airline's annual losses, which both partners anticipated would persist for the first few years. The infusion of Soviet administrators also represented a form of knowledge exchange that appears to have seemed worth the concession of sovereignty over security assets. Thus, just a year before Stalin's split with Tito, the Soviets were treated as the primary and most desirable partners in aviation development.

And yet, in a move that on its face was strikingly inconsistent, the Tito regime also founded a second airline, Jugoslovenski Aerotransport (Yugoslav Air Transport, or JAT).[12] JAT operated without oversight from Soviet officials and employed only Yugoslav citizens. Another point of difference, though minor, was that JAT flew American-made DC-3s rather than the Soviet-built version of the same aircraft. By the end of August 1947, JAT had secured five DC-3s, a smaller number than JUSTA's proposed ten. This slight difference in equipment (Li-2s versus DC-3s) set an important precedent: JAT in the future would opt for Western-made planes, distinguishing it from the other airlines in Europe's socialist states.[13]

JAT's western orientation is also clear from the international route network that the GUCVS crafted for it. While JUSTA flew the routes between Belgrade and almost all Eastern European capitals, the Belgrade-Prague-Warsaw line was in JAT's hands. At the time, flights from Belgrade to Prague and Warsaw were the only pathway for Yugoslav air passengers and cargo to reach Western Europe and Scandinavia. Because Czechoslovakia and Poland had signed the Chicago convention, the airlines in these countries (ČSA in the former, LOT in the latter) could sell tickets to and accept JAT passengers flying onward to Western or Northern Europe. Thus, as the Iron Curtain descended on Europe, Yugoslavia's JAT shared the same desire as ČSA and LOT to fly westward, even as geopolitical realities prevented direct routes from Yugoslavia.

Documents in Yugoslav archives do not clarify the thinking behind the creation of two airlines at once. One plausible basis for this both-East-and-West strategy is the ideological heterodoxy of Tito himself, who asserted independence from Stalin when crucial Yugoslav interests were at stake. Even before JAT's and JUSTA's founding in 1947, Tito drew Stalin's ire with his aggressive nationalist strategy on Trieste, which enflamed tensions with the West in ways that the USSR did not then desire. Similarly, Tito's support of a Slavic-led communist uprising in Greek Macedonia created difficulties for Soviet foreign policy, especially when the United States countered by proclaiming the Truman Doctrine, which promised economic and technical support whenever a state faced communist insurgency. Though not yet as well studied by historians as Trieste and Greece, aviation policy under Tito, especially JAT's founding, exhibited a similar independent streak.[14] The airline's existence gave Yugoslavia's leadership a tool to exploit future international opportunities independently of Moscow.

By 1947 planners at the civil aviation authority and JAT had already strategized how to embed Yugoslav aviation into the West's aerial network. Importantly, while doing so, they also intended to maintain Yugoslavia's independence from the West and its airlines: they would counter the cartography of colonialism that continued to disadvantage Yugoslavia. Their proposed solution was not Stalin's, which involved absenting Europe's East from the Chicago system and promoting a nearly hermetically sealed aviation system there. Instead, they pressed for Yugoslavia to join the ICAO and to open its airspace and airports to Western airlines. Their hope was that integrating into the West's system would attract foreign currency and enable the modernization of aviation facilities that was so desperately needed. Like in Jamaica a decade or so later, theirs was a proposal to develop through integration with the West, while still aspiring to build up Yugoslavia's own airports as potential hubs and its own airline as a competitor of Western carriers. The benefits would include Yugoslavia's increased connectedness to the world and the establishment of JAT as a viable national airline, albeit operating within Clare Boothe Luce's blueprint of bilateral treaties that often favored Western airlines.

This group promoting a Western pathway for Yugoslavia included the GUCVS's director of development, Zdravko Pudarić.[15] His two-fold plan to tie Yugoslavia to the West first involved opening Yugoslavia to Western tourists, using JAT to help develop the Adriatic Coast as a vacation destination. In a meeting with Ministry of Tourism officials in December 1947, he laid out a plan to make "tourist aviation the basis of our civil aviation transport." These Western tourists, valued because they would boost the country's hard currency reserves, would help raise the number of air passengers from thirty thousand in 1947 (the initial goal set for JAT and JUSTA) to sixty thousand by 1949. Pudarić recognized that this growth would require expanding JAT's fleet of DC-3s to twenty and adding four new eight- to ten-seat aircraft to serve smaller coastal airports. Most ambitiously, Pudarić added, "In 1949 we may procure amphibian aircraft as well, which could travel in-season," making water landings in island harbors and other remote outposts and thereby opening the entire Croatian archipelago to summer tourism.[16] Using aviation, Yugoslavia could transform the Adriatic Coast, with its hundreds of sparsely populated islands, into a destination that could compete with the Mediterranean coasts of Italy or France.

Coupled with the development of a Western-centered tourist trade in Croatia was an equally ambitious plan for the country's east, centered on the federal capital of Belgrade. Here, Pudarić believed that catering to Western airlines could stimulate massive growth. As of 1947, carriers like Pan Am, BOAC, KLM, and Air France were forced by their political disagreements with Tito and the poor state of Yugoslavia's radio and navigation services to avoid the country's airspace, even though flying over Yugoslav territory would save them precious time and money on routes to Asia. Pudarić reasoned that participating in the cartography of colonialism by replacing Belgrade's small and dilapidated airport with one boasting extensive runways, a modern terminal, and quick refueling options offered real benefits. Supplanting Rome and Athens as the preferred stopover point would bring revenue from refuelings and landing fees, while also establishing direct links between Belgrade and both the West and Middle East. Thus, unlike Tito's eastern-first vision for aviation, Pudarić and the GUCVS placed greater importance on "expanding connections with foreign countries: first with the West, then establishing routes to the Near East."[17]

As Pudarić further reasoned, once these North Atlantic carriers aspired to serve Belgrade (if only for refueling), then Yugoslavia could—in line with Tito's precepts—also invoke the Chicago convention's principle of reciprocity to secure for JAT equal access to Europe's capitals and to cities in the Middle East. In his bullish vision, the new airport would grow into a truly modern aviation hub, with as many as 120 takeoffs and landings in any given hour—comprised roughly equally of Western carriers and Yugoslavia's JAT and JUSTA.[18] Archival documents detail that the GUCVS formed a working group in May 1947 to select a site for the new airport, with hopes of including the project in Yugoslavia's first Five-Year Plan in 1948.[19]

When published, the Five-Year Plan did indeed include several of these priorities. It called for doubling domestic lines over the 1946 total and for increasing international routes to ten. As Pudarić desired, domestic growth would have been heavily focused on the country's west, with the plan directing construction of a new aerial network that would "link locations along our Adriatic coast." Because airfields with grass runways no longer sufficed, the plan also called for the construction of new airports around the country to support the projected growth in travel through Belgrade and the coast. In the tension between Tito's eastern-leaning vision and Pudarić's western-leaning goals, the plan sided with Pudarić, prioritizing routes to "several major transportation centers in Europe and in the Middle East" over those to Eastern Europe's socialist capitals. However, because prioritizing Western tourists and the desires of Western airlines would have been unsavory to admit in the Five-Year Plan, the document aligned these investments with Yugoslav workers' welfare, stressing that these investments would allow "an ever-larger number of our people" to fly to the coast on their state-supported yearly summer vacations.[20]

Ultimately, then, Yugoslav ambitions to "walk in step" with European aviation circa 1947 employed a both-and strategy that was different from Europe's other socialist states. While Tito himself prioritized an eastern-directed route system, the country's civil aviation authorities also developed ambitious western-inclined plans. This attention to both East and West was also happening in Czechoslovakia and Poland; however, Yugoslavia was unique in creating two separate airlines. The Yugoslav-Soviet joint venture JUSTA served the more modest goal of linking up with socialist neighbors, while also serving some domestic markets—mainly from Belgrade southward to Sarajevo, Titograd (Podgorica), and Skopje. Meanwhile, JAT was the preferred tool to "walk in step" with Western Europe: in the short-term it linked Belgrade with the Western towns of Zagreb and Ljubljana domestically, while serving Prague and Warsaw internationally. There was even more optimism that the airline would grow in future years, in step with the country's Five-Year Plan, opening the Croatian coast to Western tourists and exploiting routes directly from Belgrade to Europe's west and the Global South.

Turbulence from the Tito-Stalin Split

However lofty the dreams for Yugoslav aviation were, the realities in these early years were far more modest. Neither JAT nor JUSTA escaped Yugoslavia's persistent infrastructural limitations: lack of meteorological equipment, deficient radar and air traffic control systems, a shortage of night-landing equipment, and a lack of concrete runways, to name just a few. Meanwhile, a political maelstrom that was in the offing would further complicate Yugoslavia's efforts to keep pace with Europe: on June 28, 1948, Joseph Stalin commanded that Yugoslavia's communists be expelled from the Cominform. This was intended as a death sentence for the regime, a means to actively undermine Tito's rule and replace him with a more reliable ally. Stalin reinforced this threat with an economic blockade and increased military threats on Yugoslavia's borders with Hungary, Romania, and Bulgaria.

Before the split, running JUSTA had already exposed tensions between the Soviets and Yugoslavs. While JUSTA was slated to begin flying along with JAT's debut in April 1947, none of the promised aircraft had arrived. Only in late July did two planes initiate JUSTA's first route, Belgrade–Titograd–Tirana, with the other eight planes finally arriving at the beginning of 1948. Consequently, while the target of 30,000 passengers for 1947 was met, JUSTA carried just 6,421 of these.[21] In addition, even though planners had envisioned that JUSTA would lose money, the actual results from the second quarter of 1947 were far worse than planned. Financial analysts quickly revised the yearly budget: instead of a loss of 1.615 million Yugoslav dinars, the revisions now anticipated a loss of 4.115 million.[22] JAT was taking the lead in Yugoslavia's aviation development, due mainly to Soviet unreliability.

The situation in 1948 was even more dire. Despite aspirations to double the number of passengers, a mere twenty-eight thousand flew during the year, a failure that stemmed directly from the Tito-Stalin split.[23] With Stalin's announcement, JUSTA's general director quickly returned to Moscow and absented himself from decisions, while the blockade of Yugoslavia caused JUSTA's international routes to be canceled and oil supplies from pipelines originating in the east to be drastically reduced, making it difficult to keep JAT aircraft flying as well. Conditions again resembled 1945–46: canceled routes, flights operating ad hoc, and the airports (still managed by the Soviets) vulnerable to foreign attack. A report from early 1949 found this latter situation still unresolved: "JUSTA has administrative control at the following airports: Belgrade, Zagreb, Sarajevo, Titograd, and Zadar. These airports are in fact under the full control of JUSTA, such that even the clerks of GUCVS at these airports are subjugated to their rival administrative authorities from JUSTA. This situation has created the possibility that foreign aircraft have been able to land, without our proper authorities being informed."[24]

Dissolving the JUSTA joint venture became Yugoslavia's top aviation priority, superseding any plans to develop Belgrade's airport or the Adriatic Coast. By December 1948, Tito had deputized his new foreign minister, Edvard Kardelj, to negotiate JUSTA's liquidation. Financially, the resulting deal was calamitous. The Soviets repatriated all property they had brought into Yugoslavia, leaving the aviation sector short of planes, manpower, and airport equipment. The Yugoslav government also reimbursed the original Soviet investment in JUSTA and some of the company's Soviet-paid losses over 1947 and 1948. These terms placed further demands on the Yugoslav treasury, just as the Five-Year Plan was unraveling under the economic blockade and the increased military spending needed to counter a potential Red Army attack.[25]

With JUSTA gone, Yugoslav aviation was now exclusively in the hands of JAT and its fleet of DC-3s, which had now grown to ten, technically enough to maintain scheduled flights on the country's domestic and international routes. Nonetheless, tensions with Stalin resulted in hostile relations with Yugoslavia's eastern neighbors and volatile fuel supplies. As a result, JAT's international presence suffered. JUSTA's routes to Tirana, Bucharest, and Budapest were not replaced, while JAT maintained only its Prague route through most of 1948 and 1949, though with frequent interruptions.[26] When the US diplomat Melvin Turner later wrote of a "stone-age" in Yugoslav aviation, he was addressing both the bleakness of 1945–47 and the country's failure to walk in step with Europe—Western or Eastern—after the 1948 Tito-Stalin split.

The intensity of the Yugoslav Communist Party's paranoia during the Tito-Stalin conflict—which led to a series of accusations of espionage, show trials, sentences in gulags, and defections—also infected the GUCVS in 1949. Communist Party officials were suddenly suspect if they were perceived as pro-Moscow or, depending on quickly changing strategies in Tito's inner circle, as pro-Western. In the period between the split in 1948 and Stalin's death in 1953, prisons in Yugoslavia filled with political dissidents, many subjected to show trials with flimsy evidence and others receiving no trial at all. Amid this chaos, purported pro-Westerners at the civil aviation authority, including Zdravko Pudarić, were condemned by a special investigator as "enemy agents."[27] Pudarić was arrested in December 1948 and, without a trial, was transferred to a concentration camp on the remote island of Goli Otok. He spent four-and-a-half years there before being released, never to return to the aviation sector and never having been convicted of a crime. Another five named "enemy agents" at the GUCVS also presumably lost their jobs. In the panic of these volatile years, Pudarić's visions of a Western-oriented aviation sector were denounced as both financially irresponsible and ideologically misguided.[28]

Yet, just months after investigators condemned this Western orientation, decisions were made at the highest levels to tie JAT more closely to the West—albeit neither as a tourist airline for the Croatian coast nor as a competitor to Western airlines at a newly expanded Belgrade airport. Instead, JAT quickly developed a new raison d'être: linking Yugoslavia to new trade and financial partners further West. There was significant urgency to this task, since Yugoslavia was surrounded by uncordial neighbors, including the Eastern bloc adversaries blockading it; Italy (with the Trieste crisis still unresolved); and Greece (still reeling from the Yugoslav-aided insurgency). The country's lone non-adversarial border ran between Slovenia and British-occupied Austria, though even here the legacy of forced labor and genocide against Slovenes in the province of Carinthia before and during the war made the crossing tense.[29]

Flying Westward

With the overriding imperative of breaking through the country's isolation, the GUCVS and the Foreign Ministry in 1949 opened the first bilateral air negotiations with two Western states: Switzerland and the United States. The latter partner was particularly important, as it administered the airports of Frankfurt and Munich in its occupied zone of West Germany, as well as the Austrian airport of Linz. However, the Swiss discussions bore fruit more quickly, with non-scheduled service between Belgrade, Zagreb, and Zurich beginning in August 1949, even as a full air agreement was still being negotiated. Switzerland's neutrality, both in World War II and in the rapidly developing Cold War (despite its unabashedly pro-capitalist orientation), rendered it a palatable partner to Tito, who "never was hostilely oriented to Switzerland" and showed "sincere interest in practical cooperation," according to Swiss diplomats.[30] When the Swiss-Yugoslav aviation agreement was completed in 1950, it reflected Tito's long-standing desire for full reciprocity: both JAT and Swissair agreed to fly once per week, using the same aircraft type (a DC-3) and thereby assuring that neither had a distinct quality advantage. Direct service to the vital financial center of Zurich meant that Yugoslavia had a modest beachhead in the West and a pathway for forging partnerships with Swiss financiers and trading companies, which in the ensuing years served as intermediaries for Yugoslav trade with the West.

Just as the JUSTA negotiations with the Soviets had extracted a high price, so too did the Swiss deal. As the historian Thomas Bürgisser notes, an earlier economic treaty that had been finalized in September 1948 also included a confidential transportation protocol that would establish the Swiss as the virtual custodians of transportation into Yugoslavia. The protocol provided that "as much Yugoslav transit business as possible . . . to both Eastern and Western Europe would transpire via Switzerland."[31] Once established as the middlemen for such trade, the Swiss gained a means of securing Yugoslav hard currency assets to pay down Yugoslavia's debt, both from Swiss-owned properties in Yugoslavia nationalized after World War II and to pay back any additional credits lent to Yugoslavia by Swiss banks from 1948 onward.[32] In the ensuing years, cash-starved Yugoslavia turned often to Swiss financiers, who—alongside American public and private institutions—became a primary source of loans to Tito's Yugoslavia. Stalin's choice to forsake Tito in 1948 thereby created a financial reality for Yugoslavia that future postcolonial states like Jamaica would recognize all too well: these newly industrializing economies, especially those lacking reliable transportation networks to consumer markets, had to borrow heavily. Western lending institutions were typically the most reliable source for such loans.

Alongside the Swiss aviation agreement from 1950, Yugoslavia stimulated cooperation with another increasingly vital trade partner, West Germany. Here, Germany's defeat in the war left the Americans in a position to forge the beginnings of this new relationship. The aviation treaty with the United States signed on December 24, 1949, was among the first instances of postwar cooperation with socialist Yugoslavia, ushering in a new era in which the United States treated Yugoslavia as a de facto partner worthy of political, economic, and even military support.[33] This deal was ultimately more vital for Yugoslav aviation than the Swiss treaty, as it gave JAT access to three more Western airports, with the Frankfurt route now allowing Yugoslavia's citizens fast and simple connections to points further westward, including London, Paris, and New York, thanks to an interline agreement with Pan Am established in the treaty. Customers could pay in Yugoslav dinars at JAT offices for a flight with JAT to Frankfurt, and then fly further westward with Pan Am.[34]

As compensation for providing Yugoslavia and JAT this beachhead in the West, the Americans, like the Swiss, first demanded that the Tito government compensate US citizens for properties nationalized after World War II. Once this impediment had been cleared, American diplomats facilitated loans from US government sources and international institutions.[35] Even before signing the aviation deal, Yugoslavia received a US$3 million loan (in September 1949) from the IMF to close its trade imbalance, and another US$12 million loan from the Export-Import Bank, which was managed by the US State Department. Thus, while Swiss loans covered US$3 million of Yugoslavia's 1949 debt burden, the Americans helped secure US$15 million.[36]

Financial fealty was not the only thing the Americans acquired in the treaty. The State Department also demanded for Pan Am a much-desired prize for its round-the-world route: permission to use Yugoslav airspace. Of course, officials like Zdravko Pudarić would have welcomed this development, though with the stipulation that such flights refueled in Belgrade while taking on and dropping off passengers. Yet, plans for a new airport were now mothballed. As the new director of the Yugoslav Civil Aviation Authority conceded in a 1950 meeting with American diplomats, "the few tractors, graders, etc., which the Yugoslavs have are being used exclusively for construction of the expanded military airport program, and the Yugoslav government has no money to invest in the purchase of additional equipment needed for [Belgrade's new civilian] airport."[37] Given this fact, Yugoslav authorities agreed to less than ideal terms. In a move that American internationalists like Clare Boothe Luce would applaud, Pan Am won a temporary monopoly on using Yugoslav airspace vis-à-vis its Western European competitors. The airline could now leapfrog from Munich to Istanbul without the diversion through Rome and Athens. Furthermore, Pan Am had no obligation to land and refuel at Belgrade's airport. The country served simply as a fly-over space.

Other parts of the aviation treaty were more favorable to Yugoslav interests, allowing it to reflect Tito's desire for reciprocity. On paper, the treaty opened Munich, Frankfurt, and Linz to flights from Belgrade and Zagreb that Yugoslav and American carriers could exploit jointly. In reality, with Pan Am executives seeing little economic potential, JAT enjoyed a monopoly on all these routes.[38] Given JAT's profound struggles at the time, the airline needed this reprieve from competition. Overall, these new flights to Switzerland, Germany, and Austria reinforced JAT's Western orientation. Indeed, with JUSTA's dissolution and relations with Stalin still tense, the entire Yugoslav aviation system now pointed westward.

Landing Yugoslavia in the Global South

Yugoslavia's post-1948 formula for economic development was uniquely hybrid in terms of its underlying geopolitics. The country's primary economic development strategy was learned from the Soviet Union in the east: creating a command economy in which central planners allocated economic resources to prioritize heavy industry. By 1949 Yugoslavia had also availed itself of a key Western development strategy: acquiring loans and foreign aid from banks, governments, and international institutions. In addition, with Eastern European markets blocked off, Yugoslavia experienced its first major push to export goods to the West, especially to West Germany. In these first years, however, the trade westward looked similar to the Yugoslav region's historical trade under colonialism: agricultural products like pork and raw materials like timber were the only ones the West found attractive. Thus, in the early 1950s, a cadre of officials pushed Yugoslavia to add a third, more novel dimension to its development plans, by forging economic ties with decolonizing states in the Global South.

This process began in earnest in 1950, when the Yugoslav official negotiating a trade treaty with Egypt expressed hope that the Global South offered something more. Unlike in earlier trade agreements with Egypt, which were restricted to trading raw materials (mainly Yugoslav timber for Egyptian cotton), the Egyptians now sought to import Yugoslav industrial goods as well, making it "our first agreement that envisions the possibility to export products of our heavy industry."[39] Over time, this trade in industrial goods and technological know-how with the Global South grew immensely. Importantly, in this new trade nexus, Yugoslavia's historical and geographical position as a marginalized economic entity finally served as an asset rather than a liability. As a country whose respective regions also endured colonial rule and now embraced communism's strong anti-imperialist message, Yugoslavia was seen by some leaders in the Global South as a more desirable economic partner than members of the Western Bloc. The country's Cold War position straddling the two blocs was also an attractive model for many Third World leaders seeking maximal sovereignty. Thus, various states in the Global South welcomed Tito's efforts to make Yugoslavia an economic and political force beyond Europe.

Essential to these developments were Tito's newly forged relationships with India's Jawaharlal Nehru and Egypt's new leader from 1952, General Gamal Abdel Nasser. This trio shared the same commitments not only to smaller states' economic and political independence vis-à-vis the US and USSR but also to postcolonial economic development. At their 1956 summit hosted by Tito, they articulated a pathway for the Global South to build on the momentum of the 1955 Bandung Conference, where non-white leaders of Asia and Africa came together to promote common objectives. This process culminated in 1961, when Tito hosted the Belgrade Conference and, as the lone European country alongside a series of states from the Global South, helped found the Non-Aligned Movement (NAM).[40]

NAM was a loosely united grouping, rather than a formal alliance. Its commitments included pressing for nuclear disarmament and, even more prominently, resisting entangling bonds with either the United States or the USSR. With its members heavily comprised of newly independent states in Asia and Africa, NAM was also an anti-imperialist force, which hoped to advance the economic modernization of the Global South and the political sovereignty of its members. For Yugoslavia, this alignment with the Global South was motivated by its own legacy of colonization and its suddenly hostile relationship with the Soviets. As Edvard Kardelj, the regime's primary ideologue and one-time foreign minister, explained, "Yugoslavia might not have survived . . . had it not started combining with another revolutionary process that shook the entire world. That was the struggle of the colonial and all other non-self-governing and semi-dependent peoples to liberate themselves from foreign domination and economic and political dependence of all kinds."[41]

Importantly for JAT's ultimate growth, the creation of NAM also entailed economic opportunities for Yugoslavia. As the historian Svetozar Rajak stresses, Tito's extensive travels in Southeast Asia and Africa during the winter of 1958–59, which were primarily designed to secure political support for NAM, also brought economic benefits: "Tito would point out to his hosts that Soviet and Chinese aid, like that from the West, always came with strings attached." Yugoslav contracts, however, would only bolster a state's independence. "Moreover," Rajak adds, "economic cooperation and assistance between the uncommitted countries strengthened the bonds between them, something that [Tito] was keen to advance." Tito thus returned to Belgrade in 1959 with commitments for ship contracts with Ceylon (Sri Lanka) and Sudan, a munitions deal with Egypt, and a variety of construction projects (a dam, railroad, and a variety of factories and plants) with Ethiopia.[42] After all, Yugoslavia's industrial know-how—gained in its own domestic development by building dams and other electrical facilities; infrastructural projects for shipping, rail, and road transport; and entire urban neighborhoods for its rapidly growing cities—was far more advanced than that of its newfound partners. Yugoslav engineering firms sealed lucrative contracts, especially in the 1960s with oil-rich NAM member states like Libya and Iraq, to undertake such large-scale construction projects.

In sum, Stalin's banishment of Tito in 1948 had a profound impact on Yugoslavia and its relationship to the world. By the early 1950s, the country's dependence on Switzerland, the United States, and West Germany, coupled with its economically lucrative opening to the Global South, had led Tito to accept an open border strategy. Now, Yugoslavia engaged with, rather than isolated itself from, the nonsocialist world. This openness fostered not only financial and trade ties with the West and Global South, but also a unique economic migration pattern for Yugoslav citizens that persisted through the 1980s: "on the one hand, highly-skilled, Yugoslav white-collar labor (engineers, technical personal) [was] deployed to the Third World, while low-skilled Yugoslav migrant labor was slotted into the lower ranks of West European economies."[43] In both cases, such migrations meant for JAT an increased homegrown market of somewhat frequent fliers to complement the more frequent business travelers flying to the West and Global South. As such, the country's aviation needs were significantly different—hardly even recognizable—when compared to its needs both before and immediately after the "stone-age" of the Tito-Stalin split.

By the mid-1950s, JAT was maturing as a uniquely nonaligned airline: as a socialist (and in this sense eastern) airline with routes stretching westward into the North Atlantic region and southward into the Middle East. While JAT would ultimately serve cities that Pan Am, BOAC, and Air France also served (Cairo and Beirut in the south, Paris and London in the west), it did so with unique cargo: its passengers were typically businesspeople and technicians promoting products from Yugoslavia's modernization efforts that were destined primarily for similarly situated countries in the Global South and, gradually, for the West as well. JAT's routes were also novel, linking a developing country on Europe's margins directly with other developing countries in the Global South, without passing through Western Europe's hubs that served as focal points—and choke holds—of transportation under the cartography of colonialism. In this sense, JAT's growth resulted in a modest redrawing of this cartography. When JAT inaugurated flights from Belgrade through Athens to Cairo in 1954, it quickly became the young airline's most financially lucrative route.[44]

The country's overall western and southern economic strategy was lucrative for Yugoslav citizens who could find work tied to this global trade. Greater exports, coupled with the state's heavy borrowing from the West, allowed for significant GDP growth to accompany the de-escalation of tensions with the USSR that came after Stalin's death in 1953. Yugoslav GDP in 1960 was already 70 percent larger than it had been in 1956.[45] Continuing growth through the 1960s further promoted a more prosperous consumer-oriented economy, where heightened consumer expectations and increased availability of higher-quality goods produced what the historian Patrick H. Patterson refers to as the "Yugoslav dream."[46] Parents who endured the privations of World War II relished the fact that their children were more prosperous and better educated. Many citizens attained a standard of living that did not match Western Europe's, but outdistanced other socialist states' by far. These consumers of the "Yugoslav dream" were occasional leisure travelers on JAT, using their savings and their freedom to travel as far as they could afford to go. At the peak of Tito's nonalignment politics in the 1960s, citizens could travel visa-free in most of Eastern Europe (except for Albania), the West (except for Greece and the United States), and the Global South (except for Israel and China).[47]

JAT's "Walk in Step" with Western Competition

The year 1954 was momentous for JAT, as it took several important steps toward parity with Western Europe's airlines. On January 6, 1954, the Yugoslav government definitively acknowledged the westward orientation of its aviation sector by signing the Chicago convention. As a result, aviation relations with countries and airlines in the West and Global South were normalized. Joining the Chicago system entailed a commitment to open Yugoslav airspace and update the country's aviation infrastructure. In addition, entering the ICAO eased the way for JAT to expand further: the airline could now sell tickets outside Yugoslavia, and it committed itself to abide by internationally monitored safety standards.

In terms of timing, 1954 was still slightly before the rise of a Western-style consumer economy in Yugoslavia, which included "self-service shops, supermarkets, and department stores that aspired to Western ideals of luxury, choice, satisfaction, and modernity." Patterson notes that these anchors of a Western-style consumer culture "started to spring up across Yugoslavia beginning as early as the late 1950s," especially after reforms were implemented that shifted economic production toward higher-quality consumer goods.[48] Thus, when JAT in 1954 opened new routes along with its purchase of ultramodern American aircraft and with a Western standard of service aboard, it stood in the avant garde of the country's efforts to "walk in step" with the West's consumer culture.

CHAPTER 2

For JAT, this step was sealed with the purchase of three new American-built Convair-340s (CV-340s). Flights from West Germany to Paris had been initiated on DC-3s in March 1952; a flurry of activity by Yugoslav diplomats enabled flights to London soon after the CV-340s arrived in 1954, at which time the Paris route also switched over to the CV-340. Customers from these premiere European capitals thereby voyaged in a state-of-the-art American plane with double the seating capacity of the DC-3 (now about forty passengers), much faster cruising speeds, and a more extensive range of over three thousand kilometers. Once landing in Belgrade, they could remain there or continue in the same plane to JAT's first destinations in the Global South: Cairo (via Athens) and Beirut (via Istanbul), each of them served twice weekly.[49] Bilateral treaties now gave Air France and BOAC overflight rights to match Pan Am's, but they also enhanced JAT's appeal for customers who normally flew these airlines, since they could now book with JAT and board top-quality aircraft, making it to Beirut or Cairo the same night.

The same American diplomats who dismissively characterized Yugoslav aviation as being in the "stone-age" a few years before had doubts about Yugoslavia's CV-340 purchase and its expansion both westward and southward. While grateful that Yugoslav authorities chose to spend US$2.4 million for American rather than British aircraft, they also feared that the purchase was a step too far.[50] After all, airport infrastructure remained so limited in Yugoslavia that the Convairs could land only at one civilian airport in the country, Belgrade Airport. Even there, though, its concrete runway had to be hastily reinforced and expanded. There were also concerns about insufficient pilot training and the lingering lack of radio and radar equipment. Even more concerning, however, were fears that the Yugoslavs might not be able to afford the multimillion-dollar purchase.

As it turned out, embarrassed Yugoslav officials did indeed contact these diplomats just before delivery of the second and third planes to concede that they lacked the needed funds. The alarmed secretary of state, John Foster Dulles, personally intervened, stressing that Yugoslavia's political value to America—as a socialist state that broke free from Moscow—outweighed concerns about the deal. Dulles ordered the Export-Import Bank to make emergency loans available, even while lamenting that the United States' new patron was already heavily in debt: "Considering the fact (1) that Yugoslavia has already extended its borrowing capacity to the limit and (2) that the Export-Import Bank has extended a substantial loan to Yugoslavia, the payments of which it has rescheduled, it is unlikely that the Export-Import Bank would consider extending further credit to Yugoslavia unless there exist strong overriding policy reasons for approving such credit."[51]

Various US diplomats were incredulous about Yugoslavia's commitment to securing aerial independence. The nationalist globalism of State Department officials echoed Clare Boothe Luce from a decade earlier, when she advocated for "keeping America on wings all over the world."[52] When the American embassy was informed of the CV-340 purchase in late 1952, the first secretary considered the deal financially unwise and politically misguided. "The Embassy," wrote Turner Cameron Jr., "does not believe the commercial value of JAT's present foreign business warrants the indicated foreign exchange outlay at this time." He then offered an opinion consistent with Boothe Luce's own, claiming the Yugoslav government should surrender its efforts at aerial independence and instead become a dependent of Pan Am: "From a strictly economic view," he concluded, "it would probably be more practical to have Pan American work out an arrangement with the Yugoslavs for the former to stop at Belgrade."[53]

This thinking points to the double bind that smaller and poorer countries like Yugoslavia encountered in the Chicago system. First, the entry costs for such countries to create new airlines were prohibitive, forcing difficult choices about how to pay for very expensive aircraft and infrastructure improvements. In the case of Tito's Yugoslavia, part of the government's policy was to utilize its close ties with the United States and Switzerland to acquire lines of credit and then, in the words of Dulles, "[extend] its borrowing capacity to the limit." Yet, even this strategy did not prevent last-minute financial crises like with the CV-340 purchase. The second bind was linked closely to the first: the North Atlantic's preeminent carriers had long since survived the capital crunch facing the likes of JAT as start-ups, meaning they could offer developing countries connectivity at a lower cost. In fact, when doing so, Pan Am could also fall back on an additional revenue source: State Department subsidies were available to underwrite routes deemed to be in the national interest. Thus, throughout the 1950s, Pan Am insisted that it would only add a Belgrade route from West Germany if the State Department covered the projected losses.[54] In this particular case, the tension blew over when Yugoslav officials found the required funds to complete the purchase of the CV-340s from its own Central Foreign Exchange Fund.[55]

Yugoslavia's economic expansion and heavy borrowing also enabled a massive expansion of airports across the country. Work on Belgrade's new world-class airport began in 1956, while planning began for airports with concrete runways and vastly improved terminal buildings further west: in Zagreb, Sarajevo, Ljubljana, Split, and Dubrovnik. These airports, when they finally opened in the early 1960s, helped make the Adriatic Coast a major tourist destination that drew hard currency reserves into the country, while finally putting an end to grass runways and inadequate safety equipment.[56] Interestingly, this airport development strategy closely resembled plans made thousands of kilometers away in Jamaica, where the colony's popularly elected government in the late 1950s was also spending heavily on airports in Montego Bay and Kingston to ready them for the coming Jet Age tourist wave.

Even before Yugoslavia's entry into the Jet Age was complete—with the opening of these new airports and JAT's first acquisition of French Caravelle jets in 1963—Yugoslav officials still sought to expand JAT's global reach in ways that confounded American diplomats. Here, Tito's diplomatic investments in and economic ties to the Global South were again decisive. His multiple state visits and subsequent trade deals stimulated interest in yet another set of aircraft purchases, this time involving Yugoslavia's first four-engine aircraft, the American-built DC-6B from Douglas Aircraft. One of the largest and longest-range pre-jet aircrafts, seating around ninety passengers and flying as far as five thousand kilometers nonstop, this was the same model that Pan Am debuted in 1952 and continued to use on its transatlantic services and its round-the-world flights until the airline converted to jets starting in 1958. Yugoslavia's purchase of DC-6s could have allowed JAT to open routes to the Americas, an option Yugoslav officials entertained.[57] However, a confluence of factors led the new DC-6s to bolster Yugoslavia's ties with the Global South rather than initiate a North Atlantic expansion.

As planned, one of the planes was immediately designated for Tito's multi-month diplomatic and economic tour that began in December 1958. An American embassy official was again highly critical of this choice, even though the tour attracted business for Yugoslav companies and consolidated support for the Non-Aligned Movement. The diplomat characterized the plane's purchase as prestige based: "Yugoslavs place great store by [the] prestige value [of] such visits, seemingly out of proportion [to] their substantive worth." He posited that this prestige, at least in Yugoslav eyes, would "enhance [the regime's] position at home and increase [its] influence on [the] world scene." Yet, in his view, these goals were financially too costly: "One measure of [the] importance they attach to [the] prestige factor would appear . . . in [the] fact they [are] willing [to] spend [a] significant portion [of] their meager foreign exchange reserves for aircraft having virtually no commercial justification."[58]

There were somewhat similar misgivings in Yugoslav circles, though not in ways critical of nonalignment. Instead, in 1956, as the purchase was initiated, Yugoslavia's director general of civil aviation expressed concern that the preconditions for these planes' success were not yet fulfilled, especially if JAT were to initiate service to the Americas. In his view, four aircraft—not two—were needed to assure backups for overseas routes. Additionally, bilateral treaties still needed to be negotiated with countries in the Americas and Belgrade's new airport needed to be completed before delivery, which was not feasible. His conclusion was that "the investment requirements are premature for our abilities. It is particularly necessary to study the economic feasibility for transoceanic flights, given the competition with strong companies" that would be inevitable on such routes.[59] Aviation officials' reticence ultimately led the government to pay for the planes through the Defense Ministry and not the country's civil aviation authority.

With transoceanic flights temporarily delayed, JAT officials found an ultimately more lucrative use for the DC-6s: they soon replaced the CV-340s on the profitable Paris-Belgrade-Cairo route. By 1960, Yugoslav aviation officials and even American diplomats were positively surprised by the plane's success. A Yugoslav official who initially asserted that using DC-6s to fortify these routes was "not where the business was" was proven wrong after two years of operation. Even a humbled embassy staff member conceded, "The success of the DC-6 on the Paris and Cairo runs, which was originally viewed as a prestige move, may be stimulating Yugoslav interest in acquiring jets for more extensive route coverage."[60] There was momentum to Yugoslavia's engagement with the Global South, as well as with the West, that made these moves economically sound. As Yugoslav economic growth continued, it allowed such southerly air routes to flourish, even as they disrupted the West's cartography of colonialism.

A Hub for Yugoslavia's Nonaligned Airline

After the break with Stalin, Tito and Yugoslavia's Communist Party were forced to improvise, both in their international politics and their economic path forward. The only priority that remained from Yugoslavia's original pro-Soviet orientation was the commitment to developing heavy industry first, and even here the regime was forced by popular discontent in 1956 to progress more quickly toward a consumer-oriented economy. As such, by 1961 Yugoslavia was increasingly cosmopolitan in its political and economic relationships. While still committed to socialism, the regime resembled its eastern socialist neighbors in hardly any other way.

Yugoslavia's first move beyond Eastern Europe was to seal a rapprochement with the West, which quickly became the country's most important economic partner. Yugoslav firms increasingly oriented their production to the West, while the Croatian coast's growing tourist sector collected an impressive amount of foreign exchange from Western tourists. The lucrative relationship with the Global South had both a political facet, the Non-Aligned Movement, and an economic expression: the exportation of Yugoslav industrial products and engineering expertise.[61] By 1962 a third and final connection to the larger world—this time with the USSR and its satellites—was growing, thanks to modest trade relationships with the same countries that had blockaded Yugoslavia back in 1948.

This normalization took years to develop. As Tito was deepening relations with Nehru and Nasser from 1954 to 1956, he was also engaged in a process of letter exchanges, then state visits, which ultimately brought Khrushchev to Yugoslavia in 1955 and took Tito to the USSR in 1956. However, the improved relations lasted barely a year. As the historian Petar Žarković notes, the Belgrade Declaration signed by Khrushchev and Tito in June 1955 was historic for the USSR: it was "the first to regulate the relations between Moscow and another socialist country on the principle of equality," and it also "publicly proclaimed that the [Communist Party of the Soviet Union] recognized 'a different way to socialism'" that Yugoslavia was justified in pursuing. As such, Khrushchev fully disavowed Stalin's actions against Yugoslavia in 1948.[62]

However, Khrushchev proved to be an unreliable partner. In 1957, the Soviets backtracked on the Belgrade Declaration and reclassified Yugoslavia's Communist Party as a pariah. Only in 1962 did relations warm again, as the USSR's newfound interest in expanding socialism in the Global South—along with attempts to rival China for predominance in global communism—led Khrushchev to again see Tito as a potential ally. This time, Moscow's re-engagement with Yugoslavia endured through the entirety of the Cold War, thereby allowing Yugoslavia to develop a third pillar of political and economic cooperation: not just with the West and the south, but also with Europe's socialist East.

Such developments bolstered Yugoslav commitments to aviation, leading JAT to develop a three-pronged route strategy. In the 1960s, the airline both maintained and expanded its scope in Western Europe, complementing flights to major hubs like London, Paris, and Frankfurt with a handful of secondary cities. It also continued expanding into the Middle East and simultaneously opened routes to socialist capitals, from East Berlin (1960) to Moscow (1965). Even before much of this expansion, in 1964, JAT was flying to 25 international destinations and was serving 460,000 passengers annually, a dramatic improvement over the 30,000 passengers carried in 1947. By the close of the decade, the number of yearly passengers had again nearly doubled, to 880,000.[63]

Inaugurating Belgrade's new airport in 1962 ushered in the Jet Age and fostered this exponential growth. While based on the original concepts included in the 1948 Five-Year Plan, the one that Zdravko Pudarić hoped would result in 120 hourly takeoffs and landings, the 1956 plans were slightly more modest. This version rivaled the airports of Athens and Rome by accommodating up to forty-five flights per hour. It also adhered to the highest level ICAO standards, making it a legitimate competitor as a stopover on the Europe to Asia routes that Western carriers and a handful of new Middle Eastern airlines were flying.

The resulting increase just in JAT's international passenger numbers was sizable. In 1961, the last year before the new airport, the airline carried 50,000 international passengers. When JAT accompanied the opening of Belgrade's new airport in 1962 with its formal entry into the Jet Age by purchasing three Caravelle jets from France's Sud Aviation in 1963, the airline saw major international growth. The Caravelles—a mid-range jet well suited for JAT's Western European and Middle Eastern destinations—marked another improvement on the airline's prime routes linking London and Paris with Cairo and Beirut by cutting flying times in half, while freeing its DC-6s and CV-340s to develop new routes. By 1964, JAT's international passenger numbers had increased to 131,000—almost threefold over 1961.[64]

The new airport also finally lured the West's legacy carriers to Yugoslavia. Some came willingly, given that it finally met international safety standards. Others were forced: Yugoslav officials now required that airlines using Yugoslavia's airspace land at least one-third of the time in Belgrade. Pan Am, BOAC, KLM, and Sabena, among others, started serving Belgrade as a result. Even the USSR's Aeroflot, now committed to becoming a global airline, used Belgrade to refuel its Tupolev-114 aircraft—the longest-range passenger plane in the world—which flew between Moscow, Accra, and Havana.[65]

For the first several years of the new Belgrade Airport, the DC-6 remained the main workhorse of Yugoslav aviation, even as the Caravelle jets enjoyed pride of place. In 1961 JAT was joined by a second Yugoslav airline, Slovenian-owned Adria Airways, which also used Belgrade as its base for its charter-only operations on DC-6s, a plane that ferried either passengers or cargo payloads over long distances. In the 1960s, both JAT's and Adria's DC-6s pioneered new markets for Yugoslavia's share of the Non-Aligned Movement's economic trade in the Middle East, Africa, and Asia.[66]

Illustrative of the importance of the Global South to Yugoslav aviation is Adria's application for a new route to the Maghreb in June 1962. Originally envisioned as a single route from Belgrade to Tunis and onward to Algiers and Casablanca, the ultimate result was a bit different. Tunis became part of Adria's charter route to Leopoldville in 1962, while Algiers became a separate destination in 1964 and Morocco was omitted altogether. Adria's application was timed to coincide with Algeria's imminent declaration of independence, a monumental moment in the history of anti-imperialism and one strongly supported by Tito's Yugoslavia. Adria's application rosily described Belgrade's lucrative geographic position now that the new airport had opened. Executives called the city the "predestined starting point" and "natural crossroad" for routes between East-Central Europe and Global South destinations like Algeria.[67] Those planning the Maghreb route found that "the nonalignment of [Yugoslavia] in international relations is an additional contributing factor that strengthens Belgrade Airport's already optimal location." Because Tunisia, Algeria, and Morocco had all participated in the 1961 Belgrade Conference, these countries now were deemed even more viable economic partners: "Since the countries of the Maghreb will be economically strongly tied to and dependent on France for several more years, there arises the political and economic necessity that they establish good political and trade relations with the countries of Eastern Europe. Thus, the natural [geographical] bridge aligns with the political, and leads to [Yugoslavia], more precisely to Belgrade Airport."[68]

In determining the frequency for this route, Adria executives stressed that these countries' "economic structure and level of development contributes, to a certain extent, an economic complementarity, such that the material conditions exist to increase the traffic in foreign trade."⁶⁹ Adria therefore envisioned either once-weekly or twice-weekly charter flights that would be filled with "mainly businesspeople—merchants—and then diplomatic officials and couriers, engineers [providing] technical assistance, and cultural-artistic groups."⁷⁰ The report projected profitability for the route in the second year, as long as other carriers, especially Aeroflot and Czechoslovak Airlines, did not compete.⁷¹

In November 1964, Adria initiated charter service to Algiers. In its first two months, on a total of fifteen flights, the airline flew its DC-6s at capacity, with over two thousand passengers.⁷² This success eventually led JAT to add scheduled service to Algiers, alongside other Middle Eastern and North African destinations, such as Tripoli, Benghazi, Baghdad, Kuwait, and Damascus. Using Libya as an example of this expansion, ties with Yugoslavia were deep even before Muammar al-Qaddafi's coup against King Idris in 1969. Yugoslav firms had in fact constructed both the Tripoli and Benghazi airports based on the expertise they had gained in Yugoslavia's airport-building spree. As such, 3,900 Yugoslav citizens—primarily engineers, medical workers, and their families—already lived in Libya in 1968, with contracts held by Yugoslav firms in the country valued at US$160 million. These numbers would grow further after 1969.⁷³

To borrow a term from Tito's foreign policy, JAT by the dawn of the Jet Age was a uniquely nonaligned airline. The route structure it created was unimaginable under the cartography of colonialism that consigned Yugoslavia to fly-over territory, devoid of easy linkages to the vital metropoles of the global economy. Even in the cartography of the Cold War, in which the American-Soviet rivalry divided Europe between sharply segregated Eastern and Western blocs, Yugoslavia after 1948 occupied an exceptionally difficult position. It lay in between the blocs, tantamount to a no-man's-land in a time of war. This precarity pushed Yugoslavia to develop a creative foreign policy, building cordial relations with the West and eventually the East as well, while also resourcefully developing ties with newly independent states in the Global South. JAT played a vital role in this foreign policy, as it made the country a busy hub and a desirable destination in its own right. The country's geographical disadvantages became a source of vitality, as flights took off for destinations in all directions. Rather than a no-man's-land, Yugoslavia instead became like an open city in a divided world, a crossroad between the communist East, the democratic-capitalist West, and the decolonizing Global South.

Yet, despite the immense benefits that aviation bestowed, including all the ways it enabled the country to "walk in step" with Europe, there were also profound costs. The expenses required to develop a modern aviation system placed a serious strain on state coffers. This was true of the calamitous divestiture from JUSTA in 1949 and also of the 1954 purchase of the Convair-340s, when the Yugoslav government risked defaulting at the last minute. Beyond these previously discussed instances were numerous other pessimistic developments. During every year of the 1950s, the central government subsidized JAT, contributing from 20 percent to over 33 percent of JAT's earnings; the subsidies totaled at least $1 million every year.[74] On top of that, when authorities finally invested in new airports starting in 1956, another 14 billion dinars (about US$20 million at the 1960 exchange rate) were budgeted, even before the projects' major cost overruns.[75] Further into the 1960s and 1970s, even after these start-up investments were supposed to have resulted in a viable aviation sector, the government continued to subsidize JAT.

Herein lay the Achilles heel of Yugoslavia's broader ventures in the Cold War to secure political independence and economic prosperity. Despite having experienced impressive economic growth in the 1950s and 1960s, its hybrid economy—one that eschewed the basic capitalist principle of private enterprise, while nonetheless nurturing certain state-owned enterprises that competed well on the world market—could not wean itself off Western loans. On the one hand, gainfully employed members of the World War II generation were delighted when the "Yugoslav dream" offered their children better lives. On the other hand, warning signals abounded that this prosperity was not sustainable: state debts increased, going from US$400 million in 1954 to US$5.7 billion in 1971; unemployment rates remained stubbornly high at over 7 percent throughout the 1960s before worsening in the 1970s; and balance of trade deficits were a yearly reality, despite successes in exporting a wider variety of goods.[76]

These nodes of fragility amid an otherwise impressive re-rendering of Yugoslavia's aerial cartography were shared by the next case study as well. Jamaica's geographical position was considerably different than Yugoslavia's, which rested on the tectonic plates splitting East, West, and South. However, the Caribbean Basin did stand on the precipice of a significant North-South divide—between the United States and Latin

America—and it even had an "Eastern" presence once Castro assumed power in 1959 and eventually allied Cuba with the USSR. The Jamaican challenge to the cartography of colonialism was, however, not as cosmopolitan as Yugoslavia's East-West-South strategy. It was decidedly Western, even as it challenged the predominance of Western airlines and their consignment of Jamaica to the position of an overflight locale, or at best a stopover point for refueling. Here too, however, familiar elements from the Yugoslav example are visible, especially the deep tension between costly investments in aviation that would enhance both a country's economic and political sovereignty and the risk of incurring unsustainable amounts of debt.

CHAPTER 3

G. Arthur Brown
Air Jamaica's Precarious Founding

On January 28, 1962, before boarding a plane in the colony's capital of Kingston, Premier Norman Manley recorded a radio address to ready his countrymen for independence. Manley's ultimate destination was London, where he and a team of diplomats would enter final negotiations to end Jamaica's three-hundred-year legacy as a colony of the United Kingdom. His most exciting revelation was a prospective date for the festivities, August 1 of the same year, which would also be the 128th anniversary of the end of slavery on the island.[1] In Jamaica's history since emancipation, as Manley portrayed it, there had been continual attempts by "the old masters and the new freedmen" standing "side by side to work out the shape of a real society made up of people who live together as one." These efforts, he promised, were coming to fruition: "So if Independence came about on August 1st, it would be the wheel of history which made one full turn when slavery ended, making another full turn when nationhood began. There could be nothing like it, I am sure, in all the pages of all the books of history."[2]

That Manley was flying to London on a new BOAC Boeing 707 jet further highlighted the promise of this moment. Knowing that his address would air while he was in flight, he opened by acknowledging how this historic voyage also portended Jamaica's impending status as a Jet Age nation: "When you hear this broadcast I will be on a plane on the way to England for the Independence Conference." The next day's issue of the *Gleaner* newspaper coupled the speech's text with a photo of Manley's entourage at Kingston's brand-new, jet-ready airport terminal and noted their departure on a chartered "BOAC jetliner." The dawn of the Jet Age in Jamaica, which officially had begun two years earlier when the US's Pan Am and Britain's BOAC established jet service to Montego Bay, was now advancing to the capital in tandem with the final push to independence. Indeed, Kingston's first scheduled jet service, operated by Pan Am, began a few days after Manley's departure, with BOAC's first jet flights not far behind.[3]

Most Jamaican officials who accompanied the premier to London supported another Jet Age aspiration beyond Jamaica's sparkling new airports. These men wanted to form a new Air Jamaica, replete with its own jets flown by Jamaican pilots, run by Jamaican managers, and served by Jamaican flight attendants. One economist accompanying Manley found his career deeply intertwined with these aspirations, as he headed efforts to establish the new airline and ultimately served as Air Jamaica's chairman until 1978. By the time he passed away in 1993, Sir George Arthur Brown—who was most often addressed as "G. Arthur Brown" or "Arthur Brown"—had accumulated many impressive achievements. After training at the London School of Economics, Brown became Jamaica's first director of the Central Planning Unit and helped develop the first five-year economic plan (1955–62). With independence, he became the head of the Jamaica Civil Service (1962–67), thereafter serving as the first governor of the Central Bank of Jamaica (1967–77). Finally, Brown relocated to New York to work as the associate administrator of the United Nations Development Program (1978–93), where he helped channel financial and managerial know-how to countries in the Global South. Along the way, Brown also headed all of Jamaica's debt negotiations with the IMF, the World Bank, and other lenders from 1962 to 1977.[4]

Brown's extensive ties to aviation were therefore always ancillary to his primary responsibilities, though at times they were no less demanding. They began in 1961, when he chaired the government's committee on aviation, which was tasked with deciding whether and how the country should establish its own airline.[5] Then, Brown did much of the financial, legal, and diplomatic work to make sure Air Jamaica finally launched in 1966 (and relaunched again, as we shall see, in 1969). This unique career blending work on economic growth, state borrowing and debt, and infrastructural investments in civil aviation makes G. Arthur

Brown a central figure in the postcolonial history of aviation. His work especially helps explain why small, poorer, newly independent countries like Jamaica ambitiously undertook the financial risks of establishing their own airlines.

Brown's efforts to forge an independent Air Jamaica involved a rewriting of the cartography of colonialism that was different from the Yugoslav example taking place along Europe's Iron Curtain. Jamaica was unquestionably part of the Global South, but it was also in the Caribbean, meaning that its political and economic fate played out in what was known as America's backyard, where President Theodore Roosevelt, over a half century before Jamaican independence, had claimed for the United States the right to act as the Caribbean's "international police power."[6] Transportation routes were then dominated by the United Fruit Company's "Great White Fleet" of steamships, before Juan Trippe's Pan Am sought to develop a Caribbean transportation monopoly of its own in 1930. Consequently, as was true of many new states in Africa or Asia, Jamaica gained independence in a political situation where reality dictated that its loyalties to the Global South had to be mediated by fealty to the United States and its militarized Market Empire.

Castro's Cuba boldly attempted to break this Caribbean-wide alignment with the United States. His introduction of a Soviet-style economic and political system into the Caribbean (forging an eastern-oriented state, if you will) might seemingly have made the Caribbean region's position somewhat analogous to Yugoslavia's: home to fault lines where West, East, and South overlapped and created friction. Yet, the Jamaican government spent almost all the Cold War years as a loyal US political ally at the United Nations and the Organization of American States, wagering that fealty to the West's most powerful state would result in the aid, loans, and political support required for its postcolonial aspirations to develop as a modernized, independent state. Jamaica thereby largely kept its distance from the ideological investments promoted by Tito and the Non-Aligned Movement. Air Jamaica's routes also never emulated JAT's east-west-south polydirectionalism. Instead, it flew almost exclusively north-south, linking Jamaica with metropoles in the Cold War's West. By the late 1970s, Air Jamaica served not only cities across the United States and in Canada, but also London and Frankfurt across the Atlantic.

Independence-era Jamaican leaders anticipated that Americans' verbal commitments to fostering the Global South's economic development would beget concrete support for their small and needy country. The country did indeed receive American financial aid, technical support, and foreign direct investment, all designed to foster Jamaican economic autonomy.[7] However, as this chapter helps to chronicle, Jamaican hopes for greater sovereignty were not always realized, as American corporate interests as early as the 1960s resisted Jamaicanization of the island's industries and their profit streams.[8]

These conflicts grew even more extreme in the 1970s, when Norman Manley's son Michael entered the prime minister's office with sharper ideological commitments to social justice, economic autonomy vis-à-vis the United States, and an openness to embracing democratic-socialist reforms. Starting in 1972, when Manley was elected prime minister, the government cautiously began to forge ties with Castro's Cuba and deepen connections with the Global South. However, his decisive electoral defeat in 1980 foreclosed these alternatives, as did the rise of Ronald Reagan, whose policies vis-à-vis Cuba, Nicaragua, and Grenada assured that Manley's ideological straying would not be tolerated in the Caribbean. This chapter limits its focus to the 1960s and 1970s, examining how Air Jamaica's birth reflected both the loyalties to and tensions with the United States, a relationship that dominated Jamaican foreign relations.

The challenge of G. Arthur Brown's efforts to found Air Jamaica, which entailed almost a decade of hard-nosed bargaining in Washington, illustrates the downside of Jamaica's American partnership. These years show how aspirations for support were met with American duplicity: a verbal commitment to partnership that sometimes resulted in financial support, coupled with fierce protectionism aimed at maintaining Pan Am as the dominant airline in the region. This resistance on the part of the United States government proved to be costly for Air Jamaica and the Jamaican state, the majority shareholders in the airline.

Jamaican officials saw having their own airline not only as a newly won national right, but also as an important mechanism through which to seize greater financial control of the tourism sector. A national airline would keep ticket revenue in local pockets, while also helping to increase flight frequencies and open more routes to new gateways in North America and Europe. Money that previously had gone to Pan Am and BOAC could now be invested to grow the country's tourism sector, while also providing the first generation of Jamaicans working in aviation with expertise in high-tech fields and the higher salaries that accompanied such jobs.

In particular, the actions of the United States' Civil Aeronautics Board (CAB), which at the time accredited foreign airlines seeking routes into the country, reveal the extent of (neo-)imperialist thinking among policymakers and corporate interests. These entities worked to reinforce the cartography of colonialism, even when challenged by weak and undercapitalized upstarts like Air Jamaica. Acting at the behest of Pan Am, the CAB refused to permit Air Jamaica to fly into the United States, thereby delaying the airline's launch from 1963 to 1966. Thereafter, it further demanded that Air Jamaica redo its entire ownership structure by 1969.

Despite these obstacles, G. Arthur Brown's creative economic work and strategic diplomacy did ultimately allow the 1969 version of Air Jamaica to enjoy a significant, albeit quite brief, period of success. Between 1971 and 1974, it posted modest profits while robustly expanding operations and seizing market share from Pan Am and BOAC. Coupled with victories on the diplomatic side that opened more nonstop flights on both sides of the Atlantic, Air Jamaica turned the country's air network into an example of the cartography of postcolonialism: Montego Bay and Kingston both became busy hubs, from which Air Jamaica's colorfully painted jets raced to various points northward. The airline enabled the tourism sector to expand at a rapid pace, as aviation growth was coupled with investments in hotel projects, which, in turn, created more jobs and earned more foreign exchange.

These brief golden years, in which Brown's careful financial planning won accolades for its ingenuity and success, were, unfortunately, cut short by the oil shocks of 1973–74. Coupled with Jamaica's ballooning debt and Michael Manley's increasingly antagonistic relations with the IMF, these shocks forced a premature end to Air Jamaica's ambitious expansion and the optimism that surrounded it. In covering this broad narrative of aviation's role in Jamaica's first years of independence, this account focuses on a wider realm than aviation alone. It intertwines Air Jamaica's history with the country's larger struggles to attain economic sovereignty at this turning of the "wheel of history." This chapter thereby covers all facets of G. Arthur Brown's career: finance and diplomacy, as well as aviation.

Poverty, Debt, and the Structural Limits on Jamaican Development

While Norman Manley rosily envisioned independence in 1962 as a turning of the "wheel of history," the colony's official head of state, the governor of Jamaica, appointed by London's Parliament, offered a more somber assessment. In a confidential memo from 1961, Sir Kenneth Blackburne, a career diplomat who was fated to be the last Englishman to serve as Jamaica's governor, pointed to intractable problems that would plague Jamaica well beyond independence. The report cheered Jamaica's significant economic growth in the 1950s—GDP grew from just over UK£70 million in 1950 to more than £210 million in 1959— but it also warned that the "considerable prosperity [of] the middle and upper sections of the population," had "not yet, as had been hoped, penetrated to the vast mass of under-privileged people." What Blackburne labeled as "slums" in and around Kingston now held 25 percent of the population, whose living conditions were "at an abominably low level. . . . The slum dwellers cannot but contrast their conditions with those enjoyed by the more fortunate people who . . . are able to enjoy new houses, motor cars, and all the delights of a civilized life."[9] This stark divide led Blackburne to dismiss Manley's optimism. Instead, he foresaw independence as politically and socially divisive:

> For the past twenty years . . . nearly the whole population . . . has been united in its aim to secure its own independent status in the world. That aim has virtually been secured; and it is no longer possible to rally popular opinion in the struggle for the abolition of colonialism like a country which has fought a war and has been united in order to win. Jamaica is now in the "post war period" without a clarion call which will make all work for the good of their country.[10]

Despite British complicity in creating this situation, Blackburne saw little prospect that London would help rectify these inequalities. He hoped that "some help may be obtainable from the Colonial Development Corporation," which was a government institution designed to finance investments in soon-to-be-independent colonies. The CDC might finance "slum clearance," he noted, but he added that "the total amount likely to be obtainable in this way will be insignificant in comparison with the needs of the next few years." Instead, he suggested that poverty abatement be off-loaded onto the United States, though that nation's investments were more self-servingly political than altruistically focused on economic development. As such, Blackburne advocated a Cold War–inflected approach to the Americans: "The main source of capital would seem to be the United States, whose Government is rightly concerned with the dangers of the spread of communism in the

Caribbean and Latin America." If poverty abatement programs could be packaged as reducing the threat of communism, the Americans might finance them. Even so, this largesse would not come as grants, but rather as low-interest loans. Blackburne thereby foresaw that Jamaica's most pressing social and economic need, combating poverty, would require borrowing, with debt then becoming another hindrance to the new nation's economic development that would create problems well beyond independence.[11]

This context of intractable poverty and growing debt needs to be remembered when thinking about the resources devoted to Jamaica's aviation sector. When Norman Manley and his government were elected in 1955 with the greatest powers of self-rule ever granted under the British, aviation became a key investment stream to stimulate growth. Yet, the financial demands to prepare the airports alone for the Jet Age, much less to start an airline, were daunting. Before 1945, the only serviceable airports were reserved for British and American military use, with no civil aviation runways or terminals that could have handled jets. Soon after the war, the main military airfields in Kingston and Montego Bay were converted to civilian use, and loans were secured for runway extensions at Kingston, though even these updates were inadequate for the coming Jet Age. Thus, from Manley's election through independence in 1962, even more funds were allocated to make both airports jet-ready—runways, terminals, and safety equipment were overhauled. Overall, UK£6 million was spent on these airports between 1945 and 1962, mainly paid for with loans backed by the Kingston government, not London.[12]

Despite this debt and the controversial prioritization of aviation infrastructure over poverty-related needs, these investments did encourage substantial growth via tourism. Larger airports meant larger planes and more visitors, leading to a dramatic evolution in Jamaican tourism. This process began in the late 1940s with the arrival of modest numbers of wealthy Tories fleeing mainland United Kingdom's high postwar taxes, as well as Hollywood and Broadway celebrities looking to spend their winters in remote but opulent luxury. These tourists either reached Jamaica by ship, or they worked their way to New York or Miami and then took Pan Am or BOAC flights to Jamaica on propeller planes that carried around forty passengers each.

By 1962, however, the island's jet-ready airports enabled tourism to transform into a mass-marketed product focused on luring North America's middle- and working-classes. These less elite but far more numerous patrons began their vacations on passenger jets carrying a hundred or more travelers and sunned themselves at increasingly large, though still modestly sized resorts, which peaked at around one hundred beds per property. What Jamaican tourism lost in exclusivity was more than justified by the massive increases in foreign exchange and job opportunities. Indeed, when Norman Manley's minister of trade and industry, Willis Isaacs, presided over ceremonies to welcome Pan Am's first jet service into Kingston in 1962, he boasted that tourism had already doubled since the government was elected in 1955. He also predicted that tourist numbers would soon double again, which they did by 1970.[13]

Pleased with this tourism growth and a similar postwar boom in the bauxite industry, G. Arthur Brown exuded cautious optimism regarding the economy as it stood at independence. "These developments," he reported, "transformed the economy from a one-crop banana economy pre-1940, to one which . . . rested on four legs: agriculture, industry, bauxite, and tourism." Brown was closely involved with these diversification efforts through his work as director of the Central Planning Unit and chair of the ad hoc aviation committee. In fact, the latter committee's decision to establish Air Jamaica was designed to deepen this newfound economic diversity.[14]

In tandem with Jamaica's aviation investments came equally generous spending on hotel development. One of the first laws passed under the colony's first home-rule agreement in 1944 was the Hotel Aid Law subsidizing new hotel construction. When investors, whether foreign or domestic, built new hotels, they gained tax relief (no income taxes on five of the first eight years of operation), exemption from import duties (for supplies imported for construction needs), and relief from the colony's rules against repatriating hard currency earnings. These subsidies helped increase hotel inventory, most pronouncedly around the North Coast's hub of Montego Bay, which was quickly blossoming into a tourist mecca.

By 1956, the Hotel Aid Law had succeeded in increasing Montego Bay's inventory to 1187 beds, with 2809 on the entire island. Even larger hotel projects were in the works, including a proposed three-hundred-room hotel near the Montego Bay Airport that would be built by the Pan Am–owned Intercontinental Hotels Corporation. Unforeseen circumstances would delay this project's completion until 1971. Yet, it was first planned in 1949, thanks to the incentives of the Hotel Aid Law.[15] By the 1960s Pan Am had been joined by BOAC in financing a hotel of its own in Kingston. These projects were subsidized by Jamaican taxpayers, even as they became a second revenue stream for the West's legacy airlines.

Air Jamaica was born into this complex mélange of optimism and pessimism that accompanied Jamaica's independence. As Norman Manley saw it, the "wheel of history" was turning in the right direction, and even the more studied observations from G. Arthur Brown could celebrate the end of Jamaica's colonial-era "one-crop banana economy." The simultaneous pessimism was best epitomized by Governor Blackburne's report, which expressed alarm that Jamaica's poverty was worsening, even as its prosperity grew for the middle-class and elites. The "slums" that he saw growing in West Kingston were not even a mile from Kingston Harbor, where Pan Am, between 1930 and the onset of World War II, had landed its sea planes and walked passengers to the smart Myrtle Bank Hotel for a pampered overnight stay. Even Kingston's new jet-ready Palisadoes Airport (later renamed to honor Norman Manley) could be spied from Trenchtown, Tivoli Gardens, Rema, and other shantytowns in West Kingston, even though it was located on a peninsula a few miles across the harbor.

Blackburne's pessimism also contained a financial component that counterbalanced Brown's optimism: debt. Not only did he foresee debt as the main mechanism at Jamaica's disposal to address its social problems, but he also correctly pointed to the Americans as the likeliest source of such loans. Here, too, though, Blackburne envisioned limits on American largesse, except when a fight against communism was involved. Otherwise, the American and British interests that ran Jamaica's colonial-era "banana economy" were poised at independence to wean Jamaica off state aid, promoting instead development via foreign direct investment from corporations. In this model, American and British companies, including Pan Am and BOAC, could be lured by tax subsidies. While this model would foster employment and economic growth, it did not address Jamaica's postcolonial desires for sovereignty. It would not rectify foreign control of most revenue-making enterprises, as found in Jamaica's colonial era, nor would it challenge the cartography of colonialism from the prewar aviation sector. Indeed, at the dawn of independence, Pan Am and BOAC still enjoyed a near-monopoly on air routes to Jamaica, even as ticket sales to the island had been booming for nearly two decades.

The Headwinds of American Neo-imperialism

In 1961, Jamaicans surprised American and British observers—and their premier, Norman Manley—by voting to leave the West Indies Federation. According to British plans drafted soon after World War II, it was the federation, not Jamaica itself, that was to gain independence. Thus, through the 1950s, as self-rule increased in each of the individual colonies of the British-held West Indies, federal institutions were being built, including a parliament building and executive offices at the newly designated federal capital of Port of Spain in Trinidad. Manley pleaded with voters to recognize Jamaica's limitations as too small for independence on its own. Yet, its population of over 1.6 million was far and away the largest of any British colony in the region, its location was geographically isolated compared to the others, and its economy—though it lacked the oil reserves of Trinidad—was larger than its peers and growing robustly. Thus, voters opted for a go-it-alone independence plan, following the entreaties of Manley's rival Alexander Bustamante. Manley stayed in power long enough to lead the independence negotiations in London in January 1962, the event that opens this chapter. However, when he lost the next election in April, he went into opposition and gave way to his cousin, Bustamante, who became the country's first prime minister in the independence era.

G. Arthur Brown's work on founding Air Jamaica had already begun in 1961, at the same time as the referendum. As expected, the committee debated a variety of issues: Would the increased economic development that an airline might bring justify the risks of taking on more government debt to start it? Would the global aviation system, so favorable to the West's legacy airlines, really offer Air Jamaica the freedom to price seats, open new routes, and expand seat inventory? Could an unproven start-up improve on the service customers received from Pan Am and BOAC? Development, debt, sovereignty, foreign control—these variables were foremost considerations as Brown and the committee finally decided in 1963 to create an Air Jamaica that was quite unique, possessing an as-yet-untried ownership model and operating structure.

Proponents existed for all of the most viable options to provide more air service from Jamaica to North America and Europe: to bolster the Pan Am-BOAC duopoly but cajole them into continued expansion, to form an independent airline, or to co-own an airline that would serve Jamaica and its recently spurned partners from the West Indies Federation. The last of these options was unpopular among the officials on the committee. British officials had founded an airline in 1949 to serve all of the British West Indies, when BOAC created BWIA (British West Indies Airways), which they continued to own through 1961. Even though BWIA benefited Jamaicans in important ways, especially offering a handful careers as pilots, customer-service personnel, flight attendants, and technicians, the airline served as a cautionary tale for Brown and his team. As they knew, BWIA's efforts to link far-flung colonies in the Caribbean and then feed traffic onward to Miami and New York was far from profitable. In fact, overall BOAC lost UK£3.2 million on BWIA before selling it to Trinidad's government. They also expressed concerns that BWIA had become a "make work" enterprise with bloated payrolls. Thus, BWIA was the type of unprofitable, overly politicized carrier that Brown wanted to avoid.[16]

Many large hoteliers preferred to double down on the Pan Am-BOAC duopoly. These businesses already worked well with both airlines, creating mutually beneficial pipelines from airports to resorts and back. Thus, when Brown's committee ultimately voted to start a Jamaican airline, it had to appease the tourism elites' desire for continued service from these foreign carriers. By including Abe Issa as an Air Jamaica board member—among other resorts, Issa owned the Myrtle Bank Hotel in Kingston where Pan Am's prewar passengers had overnighted—Brown signaled that the new airline would respect these desires.

Overall, Brown's plans for the new Air Jamaica involved much pragmatic balancing. Expanding national sovereignty would happen, but state investments in the new airline would be both modest and prudently spent. Sovereignty was mainly boosted via the Chicago conference's reliance on bilateral negotiations. Once Jamaica had its own airline, it could finally exercise this leverage against the Americans and British to negotiate both new routes and more landings and takeoffs on exiting routes. After all, the system's primary principle was reciprocity; the starting point in negotiations was that each country's airline would fly an equal number of rotations on each route. If Air Jamaica matched Pan Am's and BOAC's capacities, it would immediately double available seats. And it could push for opening new routes by promising the same reciprocity. As a ministry paper from 1965 explained: "In the absence of Jamaica's own national carrier . . . traffic between Jamaica and any overseas country would be virtually limited to the carrier of that country only, thus resulting in Jamaica having international services with negligible, if any, effective competition. . . . Fares, schedules, frequencies, etc., would therefore rest almost solely on the decision of one airline owned in an overseas country and the Government would have little say in these matters."[17]

Brown's innovative plan for Air Jamaica, finalized in 1963, was a joint venture owned 51 percent by the government, 33 percent by BOAC, and 16 percent by BWIA, a formula that reduced the government's outlays by almost half. In fact, the partner airlines further agreed to cap the government's share of potential losses at UK£20,000 annually. This commitment made BWIA's large deficits, which committee members were loath to duplicate, a non-issue.[18] Finally, Air Jamaica also opted to wet lease BOAC and BWIA planes, meaning these airlines provided their jets fully staffed and ready to fly. This solution saved Air Jamaica money by eliminating exorbitant start-up expenses, including aircraft purchases, hiring and training of flight crews, and fleet maintenance. As a government minister noted: "The cost of a modern commercial jet aircraft is a considerable one and the annual turnover runs into millions of pounds. Jamaica has very little experience in this field, and it is clearly advantageous for the Government to ensure that, in the establishment of an airline, the experience and know-how of a large organization should be secured."[19] Thus, the agreement rightsized Jamaica's commitment to the new airline: it got the increased capacity it most wanted without massive financial investments. The new Air Jamaica would not be on par with Pan Am or BOAC, as it would not even have its own planes or in-flight personnel. However, it would serve the island's growing tourist-oriented economy well.

Air Jamaica was ready to fly in August 1963, but it lacked approval from the Civil Aeronautics Board to operate in the United States. This is where Brown's work nearly unraveled. Pan Am filed a letter of objection, which CAB officials supported, claiming that Air Jamaica was not actually an independent airline. Citing the airline's ownership structure and proposed wet lease operations, Pan Am argued that Air Jamaica was nothing more than a "paper airline." It posited that BOAC, with its 33 percent ownership stake, was the actual force behind the airline and was using Air Jamaica to get more flights for itself (albeit under Air Jamaica's name) on lucrative routes between New York and Jamaica. The CAB demanded a thorough review of Air Jamaica's ownership and wet leases, which in turn led to a protracted diplomatic fight between Jamaican officials and the CAB, with the White House and State Department ultimately intervening. This conflict delayed Air Jamaica's launch by nearly three years, until 1966.[20]

British diplomats lamented the fact that Air Jamaica had become a pawn in a larger squabble between America's and Britain's aviation giants. They surmised that Pan Am was really mobilizing against BOAC: "It is . . . clearer than ever that Pan American are determined to use these negotiations to further their object of driving BOAC out of the Caribbean." If BOAC were stripped of its ownership stake in Air Jamaica, it would fly only its long-haul routes between London and the Caribbean, since the wave of independence across the West Indies meant that BOAC was no longer a designated national carrier in the region.[21] Pan Am instead wanted BOAC replaced with national airlines like Trinidad-owned BWIA. These carriers, with small domestic markets, would predictably strain under high operating costs and ultimately become unreliable enterprises, offering service far inferior to Pan Am's. Britain's diplomats thereby concluded that Pan Am's "wish [is] to get BOAC out of the enterprise, so that no strength is left able to support Air Jamaica against the powerful blows that Pan American could rain on it."[22]

Pan Am aspired to tear Air Jamaica away from BOAC, even if it jeopardized larger American commitments to support Jamaican sovereignty and development. The CAB, after all, was forcing the Jamaican government into costly and risky commitments. The CAB finally insisted in 1966 that the Jamaican government increase its ownership in and operational responsibility for Air Jamaica, with a firm commitment that BOAC and BWIA divest. These demands would diminish Air Jamaica's competitiveness in relation to American carriers, while also pushing the Jamaican government into deeper dependence on American financiers for loans to cover the airline's inevitable debt from purchasing planes and hiring hundreds of employees.

Ever a staunch ally of the United States and eager to cast his nation as a counterbalance to Castro's Cuba, Jamaica's new prime minister, Alexander Bustamante, was initially caught off guard by the CAB's delay. British diplomats counseled their Jamaican counterparts to threaten the Americans: "In the case of Jamaica, their remedy is simple; to say to the US, 'Unless you recognize our airline, we shall not allow your aircraft to land in Jamaica.'" At the same time, they admitted this tactic's dangers: "But the Jamaicans are, one assumes, scared to do this, first because of their generally weak attitude towards the US, and secondly because they are unwilling to risk the loss of American tourists."[23] Jamaica's ambassador to Washington, Neville Ashenheim, waited until late 1964 before shaming the CAB for its neo-imperialist ways: "We allow your airlines to operate in Jamaica. We expect you to allow our airline to operate into the United States. We cannot accept a position that because you are an old and wealthy country with established airlines of its own you have the right to strangle our infant airline effort at birth."[24]

As Ashenheim's memo circulated more widely, the White House took notice and pressured the CAB to break the impasse. Ultimately, in early 1966, the CAB finally granted Air Jamaica its needed permission with its ownership and lease arrangements intact. However, it imposed a three-year time limit for BOAC and BWIA to divest. This decision finally allowed Air Jamaica to take flight, though with its days already numbered. By 1969, it would either have to fold, merge with BWIA, or rely on further diplomatic finagling to extend its lifeline.

Jamaican officials overlooked this pending turbulence when the first Air Jamaica flight took off on May 1, 1966. Acting Prime Minister Donald Sangster, who replaced Bustamante after a debilitating stroke, enthusiastically recalled that "for many years a national airline for Jamaica was a dream."[25] Yet, amid the celebration for Jamaica's taking "its place among the airline-operating nations of the world," Minister Cleve Lewis acknowledged the "very often hard bargaining" Jamaica's ambassador faced when "the representative of a small newly-independent country [was] doing business with the most air-minded country in the world."[26] G. Arthur Brown, in turn, expressed both satisfaction and caution, especially regarding the airline's future. "The introduction of service by Air Jamaica is a dream come true," he noted before adding: "What we have today . . . must only be regarded as the beginning. We have a long way to go before we have fully established ourselves but, in typical Jamaican fashion, we are proceeding with caution."[27] With renewed vigor, Brown turned immediately to Air Jamaica's future after the CAB's 1969 expiration date, exploring new options to keep the airline afloat.

Air Jamaica's Higher-Risk Second Incarnation

Air Jamaica's joint venture with BOAC and BWIA did indeed expire in 1969. Yet, Brown succeeded a year earlier in establishing a new legal entity called "Air Jamaica (1968) Limited," which would seamlessly replace it. This too was a joint venture, this time a sixty-forty split between the government and Air Canada that would last for ten years—an expiration date again mandated by the CAB. Unlike the first Air Jamaica, this new venture had more features to assure the CAB that it was not a "paper airline." Indeed, Brown formed it knowing full well that "the United States Government . . . will not compromise the financial viability of the airline"—that Air Jamaica had to own for itself the elements needed for its operation.[28]

Therefore, the airline acquired its own planes, two brand-new DC-9 jets with a capacity of around one hundred passengers each, purchased directly from the US manufacturer. While a larger DC-8 was also leased from Air Canada, it came with the stipulation that "the Board [of Air Jamaica] will have to take immediately firm decisions regarding the . . . acceptance of an option on a mini jumbo aircraft in replacement of the DC 8 in 1972," again because of the CAB.[29] Moreover, Air Jamaica's flights would boast its own flight attendants, gate agents, and baggage handlers, all of them recruited through the home office in Kingston. At the beginning pilots would be Canadians, but only until enough Jamaicans graduated from training programs.[30] Thus, with its own Jamaican employees, its own airplanes, and its own marketing plan, the new airline more credibly assured the CAB of its self-sufficiency, despite leaning on expertise and funding from Air Canada. The number of new expenses did, however, mean that this second incarnation of Air Jamaica placed greater financial burdens and risks on the Jamaican government.

The amount Air Jamaica borrowed was quite high. Another Canadian enterprise, the Bank of Nova Scotia, opened a line of credit of US$18.5 million over ten years, some of which would be drawn immediately to cover start-up expenses and planned short-term losses. Air Canada then made available an additional US$7.4 million through Air Jamaica's issue of "redeemable preference shares" of stock. While the company's so-called "ordinary shares" were held 60 percent by the government of Jamaica and 40 percent by Air Canada (with a total capitalized value of only US$800,000), a "redeemable preference share" would be given to Air Canada for every additional dollar that it invested. These shares were essentially another line of credit that could be drawn on, and, in fact, US$6.1 million was used in 1969 to pay for the DC-9s. Over time, the government bought back these "redeemable preference shares" at a premium: the base price, plus 7 percent interest, compounded semiannually. Thus, before its first flight, the new Air Jamaica had credit lines of US$25.9 million. Plus, it was already foreseen that "a further loan of U.S.$10 million will be required in 1974 but no arrangements have been concluded to obtain this loan."[31]

Because the CAB required the Jamaican government to buy out Air Canada over ten years, there were added yearly burdens in addition to debt servicing. The costs due just to Air Canada were considerable. In total, "over the ten years the outflows from the Budget could be of the order of £5,003,288 [roughly US$10 million at the prevailing exchange rate of two dollars per Jamaican pound]."[32] This amount, coupled with Air Jamaica's US$18.5 million bank loan, was disquieting to a variety of participants, including, somewhat ironically, American officials. Diplomats at the embassy in Kingston cautioned that "the prime difficulty from this Government's point of view will be . . . Jamaica['s] repurchase [of] the preferred shares at the rate of $1.1 million annually. . . . The repurchase might well constitute a politically imprudent annual charge for [the] Government to bear."[33] Totally omitted in this report was the United States' culpability in forcing this scenario on the Jamaican government. These additional risks—and debt—were dictated by the CAB.

While these were risky times for the new Air Jamaica, they were also, in retrospect, the airline's heyday, when there seemed a viable way to end Jamaica's subordination under the cartography of colonialism. Progress along these lines started with the choice of Air Canada over other viable partners from America and Britain. Several American airlines submitted joint venture proposals, and Brown's team identified TWA as the most likely of these. Diplomats in Kingston even surmised that Jamaica's new prime minister, Hugh Shearer, a member of Bustamante's political party, might press for this arrangement "in the belief that [Air Jamaica's] dealings with the CAB would thereby be smoothed." Yet, they also rightly saw a countervailing sentiment: resentment at American machinations against Air Jamaica. These diplomats were therefore not surprised by the ultimate choice: "We also know . . . that this Jamaican Cabinet, more nationalistic than its predecessors, will be attracted by the Air Canada offer, in [that] Jamaicans will own more of Air Jamaica . . . [and] Air Canada will permit a good deal of Jamaican management of the airline, whereas TWA would do virtually all the managing."[34] Thus, even in these assessments, the Air Canada partnership offered greater potential for Jamaican autonomy.

Equally vital to this era of new opportunity were the terms negotiated with the United States in a ten-year bilateral agreement governing air routes. These negotiations, completed in 1969, rendered a very favorable outcome for the Jamaicans, especially because Air Jamaica was given routes beyond New York and Miami. Chicago, Detroit, and Philadelphia were opened, and the United States also permitted extensions beyond these new cities to third-country destinations in Canada (Toronto and Montreal), Nassau in the Bahamas, and the far-off metropole of London. With this agreement, G. Arthur Brown found hope that the airline's new jets—and new debt—could pay off. As he saw it, these additional gateways would make Air Jamaica a viable long-term airline. Indeed, in forging a cartography of postcolonialism for the nation, routes that did more than replicate Pan Am's and BOAC's colonial-era trunk lines to Miami and New York were essential.

Ambassador Ashenheim's assessment was also glowing: Air Jamaica would now serve "four of the five largest cities in the U.S.," including "Philadelphia and Detroit . . . to the exclusion of U.S. airlines." He gleefully added, "if we can get the British rights [to Nassau and London], [this] could by itself turn Air Jamaica into one of the important and financially strong airlines of the world." While overstated on the latter point, Ashenheim's optimism was shared widely: "Our tourist authorities appear delighted, Air Jamaica seems to be wagging its tail in anticipation of becoming an important airline, and . . . whilst we have given the U.S. considerable freedom [flying its own desired routes into Jamaica], we have extracted a fair price for this."[35] Certainly, major risks loomed when the new Air Jamaica launched on April 1, 1969. This was the first flight in the airline's history with its own jets, decorated its own tangerine and yellow colors, with a cadre of Jamaican women serving as stewardesses, and with Jamaican pilots soon to be licensed for flying. Thus, although there were risks, as Ashenheim saw it, the potential rewards were far greater.[36]

Oil Shock and the Popping of Jamaica's Tourist Bubble

The new Air Jamaica's launch was so successful that a cover story in the trade journal *Air Transport World* feted G. Arthur Brown for his work: "The exact formula probably would be impossible to repeat. In a way, that's too bad! Because the way the Jamaican government has managed to ease into the business of running a successful flag airline has got to be one of the best yet devised." The article added that the airline in 1971, just its second year in operation, posted a profit of almost US$200,000, while its load factor (the percent of available seats sold) rose to a healthy 76 percent on the New York–Kingston route. Furthermore, the new routes initiated since 1970 (Chicago, Toronto, Philadelphia) all grew, with further expansion in the offing: "Next will come Detroit via Nassau. . . . In 1974, the sights shift across the Atlantic to a one or two flight per week service to London." The airline was on pace to carry 310,000 passengers in 1972, and there was a seeming promise of more success in the coming years.[37]

The fuller maturation of Jamaica's aviation sector invited, in turn, new commitments to larger hotels. The Hotel Aid Law of 1944 continued to help expand inventory from 2,809 beds in 1956 to 9,616 by 1969. However, almost all this growth took place at small-scale hotels. As of 1969 there were only eight properties with more than one hundred rooms and none with two hundred rooms. Air Jamaica's ambitious 1969 relaunch and its route expansion plans motivated government officials to contemplate a new phase of hotel development: building large-scale conference hotels for up to five hundred guests. To this end, Prime Minister Shearer's government passed the Hotel (Incentives) Act in 1968, which enhanced the 1944 subsidies: hotels with at least 350 beds and convention facilities now qualified for a fifteen-year tax holiday, rather than the original seven.[38]

This law finally drew in major international hotel developers, including both Pan Am's and BOAC's hotel divisions, who teamed up with local developers and broke ground on massive projects. BOAC's Pegasus Hotel in Kingston was expected to cost over US$7 million, while Pan Am's Intercontinental Hotels committed to manage (though not own) the long-planned US$17.7 million resort property near Montego Bay's airport. When it was asked to further mitigate the risks of both these projects beyond the 1968 subsidies, the Shearer government also guaranteed some of the construction loans. An even bolder commitment to hotel development came in the 1968 decision to found the Urban Development Corporation (UDC), which was owned entirely by the government and charged with increasing tourism in areas designated as high priority, including downtown Kingston, the new north shore town of Ocho Rios, and the remote Seven-Mile Beach at Negril. The UDC then laid out funding to construct convention hotels in each area, two of which—Ocho Rios and Kingston—chose Pan Am's Intercontinental Hotels to lease and manage the properties. The government was now investing tens of millions of dollars into convention hotel construction and taking on ownership of various hotels as well.[39]

Note the opening dates for these projects and their proximity to the worldwide oil crisis: BOAC's Pegasus opened in 1973, Pan Am's Montego Bay Intercontinental in 1974, its sister property in Ocho Rios in 1975, and its other sister property in downtown Kingston in 1976. Thus, this burgeoning bubble of hotel development was ready to pop right when OPEC drastically cut its deliveries of oil to the Western world in 1973 and 1974. As a country with no oil reserves, Jamaica was poorly positioned to weather the quadrupling of fuel costs. During the crisis, each of the "four legs" of Jamaica's postindependence economy shrank.

Heavy energy users like the bauxite industry were hit with drastic increases in production costs. Yet, even more detrimental was what G. Arthur Brown saw happening in industrialized countries: "The rich countries decided to cut back on economic growth and set up a deflationary policy to reduce consumption.... The deflationary policy had a serious adverse effect on demand for developing countries' products and thus began the long slide in commodity prices which in turn reduced the incomes from developing countries' exports." For Jamaica, the consequences were calamitous and multifaceted. As Brown noted, "Jamaica obviously was caught up in this vicious cycle: borrowing heavily to maintain imports, being hit by declining commodity prices, particularly bauxite and sugar and, as we got into the 1980s, being further hit by high real interest rates. This means that from reduced export earnings we had to pay for high-priced energy and the servicing of an escalating debt."[40]

The government's bold investments in convention hotels since the late 1960s now looked foolhardy. While tourist arrivals continued to increase from 1966 through 1974, "the results of this favorable trend were however nullified by a substantially faster building of new hotels and resulted in a steady decrease in year-round island-wide room occupancy, reaching an alarming low of 40% for 1974," noted a consultant for Air Jamaica. The oil shock precipitated a reckoning in the tourism sector far beyond Air Jamaica. The convention hotels, originally privately held companies, were sold to the UDC, which was now stuck paying their debts and covering their losses.[41] Faced with seeing them either closed or operating but government-owned, the Michael Manley government reluctantly opted for the latter. It was a last-ditch effort to salvage the thousands of hotel-based jobs that Jamaicans relied on.

In 1976, the minister of tourism in Manley's government, the future prime minister P. J. Patterson, announced that the UDC's most recent acquisitions of convention hotels around the island, "will place approximately 3,300 rooms under the control of Government." He added that the debt burden for these properties was especially high, since "all [of UDC's] secondary development projects," including the hotel projects it owned, "have been financed by loans with no cash equity input from Government." Also concerning was the growing difficulty finding lenders: whereas loans used to be available from banks, "now, however, long-term commercial bank financing is extremely difficult to find and medium-term funds are also scarce."[42] Patterson's address took place as Michael Manley's government, facing a broader lending crisis, contemplated bailout negotiations with the IMF. Meanwhile, labor unrest fed violence on the streets, increased crime in middle-class areas, and added to the lawlessness in West Kingston's shantytowns. States of emergency, including deployment of the Jamaica Defense Force on city streets, were commonplace in the mid- to late 1970s.

Air Jamaica's financial prospects took a similar nosedive with the oil shock. Its dependence on tourists for 80 percent of its business was unfortunate, as tourism is especially vulnerable to recessions. With more Americans forgoing vacations, Air Jamaica struggled to maintain its revenue, while also decreasing capacity and laying off workers. The company posted a profit in 1973 of JA$1.38 million and even was able to maintain financial discipline in 1974 by posting a more modest profit of JA$546,000. However, the 1974 annual report warned of losses in the following year, due to "increasing costs, low yielding fares, and the work stoppage at the start of the year." It added that for every dollar earned, an unsustainable twenty-three cents were now going to fuel costs.[43] In 1975, Air Jamaica lost a staggering JA$2.54 million and management reported even more ominous prospects for 1976: "If the world economy continues to recover without any major dislocation in commodity prices, and if crime and violence here in Jamaica abates and our industrial problems are quickly resolved, we could see the beginning of a slow recovery. If these conditions are absent, the year could prove disastrous."[44]

Unfortunately, 1976 was, in fact, a disastrous year, with economic frustrations spurring protests and numerous strikes. An exceptionally contentious and violent election campaign that year further exacerbated social tensions. Michael Manley was first elected in 1972 with an economic program summed up by his political slogan (borrowed from a popular reggae song) "Better Mus' Come." He vowed to continue his political rivals' earlier Keynesian commitments to stimulate development through state debt and state ownership of enterprises, though now coupled with more ambitious spending to combat poverty.[45] During Manley's reelection campaign, partisan tensions were far more intense, as was Manley's antagonism toward the IMF, the American government, and American companies operating bauxite mines in Jamaica. When the IMF pushed the government to accept severe austerity measures in exchange for emergency loans, Manley shared his response at a massive election rally: "The Jamaican government will not accept anybody, anywhere in the world telling us what to do in our own country." He reached his crescendo with the remark, "Above all, we're not for sale."[46]

Manley's message reverberated with voters, who delivered a decisive victory in December 1976. However, faced with no alternatives to overcome ballooning state debts and the declining prospects of finding lenders, he agreed to return a negotiating team to the IMF in 1977, headed by G. Arthur Brown. Meeting failure in the initial round, a team was reassembled in 1978, this time without Brown, and succeeded in finalizing an agreement that provided US$240 million in loans, in exchange for a 30 percent devaluation in the Jamaican dollar and further austerity measures, import controls, and tax increases.

Overall, IMF officials anticipated that the 1978 agreement would precipitate a dramatic 25 percent drop in ordinary Jamaicans' living standards, which further exacerbated the cycle of protests, strikes, violence, and states of emergency. By 1979, faced with ever-growing opposition to both the IMF and to Manley's leadership, the Jamaican government abandoned the protocols, with Manley calling them "a disastrous program" that was imposed on Jamaica "as retaliatory punishment that this impertinent little country had dared to question their wisdom." By the end of Manley's term in 1980, there was no working relationship between Jamaica and the IMF, and the country was still burdened with debt, by then totaling over US$1.3 billion.[47]

Whatever culpability lies with the Manley government's commitment to democratic socialism for the growing nationalizations and debt, it was the more conservative government of Hugh Shearer, elected in 1968, that wrote and passed the legislation that ultimately exposed the government to these risks, at least in the hotel and aviation spheres. It was also complete coincidence that the popping of the tourism bubble—as well as the simultaneous popping of the bauxite bubble—took place after Manley's 1972 election, due to the unforeseen oil crisis. While Manley's government was accused of recklessly nationalizing companies, it gained ownership of the new mega-hotels only reluctantly. The government's role as payer of last resort, thanks to corporate subsidy programs from 1968, now made it the owner of resort after resort.

These difficulties also occurred right when the government was required to buy out more of Air Canada's ownership stake in Air Jamaica.

This time at the behest of the United States' CAB—an irony that deserves more attention from those studying the Manley years—the government increased its ownership in another flagging Jamaican company. In 1974 it purchased an additional 6 percent of "regular shares" from Air Canada, and in the following year—as Air Jamaica posted its sobering JA$2.54 million loss—it raised its ownership share to 74 percent. Each year, the government also repaid Air Canada over US$1 million from its 1969 line of credit. The company's debt-to-equity ratio now reached a perilous 84:16 split, deviating substantially from the 60:40 norm that was considered healthy for airlines.[48]

It is telling to compare Air Jamaica's struggles with Pan Am at this moment of crisis. Even this most storied global airline was unmoored by the 1973-74 oil crisis, a situation made worse by its purchase of a large fleet of gas-guzzling Boeing 747 jumbo jets. For the first time ever, Pan Am had to dramatically reduce its route network. After allowing its Intercontinental Hotels in Jamaica to fall into government hands, Pan Am managers in March 1976 suspended all flights to Jamaica. The airline stayed out of Jamaica for seven years, until 1983, before ultimately going out of business altogether in 1991.

Ironically, the airline that meddled to expel BOAC from the Caribbean and keep Air Jamaica a weak, indebted competitor now unilaterally ceded its market share as conditions in Jamaica worsened. After Pan Am's withdrawal, Air Jamaica carried 75 percent of air traffic to the island, making the moribund tourism industry even more dependent on the beleaguered airline.[49] Even if the government had wanted to divest from Air Jamaica at this stage, the airline's disappearance would have been more calamitous than at any time before.

The two decades of aviation growth around Jamaican independence saw both bold successes in combating the cartography of colonialism and, unfortunately, bold failures. Massive airport expansions to make both Montego Bay and Kingston jet-ready by the country's declaration of independence on August 6, 1962, allowed the new nation to ascend into the Jet Age—albeit while still captive to Pan Am and BOAC, who brought the lion's share of the ever-growing numbers of tourists to the island. G. Arthur Brown then succeeded in crafting an artful attack on this cartography of colonialism: he created a joint venture with Britain's BOAC and Trinidad's BWIA that would allow Air Jamaica to become the new country's national airline on the cheap. The first iteration of Air Jamaica had no jet costs to assume, no in-flight employees to pay, and a guarantee that government debts would not exceed UK£20,000 in a year.

At this point, however, the Americans struck back against the Chicago aviation system's normal rules of engagement. Pan Am, eager to maintain its dominance after decolonization, attacked Air Jamaica as a "paper airline" undeserving of access to American markets, and the United States government agency in charge of issuing such licenses, the Civil Aeronautics Board, concurred. The ensuing stalemate delayed Air Jamaica's launch from 1963 to 1966, with the Americans still getting the last word. By 1969, Air Jamaica was compelled to shed its previous partners, assume more financial risk, and fly its own planes with its own crews. Even when G. Arthur Brown reincorporated the airline as a joint venture with Air Canada, the CAB here too forced Air Canada to fully divest by 1979.

Even so, for a few brief years, G. Arthur Brown's Air Jamaica (both iterations of it) seized market share on routes between New York and Jamaica. Then, as a consequence of bilateral negotiations in 1969 and thereafter, Air Jamaica was able to expand its footprint to several more gateways in the United States, as well as open up flights into Canada, the Bahamas, and even Britain. By 1973, Air Jamaica had built out the contours of what a cartography of postcolonialism looks like: Jamaica was now a hub, with Air Jamaica flights linking it directly to a dozen cities in the North Atlantic region. Despite carrying a heavy debt burden from the start-up period of the Air Canada joint venture, prospects were decent that Air Jamaica could continue to grow, and continue to earn a profit, as Jamaica's tourism industry upsized. This was now an era of mass tourism, replete with jet planes and three-hundred-bed convention-sized resort hotels.

Then came the oil crisis of 1973–74, followed by decisions by the West's central bankers to combat inflation by raising interest rates and grinding economic growth to a halt. The resulting recession was calamitous for Jamaica, as it raised energy and import costs while lowering global prices for its bauxite, sugar, and bananas. Crucially for Air Jamaica, the tourist trade, already showing signs of weakness before 1974, contracted precipitously thereafter, as consumers in the North Atlantic region cut back on vacationing. Air Jamaica never recovered from a confluence of crises: the OPEC oil shock; the costly CAB-mandated extraction from its partnership with Air Canada; and the labor unrest and politically motivated violence that was exacerbated by the country's debt and ensuing conflicts with the IMF.

All these developments are far from the turning of the "wheel of history" that Premier Norman Manley rosily proclaimed for Jamaica from a jetliner in 1962, or what G. Arthur Brown hoped for with Air Jamaica's seemingly successful takeoffs in 1966 and, again, in 1969. In the end, the challenges of developing a cartography of postcolonialism were too numerous, just as the independence-era economic challenges for this comparatively impoverished and small state were too great to overcome. Chroniclers of Air Jamaica's history may be tempted—as with the few historians who have examined aviation in the Cold War Global South—to attribute these failures to Jamaicans themselves: to the hubris of seeking national prestige through an airline, to mismanagement of a highly technical and complex enterprise, to miscalculations in developing tourist assets too quickly.[50]

Yet, Air Jamaica's failure can be traced to actions by its colonial overlords in London and its neo-imperial overlords in the United States—especially the latter. As part of a larger strategy to maintain predominance in the Caribbean, aviation officials at Pan Am and the Civil Aeronautics Board placed excessive financial burdens on Air Jamaica. Similarly, Jamaica's legacy under colonial rule, including under American economic hegemony since the early twentieth century, placed excessive burdens on the newly independent country. Incurring debt was the only way forward prescribed by the governor of Jamaica at the dawn of independence, a condition that Jamaica's local elected officials accepted as inevitable. Debt was how Jamaica was to address its stunning poverty. Debt was also how Jamaica was to develop its infant industries like tourism, including its hotels, airports, and airlines.

By the close of the 1970s, Air Jamaica had become exactly what British diplomats in 1964 surmised was the CAB's ultimate intent: an indebted airline, 100 percent owned by a Jamaican government that had "no strength . . . left [to be] able to support Air Jamaica against the powerful blows that Pan American could rain on it."[51] Unexpectedly, however, Pan Am itself was no longer around to seize on Air Jamaica's weaknesses. Instead, the tumult of the mid-1970s temporarily left the weak Air Jamaica with even less competition from US carriers—and with more obligations to supply tourists to increasingly cash-starved, government-owned resorts. In the end, nobody won from American protectionism, especially not Jamaica's taxpayers, tourism investors, nor its workers eager for jobs in aviation and tourism.

Part II

Forging Cosmopolitan Working Women

CHAPTER 4

Alix d'Unienville

The West's Strict Confines on Cosmopolitan Working Women

Part II of this book descends from the clouds of earlier discussions on aviation policy and diplomatic maneuverings to consider the lived experiences of airline flight attendants. It particularly focuses on a social development that arose as more of the world's citizens, even those beyond the United States, connected with Clare Boothe Luce's aspiration to fly everywhere: shortly after World War II, stewardesses supplanted male stewards. These women soon predominated not only in the West—across the United States, Canada, and Western Europe—but they also spread through Europe's East and the Global South at the same time new airlines were taking off in these regions. Thus, even in the pre-jet years following the war, a global cadre of women entered into the ultramodern, travel-intense, cosmopolitan profession of stewardessing.

This feminization of the flight attendant corps was yet another American innovation. Back in 1930, the future United Airlines, then named Boeing Air Transport, hired a team of women for a job that was held solely by men at all other airlines, at least at the few that hired attendants. They quickly became popular with airlines' mostly male customers and won accolades from the media as well, leading many other American airlines, though not all, to follow suit. Industry leader Pan

Am and Eastern Airlines, a major domestic carrier, kept male-only hiring policies until the labor shortage during World War II forced them to change. Yet, by the mid-1950s, men were hired only sparingly, mainly for the supervisory role of purser on international flights (a purser divides work roles among the other flight attendants, manages communications with the cockpit, and handles all paperwork on flights). Thereafter, male stewards and pursers comprised a mere 3 percent of the nation's flight attendant corps.[1]

Before the war a handful of Western European carriers also employed stewardesses, with Swissair being the first in 1934.[2] Yet, only after hostilities ended did Western European airlines opt en masse for women. Thus, when Air France returned to flying in 1946, it hired its first eleven women, including the soon-to-be celebrity Alix d'Unienville. KLM of the Netherlands returned to its prewar practice of hiring women, while Belgium's Sabena and Scandinavia's SAS followed Air France's example and hired their very first women in 1946. Britain's storied BOAC was no exception: in the same year, the airline ended its two-decade custom of hiring only men, known as "cabin boys," when reviving its routes to the far reaches of the empire.[3]

Stewardesses also became the primary choice for airlines in Europe's East and the Global South, though room remained for some improvisation at the national level. Western Europe's 1946 precedents weighed heavily on planners in Yugoslavia when they prioritized women for JAT Airways, though without closing the door entirely to male applicants. The presence of men among non-pursers at JAT was just one of the airline's several differences from treatment of flight attendants in the West. While JAT's stewardesses adhered to the same general norm that they be beautiful and charming, they benefited from socialism's stronger commitment to gender equality in the workplace. They therefore always retained the right to marry and stay working for a full thirty-year career, things Western stewardesses largely could not do.

Before the Jet Age and for a decade thereafter, there was no Air Jamaica. The only airline to hire Jamaicans as flight attendants and so-called ground attendants in the pre-jet era was British West Indies Airways. BWIA, perhaps following its parent company BOAC's newfound preference for stewardesses, reserved both jobs for women. In fact, the woman who ultimately became Air Jamaica's first head of stewardesses in 1968, Marguerite LeWars Kirkpatrick, started working a decade earlier as a BWIA ground attendant at Kingston Airport, offering extra care for travelers navigating the terminal. While thriving in this job, she also moonlighted as a beauty pageant contestant in the 1961 Miss World competition and even starred as a femme fatale in the 1962 James Bond film *Dr. No*. Through it all, LeWars Kirkpatrick became a model for later Air Jamaica stewardesses, who, like her, were trained to convey grace and poise under pressure.

The Political, Economic, and Social Stakes of Pre-jet Stewardesses

While the postwar transition from stewards to stewardesses may seem a strictly social development, there were important economic reasons undergirding this change. Airlines' rapid expansion after the war relied on thousands of decommissioned military transport planes that were now either donated or put on sale at rock-bottom prices. Lower aircraft costs allowed these resurgent airlines to charge somewhat lower fares, which in turn begat a more diverse passenger base. More women, children, and seniors now accompanied those who had always comprised the bulk of frequent fliers: businessmen. An equally important economic factor was that American and Western European incomes were growing as airlines' overhead costs declined. The West's Marshall Plan–stimulated *Wirtschaftswunder* (economic miracle) fostered a consumer spending boom, with even middle-class families now able to contemplate air travel. At this point, the economic democratization of air travel intersected with the social force of sexism, coalescing around the notion that women were more capable of serving various types of air passengers. Especially the very young and old often required more attention from flight attendants, and the presumption was that women, as supposedly natural caregivers, would best meet their needs.

Airlines from capitalist economies—those in the West and many in the Global South, including Jamaica—had an additional economic incentive to hire women. The postwar social contract that prevailed in these societies bestowed a family wage on male laborers, with labor unions (no less strong in the Caribbean than in the United States or Western Europe) ready to combat any backsliding. For airlines, which typically operated with small, if any, profit margins and with large debt burdens, designating flight attendant positions or ground attendant positions as women's work offered a reprieve from this expensive compensation scheme. Thus, to justify excluding men, airlines after World War II increasingly wrote flight attendant job descriptions to emphasize feminine skills like serving food, comforting worried passengers, caring for children, and providing a sexy look. As such, these positions became decidedly pink collar: they were now women-only and thereby lower-paying jobs offering primarily short-term employment. They were also riddled with other forms of gender discrimination, including sexual harassment, a disadvantage that their employers only encouraged.[4]

Airlines in the West were by far the worst transgressors in assigning restrictive regimens to stewardesses that were unlike anything imposed on airlines' all-male pilots or even on their few remaining stewards. Across Western Europe and North America there were bans on marrying, having children, working after a certain age (usually thirty-two or thirty-five), and being over a certain weight. These airlines also notoriously hired based on a woman's looks, with their training focusing on beauty tips as much as safety or technical expertise. The average stewardess in the United States in the 1950s worked only eighteen months, most typically "retiring" to marry.[5]

In the West, the combined effect of imposing low wages and negating long-term career options made stewardessing a low-pay, dead-end job, especially since purser positions were off-limits to women at most airlines with international routes. This discriminatory regime was considerably less entrenched in Yugoslavia and Jamaica. Instead, stewardesses in these countries demonstrate that pink collar discrimination could be ameliorated through political commitments to equality. JAT never imposed marriage bans or age-based retirement schemes due to explicit clauses in the country's 1946 constitution protecting working women, while Air Jamaica executives failed to implement such restrictions because stewardesses and their politically well-connected union pushed back.

All the same, neither JAT nor Air Jamaica addressed the rampant sexual harassment stewardesses endured on the job, nor did they undo the strict gender segregation that foreclosed women's opportunities to advance into jobs like piloting or managing. Both Jamaica and Yugoslavia kept pilot positions in the hands of men longer than in the West: Air Jamaica's first female pilot began work in 1979, while JAT never made this move before the Yugoslav state disintegrated in 1991. Meanwhile, in the West, SAS (Scandinavian Airlines System) hired the first female pilot, Turi Widerøe, in 1969, with other carriers in North America and Western Europe typically following that lead in the 1970s. Overall, then, the reality for a stewardess seeking job advancement was similarly frustrating, especially before the onset of the Jet Age, regardless of whether she hailed from the West, East, or South. This type of aspiring career woman could progress only by joining the airline's hiring committee or its training program for future stewardesses, while hoping that she, like Marguerite LeWars Kirkpatrick, would have the improbable good fortune of being selected to manage the airline's overall stewardess operations, the lone upper management spot open to women.

Overall, part II is the social counterpart to part I's political and economic content, as it details the rise of stewardesses as embodiments of their nation's strivings to attain modernity via aviation. These women, no less than the airlines who hired them, were a vital part of efforts in Yugoslavia and Jamaica to craft a modern identity in which these countries also mastered technology and fit into the cosmopolitan world that aviation fostered. Stewardesses particularly matter for what they reveal more broadly about norms of womanhood in this futurescape. They were, after all, the only cadre of working women allowed in one of the world's most cosmopolitan, most technologically sophisticated milieus. Thus, the first stewardesses in France, Yugoslavia, and Jamaica served as an avant garde for their fellow countrywomen on the ground.

Importantly, stewardesses were also working-class women, albeit with training, personal comportment skills, and a salary that allowed them to aspire to become, or at least pass as, members of the middle class. Even in socialist Yugoslavia, where social class distinctions were officially anathema, JAT stewardesses knew that their salaries, transnational mobility, and other perks (like their lavish company vacations) elevated them over other working women. Still, these were working women with a class status several notches below the airplane's other occupants, whether predominantly elite-class passengers or upper-middle-class pilots.

Such gender-based socioeconomic imbalances were especially galling in the aftermath of World War II, when women the world over—but especially in fascist-occupied territories like parts of France and Yugoslavia—took on notionally masculine roles, including soldiering, and sacrificed their lives to support the war efforts. Yugoslavia's stewardesses were at first modeled after the *partizanka*, a female Partisan soldier under Tito's command, though they surrendered this masculine-coded status as JAT's routes stretched further westward in the mid-1950s. A similar rollback of wartime roles was especially embittering for France's Alix d'Unienville, whose feats rivaled those of Yugoslavia's *partizanka*, leading to her decoration with the Croix de Guerre before she earned her wings as a stewardess with Air France.

Part II entertains this question: Why, after the decisive myth-busting of women's roles that took place during World War II, did societies in all three parts of the Cold War cosmos create a traditional rendering for the stewardess, even as she was supposed to be a quintessentially modern, cosmopolitan, working woman? One might theorize a Cold War political and social imperative to return to the prewar status quo for the sake of national security. If that was indeed the case, the situation might have been particularly pressing in France and Western Europe, perhaps even in Jamaica, which were threatened by the rise of communism. Like in the United States, it is possible that the fight to maintain the political status quo encouraged a restoration of the social status quo ante, including reverting to traditional gender norms.[6] But what could account for stewardesses' similar stylization in communist-led Yugoslavia? After all, leaders here heralded their postwar regime as the product of both a political and social revolution. The country's communists promised to introduce women's equality, and they attained power in late 1945 partly thanks to expanding the vote to women. Thereafter, they ratified a new constitution in 1946 that granted expansive new rights to working women.

What becomes clear throughout part II is that a backlash to working women's liberation took hold in all three worlds of the Cold War. Societies in the West, East, and South were all loath to acknowledge the radical and yet obvious conclusion of the war: women were just as capable as men in work roles. This included being more than qualified for higher-skilled, higher-tech jobs in aviation. As a tense compromise between progress and backlash, the job of flight attendant was carved out as the sole niche for women in aviation. Then, despite sometimes subtle and sometimes significant differences in workplace rights depending on their country of residence, these cosmopolitan working women all endured work rules that were backward looking, encountering everyday proscriptions that stunted their aspirations for equality: limits on promotion, subordination to male supervisors, grooming standards enshrined as essential job prerequisites, and vulnerability to unwanted sexual advances. None of the Cold War worlds countenanced working women's full equality.

Western Europe's Women *en vol*

A few years after she started as an Air France stewardess, Alix d'Unienville became Europe's most famous woman in the job. She first gained notoriety in 1949, when she penned a highly acclaimed chronicle of her work exploits. A work of literary journalism titled *En vol: Journal d'une hôtesse de l'air* (*In Flight: Journal of an Air Hostess*), the book indulges the cosmopolitan yearning to fly everywhere, which for d'Unienville meant New York in the west to Saigon in the Far East. It also includes various encounters, some entertaining and some confrontational, with passengers and coworkers along the way. When d'Unienville won France's esteemed Prix Albert-Londres for journalism in 1950, two things were clear: much of the public was enthralled by her account of a globetrotting, working woman, and thousands of young women across Europe were eager to join her. The book was translated into multiple European languages.

Her descriptions of working in flight combine sometimes poetic descriptions, such as her rendering of the sublime kaleidoscope of shapes and colors observed from the plane's windows, with more mundane prose about everyday annoyances, like handling overly demanding flyers. In the very first chapter, for example, she chronicles a stress-filled flight from Paris to Rome during a thunderstorm.[7] As for life on the ground, d'Unienville again accentuates the mundane challenges of her everyday routine. She catalogs various hardships of traveling, including enduring intrusive border guards, laundering her uniform in sinks late at night, and battling insomnia in noisy hotels. That said, she also includes the enjoyments of sightseeing in foreign cities and the unscripted fun of occasional late-night outings with colleagues.

Even while d'Unienville faithfully reproduces the routine of most of her workweeks, the book's publishers, as well as the committee for the Prix Albert-Londres, found her chronicle revolutionary. Their excitement arose for one reason: *En vol*'s proceedings were experienced and chronicled by a woman. As the book's preface, not written by d'Unienville, explains, "For the first time the traditional crew, formerly composed solely of men, has been complemented with a feminine presence: that of a hostess charged with seeing after passengers' well-being. The author of this memoir, who was one of the first women to practice this profession, may not always bend to the necessities and rules of commercial aviation, but this same independence gives her an original viewpoint, often unexpected, of this new 'heroic era' of aviation."[8]

Yet, even as the publishers celebrated d'Unienville's "independence" and her "original viewpoint" in this new "heroic era," the heroine at the center of this narrative is elusive. Beyond superficial coverage of her joys and annoyances, readers of *En vol* discover only scant details about d'Unienville herself and how she makes sense of her work and her travels. She does not weigh in on world politics, and even discussion of her social life is impersonal, with no friend or colleague mentioned by name. Also absent is discussion of how d'Unienville structured her private life to accommodate her globe-trotting work: what life at her Paris home looked like, how friends and family members helped nourish her through the job's hardships, or whether she dated or otherwise found romantic companionship.

Perhaps most disappointingly for feminist-inclined readers, d'Unienville also ignores the gender-based inequities of her work and how they impacted her. Readers remain oblivious to chronic abuses: distressing experiences of sexual harassment; a rigorous regime of bodily strictures (perfectly kept uniforms, strict weight requirements, girdle checks, closely governed hair and makeup regimes); myriad sexist put-downs from pilots and managers; and deeply unjust restrictions placed on a stewardess's ability to marry, have children, or to keep working regardless of age. None of these indignities appear in d'Unienville's text.

Instead, when scouring the text for inklings of a feminist consciousness, one finds only superficial accounts of gender issues. For example, when chronicling her first visit to New York, d'Unienville discusses America's sexism in an oblique way, framing her observations in a discussion of American politesse: d'Unienville admits that she and her fellow French stewardesses "kept a rather poor idea of American men, the officers or soldiers whom we had seen hanging out on the Champs-Elysées or Piccadilly Circus, rolling drunk on café terraces and whistling at girls" at the close of World War II. She adds, however, that her experience in New York nightclubs altered that perception. Here, she found American men respectfully standing up whenever a woman rose from her seat: "The American man at home is a jovial, but correct gentleman. His politeness towards women is perhaps more refined than on the Old Continent."[9]

Conveniently, *En vol* begins its narration in the midst of the action, with d'Unienville working the aforementioned flight to Rome during a storm. If she had begun with her application to Air France and the airline's hiring criteria, her chronicle would have been less inspiring to young European women. As a reporter for the newspaper *Le Figaro* detailed in 1946, women who applied at Air France had to meet exacting standards:

> What is required of [these women]? Simply all of the following: to be between the ages of 21 and 30; to measure between 1m 55

and 1m 65; to weigh between 45 and 65 kilos; to have no more than a 70cm waistline; to present all assurances of morality; to be single, widowed, or divorced without charges; to present a pleasant face, personality, and demeanor; to possess the first part of a bachelor's degree, or lacking that, a certificate attesting to either: one's initial higher-level studies, a state diploma in nursing, in social work, or in air rescue. And this is not all: one must finally speak, fluently, a foreign language, preferably English, as well as get by in the language of Goethe, Cervantes, or Dante.

He then adds with sarcastic understatement, "So do not be surprised that [the first] screening has left... only fifty of the initial applicants."[10] Note how few of these qualifications involved a woman's ability to do the work required, which entailed keeping people safe, feeding them, acquainting them with flying, and reducing their stress levels when anxious.

Norwegian Nan Hartvedt, one of the first stewardesses at SAS, recalls that almost identical physical criteria were in effect when she, like d'Unienville, applied in 1946: "We could not be taller than 1.68 meters and not weigh more than 58 kilos." She also recalls that this preoccupation with physical traits carried into the interviews: "We had to stand [in place], with our arms [fully] stretched out ... and [while doing so] we had to cross one knee over the other. And then we had to touch our noses [with a finger]." Hartvedt laughed fifty years later when recalling this strange gymnastics that supposedly proved both her beauty and dexterity: "[Somehow] I passed through!"[11] At SAS, only once these physical demands were fulfilled would a candidate be assessed for her actual work-based qualifications, which included some education beyond high school and the ability to speak one foreign language—as at Air France, preferably English—with additional language knowledge also desired.

Air France's focus on physical traits began with candidates' applications, which required the submission of two photos of themselves. The interview then opened with a comparison of one's in-person looks with their photos, with "a jury rating their general appearance with a score from 1 to 5." Only those who scored highly could sit for the language exams and then potentially continue to the interview stage.[12] For children of Western Europe's elites, including Alix d'Unienville, the educational criteria were easy enough to meet. Her schooling in the faraway island colony of Reunion, then later in Brittany, was along classical lines, and her family's move to London in 1940 to flee the Nazi invasion provided her a command of English. However, for candidates drawn from the middle or working classes, these criteria were more difficult to meet.

For example, SAS's Hartvedt, growing up middle class in Norway, had a solid education that allowed her to find office work before applying to SAS, but the airline's language demands were an obstacle. "We should be able to converse in German and French. So, I learnt a couple phrases I could impress them with . . . that was all I knew."[13] Clearly, in the case of Hartvedt and numerous others at Western Europe's less prestigious airlines, other criteria—most prominently, their looks and charm—outweighed the educational and language standards that favored elite women. Air France, however, had the luxury of rigidly applying these standards. Their first culling to fifty candidates was further whittled down to the eleven who finally were hired.

At least SAS's and other carriers' informal flexibility assured that Western Europe's new stewardess corps would have at least some class diversity. While passengers were primarily elites well into the 1960s, some of the stewardesses serving them were not. They still had to speak and act like well-schooled patricians, and under no circumstances could their looks be plebian. Yet, beyond these criteria, they needed only to share the passion for travel that d'Unienville celebrates in her memoir.

D'Unienville's Dual Acts of Subterfuge

D'Unienville had to erase more than coverage of sexist work rules to make *En vol* an uncontroversial, un-feminist, and yet exceedingly popular account of stewardesses' work. She was also silent about her unconventional personal history. After all, she was a highly decorated war hero due to her service as a spy on behalf of the French Resistance. Soon after she fled to London at age eighteen, she began working in the headquarters of Charles de Gaulle's Free French forces, initially writing propaganda leaflets to drop over occupied France. As she gained experience, however, she began training in espionage and was sent first to the Women's Auxiliary Air Force and then the Special Operations Executive.

Once trained, d'Unienville was air-dropped into occupied France with 40 million francs and a series of orders, all of which she delivered to Resistance officers. She then served as a courier over the next three months before being arrested and sent to Paris's notorious Gestapo-run prison. On August 15, 1944, in the last days of their occupation of Paris, the Nazis packed her on a train in a mass transfer of prisoners out of France and into Germany. A series of cattle cars carried 665 women and 1650 men, first stopping at Buchenwald before continuing to the women's concentration camp at Ravensbrück. D'Unienville was slated for the latter, where she would have endured forced labor, starvation, and, most likely, death. Of the Resistance fighters on these infamous "trains of death," only twenty-seven survived until the conclusion of the war, not even a year later.

However, d'Unienville never made it to Germany. Instead, she executed a perilous escape along the train route not far from Paris. When the prisoners were briefly removed from the train to cross a damaged railroad bridge on foot, she seized her chance:

> While the prisoners surged round a drinking fountain at Mery-sur-Marne, she noticed the guards not watching so she slipped into an open door. She recalled only hearing blood pounding in her temples while the guards were rounding up the prisoners outside. [She was] [h]idden by the family [who occupied the home she entered, and] they arranged for her to be treated by a doctor. A local policeman ... then looked after her until American troops arrived.

A comrade in the Resistance recalled that d'Unienville was "placid, efficient, punctual, [and] was blessed with such composure that allowed her, almost the only one amongst the deportees on the trains of horror ... to carry off a miraculous escape."[14] For her espionage activities and her escape, d'Unienville was made a military member of the Order of the British Empire and received the French distinctions Chevalier du Légion d'honneur and the Croix de Guerre.[15] Not yet finished with adventure as the war concluded, d'Unienville accepted a job with the US military in Southeast Asia, as the Americans oversaw the transfer of Indochina from Japanese occupation back to their prewar French overlords.

It was only after these adrenaline-filled years that d'Unienville—still young, husbandless, and craving adventure—discovered that her options were greatly reduced in peacetime. National security positions returned to being almost exclusively male-only. In fact, almost any jobs requiring travel, especially across borders, also reverted to men. It was this foreclosure of opportunities, even for a decorated spy, that effectively forced d'Unienville into stewardessing. Thus, *En vol*'s rosy claims heralding a "heroic era" of women's liberation rings strikingly hollow. This assertion could only be rendered plausible by concealing that the author was a former spy who escaped near-certain death at Ravensbrück. Only later, decades after her time at Air France, did d'Unienville admit to being unhappy with this phase of her life. Recalling her spy training, she wryly noted, "Specialist instructors came to teach us how to make false keys, to break locks, break into properties, poison dogs, survive in hostile conditions, in thick forests, and to find our way without a compass. I have often thought that if afterwards I had put these skills to work, my life would have been more amusing and profitable."[16]

This tension between Alix d'Unienville's actual life and her self-presentation in *En vol* reveals an important fact about the flight attendant role in the pre-jet era—namely, that the "collar" in pink-collar labor was very restrictive. For stewardesses, the freedom to fly everywhere was a geographical reality (they truly did traverse the globe), but it came with a myriad of indignities. The author's personal sequel to *En vol*, even though not written down, was cautionary. D'Unienville grew less energized by her work and then readily gave it up after just a few years. Thereafter, she fell back on her book royalties and family wealth to finance a life of leisure in the south of France, dabbling in novel writing. This woman, immensely talented and addicted to adventure in her twenties, was retired—and bored—by her early thirties. Her first acts of espionage, serving as a spy and undertaking a heroic escape, were complemented by another when writing *En vol*: she concealed these past feats to make her narrative of stewardessing more appealing to Europe's next generation of women.

CHAPTER 5

Dragica Pavlović

JAT Stewardesses at the Crossroads of East, West, and South

Dragica Pavlović's debut as Yugoslavia's first flight attendant was inflected with both the optimism and sobriety of the country's early postwar efforts to craft a viable aviation industry. Her inaugural flight in spring 1948 was designed to be yet another milestone in the country's strivings to "walk in step with Europe," in the words of aviation planner Milenko Mitrović.[1] She and four other attendants were hired as part of the country's first Five-Year Plan, which strove to make JAT a tool for bringing West European tourists to Croatia's Adriatic Coast. Thus, when Pavlović boarded her first flight just two years behind her stewardess peers at airlines further West, including Alix d'Unienville at Air France, Yugoslav officials expected to celebrate an important moment of parity. Instead, the thirty-three-year-old Pavlović never made it from Belgrade to Zagreb. A storm arose soon after takeoff, forcing the plane to turn back rather than risk landing on Zagreb's slick grass runway. The aborted flight thereby served as a reminder of Yugoslav aviation's enduring disadvantages: a lack of meteorological equipment, inadequate aids for landing in fog or darkness, and a dearth of concrete runways all played a role in souring Pavlović's debut.[2]

Of course, another storm was brewing as well, this one political in nature: within months Joseph Stalin would expel Yugoslavia's Communist Party from the Cominform and thereby initiate a sustained

FIGURE 5.1. JAT Airways' first stewardess, Dragica Pavlović, greets passengers with a Partisan salute as they board one of the airline's DC-3 aircraft. This image is undated but presumably was taken between 1948, when she began flying, and 1954.
Source: Photo by Zoran Miller, reproduced in Jovo Simišić, "The Symbol of a Profession," *JAT Airways New Review*, September 2010, 46. Permission to use this image courtesy of Air Serbia.

period of destabilization in the country. In the ensuing turmoil, JAT was reduced to a de facto charter service, its partner airline JUSTA was dissolved, and the country's civil aviation authority descended into political infighting. Dragica Pavlović was the lone flight attendant to keep her job through this chaotic period, which stabilized only in the early 1950s. Pavlović ultimately found herself with a distinguished title: she is remembered, to this day, as Yugoslavia's and JAT's first flight attendant, with her short-lived colleagues from the class of 1948 long forgotten.

Pavlović remained an active stewardess until her fiftieth birthday in 1965, at which time she moved to JAT's ground operations in Belgrade and continued working until she completed a full thirty-year career.

The length of her tenure was, of course, unmatchable by her colleagues working for Western European and American carriers. Yet, her tenure's length is only one way in which Dragica Pavlović's career differed from the traditional narrative recorded in Western-dominated aviation histories. Her nearly two decades of flying were also intertwined with the unique maneuverings of Tito's Yugoslavia between the three worlds of the Cold War. The length of her career exemplifies the country's socialist-inspired—ergo, in this rendering, Eastern—orientation, including a fuller embrace of de jure equality for working women. Meanwhile, because her job after the Tito-Stalin split increasingly focused on performing work akin to being a hostess of one's own home, that is, serving as a *domaćica* (housewife/hostess), Pavlović had much in common with flight attendants in the West.

This status as a cultural hybrid between East and West was not exceptional in Cold War Yugoslavia. As the historian Predrag Marković chronicles in his history of the city of Belgrade:

> In Yugoslavia, East and West—their ideologies and ways of life—are not something that gets imposed from the outside. East and West have been internalized in this country and in this city. Starting in 1948, in society, the economy, cultural life, and everyday life, there has been a battle underway between different forms. . . . In every sphere of life one can establish a pair of options, one which presents itself as the West, and the other as the East.[3]

Thus, especially once the Yugoslav government commissioned JAT in 1949 to begin flights to the German-speaking countries of Western Europe, the East-West cultural fluidity that took hold among JAT's flight attendants was a familiar cultural positioning.

What was not endemic to the Yugoslav region's culture and history was the third prong of Tito's foreign policy: a kinship with the countries of the Global South. With the build-out of JAT's lines across the Mediterranean, Dragica Pavlović and her peers spent increasing amounts of time on flights and layovers in places like Cairo and Beirut, and Pavlović also worked as a flight attendant for Tito's delegation during at least one of his extended tours to India, Southeast Asia, and Egypt during the late 1950s. More broadly, Yugoslav women in the 1950s were encouraged to develop a sense of curiosity about and political solidarity with their peers in the Global South. But, as a new generation of scholars attuned to issues of postcolonialism, race, and culture have pointed out, the country's government did little to address domestic racism and Eurocentrism, nor did it challenge its citizens to problematize their whiteness and Europeanness in these new relationships with the Global South.[4] Thus, while flight attendants like Pavlović were encouraged to express solidarity with women of the Global South, this sense of kinship did not render a North-South cultural hybridity akin to the East-West hybridity noted by Marković.

"This Struggle Must Bear Fruit Also for the Women of Yugoslavia"

When Yugoslavia's communist-led National Liberation Front during World War II pushed ahead in its guerilla war to expel fascism, an estimated one hundred thousand women picked up arms and served as soldiers during the war, with two thousand attaining officer status.[5] These *partizanke* (female Partisans) were stellar examples of women demonstrating their ability to be men's equals: they served with valor in all the ways men did, defying the notion that gender norms were hardwired by one's biology and therefore immutable.[6] Tito himself realized that these wartime contributions would beget greater gender equality once peace returned. In 1942, at a meeting of women involved in the war effort, he asserted: "The women of Yugoslavia, who in this struggle are sacrificing so selflessly, they who so persistently are standing in the front rows of the battle for National Liberation, have the right to establish—here, today, once and for always—this fact: that this struggle must bear fruit also for the women of Yugoslavia, that never again can anyone wrench from their hands these hard-won fruits!"[7]

Just behind the Partisans' front lines lay another vast network of female collaborators; they were organized into a communist-led umbrella group known as the Women's Anti-fascist Front (Antifašistička fronta žena, or AFŽ). AFŽ members not only supplied the Partisans with food, medical help, information, and shelter, but they also started campaigns to foster greater independence in women. Since the Partisans held territory primarily in the hilly rural areas of Croatia, Bosnia-Herzegovina, and Serbia, the AFŽ was most active precisely in the most traditional and heavily patriarchal areas of the country. Up to one million women participated in the AFŽ, taking advantage of its educational centers that taught them how to read, practice better hygiene, and improve childcare techniques. AFŽ newspapers became important instruments to mobilize women as devoted anti-fascists and future communists. Yet, while these advances were potentially life-changing for women, their location in highly traditional areas required compromise. As the social philosopher Tijana Okić notes: "The mobilisation of women into the AFŽ coexisted with traditional attitudes, and the women who contributed to the Partisan cause did so, as a rule, by performing traditional women's tasks and chores: cleaning, washing, looking after and caring for others. Thus, from the outset, the work of the AFŽ was conceived strictly as women's work."[8]

In the ensuing years, traditional notions of womanhood coexisted awkwardly with socialist-inspired and wartime-proven notions of women's equality. For the first time, women in socialist Yugoslavia were given the right to vote, and they found extensive encouragement to work outside the home and pursue the necessary education and training for lifelong careers. The subsequent changes to women's lives, when compared to both Yugoslavia's peasant-based agricultural and bourgeois-based urban societies in the prewar era, were dramatic, if still incomplete. Young women were now expected to attend school at least through high school, and universities and other institutions of higher learning opened to them more fully than ever.[9] Beyond schooling, there was further movement of women into the public sphere. In some regions of the country, such as heavily agricultural Bosnia-Herzegovina, the number of women entering non-agricultural workplaces increased by two-and-a-half times, assuring them the modicum of personal autonomy that derived from earning a wage in their own name.[10]

The highlight of women-centered legal changes in postwar Yugoslavia was the Soviet-inspired constitution passed in 1946, which included the progressive article 24 on women's rights: "Women possess the same rights as men in all realms of state, economic, and social-political life. For the same work women have the right to the same pay as men and enjoy special protection in relation to work. The state particularly protects the interests of mothers and children with the establishment of maternity hospitals, orphanages, and kindergartens, and through the right of mothers to paid leave before and after giving birth."[11] Coupled with liberalized divorce laws and other family law reforms, women gained a more solid legal footing, leading some, including Dragica Pavlović, to opt out of marriage completely. Such was the social and legal context in which Yugoslavia's first flight attendants were hired.

Gender Uncertainty at Takeoff

Planning for JAT to add flight attendants dates back to its founding year of 1947. Zdravko Pudarić, the head of expansion plans at the Civil Aviation Authority, articulated a plan to introduce "service of stewards and stewardesses" as a way of "increasing the comfort of passengers" in a meeting with the country's Main Tourism Authority.[12] The context of his comments established a Western-oriented motive for this, since flight attendants were part of a larger effort to generate an influx of Western tourists, whose home airlines already offered stewardess service. Thus, despite tight space restrictions on JAT flights, Pudarić wanted flight attendants to provide the level of comfort that was now expected in the West.

These plans moved forward just months after JAT's inaugural flight in April 1947, with the first recruiting ad placed in August. Later plans divulged in internal memos show even more growth envisioned for 1948: consistent with Pudarić's efforts to double the country's aviation miles that year, there were plans to hire an additional six "stewardesses" for both JAT and its sister airline JUSTA, the Soviet-Yugoslav joint venture.[13] The gendered designation in this text is noteworthy, especially given Pudarić's earlier gender-neutral phrasing and the wording of the newspaper ad that led to Dragica Pavlović's hiring, alongside her four shorter-lived colleagues. The ad ran in the classified section of one of the country's major daily newspapers, Belgrade's *Politika*, under the generic headline "Konkurs" (competition).[14]

The ad's wording regarding the applicants' desired gender stands out for its lack of clarity. The terms used for flight attendants around the Western world circa 1947 were almost all gendered in deliberate ways: "steward" or "purser" designated men, "stewardess" or "hostess" designated women. The Yugoslav ad, however, at first explicitly welcomed men or women to apply, informing readers: "The Main Civil Aviation Authority requires a certain number of comrades" for the position, spelling out in the original Serbian that both female comrades (*drugarice*) and male comrades (*drugovi*) were welcome to apply. The ad goes on to describe the position not as that of steward or stewardess, but rather as *službenik letač*, a novel pairing of nouns that literally translates as "serviceperson flyer" and might be hyphenated in English. Were this the last reference to candidates' gender, it would have been clear that the Aviation Authority sought applications from both women and men, and presumably on equal terms.[15] Yet, several lines later, the ad returns to the topic: "Chiefly female comrades are being considered."[16] The statement's delicate nature, coupled with the gender indeterminacy found elsewhere, leads to a clear conclusion: in this moment when the new constitution compelled ever more workplaces to discount gender in hiring, aviation planners were conforming to the letter of the law, while nonetheless aspiring to the Western standard that the field become heavily feminized.

This tension continues elsewhere in the ad, especially when compared to the criteria advertised by Air France for its 1946 class. Like Air France, the Yugoslav ad stressed foreign language knowledge, with the requirement that one know either French or English, with an additional willingness to consider German speakers. Absent, however, is any mention of one's physical appearance, whether weight, height, or waist size. Also conspicuously absent is Air France's focus on marital status. Indeed, the only criterion that was discriminatory compared to other positions available at JAT was an age restriction. Mimicking Air France, the Yugoslav authorities added that "one's age may not exceed 35 years." When coupled with its preference for "primarily female comrades," one finds here a pretext to privilege youthful, notionally attractive women when the candidates appeared in person for interviews.

Indeed, this refusal to consider candidates older than thirty-five is even more curious when compared with JAT's working manual from 1949. This document stipulates that an applicant for any other work position could be between the ages of eighteen and sixty, since this norm, in the aspirational language of the time, would "enable a socialist work discipline."[17] Only flight attendants were held to a different, decidedly less socialist type of work discipline—one that instead conformed to Western European standards.

The spirit and letter of the 1946 constitution also failed to challenge the total dominance of men in aviation positions that required extensive technical training, including the cadre of engineers, mechanics, and business planners who were essential to running an airline. The pilot corps at both JAT and JUSTA also remained male-only. While this exclusion might have been a result of women's lack of technical training and piloting opportunities (either civilian or military) before and during the war, nothing changed in Yugoslavia in the four-plus decades after the promulgation of the 1946 constitution.

Instead of forcing an end to this male stranglehold, the constitution's commitment to grant women equal access to workplaces was simply ghettoized, with women effectively limited to stewardessing and lower-level roles in administrative offices. Thus, for example, at JUSTA in October 1947, there were only seven women among the airline's ninety-two employees (less than 8 percent of the workforce).[18] When JAT's flight attendant corps finally stabilized and eventually started to grow a few years after the Tito-Stalin split, this mostly female cadre of workers became members of the sort of cordoned-off "pink-collar" labor force that exposed them to various forms of abuse. By 1958, JAT's flight attendant corps had grown to twenty-one workers, eighteen of whom were women. Meanwhile, all forty-nine pilots and twenty-one radio operators at JAT were male.[19] Flight attendants at JAT, just like at Air France, were becoming an unfortunate paradox: they were, by default, the women with the highest status in the country's aviation field, even though they inevitably lagged far behind pilots, planners, and administrators in pay and prestige.

The Stewardess as Part *Partizanka*, Part *Domaćica*

In her first decade of work, Dragica Pavlović experienced the cultural tensions facing Yugoslavia's women profoundly. On the one hand, she exercised more personal freedom than her peers in the West. At the same time, as gender historians writing on socialist Yugoslavia have stressed, the role models for women constituted a double burden. The powerful partizanka soldier was one such model, while the other was the domaćica, the housewife-hostess whose value was found in conforming to traditional gender norms as a stay-at-home—or at least a part-time stay-at-home—wife and mother.[20]

In fact, women across the Eastern bloc were experiencing the bitter reality of the legal liberation offered them by communist leaders. As historian Eric Hobsbawm observes:

> While major changes, such as the massive entry of married women into the labour market might be expected to produce concomitant or consequential changes, they need not do so—as witness the USSR where (after the initial utopian-revolutionary aspirations of the 1920s had been abandoned) married women generally found themselves carrying the double load of old household responsibilities and new wage earning responsibilities without any change in relations between the sexes or in the public or private spheres.[21]

While she chose to remain unmarried and therefore free from the most demanding duties of a domaćica, Dragica Pavlović nonetheless manifests the unrealistic expectations impacting the first generation of JAT stewardesses. Her work experience and that of her peers was an awkward combination of partizanka assertiveness and domaćica traditionalism.

As the image at the beginning of this chapter illustrates, JAT's managers amplified this confusion via the work rules and uniforms they created for Pavlović and her coworkers. In terms of her uniform, at least, JAT adorned Pavlović so as to keep alive the memory of the country's glorious victory over fascism. In the image, she is depicted during JAT's customary preflight greeting to passengers. Though her smile softens the effect, she stands atop the staircase, dressed in a military-inspired uniform, giving the Partisan salute. Visually, then, stewardesses were bedecked in the legacy of the empowered partizanka.

The Partisan salute remained a part of all JAT flights until around 1954, enduring through the Tito-Stalin split, after which it also reminded citizens that Yugoslavia's liberation from fascism was homegrown and less dependent on the Soviets than elsewhere in the Eastern bloc.[22] In other words, Yugoslavia was unique as a nation because its hard-fought victory over fascism was largely achieved by and for themselves. The eminent scholar Joseph Frankel in 1955 called the Partisans' struggle for national liberation the "crucible in which real Yugoslav unity was formed," a succinct assertion of the Partisans' legacy in the myths that strove to create a sense of brotherhood and unity among the country's fractious constituencies.[23]

Note that Pavlović's hat is a loyal replica of a Partisan's cap: all cloth, with no firmness, so that it could be removed and pocketed when duty called. It was not inspired by the rigid women's hats from earlier times, whose large size and brittle firmness forced elite women into nonactive, ornamental roles (lest their hat fall off). It is true that stewardesses in the United States and Western Europe also sported uniforms that, like at JAT, were inspired by soldiers' attire, a holdover from steward uniforms from the 1920s designed by Pan Am and Imperial Airways to imitate naval officers. However, Western stewardess uniforms in the 1940s were also typically coupled with pillbox hats, exactly the sort of rigid ornamentation that compromised their mobility and emphasized their role as fragile beauty objects.

Beyond these exterior symbols of partizanka-like strength, Pavlović also demonstrated similar assertiveness via her professional achievements, which would have been unthinkable for her peers in the West. Her thirty-year career was marked by a series of impressive highlights. Ten years in, during 1956, Pavlović tallied an amazing one million kilometers of flying, for which Tito himself decorated her with the Order of Labor, one of the country's highest honors. Furthermore, near the close of her flying years in 1963, she was elected by fellow JAT employees as president of the Workers' Council, the organization within Yugoslav companies that represented workers' interests to the company's management. While Pavlović ultimately declined the post, her election itself speaks to a profound disparity between Yugoslavia's stewardesses and those in the West: a JAT stewardesses could even, in exceptional cases, be elected to the company's most important organ of "workers' self-management."[24]

Pavlović's personal life also reflected the increased potential for Yugoslavia's new women to take on greater autonomy. From the beginning, JAT allowed stewardesses to marry at any point, a fact that gave Yugoslav stewardesses far more personal choice than their peers in the West. Yet, this freedom also made Pavlović's choice to stay single somewhat suspect. In public, Pavlović conceded that it was her work commitments that diminished her marriage prospects. For example, when asked in 1956 why she was still unmarried and childless, she cast herself as a chronic workaholic: "I spend most of my time on the ground, but even there I am busy with work involving the plane: assigning duties, overseeing things tied to my duties, etc."[25] A 2007 retrospective from JAT similarly suggested that work had replaced her family life: "Dragica was fully devoted to her job and her commitments at JAT. Although she often points out that . . . everyone in the company in the early years was like one large and united family, she never had a family of her own. She simply had no time to marry, and life passed by quickly."[26]

All the same, the very fact that Pavlović had to justify her status as single reflects a lingering traditionalism: women in Yugoslavia still experienced ample pressure to conform to the traditional norm of becoming a domaćica, complete with husband and children. This pressure was little different than what women in Western Europe and North America encountered. Air France's famous Alix d'Unienville "solved" this conundrum by staying completely—though conspicuously—silent about all aspects of her personal life in her chronicle, while Pavlović's invocations of workaholism are equally conspicuous in their attempts to mislead. After all, her assertions overlook the fact that she was already thirty-three years old when she began at JAT, meaning that her prime years for marrying were already quickly passing. If she had a deep desire to marry, she likely would have done so before starting at JAT.

Instead, a stewardess who started flying in 1956 offers a more plausible explanation: "Well, for Dragica," she claimed, "there simply was no match." In this colleague's memory, Pavlović enjoyed adventures in many forms, with her JAT years only accentuating this preexisting trait.

Once at JAT, her stellar reputation put her in line for a wide variety of out-of-the-ordinary experiences, including serving Tito, his wife Jovanka Broz, and other state officials on at least one weeks-long voyage to South and Southeast Asia. When she compared these adventures with marriage and child-rearing, Pavlović—at least in the recollections of her colleague—refused to settle for second best; a husband and children would mean forgoing a life of adventure.[27]

The interviewee stressed, however, that Pavlović's choice to prioritize her work over marriage was neither encouraged nor was it common among stewardesses. Unlike Pavlović, this colleague married in 1958, and she recalls that "every girl of my group [the class of 1956] went to work and [eventually] was married." Notably, marriage itself did not always render such women more pliant domaćice for their husbands. In this stewardess's case, a pattern of tensions with her husband and their respective families quickly arose, even on the night of the couple's engagement party. The stewardess was assigned a domestic route to Titograd (Podgorica), which would return her to Belgrade by the early afternoon, in plenty of time to attend the party. However, fog rolled in and closed Belgrade's airport, forcing her to remain in the Montenegrin capital overnight. As she remained alone in a hotel room, "my family and my fiancé's family, they had an engagement party without me."[28]

Thereafter, this stewardess reported that she was torn by attraction to her adventures as a stewardess and pleas from her family to stay home: "My mother was always worried, 'Are you in one piece?' she would ask, and so on. And my mother-in-law would chide me when I had layovers: 'Are you staying somewhere else again tonight?'" The tension between her mobile lifestyle and the traditional expectations for a sedentary domaćica was too much for this stewardess. Her marriage ended just two-and-a-half years later, in a divorce that she initiated under the liberalized laws implemented by the communist regime. Yet, throughout a series of personal choices—to marry, then to divorce—she maintained her position at JAT, something that would have been impossible for stewardesses in North America or Western Europe. Ultimately, she opted to end her time at JAT in 1962, though she moved on to what she described as equally interesting work with various embassies in Belgrade, which took advantage of her language skills and schooling in the ways of high society. She also chose never again to marry.[29]

Of course, while Pavlović and her peers partially embodied the partizanka, their ghettoization into JAT's only "pink-collar" workforce exposed them to plenty of traditional sexism. Most commonly, this involved service-oriented roles not only for passengers but for the cockpit crew as well, whether on the plane or on layovers. At times, even more overt sexism was manifest. In her earliest years, certain male colleagues, including JAT's chief pilot, felt threatened that women like Pavlović tried to forge a career in the skies. When she reported to him for her first day of in-flight training in October 1947, the pilot betrayed his personal investment in keeping the airplane a male-only space. As she greeted him, he turned to her with an unsolicited put-down: "I don't need you; I can fly without you."[30] This aggressive act demonstrated a reality that lingered for JAT's stewardesses through the coming decades: even while buttressed with legal assurances of workplace equality, they sometimes found themselves delegitimized by male colleagues and customers.

The *Domaćica* Serving East, West, and South

When JAT in the mid-1950s purchased its fleet of more modern and larger Convair-340s to serve its routes from Paris and London in the West to Cairo and Beirut in the South, its flight attendants were enlisted as public relations tools. One of the airline's first major marketing campaigns directed at an international audience crafted a Western-style aura for stewardesses and the airline. That said, it still included several noticeable cultural traces of the communist East and also a greater openness to the Global South, even though the stewardess on display conformed quite closely to Western notions of homey servitude.

Published in 1956, a high-gloss, photo-rich, four-page pamphlet titled simply *JAT* was destined for travel agencies and ticket offices in West Germany, Switzerland, and Austria.[31] Thus, the brochure's audiences were among the first Western consumers to determine whether JAT was appropriately "walking in step" with its Western competitors and to what extent JAT's connections via Belgrade to the Global South could compete with the reliability and comfort of the US's Pan Am and TWA, Britain's BOAC, and Air France.

Technology, rather than stewardesses, was chosen as the core rhetorical appeal to this customer base. The cover photo is a full-page image of JAT's Convair-340 sitting on Munich Airport's tarmac, with Bavaria's snowcapped Alps in the background.[32] When opening the pamphlet, a series of smaller images reinforce this focus on technological sophistication, offering views of the plane's spacious interior, the high-tech cockpit, and more external views of the plane. The CV-340, labeled in

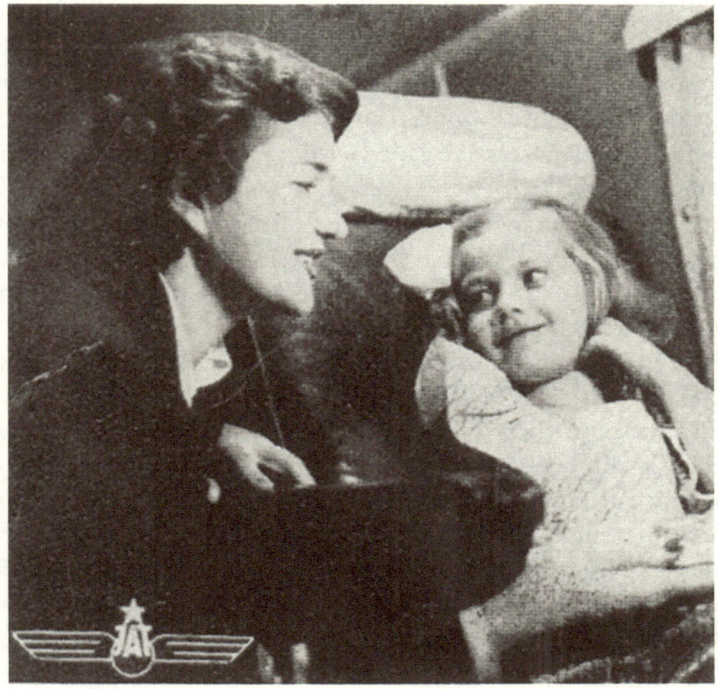

FIGURE 5.2. In JAT's first public relations materials destined for an international audience, this image of a well-manicured JAT stewardess caring for a little girl ran with the caption, "Thanks to the care of JAT stewardesses, JAT's passengers feel as though they are at home." The image reinforces how the airline strove to portray their stewardesses as beautiful, caring domaćice for international customers.

Source: This image appears in the publication JAT-Jugoslawischer Flugverkehr, *JAT* 1, no. 1 (1956), 2. It is retrievable in the Serbian National Library (Narodna Biblioteka Srbije), Belgrade, Serbia. Permission to use this image courtesy of Air Serbia.

the text as "the most modern two-engine passenger plane" available, came with both a pressurized cabin and improved temperature control, which translated to a comfortable travel environment.[33] When coupled with text detailing JAT's rigorous pilot training, the overall effect was to assure prospective passengers of a fully up-to-date experience: "Safety, comfort, and speed are the main traits which most eloquently speak to the reliability of Yugoslav aviation."[34]

The wide variety of images that included people aboard the JAT plane, both passengers and a stewardess, reinforced this trope of modernity and comfort. One image portrays a young boy happily drinking a cup of juice, while another, depicted in the above photo, shows a girl of a similar age sharing a smile with a stewardess—her hair stylish and lipstick glistening—who is kneeling down to share a comforting word. The child looks back at the smiling stewardess adoringly, as she might to her own mother. A third image would surely not have been found in marketing for Western European airlines: an older peasant man boards the plane, his hand-carved cane, Ottoman-era cap, and traditional woolen shoes typical of remote rural areas in southern Yugoslavia, offering a stark juxtaposition with the ultramodern aircraft. Seen together, these images of airlines' most physically fragile passengers (the old and young) stress JAT stewardesses' domaćica-like readiness to be a caretaker, nurturer, and voice of reassurance.

Despite such adherence to Western gender expectations, other aspects of the pamphlet diverged from what these customers might anticipate. The next photo collage involves not stewardesses, but instead passengers who were "famous personalities." However, rather than mimicking the star culture of the West that would have prioritized movie actors, singers, and literary figures, JAT's "famous" guests were exclusively politicians, with leaders from the Global South warranting primacy of place. The largest photo of the seven showed Tito shaking hands with the Indian prime minister Jawaharlal Nehru. The camera captured the two leaders on the tarmac of Belgrade's Airport, with a CV-340 behind them and the text stressing that Nehru arrived "in a special JAT aircraft." Another image portrays Burmese leader U Nu, while all the others show ministers from the European destinations where JAT's CV-340s now flew: the United Kingdom, France, Greece, and Turkey.[35]

In this projection of a Yugoslav version of the world, a few important elements stand out. First, it is immediately noticeable how significantly Yugoslav foreign affairs and its aviation sector had evolved since before the Tito-Stalin split. Tito's 1947 musing that Yugoslav aviation would be focused on linking the country to other Soviet satellites had been completely jettisoned a decade later, when countries to Yugoslavia's east were the only ones left out of the pamphlet. Meanwhile, as the images of Nehru and U Nu attest, the growth of Yugoslavia's aviation sector offered the potential to complement Tito's far-flung diplomatic activities with a corresponding flow of goods and people southward. The Cairo route into Africa and the Beirut route into Asia were initial steps in this direction.

At the same time, this display of a Yugoslav cosmopolitanism—mixing elements of East, West, and South—replicated the West's social conservatism on gender roles. Every face among the "famous personalities" is male, with Tito taking center stage. The brochure, like actual Yugoslav politics during the Cold War, did not challenge the norm that politics should be male-dominated. In fact, the image of the stewardess and little girl is the only portrayal of women, thereby reinscribing women into the separate sphere of domaćica-oriented domestic duties like hosting and childcare. The layout's overall indication was that progress in women's affairs, if progress is the correct word, lurched westward toward the same homemaking and caring roles expected in West Germany, while the transformative politics of Tito's diplomacy reached southward. Yugoslavia's holistic cosmopolitanism (East plus West plus South) thereby risked being far more forward-looking in its state diplomacy than in its cultural politics.

Yugoslavia's *Praktična žena* (Practical woman)

In the mid-1950s, Yugoslav officials started to reprioritize production goals, moving away from a Soviet-style focus on heavy industry and toward providing greater quantities of consumer products. Given their role as the main consumers of household goods, women were key participants in this transition. Various economic planners encouraged, or at least tolerated, this transition for women under socialism into citizen-consumers akin to women in Western societies. Women now had greater permission to serve as arbiters of fashion and beauty, as consumers who were justified in being selective and demanding, and as matrons of a comfortable and stylish family home. At the same time, officials began to redesign Yugoslavia's consumer market. As Patterson notes, "self-service shops, supermarkets, and department stores that aspired to Western ideals of luxury, choice, satisfaction, and modernity started to spring up across Yugoslavia beginning as early as the late 1950s."[36]

In fact, Marković finds an emphasis on women's beauty in Yugoslav publications that predates even this consumerist infrastructure, including 1951 reports in Belgrade newspapers on a Paris fashion show, replete with accounts of what designers deemed to be in style for the season. He sees these developments as indirectly tied together not just with economic decisions, but also with the easing crisis of the Tito-Stalin split, as the paranoia that followed June 1948 subsided. As Marković notes, "the liberalization of politics brought with it the widening of women's roles. Alongside mothers and laborers, at the beginning of the 1950s women were also 'permitted' to become symbols of beauty and desire."[37] Both Patterson and Marković also agree that allowing regular citizens to shop for fashions in Trieste, which became the premier shopping destination for Yugoslavs after relations with Italy normalized at the end of 1954, was yet another impetus for women to become more deeply enmeshed in the West's consumption-driven beauty culture.

By 1956, women in Yugoslavia could avail themselves of Western-style consumer tools, including fashion tips, cosmetics tutorials, and dieting regimes that increasingly appeared in the Yugoslav press. The magazine *Praktična žena* (a title best translated as *The Practical Woman*) debuted in March 1956, promising to help women negotiate their dual obligations as full-time workers and consumers. As the debut issue explained, "Today, as our women each day play an ever greater role in public life and as they, arm in arm with their comrades of the opposite sex, occupy numerous positions of responsibility in their work outside the home—their home, because they aren't authorized to lessen their work commitments, often goes neglected."[38]

Praktična žena was designed to alleviate these tensions by offering a space "in which women find advice, which may help women-mothers [and] women-as-spouses-and-housewives to manage their domestic duties and the care of their children more simply, so that a more convenient and pleasant family atmosphere can be established in their homes."[39] For the state's central planners, the magazine offered a lower-cost way to help professional women manage their excessively demanding dual roles as workers and domaćice. In lieu of high-cost solutions like increasing investments in childcare or time-off options for women, the magazine offered no-cost tips for women to excel in both their full-time commitments.

Most of the magazine's advice had a Western feel. The first issue promised that *Praktična žena* would not differ from women's magazines being published "elsewhere in the world," an oblique reference to the West that was made clearer when it promised to cover the same themes as its counterparts in the United States, Britain, or France: cooking, sewing, film, fashion, physical fitness, children's issues, and self-care.[40] Indeed, future issues frequently imitated these Western publications in their coverage of fashion shows in Paris and Rome, advice on how to dress for social and work outings, and guidance on household management and child-rearing.

Where *Praktična žena* differed from these Western magazines and instead imposed what might be considered a more Eastern (socialist) focus was its fundamental expectation that readers were working women, most typically holding full-time jobs outside the home. As such, some of its content focused on the workplace, including a regular column titled "Twenty-Five Questions" that profiled a prominent career woman's work and her strategies for managing her home life. Also reflective of this socialist orientation were open discussions of legal innovations like easier divorce and women's workplace rights that the Communist Party had introduced.[41]

While far more limited than its Western-oriented coverage, content profiling the plight of women from the Global South was also included in *Praktična žena*, marking an effort to strengthen public engagement with Tito's foreign policy of nonalignment by building solidarity with women residing in these states. This content typically appeared in a regular column called "A Letter from . . . ," which profiled a particular woman's professional contributions in her home country. The issues between 1956 and 1960 included dispatches from Syria, the British colony of the Central African Federation, Lebanon, China, and Liberia.[42] The 1957 article profiling Syria covered women's efforts to organize themselves, assert greater roles in public society, and press for greater rights. Progress at the time was impressive: regarding Syria's marriage laws, which were previously "based on old, faith-based propositions," it was now "noticeable that these shackles gradually are being broken in the actual practice of life." Additionally, working women now enjoyed access to new careers: "What a decade ago seemed unrealizable is today a phenomenon that in Syria is no longer unusual at all: women lawyers, women doctors, women architecture students, women engineers, etc."[43]

At the time, such solidarity efforts benefited from the fact that many postcolonial states, Syria included, adopted a socialist track of modernization. Thus, Syrian goals for women's reforms aligned with Yugoslavia's: to promote women's commitments to work and to advance secularist solutions against the so-called "old, faith-based propositions." Yugoslavia's postwar Women's Anti-fascist Front (AFŽ) also supported the latter goal, pressuring Muslim communities, especially those in Bosnia-Herzegovina and Kosovo, to end Sharia-based restrictions like veil-wearing and limitations on women's movements in public.[44] The similarity of such socialist-inspired reforms allowed Yugoslav women circa 1957 to look out upon the Global South and identify common elements from their own struggles against sexism and patriarchy, despite sizable cultural and geopolitical differences.

Given her relative fame in Yugoslavia by 1956, the same year Tito awarded her the Order of Labor after flying her one millionth kilometer,

Dragica Pavlović was chosen to participate in the "Twenty-Five Questions" segment of *Praktična žena*. Interestingly, in this very moment when JAT was consciously remaking its stewardesses into more stylish and doting attendants who would be more palatable to Western customers, Pavlović herself also downplayed the partizanka-like elements of the job and instead accentuated its domaćica-like characteristics. When asked to describe her work obligations for readers, she explicitly likened her work to a housewife's duties: "[What are] the functions of a stewardess? [She is] a domaćica in a home that flies. But her function, this domaćica, is no different than those on the ground. This home also has to be kept tidy, clean—and above all welcoming and hospitable to all travelers." When identifying differences with what would be expected of her as a domaćica on the ground, Pavlović was circumspect, offering only that the "service on a plane is more dynamic and therefore more interesting and is [as a result] more dear [to me]."[45]

When the obvious follow-up questions arose about the depth of her commitment to being a domaćica—whether she herself was married and had children—Pavlović was truthful, but also careful to align herself with these traditional roles. First, she assured readers that she remained committed to her extended family: "I do have a family, and I always find time between two flights for my own home on the ground." Also, when asked whether her work with JAT was so demanding as to require a maid at home, Pavlović insisted that "I love housework and thus take care of it myself." As such, Pavlović placed herself and her fellow stewardesses within the increasingly dominant norm for Yugoslav women: their work outside the home would only complement their commitment to the more traditional roles of a domaćica. She also established JAT's stewardesses as avid adherents of *Praktična žena*'s ethos that women devote themselves to both work and home. As she claimed, "This magazine has been essential for our women. Both my girlfriends and I find lots of beautiful and useful things in it, so sometimes as we leave the skies for land, we [head] to the nearest kiosk and the new issue of *Praktična žena*."[46]

Pavlović's self-characterization as a devoted domaćica, though without her own husband and children, may well have been true. At the same time, however, the portrayal of her work as "a domaćica in a home that flies" was very much oversimplified. The interviewee who started her JAT career flying alongside Pavlović in 1956 never saw her or Pavlović's experiences as reducible to the quasi-domestic tasks they performed on board. While these functions came with the job, there were always unique adventures awaiting them, especially on layovers. She claims that Pavlović particularly had a rich life beyond Belgrade, even beyond her occasional opportunities to accompany Tito on his international voyages.

"When the two of us went to Cairo—I was always with Dragica," she noted, "and she knew the best company." Pavlović's access to Cairo's high society included a close friendship with the consul of the Yugoslav Embassy, which meant steady invitations to exclusive diplomatic parties and other functions, as well as the opportunity for VIP visits to the country's cultural landmarks: "We saw the pyramids, Alexandria, it was really exquisite." Pavlović and her colleague also bonded with Egyptian officials in the Nasser administration, with the colleague adding that she even spent a vacation in the late 1950s at an Egyptian official's family villa.[47] Of course, none of these adventures conformed to the experiences of a homebound domaćica. To the extent they brought the same sense of fulfillment to Pavlović as they did to her colleague, they show that JAT's efforts to cast its stewardesses as domesticated were incomplete, if not deceptive.

Whether enduring World War II in North America or Europe, women were presented with unconventional role models to help them accommodate to a new constellation of responsibilities that pulled them, sometimes quite suddenly, into male-dominated realms. In the United States, Clare Boothe Luce offered herself as a new female political model, demonstrating that elite women could attain greater parity with men. With a combination of feminine moxie, elite class standing, and a willingness to deploy hard-nosed rhetoric, women like Boothe Luce could now elbow their way into the top echelons of power, even into decision-making on national security issues. Thus, in some ways, Boothe Luce is the elite-class equivalent to America's famous icon of working-class feminism, Rosie the Riveter. The fictitious Rosie, with tied-back hair and bulging biceps, valorized working women's contributions to America's war efforts through their assumption of men's factory roles. Their labor allowed the country to produce the airplanes, warships, and other vital supplies that helped defeat the Nazis in Europe and the Japanese in Asia.

European women, especially those in the (partly) fascist-occupied countries of France and Yugoslavia, had a more starkly militarized induction into traditionally male roles. The highly decorated war hero Alix d'Unienville offered to the French Resistance what Yugoslavia's far more numerous female Partisans, the partizanke, offered to the Yugoslav National Liberation Front. These women were so committed to the cause that they emulated the most conceptually masculine activities conceivable: that of the solider or, in d'Unienville's case, the spy. Just behind these frontline warriors, an additional cadre of supporting women were housing, feeding, and supplying these troops, with Yugoslavia's Women's Anti-fascist Front (AFŽ) overcoming the rural domaćica's traditional estrangement from the basic markers of modern citizenship. Even during the war, AFŽ women gained literacy, education, voting rights, and practice in political assembly. As Alix d'Unienville later confessed, the war years were the most stimulating of her life. This sentiment was similarly true for other women chafing against traditional gender restrictions, whether in the mode of Clare Boothe Luce, Rosie the Riveter, the partizanka, or the AFŽ member.

For the women of the West, however, the postwar years meant a retreat from the high-water marks of advancement during the war itself. Most dramatically, Alix d'Unienville went from wartime spy to peacetime air hostess in total silence, with her memoirs completely ignoring her accomplishments for the Resistance. But it is also true that Rosie the Riveter's appeal receded by the 1950s; many women in traditionally male work roles were forced out to accommodate male veterans. Even Clare Boothe Luce gave up her seat in Congress in 1947, winning just one reelection campaign before deciding that electoral politics was still too challenging for a woman to master over the long haul. She opted instead to become an intraparty influencer within the Republican Party and eventually returned to a national security role as the ambassador to Italy under President Dwight D. Eisenhower in 1953—an appointed, not an elected, position.

Regarding women in Yugoslavia, however, many war-era partizanke and AFŽ members might have hoped to serve as the foundation of a more enduring revolution. The 1946 constitution proclaimed women's equality with men, especially in the realm of work. And, indeed, for women growing up in the early 1950s, work outside the home increasingly became the norm. As one flight attendant who came of age in these years told me, women in Yugoslavia were now expected to work regardless of their marital status. "And if not, if she was not working, she had to join the AFŽ [or] a youth organization [or] a students' association." These groups then required participation on work brigades: "If nothing else, they went on these actions" to contribute their labor to larger social goals.[48] It simply was no longer enough in communist-led

Yugoslavia to be a traditional stay-at-home domaćica. Instead, one had to become a *Praktična žena*—a woman who both worked and took care of her domestic duties.

It therefore matters a lot that the earliest Yugoslav visions for flight attendants differed significantly from the experiences of Alix d'Unienville and her fellow Western stewardesses. Dragica Pavlović assumed this job at age thirty-three and continued flying until age fifty, before finding a ground-based position in which to complete her thirty-year career. All of this was a substantial improvement over the situation of Western women. So too was the fact that Pavlović and her peers could keep their jobs while making their own choices about marriage and, as needed, divorce. Even the decorative touches from Pavlović's early years of flying—the Partisan-inspired uniform and preflight salute, being awarded the Order of Labor, and her ceremonial election to head JAT's workers—established these women as empowered workers and citizens in ways that the West refused to countenance.

At the same time, however, the endemic sexism in Yugoslavia that was left unaddressed under socialism, coupled with Yugoslav aviation administrators' preoccupation with "walking in step" with Europe, ultimately entailed a backsliding on these empowering traits. When the airline first tried to market itself in 1956 to Western European clientele, it proudly cast Yugoslav geopolitics as a groundbreaking improvement over Western parochialism, with glossy images of Tito using JAT's airplanes to link himself more closely with India's Nehru and Burma's U Nu, as well as to Western officials. Simultaneously, however, Yugoslavia's progressive gender politics disappeared, as the brochure's lone stewardess lacked any trappings of her partizanka-like authority (no salutes, no military uniform or Partisan cap). She was now remarkable only for her perfect perm and lipstick, her glowing smile, and her ease in catering to a child. Also in 1956, in an interview with *Praktična žena*, Dragica Pavlović recast—indeed, arguably misrepresented—her work, stating that a flight attendant is simply a "domaćica in a home that flies."[49] Thus, regardless of Yugoslavia's increasing geopolitical convergences with the Global South, its culture regarding gender norms was converging instead with the West.

Somewhat ironically, then, Alix d'Unienville's chronicle *En vol*—captivating for its audiences and at the same time deceptive in its erasure of the author's own internal anguish regarding gender roles—served as a crucial moment in pre-jet Yugoslavia's move away from partizanka-inspired stewardesses. When French editors rereleased the 1949 classic in 1958, *Praktična žena* acquired the rights to include chapters of the work over the course of eleven issues, run under the title "Diary of a Stewardess."[50] These issues used passages from d'Unienville's book to temporarily replace another segment that was typically more attuned to Tito's foreign policy aspirations, a feature titled "Women in the World" ("Žena u svetu") that occasionally profiled women in the Global South, especially those from countries that had joined the nascent collection of nonaligned nations under the inspiration of Tito, Nasser, and Nehru.

As *Praktična žena*'s editors introduced d'Unienville's work, they barely diverged from the remarks of the original French editors, stressing how the author chronicled the expansive mobility of a stewardess's travel and the astounding speed with which her life would rush by. With no additional caveats about d'Unienville's retirement from Air France or her ignored legacy as a decorated war hero, these editors presented the same allure of the stewardess's life that mesmerized French audiences a decade earlier:

> In place of our ordinary letter from some part of the world, today we commence our presentation of a series in which French stewardess Alix d'Unienville conveys her impressions from flights around the world. While reading these pages you will travel with the French stewardess to Casablanca, Zurich, Rome, Karachi, New York, Dakar, Nairobi, Khartoum, Saigon, and Cairo. But as the author states, "I can't claim that I know, for example, the soul of India just because I spent a few hours in Calcutta." In actuality, Alix d'Unienville provides impressions of people whom she meets in passing, of passengers, of landscapes she flies over.[51]

The overall effect, especially on younger women in Yugoslavia, was the same as it was all over Western Europe. With Yugoslavia in 1958 only four years away from entering the Jet Age and with Belgrade's new airport poised to become a growing hub for air traffic heading east, west, and south, stewardesses were becoming more and more beloved. Certainly, their globe-trotting was a major part of their allure, but so too was their mastery of the touches of Western womanhood: their youthful beauty, their immaculate grooming, and their ability to serve as domaćice to the same standards as stewardesses at Air France and Pan Am.

CHAPTER 6

Marguerite LeWars Kirkpatrick
Making Jamaican Women Racially Eligible for Jet Age Labor

The earlier chapter on Air Jamaica's founding recounted the bullish ruminations from then–prime minister Norman Manley on the wheels of history that would turn once again with Jamaican independence. The first turn came with the island's 1834 termination of racialized slavery, and he rosily projected the second turn as he boarded a jet to London in January 1962, on his way to conclude negotiations with British representatives on independence. A year and a half later, Jamaica was indeed fully sovereign, and it now fell to Manley's counterpart as a "national hero" of the independence era, the new prime minister Alexander Bustamante, to remark on another moment in Jamaican history that was also transformative, though in a more superficial way.[1] On November 8, 1963, Bustamante embraced the task of congratulating a barrier-breaking Jamaican who became a newfound national sensation.

Yet, this heroine differed sharply from the "national heroes" now in power in Kingston. In fact, when Carol Joan Crawford followed Norman Manley's flight path to London on a BOAC jet, the twenty-year-old product of an elite Kingston family had no career and performed no work other than as a typist for her father's company. Her only advanced studies were at a modeling school in Canada, and she continued to live in her parents' elegant home as though in a state of perpetual

CHAPTER 6

adolescence. Reporters described her bedroom as an Ibsen-like doll's house: "The room is full of large stuffed teddy-bears, dolls, dogs and cats and on a hanger is a ballet costume which bears tribute to her years of dancing with the 'Punkie' Rowe troupe."[2] Nonetheless, adding to a national outpouring of pride, Bustamante telegrammed London in the middle of the night with joyful words for Crawford: "Please convey my heartiest congratulations to Miss Crawford on her great victory. We are proud of her."[3]

Carol Joan Crawford had just built upon her success in claiming the crown of Miss Jamaica by winning the title of Miss World, a global beauty pageant that pitted her against the most beautiful women from all over the world. Most importantly for the *Gleaner*, Jamaica's largest newspaper, Crawford's victory marked "the first time that a Jamaican girl has won an international beauty contest." It added that Crawford was also the first winner from the West Indies.[4] Another first for Crawford was less illustrious: she was the shortest winner in history, standing at five foot three (159cm), an alleged deficiency she rectified by donning five-inch heels for the competition. Finally, although the *Gleaner* never mentioned it, Crawford was the first woman of African descent ever to win a global beauty pageant. Especially in this sense, with Crawford's victory the wheel of history was indeed turning in the direction of fuller justice.

Considering that most members of cosmopolitan society in 1963 overlooked the blatant misogyny of beauty contests, it is perhaps understandable that many Jamaicans welcomed Crawford's coronation as a moment of national and racial reckoning. Moreover, here was a woman, rather than Jamaica's otherwise all-male cast of independence-era heroes, playing a direct role in making history. Of course, the amount of agency that Crawford exercised in this role was drastically limited. Due to the objectifying nature of such contests, judges and pageant organizers influenced Crawford's coronation more than she did herself; they too were the more active agents in making this symbolic strike for racial progress and greater dignity for the Global South. Regardless, with her victory, Carol Joan Crawford furnished future stewardesses at Air Jamaica with a road map to attain personal esteem and global credibility as beautiful women of color. This, however, was a road map that they too were unable to execute on their own, without surrendering the primary navigating role to sexist forces.

This chapter covers the immediate predecessors of the first Jamaican stewardesses: beauty queens like Carol Joan Crawford. Crawford's 1963 coronation as Miss World did important work to prepare the cosmopolitan world for a racially diverse flight attendant corps. That an African-descended woman could be crowned Miss World meant that other non-white women from the Global South—namely, those aspiring to become stewardesses—would now have more credibility in these roles, which also were tied to conveying poise and charm while withstanding objectification. Of course, this turning of the wheel of history is deeply problematic. The Jamaican women who sashayed from the fashion runways as beauty queens à la Carol Joan Crawford to the aisleways of Air Jamaica jets as stewardesses may have benefited from racial amelioration in the 1950s and 1960s, but they still faced the indignity of galling sexism.

While Carol Joan Crawford is Jamaica's most decorated beauty queen, the woman who served as the primary liaison between the pageant world and the aviation world was another winner of the Miss Jamaica pageant, though not of Miss World. When Marguerite LeWars won the island-wide title in 1961, she had a resume quite different from Crawford's modeling-heavy, but work-light list of accomplishments. LeWars, in fact, was a full-time employee of British West Indies Airlines (BWIA) when she was crowned Miss Jamaica, as she served as one of their ground hostesses at Kingston Airport. This position made LeWars one of the very few Jamaican women working in aviation before the nation achieved independence and started its own airline.

LeWars's job was destined to be more than a temporary fling before marriage or aging out in her thirties, like stewardesses in the United States and Western Europe. This beauty queen aspired to a lifelong career, an aspiration she would accomplish quite impressively, as she became Air Jamaica's first head of stewardesses in 1968. From that position, she solidified the linkages between Jamaica's pageant culture and its stewardess culture: she handled hiring of Air Jamaica's first stewardesses, as well as their training. She even designed their first uniforms: tight miniskirts in nearly fluorescent tropical colors that showed off ample curves and surprising amounts of non-white skin. When the Jet Age launched at Air Jamaica, racial animus was still acute, whether in Jamaica itself or in North America or Western Europe. However, beauty queens like Carol Joan Crawford had established that even African-descended women could no longer be denied their claim to physical beauty and libidinal attractiveness. This chapter traces this pathway beyond the racialized confines of cosmopolitanism, which women like Crawford and LeWars were embarking upon just as the global Jet Age was dawning.

The Wholesome, yet Exotic "Face of Jamaica"

Once she was crowned Miss World, Carol Joan Crawford became a global ambassador for her newly independent homeland. She acquiesced to pleas from the Jamaica Tourist Board (JTB) to continue her travels from London onward through Western Europe, where she promoted Jamaica in television, radio, and newspaper interviews. Crawford's sudden global celebrity was a serendipitous development for the JTB, which saw continental Europeans as an untapped market for Jamaican tourism. Media dates in France, Belgium, and West Germany were already set for unveiling a new multimillion-dollar advertising campaign that starred another beauty queen, Marguerite LeWars, so Crawford's attendance would assure even more attention.

A few months before Crawford's victory, Marguerite LeWars took time off from her day job and sat for a photo shoot. The cameras focused on her facial features: framed with a subtle, inviting smile were her light brown skin, wide eyes, and straight hair—a combination that indicated her ancestral provenance of India, Africa, and Europe. Thus, when the new Miss World journeyed to towns like Hamburg, she sat for interviews at events under posters of Marguerite LeWars's alluring visage accompanied by the headline, "The Face of Jamaica."[5] The JTB thereby offered potential visitors from Europe an enticing rendering of the new nation's racial composition: it was light-skinned, straight-haired, and female, as much European and South Asian as African. This combination, embodied in Carol Joan Crawford and Marguerite LeWars at these media events, could run the gamut from wholesome to exotic.

Indeed, a sharp dichotomy arose between domestic and international press reporting of Carol Joan Crawford's victory and its implications for questions of race. As noted, Jamaica's *Gleaner* saw a series of firsts in Crawford's victory but resisted labeling Crawford as African-descended or Black. Instead, this child of Jamaica's upper crust was portrayed just like any white, well-to-do aspiring beauty queen in England, the United States, or Canada. She even had a white idol with whom she corresponded and whom she sought to emulate, actress Joan Crawford, her namesake.[6] This tidbit, coupled with the account of her bedroom furnished to American-girl standards, reflected a decidedly elite Jamaican narrative regarding race: that light-skinned Jamaicans had, in tandem with the country's political independence, attained parity with whites.

To establish this claim more overtly, the *Gleaner* quoted the well-known London-based white businessman Billy Butlin, a judge for Miss World 1963. He offered a color-blind analysis of Crawford's beauty, stating that she "looked so fresh and so simple. The kind of girl any man would be proud to have as his daughter and prouder still to have as his wife."[7] By embodying the wholesomeness of a perfect daughter and wife, Crawford effectively broke down the cosmopolitan world's most intimate color line, the fear of miscegenation, on beauty's largest stage. Thus, just as brown Jamaicans had clawed their way to equal recognition alongside whites in the island's pageants before Crawford, they now had emulated this success more globally.[8]

Yet, a different racial narrative arose in media accounts in Europe and North America. Here, the fact of Crawford's blackness frequently became the leitmotif. The Spanish magazine ¡Hola! conjured up Jamaica's history of slavery in accounting for Crawford's exquisite beauty, which the reporter found to be characteristic of "the beauty of a nation formed in large part by descendants of African slaves transported a few centuries earlier to cultivate sugar cane in the West Indies." The reporter added, "There must be a bit of black blood in Carol Joan Crawford's veins" to account for her unique beauty.[9] London's *Daily Express* also greeted Crawford's victory with an imperialist trope that gestured to her mixed-race and African heritage, referring to her as the "exotic Miss Jamaica."[10] In turn, one American publication cast itself as proud of, rather than titillated by, Crawford's African descent. The African American glossy magazine *Jet* was eager to embrace Crawford's victory as one for all African-descended women. Even so, the chosen headline was one that Crawford herself and many other light-skinned Jamaicans would likely have disavowed: "Negro Beauty Queen Wins Miss World Crown."[11] In labeling her as Negro, *Jet* employed America's reductionist Jim Crow categories—one was either only white or only Black—in a way that ignored Jamaica's complex racial and chromatic hierarchies.

In sum, while Jamaica's *Gleaner* sought to cast Crawford's victory as a deracializing moment, erasing her blackness while affirming her parity with Europe's and America's white cosmopolitans, the press accounts from outside Jamaica continued to foreground Crawford's race: her "black blood," her "exotic" nature, and her Jim Crow status as a

"Negro." The takeaway is that the cosmopolitan world's cultural center (the West) and its periphery (the Global South) were apprehending Crawford's race in different ways. Moreover, they were doing so with strikingly discordant attractions to Crawford's mixed-race body.

The genteel readers of Jamaica's *Gleaner* saw Crawford as an ideal ambassador of the nation, at least its lighter-skinned members, with such Jamaicans increasingly countenanced as ideal daughters and wives. Meanwhile, European and American audiences still saw Crawford as exotic and titillating, an example of imperialist societies' attraction to non-white subjects, as noted by cultural theorists from Edward Said to Anne McClintock.[12] This dichotomy is significant. Like Crawford, the "face of Jamaica" whose future was closely linked with Air Jamaica stewardesses, Marguerite LeWars was also perceived simultaneously as a genteel ambassador for the new nation and as an erotically charged woman who was only a shade removed from her nation's enslaved forebears.

Aviation and the "Face of Jamaica"

Marguerite LeWars always had two profound passions, beauty and aviation, which she successfully intertwined soon after completing high school in 1958 at one of the capital city's elite institutions, Wolmer's Girls School. She almost certainly knew Carol Joan Crawford, who was also enrolled there and just a couple of years her junior.[13] Young Marguerite's role model was her older sister Barbara, who also was poised to use her mixture of good looks, intelligence, and privileged background to become famous in her own right. But, while Barbara entered university to study English and theater, Marguerite was too impatient for studies. "I read many books and wanted to travel," she noted, channeling Clare Boothe Luce's assertion from 1943 that the youth of the world were yearning for mobility. In explaining how she signed on at BWIA in 1958, Marguerite added matter-of-factly, "the least expensive way to fly was to join the airlines."[14]

Of course, for a Jamaican woman coming of age in the preindependence and pre-jet years, opportunities in aviation were exceptionally limited. BWIA was the only potential employer since neither BOAC nor Pan Am hired Jamaicans for anything but basic ground-based operations. Indeed, in 1958, American citizens of African descent were still banned from public-fronting positions with airlines in the United States, especially the in-flight positions of piloting and stewardessing.

Until the NAACP pursued high-profile cases in the late 1950s on the part of aspiring Black pilots and flight attendants, Black Americans were channeled instead into positions like baggage handling and custodial work.

For Marguerite LeWars, however, BWIA did offer the chance to fly as a stewardess, and she would have followed through on that opportunity save for the opposition of her parents. Their compromise was that Marguerite worked as the closest approximation: a ground hostess who remained anchored on the terra firma of Kingston Airport while assisting needy customers. LeWars immediately found her passion: "After the first twenty-four hours I knew I was going to make it my career and started to plan how I was going to climb the ladder."[15]

The young LeWars sisters were beautiful enough to attract national and international attention. Barbara ended up on the cover of *Life* magazine's international edition in 1959, with reporters using her image and life story to emblematize what the cover headline termed "Jamaica's new generation," who were coming of age in a soon-to-be-independent state that was a "bustling paradise."[16] In the ensuing years as a career woman in corporate communications, Barbara fell in love with and married Jamaica's most promising young politician, the future prime minister Michael Manley. Manley won his first election to parliament in 1967 during their brief marriage, though their relationship ended tragically and too quickly, when Barbara was diagnosed with cancer and died in 1968. Together they had one child, Sarah, whom the LeWars family helped to raise along with Michael and his future wife, Beverley Anderson Manley.[17]

Sarah Manley's childhood memories of being raised by her grandmother, the same woman who raised Marguerite and Barbara, offers insight into how the LeWars family negotiated Jamaica's racial politics, which preserved beauty as the exclusive domain of light-skinned women. After detailing how Gloria LeWars imposed strict regimens to help diminish Sarah's African features—no sunbathing after 11:00 a.m. and before then only with heaps of sunscreen, nightly rituals of combing out the curls from her hair—Sarah added this about her grandmother:

> I did not know then, and still work to unravel now, how these small rituals taught me from childhood about good and bad skin, good and bad hair, worth and worthlessness. She was, with each layer of Coppertone green, with each brush stroke, both creating and preserving my power, as an act of kindness and motherly love,

not an act of cruelty. It was what she knew to be true of her world. My pale yellow skin, my hair without kinks, was my power.

But Jamaica was evolving in these years at the dawn of the Jet Age. Marguerite and her sister were unmistakably products of the preindependence era when yellow skin "was . . . power," whereas their dark-skinned peer, Beverley Anderson Manley, who began helping to raise young Sarah after marrying the prime minister in 1972, had a different attitude toward race and beauty. At the Anderson Manley home, young Sarah could sunbathe to her heart's content and leave the hairbrush at her grandmother's. As Sarah registered this contrast: "The implication of this was that my 'dark' stepmother at the time either didn't know how or didn't care to raise me properly. She wanted to drag me down with her . . . [It was a] robbing of my birthright, my power, so traitorous, that my grandmother died never forgiving her for what she did to me."[18]

Raised like her sister Barbara to safeguard the power of her light skin tone and to wield this power for her own benefit, Marguerite entered the light-skinned woman's world of Jamaican beauty pageants in the late 1950s while holding down her job at BWIA. Her perseverance paid off in 1961, when she was selected to represent her local area of Kingston-Saint Andrew's at the nationwide Miss Jamaica beauty contest, the last pageant to take place in Jamaica's colonial era. As it happened, Warner Brothers' Caribbean representatives were filming the event and created a feature-length documentary, which was then distributed to cinemas throughout Jamaica.[19] Thus, when Marguerite LeWars was crowned Miss Jamaica, she also assumed the lead role in a local feature film. Her candidacy at the Miss World contest in Miami was not as successful as Carol Joan Crawford's two years later, but it nonetheless broadened LeWars's horizons and her exposure to local and global media.

Marguerite LeWars's flirtation with the film industry deepened later in 1961, when Kingston and the island's more serene beaches hosted the filming of *Dr. No*, the very first of British author Ian Fleming's James Bond stories to be turned into a movie. LeWars caught the eye of *Dr. No*'s producers as they passed through Kingston's airport and found the Miss World candidate assisting passengers in the terminal. They encouraged LeWars to try out for a small role, which did not proceed fully to plan. As she later explained, "They wanted me to try out for the part of a woman in a towel on a bed kissing a man . . . . I asked, 'Who is this man?' It was Sean Connery. I replied, 'Well, I've never heard of him.' And I stupidly said no."[20] Instead, LeWars agreed to play a Chinese-Jamaican photographer and femme fatale, Annabel Chung, who encounters James Bond in a bar and tries to seduce him and throw him off the evil Dr. No's track.

British author Ian Fleming was a longtime Jamaica resident, who spent part of his year in Jamaica at his estate famously named "Goldeneye." Fleming originally wrote a plot for what became *Dr. No* as a television show to promote Jamaican tourism, doing so in cooperation with his close friends who ran the Jamaica Tourist Board. In the end, though, *Dr. No*, in both its book and film form, became a piece of Cold War drama rather than an appeal to vacation in Jamaica. The film placed Jamaica at the center of a struggle between a sinister Chinese-German criminal overlord and the heroic duo of Britain's MI6 and the United States' CIA, with James Bond leading the charge. The film's plot played on Jamaica's proximity to the home of the American space program in Florida, with Dr. No operating a radio signal from an island just off Jamaica's north coast that was sabotaging NASA space launches.

For her scene opposite Sean Connery, Marguerite LeWars sported a stunning Chinese-inspired magenta silk dress (her character was coded as mixed-race Chinese to emulate the film's main Chinese-German villain). This dress was, however, a bolder and more risqué choice than LeWars had worn as Miss Jamaica: not only was it Chinese-inspired but it was also suggestively tight everywhere. It was sleeveless, cut above the knees, and boasted a large slit up to the hipline. LeWars's likeness appeared in many of the film's promotional posters, which placed her abstract magenta-hued figure as the last in a line of rainbow-colored femmes fatales that appear in the movie. As such, she was introducing Jamaica's elite, light-skinned beauty culture into venues that not even Carol Joan Crawford managed to enter. Indeed, Marguerite LeWars was fusing strands comprising contemporary notions of womanhood: she was a working woman, still traditionally beautiful, and she was boldly self-actualized as seductive. Marguerite LeWars thereby belonged more to the soon-to-be-unleashed era of Jamaican independence—and of Jet Age feminism—than to Jamaica's colonial era. That said, she still relied on the colonial-era marker of light skin to open these doors of career, celebrity, and sexual agency.

The year 1963 was not only important for Jamaican women due to Carol Joan Crawford's victory, but also due to Marguerite LeWars's Hollywood debut. *Dr. No* premiered in Jamaican theaters that September, including a star-studded affair with music by the ska celebrity Byron

CHAPTER 6

Lee and, of course, Marguerite LeWars and her family sitting among the guests of honor. This premiere transpired a few weeks before the film's official opening at London's Pavilion Theatre on Piccadilly Circus on October 5, where stars Sean Connery and Ursula Andress would delight the crowd.[21] While audiences looking for sexual titillation focused primarily on the famous scene when lead actress Andress rose out of the ocean sporting a white bikini while singing a calypso tune, much to the delight of the onlooking James Bond, Marguerite LeWars's sexy and seductive portrayal of Annabel Chung assured Jamaican women that they also enjoyed access to this elite iteration of sexual desire. LeWars's role in *Dr. No* also facilitated the tourist board's choice that year to use her as the "face of Jamaica," a campaign that ran all the way through 1967.[22]

This was the cultural milieu into which the first Air Jamaica was launched on May 1, 1966. Recall that this version of the national airline was a joint venture with BWIA and BOAC that used these carriers' planes, pilots, and stewardesses. Thus, when Marguerite LeWars—now known as Marguerite Kirkpatrick, thanks to her first marriage in 1965—switched her affiliation from BWIA to Air Jamaica in 1966, she became the airline's first hostess, albeit one still confined to ground duties.[23] An Air Jamaica ad from 1966 showed an eagerness to cash in on her good looks, warm demeanor, and local fame, as it neatly conflated the ground hostess position with Kirkpatrick herself: instead of referring to her job title, the text simply states, "When you're six years old, an airport can be a lonely place. That's why we have Marguerite Kirkpatrick."[24] By 1967, with the joint venture growing more successful, Air Jamaica added more ground hostesses and designated Kirkpatrick as their supervisor. Then, when the second Air Jamaica began hiring stewardesses of its own in 1968, she leaned on her decade of experience to become director of stewardesses. These women were selected and trained to fill Kirkpatrick's own shoes: attractive, self-confident, composed under pressure, and sexually energized. These so-called "rare tropical birds" (the salacious name Air Jamaica's first stewardesses were given) played their own roles as femmes fatales, akin to Marguerite LeWars when she starred as James Bond's Annabel Chung and as the "face of Jamaica."

Marguerite LeWars Kirkpatrick, Miss Jamaica 1961, shared much in common with Carol Joan Crawford, Miss World 1963. Both overlapped at an elite girl's high school in the late 1950s, and both came from well-established, light-skinned elite families in Kingston. Carol Joan Crawford's father ran a successful import-export firm, a source of income that allowed the family to settle into a spacious home next to one of Jamaica's most glamorous addresses, the Devon House estate above the city of Kingston. Marguerite LeWars's father was politically well-connected, as he served as town clerk of Kingston and ultimately as general manager of the Jamaica Hotel and Tourist Association, both positions that gave him access to political and economic power brokers.[25]

The most glaring difference between the two beauty queens is that Crawford proceeded from her victory at the Miss Jamaica pageant to win Miss World, while LeWars did not place in the global pageant's final fifteen. Yet, a more subtle difference is also evident, one which is operative for this narrative: Marguerite LeWars Kirkpatrick embodied Jet Age feminism, an updated iteration of cosmopolitan womanhood that developed in tandem with the Jet Age. Carol Joan Crawford lived under her parents' roof through at least 1964, and she worked at her father's business only sporadically, between stints at modeling school. By 1966, around age twenty-three, Crawford was married and soon thereafter was raising children as a housewife. As such, Crawford—in the years before, during, and after her glorious run as Miss World—lacked the crucial markers that young, cosmopolitan women were embodying in the early 1960s. She possessed neither a career nor a reliable source of income in her own name, and, being always under the roof of a man, she also lacked the personal and sexual independence that became de rigueur for a new generation of empowered women.

Marguerite LeWars Kirkpatrick, however, possessed all the features of the Jet Age feminism that was percolating both in American society and in Jamaica, at least among a group of better-off women like LeWars Kirkpatrick. For her, no less than for Crawford, adulation came through her physical beauty. However, her path to becoming an empowered femme fatale coupled her beauty with greater independence. LeWars Kirkpatrick enjoyed a fulfilling career that combined responsibility with a penchant for feminine charm; a desire to travel widely (even if this was somewhat unfulfilled while working as a ground hostess); a flirtatious deployment of her sexuality to eventually secure a husband and, before such a commitment, to seduce the likes of Sean Connery; and the boldness to insist on keeping her career even after marriage. Kirkpatrick thereby served as a bridge from Jamaica's preindependence, pre-jet norms for elite women to the postindependence, Jet Age norms that took root together with the launch of Air Jamaica's first flight attendants in 1969.

This chapter leaves Marguerite LeWars Kirkpatrick right at the cusp of this moment: it is 1966, she is married, working as a ground stewardess for the first iteration of Air Jamaica, and still starring as the "face of Jamaica" in ads distributed across North America and Western Europe. At work, however, Kirkpatrick is chafing against the traditions of aviation from the pre-jet age, especially those dictating her ground hostess uniform, a derivative design that Air Jamaica adopted from the staid patterns of 1950s stewardesses. At any opportunity, Kirkpatrick buttonholed Air Jamaica executives, pointing to her simple white blouse, solid-colored skirt that fell below the knee, and dainty matching cap.

She begged for their approval to radically update the garb to fit the Jet Age, with the goal of following the innovators working for Dallas-based Braniff Airways: ad executive Mary Wells and famous fashion designer Emilio Pucci. Together, Wells and Pucci introduced the first colorful and ultramodern remake of stewardess uniforms. "Look, what Braniff did with their crazy coloured planes, plastic space helmets, boots and culottes," Kirkpatrick confided when she finally convinced Air Jamaica executives to redo her ground hostess uniform in 1967 in modest but progressive ways, "It's crazy, it's great, but too flipped out for Jamaica."[26] However, by 1969, with Kirkpatrick still at the helm, such novelties were no longer "too flipped out." At that time, she finally won permission to create a uniform for Air Jamaica's "rare tropical birds" that fully synced with the Jet Age feminism of the day.

PART III

Embracing and Combating Jet Age Feminism

Chapter 7

Mary Wells Lawrence
The Launch of America's Jet Age Feminism

The legendary American crooner Frank Sinatra introduced his up-tempo ballad "Come Fly with Me" in 1958. Inviting his muse with the temptation, "Let's fly, let's fly away," the song embeds air travel into a collage of elite adventures, from sipping "some exotic booze ... in far Bombay," to a journey to Peru, where "there's a one-man band / And he'll toot his flute for you!"[1] That same October, Pan Am debuted its jet service from New York to Paris, while BOAC's de Havilland Comet jets also reentered service. The year 1958 thereby marked the onset of the Jet Age in the North Atlantic region, and Sinatra's "Come Fly with Me" became a theme song for the so-called jet set, an updated version of cosmopolitan elites: wealthy businessmen and their families, celebrities, and scions of aristocratic or robber-baron families. Their opulent globe-trotting lifestyles only accelerated with the taming of the jet engine.[2]

There was a multiyear lag before the cultural wave that arrived with the Jet Age hit the working women of the stewardess corps. Certainly, these women served on jets from the beginning, and not only on glamorous transatlantic routes. Jamaica greeted its first Pan Am jet in 1960, JAT had its own jets by 1963, intra-European carriers and US domestic airlines were converting to all-jet fleets in the early 1960s, and, before them all, Aeroflot boasted jet service as of 1956. Yet, the staid way

144 CHAPTER 7

FIGURE 7.1. Braniff flight attendant Marne Davis sports the second installment of fashion designer Emilio Pucci's uniforms for Braniff in 1966 while taking part in a flight attendant gathering in London. While quite different from Pucci's original Braniff uniforms from 1965, this version shares the modern touches of layering (a top over a sundress over tights), formfitting material, bold patterning, and vivid colors. The same cosmic influence from 1965 is also found, as Davis sports a clear plastic bubble cap. In the background, stewardesses from both BOAC and Air France are wearing their airlines' more modest attempts at accentuating Jet Age-Space Age modernity: lapel pins of the Concorde, which both airlines held contracts for by 1966.
Source: Photo B1-25-006-PB001 Marne Davis with Cutty Sark (British Aircraft Corporation neg ref MP 27731). Permission to use this image courtesy of BAE Systems.

stewardesses' employers clad them in traditional and drab uniforms marked a failure to keep pace with the times. The stewardesses from BOAC and Air France, in the back row of the accompanying 1966 image, demonstrate the stubborn persistence of 1950s fashion norms well into the Jet Age.

Part III covers the moment when stewardesses finally caught up with the Jet Age, a feat attained when Texas-based Braniff Airways radically remade stewardess fashion in 1965. Through the years Braniff created several iterations of the dramatic outfit sported by stewardess Marne Davis above. Unlike the stewardesses in the background, Davis visually conformed to the optimism and pizazz of Jet Age feminism—a novel reality for women in the 1960s that combined new opportunities regarding work, style, travel, and sex, albeit within confines still dictated by very harsh sexism. Stewardesses, in turn, were not that different from other white middle-class women entering adulthood in the early Jet Age. For this generation, working outside the home was increasingly de rigueur, while being more sexual was now à la mode—whether that meant having sex outside of marriage or just wearing fashion with elevated hemlines and lower necklines. Jet Age stewardesses were visual models for these changes.

Importantly, this evolution toward a more sexually liberated womanhood also took root among more privileged women in the Global South and in more open socialist societies. While unique in attaining near-celebrity status, Jamaica's Marguerite LeWars Kirkpatrick was far from alone in these regions when she embraced core traits of Jet Age feminism soon after high school. Her subsequent roles as a career woman, as a model and beauty queen, as a silver-screen sexualized femme fatale, and as a connoisseur of tighter and brighter fashion fulfilled yearnings that many women held across the globe. In Yugoslavia, no less than in Jamaica, Jet Age feminism's sexualization and stylization found adherents. Yugoslav women's lives were increasingly spent at beauty pageants, movie theaters showing glitzy domestic and Hollywood films focused on silver-screen divas, and department stores filled with more adventurous fashion choices. This more financially secure and more sexualized generation differed significantly from their pre–Jet Age mothers, even as the amount of sexism they endured remained constant.

This chapter situates Jet Age stewardesses within the larger cultural developments that forged Jet Age feminism in the United States. It focuses particularly on advertising executive Mary Wells, who was already one of the most acclaimed women working on Madison Avenue before her work for Braniff. When Wells's firm placed her in charge of the Braniff account, she assembled a potent triumvirate of jet-setters, teaming up with Florentine fashion designer Emilio Pucci and US-based interior and graphic designer Alexander Girard. Braniff was an otherwise overlooked airline based in the then-obscure commercial center of Dallas, Texas. It needed what its CEO, Harding Lawrence, termed a "very big idea" to transition to the Jet Age.[3] Lawrence wagered that a marketing makeover was the only way to draw in an influx of new passengers to pay off the debt he had accrued when transitioning Braniff to an all-jet fleet. As such, Wells's bold stewardess makeover and the financial exigencies of the Jet Age were intimately intertwined.

Wells's final product, a visual overhaul presented under the slogan "The End of the Plain Plane," left no stone unturned.[4] Girard provided a strikingly bold and contemporary logo, bright and stylish interiors for Braniff's airport lounges, jelly-bean colored marketing placards, and vibrant plane interiors. Wells then made racy new ad materials, and—most important for the cultural questions tied to working women—she and Pucci crafted a novel way of presenting Braniff's stewardesses. Aesthetically speaking, this stewardess makeover was playful and colorful, but also contemporary and expensive-looking, the equivalent of bringing Pucci's runway creations, worn by jet-set elites like Jackie Kennedy and Sophia Loren, to provincial Dallas.

Braniff's and Mary Wells's creation—cosmopolitan, stylish, and sexually overt—became a fad in global aviation, not just in the United States. By 1970, Western European stewardesses' staid uniforms had evolved. Beyond the North Atlantic region, too, such uniforms spurred on Marguerite LeWars Kirkpatrick's 1967 redesign of her ground hostess uniform and later inspired her to create even bolder uniforms for Air Jamaica's first stewardesses in 1969. By then, the airline was finally ready for uniforms that, as she regretted back in 1967, were at first "too flipped out for Jamaica."[5] Yugoslavia's JAT opted for a more soft-core rendition of the sexy stewardess, but here too one finds a greater sexualization. In both film and popular music from Yugoslavia's early Jet Age, JAT stewardesses were cast as heartthrobs who rivaled fashion models. The same happened in JAT advertising and in a bold uniform redesign from the mid-1970s. While not as colorful, formfitting, or whimsical as Pucci's creations, the uniforms created by local designer Aleksandar Joksimović modernized JAT stewardesses for the Jet Age. With certain concessions to modesty, JAT helped bring Jet Age feminism to the threshold of Europe's socialist East.

Importantly, women like Mary Wells, Marguerite LeWars Kirkpatrick, and indeed a vast majority of stewardesses in the early Jet Age saw themselves as more liberated women. They enjoyed increased economic, social, and sexual agency over previous generations and were therefore, in this limited sense, feminists. But these women were still, to use LeWars Kirkpatrick's words, too flipped out for the more rigorous Second Wave feminists of the 1960s. In the United States by 1963, such feminists were already warning against the dangers facing women who allowed the sexist metrics of good looks, youth, stylish dress, and sexual availability to dictate their value to an employer. One of the leading voices of America's Second Wave was Betty Friedan, whose book *The*

Feminine Mystique attracted many women—especially younger, middle-class, white baby boomers—to the feminist movement by stressing how such beauty regimens undermined women's freedom.

However, Jet Age feminism differed from Friedan and other more rigorous feminists on these points. This too-flipped-out iteration of empowerment also appealed to the same young, primarily middle-class white women coming of age in the 1960s. They instead followed a vision of womanhood espoused by another American, Helen Gurley Brown, the longtime editor of *Cosmopolitan* magazine. To be a so-called "*Cosmo* girl," as Brown fondly called her readers, was to be a working woman who confidently used her good looks and sexual agency to advance her career.[6] Of course, as the pages of Brown's magazine privileged young, white career women, this American version of Jet Age feminism had clear confines. They were the same classist and white supremacist reflexes that had historically been used to demarcate true womanhood in the United States and elsewhere in the Western world.

To be clear, Jet Age feminism was a highly skewed version of women's liberation. It harmfully celebrated sexuality in the workplace, while also whitewashing the emancipatory demands of working-class women and women of color. Additionally, it failed to problematize how this libidinization of women was done, first and foremost, to gratify straight males' desires. Nonetheless, Jet Age feminism was an effective marketing strategy for Madison Avenue and its global counterparts. In fact, the ethos found an ample number of adherents among women in America's, Western Europe's, Jamaica's, and Yugoslavia's middle classes.

Thus, Friedan's Second Wave feminism and Jet Age feminism were sparring partners competing for prominence in the 1960s, with their most intense competition for the hearts and minds of liberation-minded, cosmopolitan young women. Indeed, Friedan's *Feminine Mystique* and Helen Gurley Brown's Jet Age feminist manifesto, a book titled *Sex and the Single Girl*, were released within months of each other in 1962-63, and both ascended to bestseller status.[7] They thereby staked rival claims on the soul of cosmopolitan women (or "*Cosmo* girls") inside and beyond America's borders. To appreciate the magnetic appeal and repulsion of Jet Age feminism, one need only inspect the photo above. Here, the camera is transfixed by Braniff's Davis, but so too are the other stewardesses. Perceptible in their gazes is a rich mixture of emotion: envy, perplexity, contempt, jealousy. These women, like young women around the globe, were engaged in an intense, though often internalized debate on the virtues of Jet Age feminism.

CHAPTER 7

A Runway for Jet Age Feminism

Frequently in the Cold War years of massive aviation expansion, runways supplemented their utilitarian purpose with something more festive. Whether for christening new routes or unveiling new aircraft, they and their adjoining aprons hosted water cannons welcoming a landing plane, grandstands of dignitaries cheering a sparkling new livery, and rolling cameras capturing the takeoff of an inaugural flight. But in July 1965 aviation history marked a revolutionary moment on a different kind of runway, one that was indoors and in a grand Renaissance-era palace: the famous Palazzo Pitti in Florence, Italy.

On a fashion runway assembled in one of the lavish ballrooms, designer Emilio Pucci, a native son of Florence and a scion of one of the republic's governing families, introduced his fall haute couture collection. Alongside his elegant evening gowns, he also debuted the fruit of his months-long work for Texas's Braniff Airways. The new ensemble of stewardess uniforms he unveiled embodied, in the words of *Vogue* magazine, the geographical fluidity and extraterrestrial yearning of the Jet Age: "In look, a combination of Texas, Florence, and Mars, the clothes [Pucci] has worked out are meant to meet every possible exigency—including the future."[8] Braniff's public relations team added a similar point, stressing that Pucci was "a decorated Italian pilot"—he flew a fighter plane over North Africa for the Italian Air Force in World War II—who now "is blazing a new space-age trail for erstwhile earth-bound fashions. His concept for in-flight hostess attire is completely new, completely contemporary, and completely in accord with his credo: 'When I design, I think of a woman in motion.'"[9]

There was considerable gimmickry in this presentation, designed as it was to raise eyebrows and generate publicity for the airline. Cutting through the self-aggrandizing marketing copy, what really happened in July 1965 was that flight attendants at a rather obscure airline got an expensive makeover to sell more seats. Yet, scholars and social critics also see in this moment a rupture along important cultural fault lines in the 1960s.[10] This rupture occurred right where Braniff's public relations materials and media reports suggested: it was about the state of women in the Jet Age, about women's identity for "the future." In this future, women would participate in a cosmopolitan world—replete with airplanes, border crossings, more financial self-sufficiency, and bolder fashion. The Braniff stewardess was Pucci's exemplar of this Jet Age "woman in motion."

Emilio Pucci's work was done at the behest of Mary Wells and her "End of the Plain Plane" campaign. It was a response to her research, which exposed a deep concern among travelers, one shared by many airline executives at the dawn of the Jet Age, that the jet, especially because its expanded seating capacity made air travel less exclusive, was spoiling customers' enthusiasm for flying. Since flying was becoming "plain," especially for frequent flyers, Wells devoted herself to renewing their excitement and driving more of them to Braniff. Pucci's creations added a needed element of panache to enliven passengers' experience.

For stewardesses themselves, Pucci's and Wells's new creation provided a novel makeover, but it also reinforced their workplace inferiority. Their value as beauty objects was accentuated, while their standing as safety professionals diminished further. At the same time, however, when clad in Pucci's outfits and profiled in Wells's racy ads, Braniff's stewardesses became paragons of Jet Age feminism. Even while enduring more risks due to their increasing sexualization, these "women in motion" embodied a life freed from the constraints of home and the traditional mores that had previously governed women's sexual practices.

Color and Sophistication for the Masses

For several months in 1964 and '65, Mary Wells and her team researched the aviation industry in search of the "really big idea" that Braniff CEO Harding Lawrence needed for Braniff to attract more passengers and thereby pay down its jet-induced debt. Wells's team was most struck by the monotony of air travel. In particular, she noted, "there was no color. This was the sixties, mind you, when color was a hot marketing tool." Elsewhere in Wells's jet-set lifestyle, color was everywhere: in the boldly patterned, Pucci-designed cocktail dresses she saw at Upper East Side parties and at the ultramodern, Alexander Girard–designed restaurant Fonda del Sol that she frequented in Midtown, which she described as "a high-octane color montage of Mexican and modern."[11] As the fashion historian Shirley Kennedy notes,

> One could not help but notice color everywhere.... Colors vibrated and seemed to explode on the Pucci silks, as they did on the Pop Art canvases of Lichtenstein, Warhol, Wesselman, and Rosenquist, the ad art of Peter Max and Milton Glaser, psychedelic rock concert posters, and the Beatles' cartoon movie, *The Yellow Submarine*. Color—hot, bright, and clear—and shapes—rounded and sensually

curved—were key elements of 1960s furniture designs produced by Americans and Europeans.[12]

With color now foremost in her thinking, Wells returned to Lawrence with a pitch. As it turned out, "He liked thinking about color; he reminded me that Braniff would be flying to places associated with brilliant color, Mexico and South America," thanks to these regions' vibrant premodern artistic traditions that used bright colors in their textiles and architecture.[13] As Wells put it, "Color was my idea, but not really. There's no magic talent in advertising. Too many people don't do their homework and find the obvious need."[14]

Color would ultimately infuse everything that Wells remade in her pursuit to end the "Plain Plane": the ticket counters, first class lounges, gate areas, and print materials that she outsourced to Alexander Girard, as well as the stewardess uniforms that she entrusted to Pucci. In the end, hardly a single Braniff space was left colorless. The original burst that led to this embrace was an idea for the planes themselves. As Wells notes, she and her staff considered painting the planes one bold color—perhaps a fleet all in yellow, or orange, or indigo. Her partner and art director, Stewart Greene, was drawing large renderings of planes in these individual colors, then placing them on the office floor for the staff to critique. "Then I asked him to do one with all different-colored planes," recalled Wells. "When that sketch hit the floor," she added, "it was a thunderbolt, there wasn't a doubt in my mind . . . the sketch of the solid-colored planes in seven different colors was the hit show." As she explained, "Seven colors looked like a big idea and wow and friendly and it would be big news. People would go out of their way to see them." She again found that Lawrence was very receptive: "When he studied the sketches of his planes in seven different solid colors he was quiet for a minute. I don't think I breathed. Then he laughed. He said, and I will never ever forget it, 'That will do it!'"[15]

Thereafter Wells made her second vital move, one that tied the universally accessible inclination to embrace color to the more exclusivist impulses of elite cosmopolitan society. After all, Wells did not employ a childlike idea of color as one might find in a nursery school, or even the notionally "primitive" collage of colors from Incan or Aztec textiles. Instead, she delegated the implementation of Braniff's color infusion to two of America's and Europe's top-name designers. By effectively purchasing their aesthetic for use at the airline, she guaranteed that Braniff's colors had a patina of elitism.

Pucci's explosively colorful cocktail dresses were famous primarily because of the celebrities who wore them. He had a large coterie of exceptionally rich patrons who would buy directly from his boutiques in Florence or the jet-set hideaway of Capri. By the mid-1960s, he was also exporting to major department stores in the United States. But, as Helen Gurley Brown recalled, Pucci's price point was prohibitive: "I remember seeing my first Pucci dress in Burdine's department store in Miami in 1963 when I was on a book promotion. 'How long has *this* been going on?' I asked myself and, though I didn't think I could afford one—$190 for one little skimp of a dress—I tried on four in fifteen minutes for sheer pleasure."[16] That Brown, wealthy thanks to her best-selling book, decided she could not afford Pucci's creations speaks to the designer's exclusivity. Moreover, as a well-to-do celebrity in his own right, he already belonged to the jet set. Thus, Wells's choice of Pucci meant that Jet Age stewardess fashion would be designed by a jet-set celebrity.[17]

Ironically, this deployment of a jet-set aesthetic was also Braniff's tool for democratizing air travel. Braniff's new customers would be drawn from two divergent income groups. The first was composed of those who were wealthy enough to partake in Girard's and Pucci's worlds as consumers. Since this wealthy group already flew quite frequently, Braniff's embrace of jet-set glitz might help lure them from their competitors. Yet, more numerous were customers with considerably less spending power, many of them first-time flyers. In their case, too, there was real appeal in the Braniff aesthetic. In the strictly regulated US aviation market of the time, customers typically found only two airlines flying to any desired destination, both offering the same fares. For Braniff's most lucrative routes linking Texas with Chicago and New York City, the main competitor was the well-heeled legacy carrier American Airlines. The only difference was American's stronger reputation and its earlier adoption of jets—hence Braniff's desire not only to match the competition with an all-jet fleet, but also to surpass it with a fashionable makeover that generated a media buzz.

When ad executives for Pan Am researched travelers with limited budgets just a few years later, they found the following: "Once they [are committed to] pay full fare, they are prepared to shop among competitive airlines on the basis of the comfort, service, and enjoyment aspects of the trip."[18] With its new jets and Wells's stylish overhaul, Braniff seemingly offered more for the money: upon paying what by all accounts were expensive fares, these customers were treated a bit more like the jet set themselves. They lounged in Girard-styled airports, boarded planes that boasted bold fabrics and even Latin American artwork on the walls, and were served by hostesses who sported the same sort of Pucci-designed outfits as movie stars. Overall, these middle- and working-class customers purchased a voyeuristic opportunity to partake in the cosmopolitan ambiance they saw in movies and read about on celebrity pages.

Braniff's choice to turn their stewardesses into Pucci-clad hostesses also addressed—or at least diverted attention away from—a growing crisis tied to the democratization of jet travel. With larger and faster aircraft, customers feared that flying would become more like mass transit: utilitarian rather than exclusive, crowded and impersonal rather than enjoyable. In the parlance of Mary Wells, the fear was that air travel would occur increasingly on a "plain plane." When the ad executives later working for Pan Am surveyed middle-income consumers, they heard concerns that jets were becoming too large: "The impression of mass travel also underlines their basic concern about de-humanization. They feel the individual passenger will be one of a mob and will not have the kind of personal attention they seek."[19] Braniff's largest pre-jet plane, the DC-7, seated a maximum of 75 passengers, while its new Boeing 727s seated 154.[20] Thus, passengers hoping for intimacy and a personal touch were more likely to be disappointed.

Unattainable expectations were now falling on the shoulders of stewardesses. As the Pan Am report summarized, consumers "desire to be treated as individuals. Some of them are even sensitive to 'cookie cutter' pleasantness on the part of the stewardesses. They don't want a mechanical greeting no matter how pleasant. They want to really feel that someone cares about them as individuals."[21] However, providing this sort of individualized attention was increasingly difficult. Stewardesses now cared for more people and undertook the same list of tasks with reduced flying times. Braniff's Pucci-designed stewardess outfits offered a potential remedy to this crunch. By turning the aisle into a fashion runway, passengers would think of themselves as spectators rather than guests in an intimate space. They would still take part in jet-set cosmopolitanism, but more passively, as befitted the financial exigencies of Jet Age travel.

Jet Age Feminism Takes Off

The early 1960s saw the first rumblings of a second wave of feminism in the United States. As Betty Friedan's 1963 best-selling book

The Feminine Mystique explained, many middle-class and working-class housewives were depressed, even as their families prospered economically. Being a loving wife and mother, Friedan noted, left some women incomplete: "Each suburban wife struggles with it alone. As she made the beds, shopped for groceries, matched slipcover material, ate peanut butter sandwiches with her children, chauffeured Cub Scouts and Brownies, lay beside her husband at night—she was afraid to ask even of herself the silent question—'Is this all?'"[22]

This driving question from 1963 about whether American women could partake in a life outside the home converged with a political advancement in 1964: the Civil Rights Act, rather unexpectedly, passed while including workplace protections for women. This marked the first time in American history, at least legally, that companies could not discriminate against women when making choices to hire or fire personnel for almost any job.[23] As a result, Second Wave activists increasingly pressed the federal government and companies to establish the Civil Rights Act in practice, founding the National Organization for Women (NOW) in 1966 to undertake this work. Thus, the Second Wave's first impetus was to place women in careers that were engaging and on par with men in terms of pay and responsibility. This goal was soon accompanied by additional efforts to secure reproductive rights, combat sexual violence, secure women's healthcare, and promote consciousness-raising about sexism's impact on women's private lives.

Braniff's revamped marketing was out of step with these feminist priorities, especially regarding workplace equality. Wells's work did nothing to address the airline's persistent policies that kept stewardess jobs short-term. Additionally, the airline maintained its beauty-based hiring standards. In 1962, Braniff hired only women who were no larger than "5'7" and 130 pounds" and possessed "an attractive, wholesome, well-groomed appearance." It openly acknowledged its no-marriage policy and even promoted it as advantageous for stewardesses, noting that "the wealth of knowledge and experience gained from their enriching and challenging career as a Braniff hostess [will have] contributed immeasurably to their later success as a homemaker."[24]

By 1968, despite the Civil Rights Act, these standards had changed only slightly, with women two inches taller and five pounds heavier now allowed to apply. Also, the no-marriage policy, while still in place, was loosened a bit, in that widows and divorcees were now invited to apply:

> [A] young lady is qualified for employment as a Braniff hostess if she is 20 to 27 years old; from 5 feet, 2 inches to 5 feet, 9 inches tall with weight in proportion to her height and not over 135 pounds; single, or a childless widow or divorcee unmarried for one year or more; has 20/50 vision in each eye without glasses; has at least a high school education and good character, and is blessed with sound judgement, an attractive appearance with a clear complexion and an attractive smile, a pleasant disposition, even temperament and a pleasant sounding voice.[25]

Thus, rather than evolve with the Second Wave, Braniff's marketers ultimately chose to mock the feminism of Betty Friedan and NOW. When it opened a new training academy for flight attendants in 1967, the airline described it as an "ultra-modern and beautiful edifice [that] has been artfully designed with the feminine mystique in mind." Taking Friedan's own term—which referenced women's degradation due to harsh beauty norms—the airline sarcastically, but proudly professed to embody exactly what Friedan fought against.

While Second Wave feminists encouraged women to see a university education as the foundation for a lifelong career, Braniff again ran in the opposite direction. Its new training facility was christened the "Hostess College," which was a "Girl's Dream World." While noting that the five-story building possessed a meager five classrooms for training sessions, the airline's marketing materials focused on the extensive facilities aimed at beautifying the stewardess-to-be: "The college has everything for the girl's training, aesthetic, and physical needs." There was a boutique where trainees would acquire their Pucci-designed outfits and the so-called "Powder Puff room—where girls learn the secrets of makeup and flawless complexions." This supplanting of college learning with indoctrination into a beauty regime continued elsewhere: "Another few steps away are the rows of electric hair dryers where she may do some homework on jet aircraft passenger configurations while her hair dries."[26]

Braniff's flight attendants fit more closely with Helen Gurley Brown's vision of feminism than with Friedan's, especially in the ways that their workplace was increasingly sexualized. Despite the salacious title, *Sex and the Single Girl* had a core message that supported women entering careers and striving for financial independence. However, it also correctly recognized that workplaces were filled with unsolicited sexual advances from men. They were becoming, in her words, "sexier than Turkish harems, fraternity house weekends... or the Playboy centerfold."[27] Rather than decry this reality, Brown instead encouraged women to build long-term careers in these sexualized offices. She instructed them on how to dress, how to conduct themselves in meetings, how to manage money, how to vacation, how (and how not) to date office colleagues, and when (and when not) to have sex. Most importantly, Brown encouraged working women to hone a skill set with which they could playfully dismiss most men's sexual advances, while assenting to the ones that could further their careers or financial well-being.

The historian Patricia Bradley notes the large audience for such advice: "When Brown published her book, women between ages twenty-five and fifty-four were on the cusp of exploding into the workforce, a group that increased 45 percent from 1962 to 1975."[28] This increasing audience ensured that Brown stayed in the public eye and was still promoting her version of feminism well after 1962. In 1965 she became the editor of *Cosmopolitan* magazine and proceeded to revamp it as a standard-bearer for single career women. She remained in this position for the next thirty-two years, during which time she consistently encouraged readers to aspire to financial independence, while eschewing the Second Wave's attacks on the feminine mystique. The so-called "*Cosmo* girl" or "single girl" (synonymous terms for Brown) was comfortable being sexy, dressing in conventionally feminine ways, and being sexually active. As long as they overlooked the fact that Braniff's stewardesses were compelled to be short-term workers, Brown and her devotees could treat Emilio Pucci, Mary Wells, and Braniff stewardesses as model innovators of the "single girl" lifestyle, as fellow practitioners of Jet Age feminism.

Consistent with such views, Brown considered Emilio Pucci a liberator of women. She saw an almost political ferment in his fashions, likening his impact to the flapper look of the 1920s. "I think Emilio, some thirty years later, had somewhat the same effect on American women. No, we weren't exactly constricted or restrained by fashion or society like those twenties women, but he did help us express ourselves ... experience a new freedom, a sensuousness we hadn't felt or shown before," she noted. The key to enabling this result was that "the dresses were spare, sexy, and liberating!"[29] In the 1950s, Pucci was already innovating fashion to empower women's mobility. He is credited with streamlining undergarments by marketing a lightweight girdle that highlighted a woman's natural curves. He also successfully blurred the line between sportswear's casualness and high fashion's formality.

By the 1960s Pucci had further refined his aesthetic for active women, often opting for either miniskirts or tights, or both in combination, as in his creations for Braniff. "Motion and movement are very important in our lives," he noted, before adding more controversially, "A woman can run to get a taxi in a short skirt and still look elegant, but if she runs in a long skirt, she looks gauche."[30] This assertion betrays ambivalence about women's liberation. On a positive note, Pucci embraced how women's lives now included moving through cityscapes with the earnestness and speed that only men previously could. Less progressive, however, was his subjective assessment of what looks gauche. Here, he opened space to design for women still captive to the feminine mystique—to socially determined, sexist criteria of what is beautiful and what is gauche. Despite such contradictions, Pucci's creations were nonetheless emblematic of the age. As the author Marilyn Bender stresses, they appeared at "the threshold of the Jet Age," making "the Pucci dress . . . both symbol and passport of the new era. Fragile-looking but indestructible, chic and sexy, it was the capsule wardrobe for the mobile woman glorying in the body beautiful."[31]

In media interviews, Pucci expounded on his ambivalence about women's liberation, asserting that he strongly disagreed with central goals of the Second Wave. When interviewed by *Life* magazine, he started with a sentiment that progressive feminists might applaud, as he called for appreciating a subtler form of feminine beauty: "America has been left with the idea that a woman is sexy if her bust sticks out or if she has a thin waist." Exalting the petite, androgynous Audrey Hepburn as a role model, Pucci insisted, "It's not the inches of bust that make the difference, but what is inside." As for Hepburn, Pucci added, "Everything she has is fire inside."

Nonetheless, Pucci would have disappointed Hepburn when he dismissed women's aspirations for parity with men. He continued, "What is natural to the American woman is to compete with the man in all fields. I think this makes her unhappy. If the end of man is work and creation, the end of woman is home, children, friends, and culture, things that man hasn't time to pursue." He readily perceived that "American women won't accept" his views, which were steeped in the traditional ideology of separate spheres. Yet, he persisted in blaming women for their own unhappiness, especially deriding their efforts to enter men's spheres and vacate their own. While Second-Wave feminists like Friedan encouraged housewives to attend to their yearning for something more when haunted by the question "Is this all?," Pucci instead saw this sort of discontent as wrongheaded: "Something has been missed over there [in America]."[32]

This disregard for working women also informs an analysis of Pucci's Braniff designs. His dismissal of Second Wave feminism helps make sense of his efforts to craft a Jet Age identity for stewardesses that was a separate sphere: a feminine realm in the plane cabin focused on nurturing, socializing, and sparking the potential for male-female eroticism. Yet, at the same time, as with Pucci's other creations, his Braniff commissions allowed these active women to negotiate the public spaces of modern life with agility and elegance.

From Runway Elegance to "Air Strip" Debauchery

Pucci's first reflex was to feminize Braniff's stewardess uniforms. He did so in part by erasing the military-like elements that had been fixtures of flight attendant uniforms from their earliest days. Gone were the drab colors and androgynous fits, as well as the stripes on the cuffs and wings on the lapel. These were introduced in the 1920s when only men served as flight attendants, with crew dressed in military-style uniforms and given ranks akin to sailors on naval ships. For Pucci, these symbols of male-oriented military status were undesirable. In justifying his radical overhaul to the press, however, he suggested merely that the uniforms were outdated: "Most airplane stewardesses are dressed as if they are traveling by bus in the year 1925."[33]

Yet, Braniff's copywriters pushed further on this point. They began by stating that the airline's first hostess in 1937 was attired oddly, "looking as if she probably could fly the plane herself." They then credited Pucci with replacing "the severe, mannish uniforms" with feminine touches of color and "culottes, leotards, wraparound skirts, scarf hats, derbies, serving dresses."[34] Pucci now attired stewardesses as though they were at social events, the environs where he felt women should focus their lives. Braniff executives further fortified this division of spheres between the cockpit and the cabin by jettisoning the term "stewardess," with its origins in the navy, and opted for "hostess" instead. "Stewardess is a 'hard' word. Hostess is a warm, friendly word," noted CEO Harding Lawrence, "We train our hostesses to be just that—hostesses, and to approach our passengers as friendly visitors in their home."[35]

CHAPTER 7

Pucci would add to this sentiment by eschewing the term "uniform." Instead, his multi-piece creations comprised what he called a "couture collection." After all, while each item of his 1965 creations included a hemline just above the knee, the collection allowed these women to sport four distinct looks on the same flight: an exterior layer anchored by a winter coat, a suit with a wraparound skirt and zippable blazer, then a lighter layer of culottes and a turtle-neck blouse. The fourth item, nicknamed the "Puccino," was a colorful smock to don when serving food. Each of these items embodied the combination of elegance, casualness, and sophistication that made Pucci's designs so desirable among jet set celebrities and the "single girl" set alike: formfitting, above-the-knee styles that supposedly made women attractive while in motion.

The multilayered nature of Pucci's creations ultimately inspired the most controversy, though Pucci himself was not to blame for this. In his view, the layers reflected the wonder of jet travel, allowing stewardesses to stay stylish along their surprisingly quick half-day transition from the icy climate of the northern United States to the balmy beaches of Latin America. Furthermore, by employing formfitting but breathable and easily washable fabrics, he added further flexibility for stewardesses' nomadic lives. He was proud that the entire ensemble fit into an overnight bag. "In the future," he noted, "all an international traveler would need add to such an ensemble would be a dress or two and accessories for evening occasions."[36] Such visions enabled not only stewardesses' mobility but also that of Jet Age passengers, including millions of women who were adherents of Brown's "single girl" ethos. By 1964, there were thirteen million single women in the United States and another twenty-three million married women working outside the home. These women were more likely than ever before to have the financial means to fly, paying for this privilege without the support of a man.[37]

It was actually Mary Wells who devised an alternative use for the uniform's layers, turning them into the basis for a burlesque attraction that she labeled the "Air Strip." For Wells, the "Air Strip" served as a titillating opportunity to appeal to Braniff's core customer base: the unaccompanied man flying for business. It was these frequent fliers, many of whom paid for full-fare first class tickets, who experienced the most fatigue with flying. If the "End of the Plain Plane" was to succeed, these men needed to buy in, shifting their travel to Braniff from its competitors as the airline invested in new jets. Thus, as stewardesses discarded each layer of clothing while in flight, they were told to do so in the aisles, in full view of gawking passengers.

Business Week, one of the most-read publications among businessmen, immediately voiced approval for the "Air Strip." It first quoted Harding Lawrence, who articulated the motive for this innovation: "We are adding sheer pleasure to the experience of flight." The author then added his own experience: "Indeed, a passenger might easily feel that he's attending an airborne striptease show when, right after takeoff, the hostesses peel off their pink uniforms to reveal the blue ones underneath."[38] Correspondent Stan Mays of London's *Sunday Mirror* linked the "Air Strip" with the recently released hit movie *Boeing Boeing*, in which actor Tony Curtis played a man secretly dating three stewardesses at once. "The things they get up to in the air these days!" Mays began. "There was I, minding my own business, 32,000 feet up on a flight from New York to Mexico when . . . Boeing-Boeing. She did it." He continued, "The air hostess. She started to undress. Bang in the middle of the aisle. Fasten your seat belts. There's more to this than meets the eye. Because four other hostesses were doing a similar air strip in other parts of the giant Boeing 720 jet." Mays added a supportive comment from a stewardess: "It's zip zip zip all the way. The passengers seem to love it, and we think many fly Braniff just to see our act."[39]

Wells made sure the "Air Strip" received prominent play in the "End of the Plain Plane" advertising campaign. She devised a media plan with a two-step newspaper strategy: on the first weekend, at the end of November 1965, color ads boasting the "End of Plain Plane" would run in forty-one newspapers in thirty-three cities. Then, "A week later our second color newspaper ad will run in the same 41 newspapers headlined, 'Introducing the Air Strip' (It talks about the hostess quick change of course)." To maximize Braniff's exposure to the core audience of businessmen for the "Air Strip," Wells followed up with TV ads during football broadcasts over the winter holidays: "Braniff will be one of the sponsors of seven football bowl games, in fact all the major ones except the Orange Bowl and the Rose Bowl."[40]

The television ad began with the sort of whistling music common to striptease acts from the burlesque era and then proceeded to show a stewardess, suggestively smiling at the camera, in the process of disrobing through her various layers of colorful Pucci designs. It concluded with a male voice-over—in the deep, slow tone of an MC at a stripper bar—intoning, "The Air Strip is brought to you by Braniff International, who believes that even an airline hostess should look like a girl."[41] The print ad attributes to Pucci himself the claim about hostesses looking like a girl, but it ends with a similarly suggestive statement, "If the flight seems all too short, that's the whole idea."[42]

It says much about the preponderance of straight male sexual privilege that the debut of the "Air Strip" found no opposition in the mainstream media. When the topic was covered, there was often mention of buy-in from stewardesses. For example, one stewardess stressed a newfound freedom in Pucci's clothes, noting, "We love the new outfit. It makes you feel like a real female and not a busboy."[43] Most importantly for Braniff, the "Air Strip" was a commercial success, playing a key role in selling more seats on the new jets. By June 1966, the airline's passenger traffic was up 48.7 percent over the previous year, while its revenue in the first full year of the campaign rose by 42 percent.[44]

Mary Wells Lawrence and the Turbulent Legacy of Jet Age Feminism

In a passage reminiscent of Helen Gurley Brown's *Sex and the Single Girl*, Mary Wells confesses in her autobiography that her work with Braniff inspired romance. She traces the spark of the affair to the very moment in mid-1965 when Harding Lawrence agreed to paint Braniff's jets in a jelly-bean bowl of colors. "That had to be the moment I fell in love with him," she notes,

> I knew I looked perfectly calm, he told me later I was discouragingly professional, but I was keeping a lid on emotions that seemed extremely dangerous to me. I felt powerful undercurrents zinging back and forth between us that could mess up my life, his life, a lot of lives. . . . I didn't want trouble, I wanted to build the best advertising agency in the world, I didn't have time for life-altering love.[45]

Disregarding these warning signs, Harding Lawrence and Mary Wells over the next two years engaged in one of America's most high-profile office romances. As both worked their way through divorces to their first spouses, they also worked together to mold Braniff into one of America's fastest-growing airlines. When they wed in November 1967, Harding and Mary Wells Lawrence (she adopted her husband's last name as an addendum) became—like Henry and Clare Boothe Luce a generation before—one of America's most prominent power couples.

Each kept their careers that pulled in respective salaries of over $100,000 per year, near the peak of executive pay at the time.

Mary Wells Lawrence thereby served as a corporate-class expression of Jet Age feminism, which is both similar to and different from the working-class variety embodied by Braniff's stewardesses. Because she was married even before meeting Harding Lawrence, she was not exactly a bona fide "single girl" like stewardesses were, but in 1965 she was still relatively young (aged thirty-seven) and very much a working woman. Indeed, she had succeeded quite spectacularly in the otherwise male-dominated field of advertising.[46] She also exercised a sexual agency that would endear her to Helen Gurley Brown, as she managed the minefield of come-ons from powerful men in the office and strove with her first husband to make marriage work in a dual-career household. Wells and her first husband also tried an unorthodox form of child-rearing for the time, raising two adopted girls with the aid of a live-in nanny. All the while, Wells maintained her financial independence and built her career.

As with Pucci and his work for Braniff, Wells Lawrence was a polarizing figure in Second Wave feminist circles. On the one hand, she built a wildly successful career in a male-dominated world and also boldly reworked marriage norms to accommodate her profession. Yet, she also problematically built her own success by promoting sexism in various marketing campaigns, especially those for Braniff and other airlines. Among Second Wave feminists, even her marriage to Harding Lawrence constituted grounds for attack. Author and activist Gloria Steinem quipped, "Oh, well, Mary Wells Uncle Tommed it to the top," thereby attributing her formidable career successes to her cozy relationships with men like Lawrence and her willingness to perpetuate sexism against other women.[47] Furthermore, in her studied assessment of Wells Lawrence's career, the historian Patricia Bradley finds that she "took no position on feminism, took no particular interest (judging by her memoir) in promoting professional women's careers at her agency, and was not involved in the push to change women's images in advertising."[48]

Fundamentally, however, Wells Lawrence shared much in common with her working-class counterparts at Braniff, despite enjoying far more class privilege. She too experienced unwelcome come-ons from men, including when she landed her first job on Madison Avenue, where she was hired in part because her boss found her attractive. As she recalled, during the job interview the man "watched me cross his office without expression, but then I saw him think 'Huzzah!' and I knew he was going to be a fan." While unnerved, she also sensed his attraction could work to her advantage, just as Helen Gurley Brown counseled in *Sex and the Single Girl*: "He was wildly flirtatious but in that safe, careful, old-fashioned way."[49] This sort of wagering about the risks and benefits of men's workplace attractions was all too familiar to her working-class counterparts in the stewardess corps. Those who were savviest could artfully negotiate flirtations from pilots, managers, and passengers. But, if the man's unreciprocated interest escalated, stewardesses, like women who were business executives, were forced to manage an unwelcome and potentially dangerous workplace situation.[50]

In at least one instance, Wells Lawrence became painfully aware of another commonality with stewardesses: because she was a woman, she was overlooked for advancement. Stewardesses were ghettoized into a pink-collar career that was devoid of promotion opportunities. Marriage to a wealthier man was the only vehicle for their economic ascendance. Wells Lawrence's case was quite different in its contours. Just as her work for Braniff came to fruition in late 1965, she left the firm where she was working, Jack Tinker and Partners. The split was not amicable, as the company had reneged on its original offer to make her president: "I joined Tinker because I'd been promised I'd be president and run it," she noted. In her first year with them, however, "They became so successful they didn't want to rock the boat," fearing that having a woman in charge would deter future clients from signing on. Wells's ambition could not be satisfied if she were stuck under corporate America's glass ceiling: "I had a terrible need to put together my ideas and run my own company, ideas that would go out the window if I [stayed]. Instead I resigned."[51]

In her case, however, resigning resulted in more opportunity, quite a difference from Braniff's stewardesses. She cobbled together partners for a totally new firm—Wells Rich Greene—with her at the helm as president. Crucially for the new firm, Harding Lawrence felt a strong personal loyalty to Wells (whether coincidental or not, their courtship had already begun by this time). He agreed to move Braniff's business, supplying Wells Rich Greene with their first client in 1966, just as it opened its doors. The $6 million in billings was enough to float them until their success with Braniff begot other clients.

Wells Lawrence stayed on as Braniff's account executive for about a year after her marriage. During this time, the couple moved her children to Dallas to live with Harding and attend school, while she maintained her home and office in New York. She flew back to Dallas most Fridays, often meeting the family at the airport, so they could all continue on Braniff's evening flight to Acapulco. Between homes in Dallas, New York, Acapulco, Arizona, and the Cote d'Azur, the family led a decidedly nontraditional life: "Harding and I are both naturally nomadic and our timing was good," she summarized. "The jet was cutting the world in half, in fact the world was fast becoming small."[52] The Jet Age stimulated social forces that unleashed not only new iterations of feminism, but also new constellations of marriage and family, including the so-called long-distance marriage.

Meanwhile, executives at Braniff publicly maintained that the Lawrence-Wells marriage created no conflict of interest. "Anybody who thinks like she's acting like the boss's wife in there is wrong," said one. "She gets a little loud at times. As for us, and that includes Harding, it's no holds barred." It was, however, harder to manage voices concerned with the potential conflict of interest that arose from outside the company. As *Fortune* magazine stated, "The legion of Mary Wells watchers was immediately fascinated by the comic possibilities arising out of a situation in which the client was married to the president of his agency."[53]

With the writing on the wall, Wells Lawrence orchestrated an exit from Braniff, though here again this was very lucrative. She resourcefully lured a rival airline, TWA, to sign on with Wells Rich Greene before canceling the Braniff account. As TWA was a larger airline with a larger advertising budget, the payout for this exchange was impressive: "In economic terms, the agency would give up about $7.5 million in billings (its share of Braniff's $9 million in advertising expenditures) and take on $22 million."[54] The deal elicited jealous and misogynistic venom from competitors. The day the deal was announced, Wells wrote, "was the day some of Madison Avenue's old guard decided women were dangerous to the advertising community and that I was not only an arriviste but the queen of black widow spiders. I don't think I am overstating it."[55]

For Wells Lawrence—the Jet Age feminist in Braniff's boardroom—marriage was an effective business tool, enhancing her exposure to the aviation industry by combining her already impressive connections with her husband's. Rather than an off-ramp into a life as a full-time wife and mother, as was the expectation for stewardesses, Wells Lawrence's marriage propelled her career ever higher. All the while, she maintained her financial and social independence. As Wells Lawrence explains, "In

1967 when Harding and I married it never entered his mind or mine that I would leave Wells Rich Greene, that we would have a traditional marriage living and working in the same town." This reality, for her, was vitally important to the cause of feminism, even to the Second Wave activists with whom she often clashed:

> Betty Friedan established NOW in 1966 and although she was already focusing on the ERA and the right of women to control their reproductive lives, the psychological shift that the women's movement brought to society had not yet changed it. Long-distance marriage was major news, and we were forever being interviewed about the details of ours. There was just enough awareness about what Betty Friedan called "the problem that has no name," the growing sense that motherhood and housework were not enough for some women, that our marriage was examined with respect, if not awe.[56]

What is missing from Wells Lawrence's own assessment of her contributions to feminism is a sense of cross-class solidarity. She was quite proud that both her trailblazing career and unconventional marriage pushed the boundaries of feminist-inspired changes and enabled her to become a model for other women entering high-powered careers in the ensuing decades. Yet, her work for Braniff, especially the "Air Strip" campaign that further objectified stewardesses, only reinforced an already sexist culture in aviation. Working-class women at Braniff had no opportunity to emulate Wells Lawrence's successes, whether on the job or in her marriage. As such, Jet Age feminism disproportionately favored women in the corporate class.

Others were left to press for equality for Braniff's stewardesses. More progressive feminist groups, including NOW, took up stewardesses' growing number of grievances against their sexist treatment. In the late 1960s, a homegrown feminist group named Stewardesses for Women's Rights (SFWR) built up a network of stewardesses from across the industry to protest and to initiate legal challenges against the overt sexism in their workplace. Their fight boiled down to one central claim: that flight attendants were, first and foremost, safety professionals conducting a job that required authority and responsibility, both of which were compromised by the sexist treatment of stewardesses. Over the next decade, this feminist vision gradually prevailed in American aviation, leading airlines like Braniff to jettison the colorful, sexy uniforms of the Jet Age feminist era and replace them with admittedly drabber, but also more professional attire appropriate for a serious workplace.

Second Wave feminism's rise in aviation also meant that all airlines, including Braniff, would stop forcing stewardesses to retire upon marriage or pregnancy by the mid-1970s. Wells's efforts in 1965 to stimulate profit by deploying sexual arousal were ultimately replaced by more serious commitments to women workers' equality. Yet, for the better part of a decade, her marketing creations were one of the hottest trends in American and global aviation, spreading the deeply compromised notion of Jet Age feminism well beyond American shores. What follows is a chronicle of how Jet Age feminism hit stewardesses in more distant parts of the globe, including in socialist Yugoslavia and in Jamaica.

Chapter 8

Love, Fashion, and the *Stjuardesa*
Yugoslavia's Jet Age Feminism

A large assembly of officials turned out on April 28, 1962, for one of the most triumphant events in the history of Yugoslav aviation: the ribbon-cutting ceremony for Belgrade's new international airport. Like a smaller facility that would open just a few months later in the coastal tourist destination of Dubrovnik, the federal capital's airport was built to the ICAO's top "A category" specifications, meaning that it was equipped with the highest quality navigation and safety tools and was ready to accommodate frequent landings and takeoffs with heavier payloads, as was needed for the arrival of the Jet Age. The ribbon cutting culminated a planning process dating back to 1947, when Yugoslavia's Civil Aviation Authority devised plans to overtake Rome and Athens as a gateway for routes between Europe and the Middle East. Belgrade's new airport was smaller, but in other ways it compared well with Rome's new airport in the coastal town of Fiumicino that had opened a year earlier, and for several years it outpaced its rival in Athens, where a new and larger Eero Saarinen–designed terminal opened in 1969. Also beyond Belgrade and Dubrovnik, Yugoslavia in 1962 was engaged in a massive airport-building spree, with construction underway on new facilities in Ljubljana, Sarajevo, Split, Mostar, and Rijeka, and major renovations taking place in Zagreb, Skopje, and Titograd (Podgorica) to make them jet-ready.[1] The country's

LOVE, FASHION, AND THE *STJUARDESA*

FIGURE 8.1. When Yugoslavia's head of state, Josip Broz Tito, opened Belgrade's state-of-the-art airport in April 1962, a JAT stewardess accompanied him. She sported white gloves and a newly designed uniform, complete with a cap designed by Paris's Christian Dior.
Source: Permission to use this image courtesy of Belgrade Airport.

progression in aviation from what an American diplomat called the "stone-age" to the Jet Age was taking place in one socialist-led great leap forward.[2]

Amid the assembled dignitaries at Belgrade airport, two uniquely dressed individuals stood out in the otherwise monochromatic assembly of men in drab suits. The first was the head of state, Josip Broz Tito, whose camel-colored trench coat and dark sunglasses allowed him to cut a stylish figure, even if the ensemble was more muted than his oft-employed white suits or military uniforms. The second person to steal the show held an admittedly more modest role: a young JAT stewardess accompanied Tito while holding the ceremonial ribbon-cutting scissors on a plush pillow. Yet, her white gloves, smart navy blazer, white blouse, and dainty beret allowed her to stand out as Tito's visual counterpart. While Tito was the diplomatic mastermind ushering Yugoslavia into the Jet Age, the JAT stewardess embodied a new generation of women equipped with the style, beauty, and independence of the new era—Yugoslavia's own version of Jet Age feminism.

This event transpired a few years before Mary Wells and Emilio Pucci revolutionized the "plain plane" by injecting a massive dose of color. Instead, what set these new stewardess uniforms apart was just one element of Wells's and Pucci's creations: a patina of Western elitism. JAT's new uniforms were still designed and produced locally and the new iteration had the same drab navy blue skirt and blazer over a white blouse. They were in most ways a continuation of the military-inspired outfits that JAT stewardesses had worn since their first flights. However, there were two new elements that added a distinguished flair to the stewardess alongside Tito. First was her new cap that was flown in from Paris, as the airline had secured the rights from Christian Dior to use the same ones commissioned by Air France.[3] They were firm and exclusively decorative, a distinct move away from the partizanka's foldable cloth caps sported a decade earlier by Dragica Pavlović. There were also newly issued white gloves, which further reinforced the airline's ties to elite sophistication.

Thus, the JAT stewardess's look was more fashion-forward than ever, thanks especially to the tie-in with Christian Dior. They were nonetheless still more traditionally elegant and far staider than Pucci's 1965 Braniff creations. When JAT received its first jets a few months later in January 1963, Yugoslavia's first Jet Age makeover was complete. JAT could now credibly assure its passengers boarding a jet in Paris, stopping at the ultramodern Belgrade airport, and then progressing across the Mediterranean of equal sophistication to Air France.

Like with the photo above, understanding Yugoslav cosmopolitanism in the Jet Age requires two distinct but interrelated focal points. On the one hand, one must consider the economic and political developments, embodied here by Tito, that allowed the country to move beyond the obscurity imposed on it by the cartography of colonialism. Only part of this transformation involved aviation since the main driver was the country's increasing economic progress and its corresponding insinuation into the economies of the West and Global South. Most exemplary were the country's engineering firms, which developed crucial expertise building factories, roads, housing projects, airports, and hydroelectric dams during the country's rapid postwar industrialization and urbanization. These firms then exported their expertise to similar projects in the Middle East and Africa. By the 1970s, their reputation for quality work at lower costs also opened up footholds in Western Europe. For example, the housing complex for men's athletes at the 1972 Munich Olympics was built by the Belgrade-based firm Energoprojekt.[4]

JAT followed these engineering firms into new destinations, especially in oil-rich nonaligned countries like Iraq and Libya, where thousands of Yugoslavs were now stationed as architects, engineers, and skilled carpenters. Along with the simultaneous development of the Adriatic coastline for mass tourism, including efforts to attract wealthier Western European visitors, JAT also increased traffic into the new coastal airports of Dubrovnik, Split, and Rijeka. JAT's route network expanded near and far, while its customer base attracted ever wealthier foreigners and domestic citizens. In these ways, JAT found a market-driven motive for expanding and enhancing its service, which set it apart from its more politically motivated Eastern bloc competitors at Aeroflot, Poland's LOT, and Czechoslovak Airlines (ČSA), all of which also expanded in the 1960s to the West and Global South.[5]

In other ways, Yugoslavia's greater connectedness to the international economy reflected less of a challenge to the cartography of colonialism than the country's growth as an aviation hub. In fact, there were disturbing signs of continued dependence on the West, akin to the region's status during the colonial era. In the Cold War years, the out-migration of lesser-skilled citizens to the West remained unabated, continuing a practice from the past century and foreshadowing the current age of neoliberalism. While most of these migrants relocated as *Gastarbeiter* (guest workers) in the German-speaking lands of West Germany, Austria, and Switzerland, and rarely flew with JAT, others migrated further afield—to Canada, Australia, or the United States.[6] There was a silver lining in this unfortunate development for JAT: these far-flung diasporic communities offered the airline yet another expansion opportunity. They were a built-in market of people, though mainly of more modest incomes, eager to spend holidays with family back home. They helped fill seats in JAT's coach class, while the growing number of businesspeople and higher-end foreign tourists settled into JAT's more exclusive Adriatic class on its first intercontinental flights to Sydney, New York, and Toronto in the 1970s.

This outflow of economic migrants was a warning sign for Yugoslavia's economy. After all, the need to work abroad reflected a discouraging inability within Yugoslavia to modernize with the speed and commitment to equality that would have allowed its poorer citizens to prosper at home. These economic failures prefigured the even more dire economic upheavals that rocked the country in the 1980s and played an important role in its disintegration into violence by 1991. Indeed, both Yugoslavia and Jamaica share the dubious distinction that by the late 1970s they were both early targets in the International Monetary Fund's efforts to address runaway debt through often draconian "conditionality agreements."[7]

In the 1960s and 1970s, however, before debt became a full-fledged crisis, this sizable out-migration of Yugoslav citizens—more than one million out of a population of roughly twenty million pursued opportunities outside the country—served, somewhat ironically, as a badge of honor in relations with the West. Open emigration policies and open borders aligned Yugoslavia with Clare Boothe Luce's cherished freedom to fly everywhere, whereas the rigorous emigration and border regimes in Europe's other socialist regimes exposed them as fearful of granting basic human freedoms. For JAT, this era of almost entirely visa-free travel to and from Yugoslavia was yet another boon, stimulating greater circulation of passengers who filled the new Jet Age terminals across the country.

While these economic and diplomatic developments are vital for understanding the maturation of Yugoslav cosmopolitanism in the Jet Age, this chapter instead concentrates on the photo's other focal point, the JAT stewardess. She represents how the Jet Age brought about changes tied to women's roles as the country grew increasingly open to the larger world's economic and social realities. In particular, a series of social innovations ended up fostering a homegrown version of Jet Age feminism that lacked the overt raunchiness of Braniff Airways' "Air Strip," even while objectifying women and fetishizing their increasing sexual availability. All along, JAT stewardesses continued to benefit from the communist-inspired push for women to forge lifelong careers. This mix of work plus objectification plus sexualization led to a convergence of women's roles in Yugoslavia with those further West in the Jet Age. JAT's stewardesses worked amid this complicated confluence of regressive sexism and more progressive impulses for greater independence. This chapter details how Yugoslavia's constituent cultures developed a growing openness toward candid sexual expression starting in the late 1950s and how JAT's stewardesses became symbols of this change. As such, JAT stewardesses in the Jet Age exhibited certain similarities with Braniff's stewardesses, even as the Yugoslav iteration of Jet Age feminism remained distinct in important ways.

A Yugoslav Sexual Revolution

Through the mid-1950s, Yugoslavia's government was conflicted as to how much sexual liberalization to permit. Some changes that increased women's independence had already occurred in 1946, including amending divorce laws to help women escape from toxic marriages and pushing more women into wage work. Abortion laws also changed between 1952 and 1960 to allow greater reproductive choice, while other contraceptive tools also became available. As an example, Belgrade opened its first contraception clinic in 1955. These developments allowed young people more autonomy, including empowering them to have sex when they desired, even outside of marriage, while deferring pregnancy. Socialist Yugoslavia was therefore building out the legal and healthcare infrastructure necessary for a sexual revolution.[8]

The country's popular culture was somewhat slower to embrace such changes. Into the late 1950s, communist authorities strictly prohibited sexual content in films and other media. The historian Predrag Marković notes that change came only in 1957, with the release of the film *Saturday Evening (Subotom uveče)*. Its attack on conservatism began when the film portrayed a common policing practice, with a young Belgrade couple who were kissing arrested for public indecency. However, the film—and the communist authorities who permitted its release—struck a blow against the regime's puritanism by casting the couple, not the police, as the protagonists. Further liberalization came quickly: "By the mid-1960s everything had changed," notes Marković, as exemplified by the fact that "after the official program celebrating the Day of Students in 1965 [at the University of Belgrade] a striptease was performed."[9] Despite obvious differences between a one-time event among students and the airing of Braniff's "Air Strip" commercial on national television, both episodes from 1965 illustrate that sexual expressions like striptease acts were becoming mainstream, in Yugoslavia as well as the United States.

Like their counterparts at Braniff, stewardesses at JAT were public personalities in this sexual revolution, as embodiments of physically attractive working women in the era of Jet Age feminism. Turning JAT stewardesses into sexy exemplars of cosmopolitan womanhood depended first on wider social changes, including the maturation of a consumer economy. In fact, Marković asserts a direct link between the transformation of sexual norms and Yugoslavia's economic reforms in the late 1950s, which elevated living standards for many people. Just as new women's magazines like *Praktična žena* led women to become empowered consumers, a younger Yugoslav generation became more sexually open: "a higher living standard leads to greater independence and, thus, to freer behavior."[10]

One of postwar Yugoslav cinema's first blockbusters illustrates how this spirit of greater sexual openness could be coupled with fetishizing aviation and stewardesses in alluring ways. Entitled *Love and Fashion (Ljubav i moda)* and released in 1960, the film broke not only from Yugoslav cinema's heavy dependence on communist-inspired themes, but also from the puritanism critiqued in *Saturday Evening*.[11] As the film critic Dinko Tucaković details, *Love and Fashion* marked a moment when Yugoslav cinema, which previously was "full of Partisan films," produced films that "tried to talk about a brighter side of life, which were made in technicolor, which tried to introduce a bit of glamor, and to replace the ... heroes from the Partisans or the working class."[12] *Love and Fashion* mimicked the highly popular Hollywood musical genre that made megastars of actors like Ginger Rogers and Judy Garland. It played a similar role for seventeen-year-old Beba Lončar, the film's lead actress, who even today remains popular among older generations across ex-Yugoslavia for her numerous films.

Lončar's character, Sonja, was coded as a modern young woman: she was beautiful in a traditionally feminine way, but she also studied architecture and spent her free time learning to be a glider pilot. Consequently, many of the film's scenes followed Sonja to Belgrade's soon-to-be-replaced airport and boasted cameos of JAT's airplanes and crews. Yet, even before this entwinement of femininity and aviation, the film opens by highlighting various tenets of Helen Gurley Brown's Jet Age feminist manifesto, *Sex and the Single Girl*. In the very first scene, Lončar is portrayed as iconically beautiful, impeccably stylish, highly mobile, and focused on finding romance. The film's first sounds are a catchy, jazzy song, "One Young Woman" ("Jedna mala dama"), whose lyrics yearn for love to overcome loneliness: "A young woman always walks alone. Why is this? Why is this? Why ... when she's a beautiful woman?"

Unlike the song's fictional persona, Lončar's character Sonja does not walk, nor is she alone for more than one minute of the film. Instead, with the song playing, Sonja is shown coasting through central Belgrade on a sky-blue Vespa, making her way to the university's architecture faculty. As conspicuous as Lončar's flowing blonde hair and her stylish ride is her brilliant sundress, a red-and-white checkered sleeveless design with a deep neckline and a full skirt that flitters in the breeze. It would have been just as trendy on a young collegiate in New York in 1960. Before making it to the university, Sonja first encounters the male lead by nearly running into him as he carelessly crosses the street against a red light. She curses at him, full of indignation, but also confidence. Then, in the following hour-plus of playful adventure, the two progress from initial distaste for each other through various comedic interludes and impromptu moments of breaking into song, to finally end up in a fully sprouted romance.

Love and Fashion boasted Vespas from Italy, dress styles inspired by Paris, upbeat jazz music popularized by Hollywood, and the youthful Yugoslav woman, who was empowered as a fashion connoisseur, a university student, and a glider pilot. However, the fusion was still a bit fantastical as of 1960, even for the children of relative privilege who came of age in urban Yugoslavia. So fashion-forward were Lončar's dresses that the film's costume designer had to create them herself. As she recalls: "Nowhere [in the country] could you, say, buy a brightly colored V-necked sweater. My mother stitched together many of the dresses, and a good number of them were done by seamstresses from theaters. Maybe it all looked glamorous and very unique at the end, but back then it was really difficult to make these outfits."[13]

The fact that Lončar's clothing was unattainable for most women made JAT's Jet Age stewardess, to be clad just two years later in imported Parisian extravagance, even more privileged and desirable. Even in 1960 they spent every working day in stylish uniforms designed by Yugoslavia's top fashion brands. They also had a salary supplement for cosmetics to allow them to purchase superior imported Western beauty supplies. It is therefore not surprising that JAT and its stewardesses played important cameo roles in *Love and Fashion*. At various points, JAT's most modern airplanes fill the film's backgrounds, with the massive DC-6s that were purchased just before the film's shooting receiving pride of place. Audiences saw the engines igniting, the planes taking off, and pilots and stewardesses bidding farewell to passengers as they deplaned. The allure of air travel was a key part of the fantastical romance that Yugoslav audiences were having with this cosmopolitan iteration of Yugoslav womanhood. The author and journalist Sonja Ćirić summarized the film's impact on teenagers in this way:

> For just a few months, from Triglav [on the borders with Austria and Italy] to Đevđelija [on the border with Greece], there wasn't a living thing uninfected by the film: young women thought that if they wore a dress in [the same] design, they would be beautiful like Beba Lončar; young men thought they would meet her if they rode around the city on a Vespa; undiscovered singing talents were convinced they would become famous if they learned the songs

from the film . . . ; and those a bit older of both genders indulged in the sweet images on the screen that they didn't actually possess in real life.[14]

Importantly, *Love and Fashion* also marked the debut of JAT's stewardesses in film, albeit in a minor role. Unlike with Lončar's character, the focus was exclusively on beauty, rather than on technological prowess. The scene is set at the airport's outdoor restaurant, where crew and passengers were assembled awaiting their flights. It opens by following characters already introduced, the all-male managerial team of a Belgrade fashion company called Yugochic (Jugošik), who await their colleague's arrival from Rome. At another table, an unnamed JAT stewardess and pilot dine together as they await the return flight to Rome.

The scene stresses the glamor of flying. It begins with gratuitous coverage of a JAT DC-6, before cutting to the well-dressed crowd of passengers and JAT employees enjoying meals or drinks on the sun-soaked terrace. As though coincidentally, Yugoslavia's most famous singer and actress, Gabi Novak, joins the crowd, playing herself in the film. Everyone turns to catch a glimpse of the star. As appropriate for a member of Yugoslavia's small but growing jet set, Novak announces that she is on JAT's flight to Rome.

In the meantime, the Yugochic team has noticed that the JAT stewardess is now sitting alone. The commercial director, played by the comedian Miodrag Petrović, decides to go over and court the woman. Typical of slapstick comedians, he does so in a way that is overdone, such that his performance would likely elicit both awkward unease and, potentially, laughter from the film's viewers. The basis for such immature behavior is the irresistible beauty of the stewardess, which turns him into a bundle of nerves. Ultimately, the courteous smile wears off the stewardess's face so that she can put an end to the uncomfortable encounter: "Oh! You're so aggressive! I wouldn't allow myself to go on the plane with you." To defuse the tense situation, Petrović's character apologizes and admits defeat in his courtship efforts, just as an announcement comes that the flight to Rome is boarding. The stewardess rises to join the flight crew, but before leaving, both characters grab their glasses of *šljivovica* (plum brandy) and toast each other. While not the sober comportment required of flight attendants, the concluding toast fit with Petrović's comedic role: it signaled to viewers that his awkward advances, which bordered on harassment, were written off and forgiven.

FIGURE 8.2. A JAT stewardess, played by actress and model Ljubica Otašević, is courted by comedian Miodrag Petrović (popularly known as Čkalja), who plays the commercial director of the fictitious fashion firm Jugošik in the 1960 film *Love and Fashion*.
Source: Permission to use this image courtesy of Avala Film Way.

Despite the brevity of JAT stewardesses' film debut, it nonetheless crystallized for audiences the notion that stewardesses were young, beautiful, and sexually available. The only items missing from Mary Wells's Jet Age redesign of Braniff stewardesses were a colorful and high-style uniform and the raunchiness of the "Air Strip." To further accentuate the stewardess's beauty, the filmmakers cast a well-known local heartthrob who returned from Hollywood to play the role. Model and actress Ljubica Otašević came of age playing basketball for the sports club Red Star Belgrade, where she befriended several prominent men, including Yugoslavia's Nobel Prize–winning author Ivo Andrić. In her mid-twenties she was discovered by a Hollywood talent agent and in 1958 she served as the double for Sophia Loren in the romance *The Key*. Casting Otašević further elevated JAT stewardesses as objects of desire for straight men and objects of envy for many women, who yearned to be like either the skilled glider pilot Sonja or the stewardess who enjoyed access to Yugoslavia's jet set via her work and beauty.[15]

A similar pop culture rendering of JAT stewardesses came two years later, in 1962, when singer Đorđe Marjanović released a popular song in the Schlager style of Frank Sinatra. Titled "Stjuardesa" (the stewardess), the song recounts a man's infatuation with a stewardess. It is sung from the viewpoint of a passenger who has not flown before. He approaches a stewardess in the terminal to ask which plane is his; however, before he addresses her, he falls for her: "These eyes more blue than the sky we sail, more brilliant than the sun, eyes full of dreams."[16] Unlike the stewardess portrayal in *Love and Fashion*, Marjanović's song describes an infatuation based on more than looks. This was a woman who, due to her vast experience with flying, was more self-assured than the man. The lyrics continue with the man, now sitting on the plane, worried for his safety and needing the stewardess to calm him: "With her I would never be afraid of anything. All the way I would look into her eyes." The woman's strength sparks this man's desires, which catch fire even though he forgot to ask the stewardess's name. Thereafter he is haunted by her memory: "Everywhere I seek your eyes, every airplane I await."[17]

In the five years between the 1957 film *Saturday Evening* and the 1962 song "Stjuardesa," socialist-era Yugoslavia's popular culture had jettisoned much of its sexual puritanism. While overt sexual scenes or references to them were still absent from both *Love and Fashion* and "Stjuardesa," sexual attraction was now an accepted leitmotif. There may have been a socialist inspiration to this development, at least in this sense: these works portrayed fashionable and infatuation-ripe women as engaged in modern careers like stewardessing or as architects in training. Yet, as more women in North America and Western Europe also entered lifelong careers, the differences between women in socialist and capitalist societies were blurring. Whether in the United States or Yugoslavia, role models like Helen Gurley Brown, Mary Wells, Beba Lončar's Sonja, and Ljubica Otašević's stewardess were promoting a Jet Age feminist vision that coupled style and sexual availability with a commitment to serious work outside the home.

Sexual Infatuations Enfleshed

A JAT stewardess who flew both before and after the release of the song "Stjuardesa" in 1962 found these to be thrilling years. She also believes that this excitement derived from the sources that the song covers: men fell for her not only because of her beauty, but also due to her feminine strength. First and foremost, she claims, many men fell for her attractiveness. As she divulged, "Well, among men we were more popular than even some actresses," before continuing, "To get to the old . . . airport in the morning I had to walk a fair way from the bus stop to the terminal.

There was a student who met me there every morning, who would politely ask, 'May I accompany you to the airport?' It was a total crush!"

In the next breath, she added a second compelling trait that also attracted men: "Well, also bravery. Of course, I was very brave for the time." In her case, this bravery had two aspects, including how she endured the risks of air travel and exuded confidence to less seasoned passengers. However, she also saw herself as brave because she defied her parents' will by entering this career. Knowing her mother's fears of air travel, she kept her work secret for an entire year. "I just told [my parents] that I work at the airport and that this work requires me to be there day and night." This lie accounted for her frequent overnight absences without revealing that she was sometimes staying in cities hundreds of kilometers away. For her, gaining more freedom from familial restraints was one of the main appeals of stewardess work.[18]

This balance of expressing both physical beauty and independence is also found in the memoirs of another JAT stewardess hired at the time, Milica Lukić. According to her book *Recollections of a Stewardess* (*Zapisi stjuardese*), Lukić was already working an office job for an import-export company when she applied at JAT in 1962.[19] While she was confident in professional settings and financially secure, she found that applying for the flight attendant job was unsettling due to JAT's rigorous beauty standards: "I know I tried in those days to look beautiful. Simple, but beautiful," but she was not sure that would suffice. Yet, as she entered JAT's headquarters for her interview, she had a bit of good luck, "As I waited for the elevator, in the lobby I heard a few people saying: 'She's surely a stewardess!'" Overhearing these compliments "emboldened me," Lukić added, "and I think because of this I was able to present myself a bit more confidently before the [hiring] commission."[20] The fact that this young career woman was anxious about her appearance demonstrates how JAT's focus on beauty grew more intense as *Love and Fashion* tied stewardesses to Hollywood-caliber beauty and songs like "Stjuardesa" made them objects of infatuation.

JAT's marketing initiatives starting with the dawn of the Jet Age in 1963 also cast stewardesses in more sexually alluring ways, though in ways that again fell short of Mary Wells's "Air Strip." Figures 8.3. 8.4, and 8.5 illustrate different renditions from the mid-1960s and early 1970s in which women were centered. Even while employing a tamer strategy, they still establish a feminine mystique, if you will, tied to jet travel. The first two images employ a sort of victimless objectification: they use animation rather than photography to elicit desire for stewardesses.

178   CHAPTER 8

FIGURE 8.3. This stylized promotional material features a combination of images: a smiling stewardess, a silhouette of a jet plane, the abstracted shape of a plane window, and a JAT logo. Created in 1963, this image subtly pays tribute to JAT's acquisition of Caravelle jet planes that year, even as the stewardess remains the central focus.
Source: This image is part of the online collection of JAT promotional materials curated by the Ex-YU Aviation News website. https://www.exyuaviation.com/p/ex-yu-vintage-photos.html. Permission to use this image courtesy of Air Serbia.

The first image from 1963 shows a woman animated from the neck up, while nonetheless highlighting her perfect hair, eyes, and lips.

The woman's face on a poster that otherwise brags of JAT's first jets is still jarring: why promote the airline's technological advancement via stewardesses? A closer look reveals that there are actually two competing circular orbits that vie for the viewer's attention. The less prominent of these is a perfect circle, colored in red, that the airline's new Caravelle jet is intersecting—perhaps an homage to jet technology's ties to space exploration. Yet, a competing orbit, oblong and perpendicular to the red circle and traced in black ink, frames the stewardess's face. This second orbit is also part of Yugoslavia's ascent into the Jet Age; in fact, the pull of this feminine orbit is just as intense as the jet

LOVE, FASHION, AND THE *STJUARDESA* 179

FIGURE 8.4. Like figure 8.3, this promotional poster originates from JAT's first decade after entering the Jet Age, though it is undated. Updates from its predecessor (figure 8.3) include a full-body image of a stewardess sporting a much higher hemline for her skirt. That the stewardess sits atop a globe hearkens to the reality that JAT's route network expanded substantially in the decade following 1963, including more extensive routes to the Middle East, socialist Eastern Europe, and Western Europe. The airline also began charter service to North America, Asia, and Australia in this decade.
Source: This image is part of the online collection curated by the Ex-YU Aviation News website, https://www.exyuaviation.com/p/ex-yu-vintage-photos.html. Permission to use this image courtesy of Air Serbia.

plane's—maybe more so, given that the woman's face and her oblong orbit is more prominent. That these two orbits commingle suggests that two tracks of male desire converged with JAT's ascent into the Jet Age. The moment marked the fruition of technological mastery (the success of man's exploratory drive) and of sexual desire (with its link to man's drive for sex).

The next two images date from the years 1968 to 1973, at least a half-decade later than the first. The focus here is on JAT's above-the-knee

180 CHAPTER 8

FIGURE 8.5. Ksenija Pavlović, a stewardess from JAT's flight attendant class of 1969, anchors this undated image from JAT's promotional materials. While she still sports JAT's pre-1975 uniform, Pavlović is positioned so that her bare legs serve as the visual anchor for the city of Belgrade's most iconic landmark, the statue of the *Victor* (*Pobednik*) perched above the city's rivers at the city's historic fort, Kalemegdan.
Source: This image is part of the online collection curated by the Ex-YU Aviation News website, https://www.exyuaviation.com/p/ex-yu-vintage-photos.html. Permission to use this image courtesy of Air Serbia.

uniforms, which debuted in the latter part of the 1960s, after Emilio Pucci's Braniff designs had been introduced. One image retains certain elements of the first: the use of animation, the same depiction of the Caravelle jet, the same fonts. But here, the notion of "cosmic" is attained not by orbital lines, but rather by a depiction of a globe, drawn from the perspective of space. The woman, seated upon it, is now a full-bodied temptress, akin to Marguerite LeWars Kirkpatrick's role in *Dr. No*: her hand accentuates her exposed knee, and her straight hair is complemented by a straight face (no smile) and a direct stare. The result is a seductive invitation from the stewardess to explore her, in the spirit of jet pilots or astronauts. At the same time, the warm colors most prominent in the image emanate from her skin, especially from her legs, which are now exposed above the knee for the first time in the airline's history. For all the movement and progress of the Jet Age, this image suggests that the movement of stewardesses' hemlines, ever upward, is a parallel achievement.

The third image fleshes out a similar narrative, though this time using an actual photo. This poster from the early 1970s emphasizes the exposed legs of stewardess Ksenija Pavlović, which blend visually into the column supporting the city of Belgrade's most famous monument: the *Victor* (*Pobednik*), forged by the modernist Croatian sculptor Ivan Mestrović after World War I.[21] Audiences in Yugoslavia would have immediately recognized this streamlined statue, which soars over the city, arising out of the ancient foundations of the city's fortress and projecting itself far above the streets of Tito's modernist New Belgrade (Novi Beograd), which lay across the Sava River. Images of jets are absent in this photo—what remains is a focus on the beautiful stewardess, especially her legs, which are craftily synced with the iconic *Victor*.

In the early 1970s JAT was engaged in yet another expansion that marked the next phase of its immersion into the Jet Age. Since 1963, the company had operated Caravelle jets, whose range maxed out with the distances between Belgrade and London in the West and with its trans-Mediterranean destinations of Cairo and Beirut. By the 1970s, however, the airline was eager to follow the country's growing economic ties and its sizable emigration flows even further afield, to New York, the airline's first destination in North America, and via a variety of Middle Eastern and Asian stopovers all the way to Sydney. It would not be until 1975 that the airline found enough demand on these transoceanic routes for scheduled service. However, as early as 1970, thanks to the purchase of used Boeing 707 jetliners, JAT was able to begin charter service to the United States and Australia. By 1975, JAT also had added a fleet of three new Boeing 727s, which were equally capable of traversing the Atlantic and the Pacific.

In 1973 the Belgrade-based illustrated news magazine *Ilustrovana politika*, with one of the country's largest readerships, profiled a pleasant side effect of this expansion: JAT's largest class of flight attendants to date—sixty women and men, though heavily dominated by women—reported to JAT's pilot training facility. The article opened by remarking on a profound change when this group arrived: "Instead of handsome, brave young men impatiently awaiting to twist up into the sky by airplane . . . we met a bouquet of young women. One was more beautiful than the other, and all of them were gorgeous, as though a selection show for Miss World was soon to take place here." Reinforcing this emphasis on physical beauty, the article and its accompanying photos ran under the headline, "The Sky's Most Beautiful Crew."[22] In imitation of a haute couture fashion shoot, the magazine's photographer set the recruits in a misty forest among the leafless trees of winter, creating an edgy effect accentuating their physical forms.

As the reference to the Miss World pageant indicates, the association of stewardesses with beauty reflected more than just Yugoslav norms. After all, Jamaica too, through the likes of Carol Joan Crawford and Marguerite LeWars Kirkpatrick, aspired to the Western-dominated ranks of feminine beauty through such pageants. While the nationwide Miss Yugoslavia beauty contest dated back to 1927, the communists disallowed its return for two decades after World War II. Only in 1966, in the years of sexual liberalization, did the pageant return, with the winner joining the Miss World competition. This return marked a key moment when the Western-influenced objectification of women entrenched itself more deeply in the socialist state, especially when the first postwar Miss Yugoslavia, Dubrovnik's Nikica Marinović, became not only the first candidate from a communist country to compete in Miss World, but was also crowned runner-up. Marinović immediately became a celebrity in Yugoslavia. Though she turned down movie roles, she married the well-known Belgrade film director Vuk Vučo and remained a prominent fixture of Belgrade's jet set for the next decade.[23]

Readers of Yugoslav fashion magazines also knew that Western stewardesses were increasingly engaged with pageant-style beauty norms and the free-wheeling sexual libertinism glamorized in Hollywood in the 1960s. While the 1967 best-selling book *Coffee, Tea or Me?* was not translated into Serbian or other Yugoslav languages, readers of the Belgrade fashion magazine *Bazar*—the same publication that managed the Miss Yugoslavia contest every year—were introduced to its contents.[24] The American book offered a mildly salacious account of stewardesses' carefree sex lives, as embellished by flight attendants Trudy Baker and Rachel Jones, the alleged authors who, it later was revealed, covered for the male public relations specialist who actually wrote the book. In August 1969, *Bazar* ran an extensive interview with Baker under the provocative headline: "Stewardesses on Passengers: Italian Men Undress You with Their Eyes," detailing the book's premise and some of the stewardesses' exploits.[25]

All the same, the *Ilustrovana politika* profile of JAT stewardesses still took pains to distance Yugoslavia's stewardesses from the worst sexist excesses faced by their Western peers. While the article did proudly point out that part of their training involved lessons on "aesthetics and cosmetics, which are taught by experts from *Dior* who arrive directly from Paris," it also complicated this focus on beauty with a quote from stewardess candidate Slavica Radulović, who asserted, "We're not all failed film divas, like many think of us." The journalist proceeded to note that Radulović, like many of her fellow trainees, was a university student. In her case, it was her love of world literature that led her to apply for the job: "I love reading most of all, so I want to head to Paris, London, and Moscow to find books that interest me . . . I'll be registered at all the world's libraries, and who can do that any better than a stewardess," she added.

Another trainee, Ružica Milosavljević, followed the examples of her uncle, a JAT pilot, and her aunt, who flew agricultural planes, by receiving a sporting pilot's license before starting her stewardess training. She even confessed to being unsure whether she preferred piloting over stewardessing. The uncertainty was something she felt deeply: "I'm not even sure myself if I'd like to become the first female pilot for our passenger aviation, [as] there's also something holding me back." When elaborating on this uncertainty, she added, "I'm so calm when I'm piloting, I'm collected and happy as if I were reading a beautiful book at home. But is this really something for a woman or not?"[26]

Note that the article's author artfully placed this uncertainty in the thoughts of the woman herself, as though it was a strictly personal decision to exclude herself from the pilot corps. In reality, of course, there was an interwoven set of factors in Yugoslavia that prevented women from becoming pilots—a web so strong that no woman was ever hired in JAT's entire history. Of course this exclusion violated the article from the 1946 constitution that legislated women's full equality in workplaces. Thus, crediting the woman's choice of stewardessing over piloting as her own personal decision was the only way to hold the socialist state blameless for this failure.

Instead of critiquing the state, the article instead differentiated JAT's stewardesses from their Western peers in a way that suggested important benefits for women under socialism. Thus, on the one hand, the journalist objectified these women as the "most beautiful crew in the sky"—supposedly outdueling the West's women on this metric. Yet, on the other hand, he also emphasized JAT applicants' backgrounds as university students, certified pilots, or already successful career women. He also stressed their better treatment at JAT: "In our society, there is no set maximum working age for stewardesses. Additionally [the veteran stewardesses who were training the newcomers] are both married and they have children. Neither of these things in our society is considered a hindrance to being a good stewardess."[27]

If the author had opted to, he could have also mentioned that these restrictions on Western women were now more contested than ever. At the time he was writing, the European Court of Justice (ECJ) was hearing a case from Belgian stewardess Gabrielle Defrenne, who sued her employer, Sabena, when they fired her for turning forty.[28] It would take the ECJ another few years, until 1976, to finally side with Defrenne and eliminate forms of "indirect discrimination" like marriage and pregnancy bans as well as early retirement rules that were policies "hiding the danger that primarily members of only one gender were disadvantaged."[29] Only after this were airlines in Western Europe's European Economic Community (the future European Union) required to match Yugoslavia's workplace policies for flight attendants on age, marriage, and pregnancy.

Even in other areas pertaining to a stewardess's physical appearance beyond the scope of the *Ilustrovana politika* article, JAT's treatment was indeed less draconian in 1973 than in Western Europe and North America. Interviews with JAT stewardesses who flew at the time added details on JAT's weight policy, which was a panic-inducing reality further west. Whereas supervisors at airlines like Braniff, Pan Am, BOAC, and Air France had the right to weigh stewardesses at will and frequently did so, JAT's stewardesses were weighed once per year in their annual medical exam. New applicants who were over the airline's rigorous weight targets were screened out during the interview process, but active stewardesses risked only probation, most often with the right to continue working, if they failed their annual check. Thus, whereas weight violations were common grounds for dismissal at North Atlantic carriers, interviewees recalled no one at JAT losing their job for such transgressions. They were even unsure if termination had been an option for the airline.

Overall, then, like the somewhat clumsy and contradictory *Ilustrovana politika* article, JAT adhered to an inherently awkward formula when overseeing its stewardesses in the era of Jet Age feminism. It imposed demeaning and objectifying standards on these women, while nonetheless falling short of Western airlines' rigorous enforcement of them. Thus, even as the article's author boasted of JAT's more enlightened legal policies on marriage and age, he still expected stewardesses to make the more enlightened choice to quit on their own: "These young women know that the job of a stewardess, like that of a ballerina, can't be done for the entirety of one's working years." He simultaneously praised and devalued one of the most progressive features of JAT's stewardess corps: like the first JAT stewardess, Dragica Pavlović, stewardesses in the 1970s could still potentially work a full-length career.[30] Yet, in this era of Jet Age feminism, the greater priority seemed to be for women to represent Yugoslavia well at pageants like Miss World and for JAT stewardesses to be "the sky's most beautiful crew."

Yugoslavia's Pucci

Fashion is one area in which this chapter's original dual foci—politics and economics, plus gender—reconverge. After all, fashion was, first and foremost, an economic enterprise targeted by Yugoslavia's central planners as a major focus of industrialization and, in time, a designated export field. At the same time, fashion's role as a consumer product and a locus of aesthetic choices allows an examination of how Yugoslav women meshed with cosmopolitan trends during the Jet Age. Thus, when JAT seized on its 1975 launch of scheduled routes to Australia and the United States to overhaul its stewardess uniforms, the moment underscored the gender-based consequences of Yugoslavia's rise as a small, but disproportionately influential global power. The resulting uniforms resisted simple conformity to the West, including Pucci's work for Braniff. Instead, JAT's uniforms strove for what we might consider a nonaligned iteration of fashion, with inspiration from each node of the Cold War cosmos: East, West, and Global South.

The key actor in the 1975 redesign was one of the country's major fashion designers, Aleksandar Joksimović. His career began in the 1950s and tracked the maturation of Yugoslavia's fashion industry from its original focus on low- to medium-quality everyday workwear to higher-end, export-oriented ensembles. Joksimović's first work was to design simple patterns for ready-to-wear women's professional dresses and suits. At the time Yugoslavia utilized its access to Egyptian cotton to open textile mills focused on staple fashions for the domestic market. These mills served not only to clothe its urbanizing citizenry but also to open more factory jobs for lower-skilled women workers.[31]

By the mid-1960s, Joksimović's work had matured alongside the country's textile companies, which were now aspiring to capitalize on the country's low-wage structure to export higher-end products to the

West and Global South. Joksimović, who apprenticed under Christian Dior in Paris, was now creating clothing for women's professional and leisure needs, and he eventually headed the design team at one of Yugoslavia's major export-based fashion houses, Centrotekstil. His employer in turn sent his designs to target markets like Paris, where, in the words of the magazine *Praktična žena* in 1965, "*Paris-Jour* and *Elle* are rushing to ensure that their pages are devoted to the models of Aleksandar Joksimović," since his designs have "quickly ... conquered the world metropole."[32]

Undoubtedly, part of Joksimović's appeal both to consumers in Yugoslavia and abroad was his loyalty to trends that designers like Emilio Pucci and Christian Dior had already been offering women in the West. As though echoing their work, Joksimović affirmed in a 1965 interview that "the fundamental mistake of our women is that they think that quantity [of fabric in an outfit] renders elegance. This leads to imbalance and tackiness in clothing." Joksimović pressed Yugoslav women to embrace a greater simplicity in cut: "I personally ... love a simple uncut dress, as it alone enables clean lines to stand out. And when clean lines are revealed, you have an elegant style even without any sort of jewelry."[33] The sketches Joksimović included in *Praktična žena* with his comments portrayed the sort of formfitting, streamlined look best suited for the "women in motion" that Pucci designed for.

The key difference between Joksimović and Pucci involved color. Whereas Pucci's jet-set creations employed color for its boldness and exoticism, Joksimović instead cautioned that "the question of color is a very delicate one" and that "an affinity for playing with color requires a truly refined taste." If she lacked this sort of mastery, then "a woman needs to favor classic and dark tones. These assure simplicity." After all, concludes Joksimović, returning to echo Pucci after defying him on color, "it is simple lines and details that are magically transformative—this is the truth that every woman needs to acknowledge."[34]

Joksimović spoke of fashion in a distinctly Western, capitalist way, stressing a woman's transformation and emancipation through clothing and even naming dressing up as a process that is "magically transformative." This sort of vocabulary mimicked—though with the opposite intent—the way Karl Marx had critiqued the industrialized world's "commodity fetishism" a century earlier.[35] At the same time, however, Joksimović was aware that Yugoslav women, as well as their middle-class and working-class counterparts in the West, were different consumers than the jet-set elites who bought Pucci dresses in high-end boutiques. His emphasis on simplicity was based on the reality that one dress needed to satisfy multiple needs for his customers. He knew that "every woman has to have one dress that can be worn in any situation. This has to be a simple dress of good material . . . which will stay in style through the whole year and for any celebratory occasion: for a concert, for a visit to the theater, and for any sort of evening party."[36] This imperative to design such "magical" clothing for women living in relative austerity was a skill that Joksimović learned not in Dior's Paris workshop, but rather in the design studio of a socialist, state-owned enterprise in Europe's East.

By the time the Jet Age had taken hold in Yugoslavia, the country's textile industry had matured even further, to the point that state planners saw opportunities to enter Western markets with haute couture ensembles. In the late 1960s youth-inspired fashion movements were taking over traditional centers like London's Carnaby Street with not only bolder colors, but also bolder fabric choices.[37] Yugoslavia's well-developed fur and leather fashion sectors saw a boom in these years and began attracting high prices in the West for more eccentric, well-designed, and expertly manufactured goods. Thus, Joksimović again joined a cadre of fashion pioneers in Yugoslavia, as he was commissioned by Centrotekstil to design one of the country's first high-end collections for the export market.

It was in these projects starting in 1967 that Joksimović, while now designing for a similar clientele as Pucci, looked beyond both capitalism and state socialism for inspiration. Analogous to Pucci's borrowings from the color patterns of Latin America and Southeast Asia in his high-end designs, Joksimović also developed a style that the fashion historian Danijela Velimirović aptly calls "grandiose exoticism." As she notes, this choice was more typical of fashion arising from the Global South, where designers resurrected pre-European motifs (saris, kente cloth) and infused into their designs a mix of the archaic and modern.[38]

Unlike Pucci's appropriation of aesthetics that he collected as a tourist in the Global South, Joksimović sought "grandiose exotic" roots within the Western Balkans' own folk legacies. His debut haute couture line "Simonida" was a modern rendition of the monastic-like costumes worn by Serbian medieval royalty, while one of his 1968 collections, "Vitraž," derived inspiration from the stained-glass windows of the region's Catholic and Orthodox churches. In all these works, Joksimović fused medieval inspirations with modern fashion elements that meshed well with the innovations arising in the West's trendiest fashion centers. His works from the late 1960s and early 1970s were disorienting in their combination of retro and hip, but there was also something primordially local and pre-bourgeois in their folkloric inspirations. As Velimirović points out, this style was well-suited for Tito's engagement with the Global South: "Given that this international movement [nonalignment] was composed primarily of postcolonial nations whose politics of fashion included forms of exoticism, including wearing traditional dress or an adaptation of it combined with elements adopted from Western fashion systems, fashion in the 'national style' was the perfect equivalent to the clothing of the nonaligned countries."[39] The otherwise white, European Yugoslavia could thereby express its own form of "grandiose exoticism" alongside its allies in the Global South.

When Joksimović agreed in 1974 to produce new uniforms for JAT, the airline was hoping for a similar balance between retro and hip, but it also desired a homegrown way of matching Pucci's appeal at Braniff. By that time accustomed to working almost exclusively on haute couture fashion, Joksimović found the task of designing stewardess uniforms a challenging return to his past pursuits of eveningwear outfits and workers' clothing. As he admitted, "Work uniforms, which stewardess outfits truly are, are not an unfamiliar theme, since I started my career creating work clothes. However, this task was more delicate than I imagined."[40] Stewardesses used their uniforms more frequently and in far more trying settings than the wealthy clients who purchased his typical runway items. "The fabrics have to be durable," Joksimović asserted, "they can't ball up, they can't be too hot for the temperature on the plane or for the differences in climate. The uniforms have to be both beautiful and comfortable." He then added a comment that strongly differentiated his work from Braniff's, noting that the uniforms "also can't be too flirtatious because they're actually uniforms."[41]

As his last line suggests, JAT's socialist work norms made Joksimović's task more challenging than what Pucci had faced at Braniff a decade earlier. Pucci was not required to respond to stewardesses' input, and the company's marketing team actually reveled in having a flirtatious quality to their outfits. At JAT, however, the stewardesses themselves—working through the auspices of the company's Workers' Council—would have the final say on which uniforms to adopt. As one journalist noted, these stewardesses would "understandably also have the desire that their appearance be beautiful and elegant—like a model." At the same time, though, the practical concerns Joksimović cited would be equally compelling: "They themselves would know best which uniforms are most suitable for their work."⁴² Thus, Joksimović had to respect these socialist exigencies, even as he developed an aesthetic for JAT's new flights to New York and Sydney that reflected the high-style glamor of the Jet Age West and also embodied the "grandiose exoticism" that bespoke the country's alignment with the Global South.

Ultimately concluding that such a balance was unattainable, Joksimović and his promotions team at Centrotekstil opted instead to

FIGURE 8.6. Aleksandar Joksimović created a wide range of prototypes for JAT stewardess uniforms, which he then showcased in winter 1975 at the Belgrade Fashion Fair. In many ways the prototypes shown here, designed as a unified ensemble that a team of stewardesses would wear on the same flight, are the most staid. The other prototypes included medieval-like flowing robes and headpieces and scarves worn in ways reminiscent of a medieval Serbian princess or an Orthodox nun. While one of the pictured models does sport such a scarf, the uniform submissions here limit the amount of fabric and rely on just the three colors of the Yugoslav flag.

Ultimately, even these designs were not selected by the stewardess committee overseeing JAT's choice. The uniform features were still too ornate for stewardesses' work in tight aisleways, and the colors—especially the ample use of white—would have made them too difficult to keep clean. The winning design was far simpler, while also retaining some of the "grandiose exotic" and folkloric flair that Joksimović included in his various prototypes.

Source: Permission to use this image courtesy of the Museum of Applied Art, Belgrade, Serbia.

craft what were in effect two collections of JAT uniforms. The first such collection, which included the samples shown above, were boldly colorful and ornate. Joksimović anchored each of these uniforms in JAT's traditional navy blue, but he also added striking accents of red and white, the other colors of the Yugoslav flag. In some mockups, the fabrics also flowed generously, mimicking (with flowing capes and coats) styles typical of medieval Serbian royalty, or (in terms of headscarves) peasant women across Yugoslavia.

Yet, any touch that was too "grandiose" (bold colors, flowing coats) made these designs too impractical for stewardesses. Upon seeing these images, no stewardess I interviewed who worked in 1975 recognized them, but they also had immediate thoughts on why: uniforms with too much white or red fabric would be impossible to keep clean, while flowing fabrics would catch in the aisleways and be too difficult to store in cramped storage bins. Any element that was too "exotic" also detracted from these stewardesses' need to have uniforms that were easily washable and wearable. That said, Joksimović and Centrotekstil still employed these impractical, but stunning uniforms for public relations purposes. During Belgrade's Fashion Fair in 1975, the designs attracted significant attention, allowing Joksimović to employ them to elicit both media attention and plentiful feedback from audiences comprised of the general public, fashion wholesalers, journalists, and specially invited JAT stewardesses and officials.[43]

Within a few weeks, however, Joksimović had readied a final version of uniforms that were much simpler than those from the Belgrade Fair. Responsive to stewardesses' needs for a color scheme easier to keep clean, Joksimović jettisoned the ample use of white and red, instead coupling an almost black navy-blue skirt with a stewardess's choice of blouses: one in the same dark navy color and another composed of a slightly lighter shade of blue that also boasted a white collar with red and navy touches. A red, white, and blue scarf was available for those wishing to complement the monochrome skirt-blouse combination. In the end, Joksimović professed himself satisfied with the color palette: "The color of the outfit is of foremost importance . . . I embedded a discreet Yugoslav tricolor, while the dark blue agrees with any color of skin and hair."[44] Of course, his use of the term "discreet"—a significant contrast from the "grandiose" nature of so many of his creations—marked for Joksimović a significant concession to stewardesses' demands for practicality.

FIGURES 8.7 AND 8.8. The final version of Joksimović's stewardess uniforms, which debuted on JAT's first scheduled transoceanic route to Sydney in late March 1975. Note that these uniforms still had minor touches of "grandiose exotic" flair: the flowing skirts and the tricolor collar and optional scarf. Nonetheless, in adherence to stewardesses' feedback, the colors were now more muted and thereby easier to keep clean when working.

Source: These images appear in "Novo ruho stjuardesa," *JAT Revija*, Summer 1975. Permission to use these images courtesy of Air Serbia.

Also jettisoned in the final JAT uniforms were the "exotic" elements that predominated elsewhere in Joksimović's work. In particular, scarves were now worn around the neck, not atop the head, while blouses were quite modern in that they were tapered to fit tightly. A slight move away from Pucci's embrace of formfitting, mobility-enhancing styles was found in Joksimović's choice of skirts, as he jettisoned Pucci's preferred above-the-knee versions in favor of a longer and more freely flowing design that was at least reminiscent of traditional peasant styles. This cautious retro-extravagance then returned at the neck, either with the oversized blue, white, and red collar or the similarly colored scarf.

Thus, even as the uniform's overall effect was more modest than "grandiose" and more contemporary than "exotic," there was still a subtle contrast between elements of the traditional and the modern that attested to JAT's and Yugoslavia's unique efforts to forge a Jet Age fashion ensemble that was at once born in the East, appropriately glamorous for the West, and tradition-inspired and exotic enough to be allied with the Global South. Joksimović's own analysis of the uniform stresses these contrasts, suggesting that Yugoslavia's national ethos (to the extent such a thing existed) resided therein: "The uniform of a stewardess symbolizes in a way the country, the climate of the company, the nation, the race. It must attain a synchronicity of aesthetics and the demands of work. The uniform is both practical and elegant."[45]

The stewardesses interviewed for this chapter were unanimous in praising Joksimović's 1975 creations. Many cited their practicality. Like with Pucci's creations for Braniff, they could be washed easily in a hotel sink on an overnight layover, while the separate skirt and blouse made them easy to pack in a carry-on. There was even room to pack extras of both for longer journeys. The mix-and-match components were also quite popular, as stewardesses had a degree of autonomy to compose a wardrobe slightly different from their peers or from what they had worn the day before. In addition, many of the women appreciated the unique style that the uniforms gave them in contrast to other airlines: they were one of a kind, designed and produced in the home country, and they embodied both simplicity and elegance. One stewardess stressed that she had enjoyed almost all her JAT uniforms through the years, as they always made her feel "feminine and distinguished . . . [and very] stylish." But Joksimović's creation was her favorite, as it was all these things plus "comfortable and modern" and, quite practically, "it was easier to clean" than the uniforms both before and after.[46]

More than one stewardess confessed pride in their work and in the way that JAT competed with other world airlines, even as they knew their work lives were both "different and similar" to stewardesses at the West's more storied airlines. While the work itself was "very very similar" around the world and the women in these positions "shared the same problems," according to one stewardess, it was Yugoslavia's socialism that was so different. At one stewardess conference she attended in London, "there were two of us [from JAT], and we were the only participants from a socialist country." When recognizing this fact, she noted, "In a way, I was proud, very proud. Because many things were ok in this socialist system," and she was therefore pleased to be part of a socialist enterprise that allowed her to stand as an equal on the global stage. She proceeded to acknowledge plenty of problems in this system, but added a benefit that, in her view, outweighed these negatives: the "absence of nationalism" was, for her, "one of the great things about socialism, real socialism."[47] Thus, being at the conference as a product of both socialism and the multinational Yugoslav experiment was an honor for her, at least in these peak years at JAT.

Yugoslavia's Jet Age officially commenced in 1962 with the opening of the new jet-ready Belgrade Airport. Within days, the first foreign-operated jets landed in Belgrade, while just a few months later, JAT put its own jets into service. At the ribbon-cutting ceremony, the JAT stewardess accompanying Premier Tito modeled a new uniform, one mimicking Christian Dior's designs for Air France stewardesses. She thereby exuded a cosmopolitan, Parisian sophistication that reinforced the country's ascent into the world's elite echelon of Jet Age states. Just a few years later, however, both the airline based in the West's fashion capital of Paris and its smaller Eastern nearby neighbor based in Belgrade—indeed, all airlines in the world—struggled to catch up stylistically to Emilio Pucci's creations for Braniff. By the late 1960s, nobody wanted to be flying on a "plain plane" and served by a stewardess that, in Pucci's words, looked like they were "traveling by bus in the year 1925."[48]

Airlines with primarily domestic routes in the United States or leisure-based international routes—think carriers like American Airlines or Southwest Airlines or, indeed, the heavily leisure-focused Air Jamaica—followed a fairly consistent strategy in the resulting fashion competition: they kept Pucci's emphasis on color, while raising stewardesses' hemlines further up and lowering the necklines further down.

Thus, by 1970, leisure travelers found an orgiastic explosion of female allure on display while on their vacation getaways. This was all much to the delight of certain straight businessmen, the world's most frequent fliers and most lucrative customers, who now had intimate access to skimpily clad stewardesses.

However, international flag carriers that were not heavily leisure-oriented had a more sophisticated and cosmopolitan reputation to uphold. The Pan Ams, BOACs, and Air Frances of the world had no desire to mimic Mary Wells's "Air Strip" raunchiness, as it was deemed to be too pedestrian for their more culturally conservative clientele. The fact that some of the world's great national flag carriers were state-owned (Pan Am was an exception here) mattered as well, since state institutions generally had less latitude to engage in marketing that so overtly exploited women. Instead, these more elite international airlines strove to embrace aspects of the Braniff revolution without the same crassness as domestic competitors or international leisure carriers. For the world's leading non-Western carriers, one option was to adopt the "grandiose exoticism" of national dress: Japan Air Lines adorned stewardesses in kimonos for part of their flights, while Air India dressed their stewardesses in saris—and, in a nod to "Air Strip"-style playfulness, even briefly clad them in paper saris, which passengers could also buy and take home.[49]

Legacy carriers in the West, however, more typically adhered to aspects of the Braniff formula that did not include overt sexualization. These airlines in the late 1960s or early 1970s hired top-name fashion designers to rival Pucci (Evan-Picone for Pan Am, Clive Evans for BOAC, and Carlos Balenciaga for Air France) and then encouraged them to creatively play with color and cut. The results fell short of Pucci's work in terms of palette—most kept to shades of blue or tan—but none of them crafted outfits that would be confused with 1925 bus attendants. Instead, the designers combined chicness, a tighter fit, and a fresher color palette while remaining within the cosmopolitan confines of traditional sophistication.

Not surprisingly, just as JAT imitated Air France at the dawn of the Jet Age, so too did it at the peak of its Jet Age in 1975, when it initiated flights to North America and Australia. Like Balenciaga at Air France, JAT's chosen designer Aleksandar Joksimović never aspired to the same color explosion and suggestive layering (and disrobing) that Pucci and Mary Wells created for Braniff. Instead, he went a different direction. While still embracing the Pucci model of styling outfits for a "woman in motion," the final product for JAT—revised with input from stewardesses on the company's Workers' Council—aspired to a very different cosmopolitanism, one not so captive to the oversexualized male gaze of the 1960s. Indeed, and here his work contrasted even with Balenciaga's at Air France, Joksimović worked at the intersection of Yugoslavia's commitments to West, East, and South. He thereby expressed a cosmopolitanism that was more universal in inspiration than Pucci's and Braniff's, or even Air France's.

JAT's stewardesses ended up clad in outfits that were well-suited for the hyper-mobile lifestyle of Jet Age feminism: they were now career women with unprecedented access to mobility, to greater sexual autonomy, and to amassing modest wealth for themselves, even as they embraced the long-standing expectation of cultivating their own feminine beauty. All the while, however, Joksimović subordinated choices like color and skirt length—at the knee, not above—to workers' dignity, as one would expect of socialist-inspired design. In contrast, Balenciaga's palette at Air France included uniforms in light blue and white that were difficult to keep clean and launder in a hotel sink. Moreover, to the modest extent that Joksimović's touches of "grandiose exoticism" remained in the final product, the uniforms established an affinity with fashion from the Global South. In these ways, the JAT uniforms from 1975 were more than visual counterparts of Air France's. In fact, Yugoslavia's and Joksimović's ideological investments were more global than those that influenced Balenciaga, Pucci, and the West's other designers of Jet Age stewardess outfits.

That said, even this softer adoption of the West's Jet Age feminism left Yugoslavia with a growing problem that was becoming increasingly global in scope: women were becoming more objectified as the 1960s progressed, more entrapped in what American Second Wave feminist Betty Friedan called the feminine mystique of being valued mainly for their beauty. Furthermore, women in Yugoslavia were increasingly frustrated with failures impacting their lack of equality that arose from within the socialist state itself: maternal leave plans, kindergartens, and day care centers all remained underfunded, while the state also failed to integrate women into some of the country's highest-paying and most technically skilled professions, including piloting. These shortcomings made a mockery of the 1946 constitution and the socialist state's supposedly all-out commitment to equality for women workers. Yugoslavia's women were left underpaid, with few career options, and saddled with the unrealistic double burden of a full-time job and full-time family commitments. With the state's embrace of Western-style sexual objectification in the 1960s, the list of women's grievances grew, which in turn begot a new and more vocal wave of Yugoslav feminists. As in the West, Yugoslavia's feminists found even greater urgency in the Jet Age to intervene against the worst outcomes of men's sexual aggression: domestic abuse, rape, sexual harassment, and unwanted pregnancy.[50]

As with stewardesses in the United States and Western Europe, most JAT stewardesses themselves did not identify with this new wave of more radical feminism that was slowly taking hold. Instead, they were more allied in their hearts with Helen Gurley Brown's "*Cosmo* girls"; they were typically happy with the guidelines set by JAT requiring them to be young and beautiful and commonly aspired in their work to emulate the moxie of Beba Lončar (who played the main character, Sonja) in *Love and Fashion* or even the more passive, more objectified beauty of the JAT stewardess played by Sophia Loren's look-alike, Ljubica Otašević. Nonetheless, many of these women privately chafed against the unrealistic norms of Jet Age feminism and the shortcomings of the socialist state that made their work exceptionally challenging. On the outside, they were model cosmopolitans—Yugoslavia's entrants into the global pageant of Jet Age feminism, if you will—but on the inside, they cleverly developed coping strategies to compensate for their insufficient pay and advancement opportunities, their lack of adequate childcare, and their frequent run-ins with unwelcome sexual advances and sexual abuse.

CHAPTER 9

"Rare Tropical Birds"

Postcolonial and Neo-imperialist Legacies of Jet Age Feminism

With a new Air Jamaica in 1968 feverishly preparing to take off, Marguerite LeWars Kirkpatrick received a major promotion. The former head of the airline's ground hostesses, who had also redesigned the team's uniforms the year before, now became the airline's first-ever head of stewardesses. Air Jamaica, after all, was evolving in 1968 due to the ruling from the United States Civil Aviation Board (CAB) that forced the airline to terminate its joint venture with BOAC and BWIA. Sir G. Arthur Brown incorporated a new company that year, Air Jamaica (1968) Limited, that now included Air Canada as a minority shareholder. Per CAB requirements, this new Air Jamaica had to fly its own jets, hire its own pilots, and train its own flight attendants for the first time. Kirkpatrick had the task of hiring, training, and then introducing the first Air Jamaica stewardesses to the world.

Having never worked aboard aircraft, Kirkpatrick lacked the necessary safety background and catering expertise to train flight attendants. However, the new airline wanted her to imprint on stewardesses something equally valuable, in their estimation: her beauty pageant skill set. While teams of Air Canada stewardesses handled the skills portion of the training, Kirkpatrick taught Air Jamaica's first stewardesses how to dress to code, exhibit good posture, apply makeup elegantly, interact

CHAPTER 9

with customers tactfully, and even model confidently for the airline's new in-flight fashion shows. She was the airline's voice of Jet Age feminism, ensuring that a contemporary sexual appeal would be infused into this workplace, for the delight of customers.

Air Jamaica's management, working in sync with the airline's New York–based marketing team at Ketchum, MacLeod, and Grove (hereafter Ketchum), also finally granted Kirkpatrick the artistic license to design the "too flipped out" flight attendant uniforms of her dreams. Her debut ensemble took both Pucci's bold colors and Mary Wells's "Air Strip" raciness and melded these elements with Caribbean-inspired touches. The result was a color palette befitting a Jamaican sunset: yellows, oranges, and pinks. Her original uniforms also included lime green. Kirkpatrick's extravagance compared to Pucci came in choices to make these tropical colors gleam with a nearly fluorescent sheen, raising the hemline a good fifteen centimeters above the knee, and further tightening the fit through the stewardess's chest, arms, and waist.

Mary Wells's "Air Strip" was modeled on an American striptease bar, while Kirkpatrick's and Ketchum's stewardesses, whom they christened "rare tropical birds," were styled after Jamaican beauty queens—though a far more risqué version than Miss World 1963, Carol Joan Crawford. This creative team then added an in-flight fashion show, a wholly new feature in global stewardessing. The women working each long-haul flight paused their flight attendant duties to don outfits from the various rounds of a beauty pageant, from eveningwear to swimwear, often leaving them bikini-clad while parading down the plane's narrow aisleways. This novelty further established the "rare tropical birds" as descendants of a complex duo: the island's decades-long embrace of beauty pageants, coupled with its continuing role in the West's neo-imperialist imagination as a space of eroticized othering. Jamaican women's long-standing role of sexually titillating North Americans and Europeans was now expressed through a "too flipped out" technicolor ensemble and an irreverent cheekiness.

This neo-imperial outfitting of Jamaican women was hardly consistent with the country's postcolonial aspirations. After all, the "turning of the wheel of history" that Premier Norman Manley predicted back in 1962 for the soon-to-be independent Jamaica was supposed to stimulate greater parity with the privileged nations of the West by fostering greater economic development, enabling more political autonomy, and promoting continuing progress against racism and other imperialist mentalities that disadvantaged Jamaicans socially. Thus, as Air Jamaica executives and their American advertising company pressed forward with exoticizing Air Jamaica stewardesses, their efforts increasingly conflicted with newly emergent and more radical postcolonial strivings in Jamaica.

The year 1968 also saw Jamaica's first racially and economically motivated riots to cross the country's otherwise rigid class boundaries. Many intellectuals and students joined these riots thanks to the Black nationalist and Marxist historian Walter Rodney, a Guyanese citizen teaching at the University of the West Indies, who pressed for profound changes to West Indian societies. Rodney backed up his intellectual critiques of Jamaica's systematic oppression of its poor Black underclass by building alliances with Rastafarians and other residents of West Kingston's shantytowns. Thus, when the government expelled Rodney from the country, both the campus and the shantytowns erupted in violence, worsened by the police's aggressive tactics.[1] For Rodney's followers, these weeks-long riots were a clarion call to force the country's brown elites to address the needs of the country's long-disadvantaged poor Black citizens.

The Rodney riots gave way to a cultural revolution promoted by reggae artists preaching Black nationalism and economic justice in their songs, the most famous of these being Bob Marley. Then, in 1972, motivated in part by the Rodney riots, Jamaicans voted in Michael Manley, who embraced aspects of this postcolonial sea change for Jamaica, as prime minister. Manley ultimately aligned his People's National Party (PNP) with the economic plan of democratic socialism and prioritized efforts to address the plight of Black Jamaicans caught in a cycle of poverty. He even challenged the bedrock foreign policy commitment of unwavering fealty to the United States by expelling Ambassador Vincent de Roulet in 1973, soon after formalizing relations with Castro's Cuba.[2]

Manley's new wife, Beverley Anderson Manley, also assumed a prominent political and social role in these years. The two married in the first months of his prime ministership, a few years after the tragic death of his first wife, Marguerite Kirkpatrick's sister Barbara. Beverley became the country's foremost representative not only of an empowered darker-skinned citizenry but also of a growing number of Jamaican women committed to promoting feminism. Thus, Air Jamaica's neo-imperialist launch of its "rare tropical birds" on April 1, 1969, quickly garnered controversy, as it flew directly into the headwinds of a more progressive postcolonial social and political moment in Jamaica. The airline's imposition of Jet Age feminist axioms was soon challenged, not least by Air Jamaica stewardesses themselves.

Preflight Turbulence for the "Rare Tropical Birds"

The new Air Jamaica was even more attuned to the proclivities of North American customers than its earlier version had been. Minority partner Air Canada brought expertise on penetrating the American and Canadian markets, while earlier media campaigns from the Jamaica Tourist Board (JTB) in these countries offered insights on how to successfully promote the island. In fact, the JTB's experience using beauty queens like Carol Joan Crawford and Marguerite LeWars Kirkpatrick, who was the "face of Jamaica" on posters and billboards for several years, established the precedent for using stewardesses to similar ends. Of course, Braniff's wild success in the United States at the time offered further encouragement for Air Jamaica's team to highlight skin and seduction when promoting their stewardesses.

The first major media event along these lines took place a month before the new Air Jamaica's first flight on April 1, 1969, just as the first fifty-six stewardesses finished their training at Air Canada facilities in Montreal. Ketchum had organized press conferences in both New York and Miami, to which "all the food and fashion [reporters] from America's leading magazines (e.g. Vogue) have been invited." The assembled journalists met with the company's new executives and sampled Jamaican food. But the main attraction involved "Mrs. Kirkpatrick along with three of her stewardesses," who presented, "a fashion show modelling high fashion creations from Jamaica's top couturiers."[3] The former Miss Jamaica and Bond femme fatale herself donned the pajamas she had designed for pursers to wear in flight, explaining that the boldly colored and relaxed stylings "are designed to help bring the sunny, pleasurable atmosphere of our country to travellers the minute they step aboard an Air Jamaica jetliner."[4] Thus, in this seminal moment when the first Air Jamaica stewardesses were introduced to the American public, tropes for the future were already in place: the stewardesses, via Kirkpatrick, were inheriting Jamaica's global beauty pageant fame, and they were also linked to exoticized and eroticized fantasies of "sunny" and "pleasurable" tropical escapes.

Consistent with this embrace of beauty pageant norms, Air Jamaica required its stewardesses to meet rigid physical criteria: they had to be between the ages of nineteen and twenty-five, between five feet two and five feet eight, between 100 and 132 pounds, be unmarried (and, at least at first, had to remain so during their working tenure), and have perfect vision. The airline also shared that the sole criterion for the first cuts would be aesthetic: "At the first interview the girls will be requested to walk around a room in the presence of two members of the Air Jamaica staff, one of whom will be Mrs. Marguerite Kirkpatrick."[5] Only those who passed this beauty test would be welcomed back for a second interview to scrutinize the candidate's personality and aptitude for flight attendant work. Compared to their global peers, these hiring criteria conformed quite closely to Braniff's requirements and were more rigid than JAT's in Yugoslavia.

To keep the stewardess corps young over the long-term, the airline devised an incentive structure to encourage them to leave the job in a timely fashion. According to the company's directors' meeting minutes from November 1968, "as a general rule [stewardesses] would not be employed for longer than five years."[6] When the company articulated this policy to the public, an executive stressed that "world research has revealed that stewardesses rarely want to fly five years." He added that at the time of their termination, "the girls will be given a bonus which the Company feels might come in handy as a nest egg, or perhaps to finance training in some other field."[7] In reality, of course, this policy was designed to retain only the most promising women beyond their early adulthood—women like Marguerite Kirkpatrick, who by 1968 was a full decade into her aviation career, married, and around thirty years of age, yet still modeling and performing at an exceptionally high level.

These criteria also created Air Jamaica's first public relations crisis, due to the divisive ways that racial identity and skin complexion continued to disadvantage dark-skinned women at Miss Jamaica and other beauty pageants. This discrimination persisted even after breakthrough moments for light-skinned Jamaicans such as Carol Joan Crawford's victory at Miss World in 1963 and Marguerite LeWars's role in *Dr. No* and as the "face of Jamaica." When Air Jamaica's first recruiting ad called not only for good posture and good teeth, but also "good complexion . . . [and] attractive hair," many readers saw commonly used euphemisms that excluded darker-skinned candidates.[8] The blowback was swift. A Garveyite-inspired leader on the island, Dr. M. B. Douglas, president of the Council for Afro-Jamaican Affairs, penned a sharply worded letter to the airline's directors requiring "assurance that black girls with black hair would have a chance of being employed."[9] Even the government's own powerful minister for communications and works,

Cleve Lewis, whose portfolio included civil aviation, condemned the airline for their insinuations.[10] In response, the airline quickly moved into damage control, with an executive reaching out to Douglas to assure him that "there would be no discrimination on the grounds of race, colour or creed." The directors also dispatched the airline's managing director to meet with a *Gleaner* newspaper reporter to stress the same.[11]

Amid this tumult, the airline did indeed hire a handful of dark-skinned women, though by no means in proportion to their numbers in the population. Other hiring criteria that were supposedly color-blind already skewed the number of qualified applicants to overrepresent Kingston's privileged light-skinned minority. These factors included passing O-level exams at the end of high school and possession of "good diction" in speaking, which were grounds to exclude those who spoke forms of Jamaican patwa (patois) from the countryside or impoverished urban areas.[12] As one longtime flight attendant noted, the job's most effective language speakers were those who had been trained in families and schools to speak "what we called the 'Queen's English.'" She quickly added that another language skill was required, but less frequently, as stewardesses needed "to break down into patwa when you had the ... odd Jamaican who, you know, was giving trouble."[13]

In lieu of having a fully proportionate number of darker-skinned hires, Air Jamaica executives instead carefully drew attention to the few such women at press events. One reporter who covered a reception with new hires noted, "There was special attention to petite Lilla Bennett, whose 'Afro' hairdo was the perfect answer to those who had seen something sinister in the Air Jamaica advertisement's reference to 'attractive hair.'"[14] In advance of Air Jamaica's relaunch, its soon-to-be president, Guillermo Machado, also gradually fed the new stewardesses' biographies and headshots to the press. He thought this tactic would keep the airline in the news and "help to dispel any previous doubts as to [the] number of dark girls being used."[15]

Overall, the collection of brown Jamaican and white Canadian men calling the shots at Air Jamaica were initially caught flat-footed, unaware that demands for greater racial equity had increased. Racial victories for light-skinned Jamaicans, like Carol Joan Crawford's 1963 coronation as Miss World, no longer sufficed. The *Gleaner*'s profiles of the fifty-six women who made Air Jamaica's final cut was, therefore, hollow reassurance for racial progressives. The article notes that the women included "two Caucasian types ... and one of Oriental origin," and, employing vague language, "the others run the Jamaican chromatic scale." Seemingly of greater appeal than racial identity, at least to this reporter, was that "at least three were entrants in last year's 'Miss Jamaica' contest."[16]

Both Ambassadors and Neo-imperial Fantasy Objects

There clearly were divergent ways that the public evaluated Air Jamaica stewardesses upon their debut. On the one hand, both Air Jamaica and the women who worked as stewardesses were treated by many—certainly by the elites who ran media outlets like the *Gleaner*—as a source of national pride. For them, the stewardesses heroically represented their small country, and especially Jamaican women, on the sophisticated world stage of aviation. All the while, they delivered high-quality service with a unique gusto instilled in them by masterminds like Marguerite Kirkpatrick. Thus they were, in the words of the Air Jamaica executive team, "girls [who would] portray Jamaica to visitors and local passengers" and serve as "ambassadors of goodwill for Jamaica."[17] On the other hand, however, the airline openly encouraged potential customers to exoticize them. Thus, when these women appeared in a special supplement to the *Gleaner* celebrating the airline's first flight, the stewardesses' headshots and bios ran under the demeaning headline "Air Jamaica's Rare Tropical 'Birds.'"[18] Not only were they labeled with the imperialist-era exotic designations of "rare" and "tropical," but they were also reduced to subhuman "birds"—which, not coincidentally, was a trendy slang term in the 1960s for loose women.

This headline arose from intentional work at Ketchum, Air Jamaica's New York–based marketing firm, which worked closely with Marguerite Kirkpatrick on her uniform designs and on other stewardess-related promotions. This predominantly American team was aware of Mary Wells Lawrence's success in 1965 turning Braniff from an obscure airline into an effective upstart, and they felt that Air Jamaica's status as a new arrival called for a similar formula. Ketchum also researched American customers' preexisting knowledge of Jamaica and found an array of simplistic and exotic tropes: catchy calypso music (thanks to the likes of Harry Belafonte, who catapulted to fame in the calypso craze of the 1950s), intoxicating rum, an unusual dialect of spoken English, a tropical setting for the James Bond film *Dr. No*, and Carol Joan Crawford—the first "Negro" crowned Miss World. Rather than challenge the ways these elements had become stereotypical and derivative when circulating in America, Ketchum opted instead to indulge these simplifications. If challenged by customers who might see through this pastiche, they could pass off the simplistic portrayals as part of a tongue-in-cheek, fun vibe, akin to Mary Wells Lawrence's bawdy "Air Strip."

The overall in-flight experience at Air Jamaica was thereby scripted to play on many foreigners' incomplete conceptions of Jamaica, with the purported goal of making passengers feel that "their Jamaican holiday [begins] the minute their flight stewardess says 'welcome aboard' in New York and Miami."[19] Ketchum's first ad, placed in *Life* magazine, detailed elements of this exotic, playful experience on board: passengers are greeted with "soothing island music [which] . . . accompanies every Air Jamaica take-off and landing," are served by "stewardesses so pretty and graceful, we call them Rare Tropical Birds," are offered a special cocktail known as the "rum bamboozle . . . to warm the inner you," and finally can sit back and enjoy the airline's "flying fashion shows, a showing of the latest island creations." The fashion show justified encouraging customers to "have your Travel Agent book you a seat on the aisle." After all, as the text noted, "Modeled by our Rare Tropical Birds, it's quite a sight."[20]

Like Mary Wells's work, the in-flight experience at Air Jamaica was part of a larger branding strategy promoting a sexually flirtatious air, though with a tropical vibe. The jets were coated with stripes of orange and gold to complement Kirkpatrick's multicolored minis, and the new logo—inspired by a doctor bird, a hummingbird species native to Jamaica—was painted on all plane tails. To maintain a sexy flair, the logo was christened the "love bird." Such touches allowed Ketchum to double down on sex and exoticism in their 1972 ads: "Our Rare Tropical Birds model the latest resort wear to authentic island music. And then spare that little bit of extra time soothing and serving you in a special, Jamaican way."[21] By then, the airline's main advertising slogan had become racier as well: "We make you feel good all over."[22]

Former stewardesses' reactions to being marketed in such ways were complex. One employee from the first stewardess class, when speaking fifty years on, recalled this sort of sexual objectification with incredulity. When first asked for her reaction to the "rare tropical birds" moniker, she admitted that "it didn't seem unusual to us at all. . . . We were excited and we were accepting of it." There was, after all, esteem to be gained from the beauty queen aspect of the job, and folding these elements into a cheeky marketing campaign was common in Jamaican entertainment venues catering to foreigners. She added that the marketing scheme elicited some unusual conversations:

> You know, I remember there was just, uhm, not controversy, but a lot of talk about flight attendants and what they should be called. The airline itself was called, oh god what was it now? "The love bird." But we were the "rare tropical birds" (*laughter*) . . . And it was, like, passengers would come on, and they want to say that [we were the "love birds"]. And [we corrected them]. No, we were the "rare tropical birds," we're not the "love birds" (*laughter*).[23]

This woman's ability to laugh while discussing her situation is, on the one hand, consistent with a key tenet of Jet Age feminism circa 1970: that sex, especially sexual innuendo, can be fun, playful, and free from dire consequences, even when it occurs in a workplace. Yet, there was another motivation for her laughter. Fifty years on, she saw this sexualization as an anachronism, one inconsistent with the more progressive feminist norms to which she now ascribes.

Another former stewardess from the class of 1970 shared mixed memories of the in-flight fashion shows. Her account was also filled with laughter, both at the anachronism of the premise and at the comically challenging work demands it placed on stewardesses. She noted that each flight's crew had a limited number of women scheduled for the show: "When they were making up the roster, you would have several people who were scheduled to 'do fashion,' as they called it." The first stress point when scheduled to "do fashion" was changing into the clothes: "Now, we changed in the first-class washroom (*laughter*), and it was very tricky. I mean, we were kind of contortionists, because (*laughter*) there we were, all of us in this little tiny washroom trying to change. Well, one at a time, of course. And then you would maybe bring out your uniform and push it somewhere, then you would go back in, you know. It was kind of weird (*laughter*)." More laughter arose when this former stewardess recalled the chaos that sometimes resulted:

> I remember once coming out after a fashion show, this young lady she was—I mean, I still am a small person—and she was much bigger than I am. And I put on my uniform quickly because, of course, by this time the flight is getting ready to land, and you have to be in your assigned seats for landing. And I come out of this washroom, and I am feeling, "Mmhmm . . . this doesn't feel right on me."

And I look down, and I have on this dress that is so big for me! (*laughter*) And I turn around and look at her, and she is squashed into my little tiny uniform (*laughter*). We just took one look at each other, and then we had to bolt and dash back into the tiny little washroom (*laughter*) to change out . . . and swap clothes.[24]

Regarding the fashion show, stewardesses were divided about their value, even at the time: "Let's put it this way, some people liked the fashion show. It took the passengers' minds off the flight. But I, for one, [that was] the main reason why I applied to be a purser as soon as I could, after two years." Pursers, the flight attendant in charge of supervising all other stewardesses' work, "did the commentary and not the actual fashions."[25] While laughing may have been a temporary coping strategy for women like this interviewee, it was not a long-term solution. Moreover, the vulnerability of stewardesses during the fashion show to sexual harassment in the form of both verbal abuse and unwanted touching was keenly felt.

The frivolity of these parts of their job made it more difficult for stewardesses to serve as dignified ambassadors for their country. Nonetheless, even some Jamaican elites involved in the country's civil rights struggles, including the journalist Evon Blake, were eager to compliment them as such. Blake is remembered for his protest in 1948 to dismantle the unofficial segregation practiced under British officials and local brown elites. As a dark-skinned, but well-off Jamaican, he held precarious access to places like the Myrtle Bank Hotel, the most elite address in Kingston. He secured a day pass to the pool from the front desk, but he then created a disturbance by diving into the water. Guests gasped and staff members cursed at him while trying to extract him from the pool. Blake stayed put and defiantly screamed, "Call the police! Call the army! Call the owner! Call God! And let's have one helluva big story."[26]

Firmly established by 1970 as both a member of Jamaica's elite and an advocate for Black Jamaicans, Blake expressed enthusiasm for the Air Jamaica stewardesses working his flights between Montego Bay and Miami. "Being a critic by nature and profession," Blake's review began, "I went aboard each flight deliberately looking for faults to criticize and later complain about." But the stewardesses more than passed Blake's examination: "Believe me, . . . your stewardesses are, as we Jamaicans say, 'class.' I watched them perform with a feeling of pride." First and foremost in his compliments came the issue of race: in terms of their selection, "they are a true cross-section of the finest of our people, and each is a beauty." Beyond that, he added, "they are obviously superbly trained: beautiful of speech, without any 'put-on,' smooth and graceful of movement, solicitous and friendly without being familiar, patient, pleasant-mannered and alert." Blake tied these women's performance not only to a general sense of national pride, but particularly to Black nationalist pride: "If you had been saying out loud as long as I have, that given an equal break and proper training, the Jamaican, especially the non-white Jamaican, can be as good as any worker of any nationality anywhere, and then had the opportunity of watching coloured Jamaican girls handle a planeload of nervous homebound white American tourists with such éclat, you would know why I am writing this letter."[27]

One of the culminating moments for stewardesses' recognition as ambassadors of the nation came in 1972, when the Jamaica Post Office

FIGURE 9.1. In 1972 the Jamaica Post Office issued a stamp honoring the stewardesses of Air Jamaica.
Source: Details of the stamp are found in "Stamps in the News: Air Jamaica Honored," *Reading Eagle* (Reading, PA), June 11, 1972, 74. Permission to use this image courtesy of Neftali / Alamy Stock Photo.

honored them with a stamp. Yet, even with this honor, a tension was readily apparent between stewardesses' eroticized work personae and their more reputable role as ambassadors. The creators of the stamp conspicuously desexualized the stewardess.[28] While the uniform was depicted in a somewhat more muted but still correct bold color, the stamp portrayed the model in a dress with far more fabric than the actual uniform—enough to hide her curves. The stewardess also now held a pen and paper, so that she could be confused as a schoolteacher or a minister's wife, not someone serving "rum bamboozles" and changing into beachwear aboard the plane. That stewardesses had to be classed-up when embodying national pride for a domestic audience betrays how wide the gap remained between local standards of reputable womanhood and the airline's rendition of Jet Age feminism, one that was especially exoticized and sexualized to attract foreign tourists.

Air Jamaica Confronts the Nation's Postcolonial Turn

In the February 1972 national elections, Michael Manley of the People's National Party (PNP) scored a decisive political victory over Alexander Bustamante's successor as prime minister, Hugh Shearer of the Jamaica Labour Party (JLP). Seventeen seats of the fifty-three comprising Jamaica's House of Representatives changed hands, as Manley garnered what was at the time the most lopsided victory in Jamaican political history. While still retaining a share of elite and middle-class voters, Manley employed his personal charisma, ideological openness to more radical ideas, and commitment to improving conditions for the country's poor Black majority to draw poorer voters to his side. His campaign slogan "Better Mus' Come," borrowed from the lyrics of reggae artist Delroy Wilson's 1968 classic, captured many Jamaicans' impatience. Ten years on from independence, society remained polarized along both class and color lines, and poverty was intractable for the nation's large underclass.[29]

"Better Mus' Come" was also a social slogan in 1972, as director Perry Henzell released his collaboration with reggae artist Jimmy Cliff, the Jamaican film classic *The Harder They Come*. Set largely in West Kingston neighborhoods, the film showed a side of Jamaica drastically different from the one where elites like Carol Joan Crawford and Marguerite LeWars Kirkpatrick lived. This was a place of shanty towns, guns, drug deals, organized crime, corrupt police, rampant illiteracy, negligent social services, and seemingly inescapable poverty. The other person who made 1972 a monumental cultural year was Beverley Anderson, a young, dark-skinned model and popular broadcaster who also played a small role in *The Harder They Come*, albeit as a decidedly middle-class housewife. In June 1972, Anderson married her boyfriend, the same Michael Manley who was now prime minister. The marriage of the most prominent politician to his celebrity wife was a star-studded affair that effectively saw the thirty-year-old Anderson supplant the much lighter-skinned Marguerite LeWars Kirkpatrick and Carol Joan Crawford as Jamaica's foremost image of womanly beauty.

Anderson's ascension to first lady was therefore the next step in the evolution of Jamaica's racialized beauty norms. But this was a political evolution as well, as she used her position to project a far different voice than her predecessors, one that was decidedly political and feminist. She was highly supportive of redistributive justice for darker-skinned Jamaicans and sympathetic of her husband's eventual embrace of democratic socialism and improved relations with Castro's Cuba. Most importantly, she enjoyed her husband's support in engaging in feminist politics, and she soon became the head of the PNP's women's movement. Anderson Manley used this position and her platform as first lady to press for various reforms to support women, including passage of a law providing for paid maternity leave in 1979.[30]

At Air Jamaica in 1972, however, it was business as usual. The company kept its stewardesses in miniskirts that had changed only slightly from the ones Marguerite LeWars Kirkpatrick had designed in 1969, it continued to use them in seductive fashion shows, and it still employed the sexist "we make you feel good all over" ad campaign. Yet, each of these marketing ploys was increasingly out of step with the more energized postcolonial voices influencing Manley's government.

Thus, over the course of Manley's initial tenure as prime minister, which lasted from 1972 to 1980 (he returned as prime minister for a second time in 1989, though with a less progressive political plan), Air Jamaica officials struggled to recalibrate their marketing techniques to adjust to this new environment. Stewardesses, too, though never as full-throated as Anderson Manley or the new feminist groups that arose in the 1970s, pressed for their own renegotiations of harsh workplace rules. They first took aim at the airline's marriage and maternity bans and, by the end of the decade, at the in-flight fashion shows as well.

Jamaican tourism slumped in the mid-1970s. Even before Manley and the PNP gained power in 1972, the exponential growth in tourism that had persisted through the 1950s and 1960s started to slow.

As Air Jamaica's chairman G. Arthur Brown confided to officials in 1970, 1969 brought a larger loss for the airline than anticipated. With the start-up costs and purchase plans for new jets, the airline was projected to lose JA$1.33 million, but the losses ended up totaling $1.52 million. While technical issues explained some of these overruns, a larger concern was the decline in tourism growth. As Brown detailed, "It is a fact . . . that the travel market to Jamaica did not increase by more than 7% for the year when it had originally been estimated that the total travel market would have increased by 15%."[31] Later, when the oil shocks of 1973–74 exacerbated this cooling off, the Manley government sounded the alarm.

Committees worked throughout 1974 and 1975 to generate a report for parliament with recommendations for the future of tourism, and the results cautioned leaders to expect a further slowing. It also called for a reckoning with the historical "lack of planning of Jamaica's tourism development, resulting in haphazard construction of visitor accommodation."[32] In addition to the damaging economic consequences of overbuilding, including decreased occupancy rates and increased debt, the final report added a new cultural dimension. It lamented that "the presence of huge numbers of foreigners on the local society and culture must result in a certain amount of social deculturation."[33] This newfound concern for cultural loss then led to embracing a new priority for the future: "promotion of indigenous values in the [tourism] industry."[34]

As though directly countering Air Jamaica's marketing, the report was particularly damning when describing choices that play into neo-imperialist stereotypes. As it articulated, "Much of the development of the Tourist Industry in the past has been determined by external influences. This has been reinforced in some instances by an excessive willingness to provide what it was imagined the visitor wanted." Rather than catering to these false expectations, it counseled, "The raison d'etre of a vacation in a foreign country is precisely its foreignness—the climate, physical configuration, and culture which are native to the destination. Jamaica must preserve a distinctive Jamaican aesthetic."[35] While this parliamentary investigation focused primarily on Jamaica's land-based assets like resort areas, the priority placed on "indigenous values" over "what it was imagined the visitor wanted" also pertained to Air Jamaica.

The earliest and most notable evolution in this direction came when the airline sought to rectify an entertainment gap in its in-flight service:

not until Manley won election in 1972 did Air Jamaica develop its own in-flight magazine. In the age before passengers enjoyed various media alternatives, other airlines turned to in-flight magazines to assuage passengers' boredom. The first goal for such magazines was to offer a diverse array of articles that would entertain a broad swath of people, but they also introduced an airline's destinations to flyers, often providing in-depth coverage of sights to visit. When finally filling this gap, Air Jamaica's management made a very different choice than it had in 1969. Rather than turn to its marketing team at Ketchum, it instead hired a Kingston-based firm to produce the new *SkyWritings* magazine. This firm, Carter Gambrill Robinson, then formed a subsidiary called Creative Communications Incorporated (CCI), which published *SkyWritings* over the ensuing decades, with Jamaican ad executive Anthony Gambrill at the helm.

This separation from Ketchum allowed the production team to have a wholly different premise for the magazine. Stated one longtime CCI employee, "It read really like it wasn't pushing the marketing [aspect]; it was just pushing a great story."[36] Moreover, the content also was more indigenous than Ketchum's work, which replicated American cultural stereotypes. As Odette Dixon Neath, a longtime editor, explained, "*SkyWritings* was conceived with two guiding principles: that Jamaica is a symphony of vibrant textures, and that there are so many ways to tell a story." She added that the magazine's very first issues came out when Jamaica was deeply engaged in "the national pursuit of self-definition."[37] CCI's local leadership, which was well connected with Jamaica's literary, artistic, and political community, eagerly participated in this process, as was evident in the first two issues produced in late 1972.

When Gambrill and his associates pitched their ideas to Air Jamaica executives, they offered something unique. Said one collaborator, "Of all the agencies . . . trying to do marketing, we wanted [our work] to look like it was indigenous. We weren't doing just the cookie-cutter, copying of British- or American-type advertising and just calling it Jamaican."[38] Instead, the materials they developed for their pitch, which ultimately were published in *SkyWritings*' inaugural issue, challenged Air Jamaica's customers to acquaint themselves with the island's complexities—not only its beaches, nightlife, and beautiful women, but also the vibrant but impoverished village life and even the harsh legacy of slavery.

The first issue boasted an unexpected cover photo: a stylized painting of a mountain village, a part of Jamaica that the vast majority of beach-seeking tourists never visited. A description of the painting noted its provenance from the artist Kapo, who was a "self-taught 'primitive' painter" and "spiritual leader of a flock of highly religious cultists." Kapo's embrace of African dress and religion was just one way in which "his work has done much to bring prestige and acceptance in Jamaica for the Black poor." This description in turn aptly introduced the accompanying article from the accomplished Jamaican novelist John Hearne, who profiled Jamaica's hill regions and their role in promoting Black Jamaicans' autonomy, both during slavery and after emancipation.[39]

Hearne stressed that Jamaica's mountains forged a fierce independence in its citizens, whose Maroon ancestors fought off white encroachment and whose later ancestors, when freed from slavery, escaped the seaside plantations to engage in farming for themselves: "Within thirty years a slave people were metamorphosed into a hard-edged, responsible and sceptical [sic] peasantry," Hearne explained, before asserting that the resulting "quirky, independent personalities" of the hill country "are what we play from now." With more than a tinge of regret, Hearne added that in today's Jamaica, "Kingston, Montego Bay, and the tourist complexes have begun to re-attract the best of our young." These more modern locales are "refashion[ing] them into either a lumpenproletariat or rootless metropolitans."[40] It is not difficult to imagine the average tourist's response to this claim. Those not perplexed by the Marxist terminology might have felt either shame or resentment that their choice of a beach vacation was subtly implicated in the degradation of Jamaicans' independence.

The second issue of *SkyWritings* turned its focus to Jamaican women, offering a very different vision from the beauty queen narratives that otherwise attracted media attention. On the cover was Beverley Anderson Manley, with the ensuing profile and interview focusing on her commitment to feminism and the way she "personifies the new mood of Jamaican women." At this early moment, Anderson Manley walked a fine political line on feminist ideas. The author noted, "Although she declines to be categorized as a women's liberationist, she is concerned about and actively involved in issues that should 'liberate' Jamaican womanhood from traditional economic and social prejudice." The first lady then mentioned a series of changes she supported, all of which were feminist staples: "Family planning. Early childhood education programmes. Legal discrimination. Job equality. These are well-defined targets. More difficult to confront, she says, are the 'unwritten laws.'" Also noteworthy was how the magazine characterized Anderson

Manley's marriage. Rather than conforming to traditional modes, the couple was instead a "team, the two of them working together," a sentiment that Jet Age feminists like Mary Wells Lawrence, and even Clare Boothe Luce a generation earlier, would have applauded. Yet, the report also clarified that this partnership still had Anderson Manley "in a supporting role."[41]

The remainder of issue 2 profiled working women in various careers, from the arts to the business world. It culminated with a profile of Air Jamaica stewardesses that provided small elements of a feminist counternarrative to the airline's other marketing materials. That said, the profile was still quite sexist in places. Its introduction could have come from Ketchum's New York–based copywriters: "Like women everywhere, the stewardesses on Air Jamaica's Love Birds are attracted to the male of the species." Mention of the on-board fashion shows followed, with the claim that they gave men permission to "safely concentrate on shapely Love Bird curves" and offered moments "when most male passengers on the Love Birds are really glad to travel in a 'woman's world.'" A few paragraphs later, however, the author shared one disadvantage of these working conditions. He frankly stated that men are "the source of most of [stewardesses'] extra work on board," adding a quote from a stewardess who said that "men are very nice, but very demanding and prone to be a bit troublesome after a few drinks." The airline's in-flight services manager then shared how she monitored the boarding process on flights very closely: "More men than women and most stewardesses begin to worry a little bit."[42]

In sum, both of the first two issues of *SkyWritings* as well as subsequent issues beyond 1972 offered a far richer, more nuanced and politically engaged perspective of Jamaica than the airline's reductive marketing schemes. The airline was now more equitably straddling the cultural divides in its home country, which in the Manley years were widening. Challenges to sexism were now mainstreamed, with women's liberation finding a powerful advocate in the first lady. The magazine's more complex presentation not only of gender inequality, but also of Jamaica's struggles with racism, classism, colonialism, and its legacy of slavery challenged the racist and imperialist mentalities that some American and European customers brought on board with them. A former CCI employee, when asked about why they opted to make *SkyWritings* so political in the early years, responded, "Well, it [i.e., political change] was in the water, it was in the air. You have to understand too that . . . the People's National Party was now in control. . . . And they were very progressive, and there was a left wing of that party as well that was for democratic socialism. So, there was a lot going on."[43]

Stewardesses and the Postcolonial Turn: Confronting Sexism

Many early stewardesses were enthralled to be entering a workplace replete with beauty queen–caliber hiring criteria and in-flight fashion shows. There was a sense of pride among the rare women who met these exacting standards. As one woman who began work after competing in the 1971 Miss Jamaica contest noted, her uniform looked exquisite and gave her confidence: "You know, the green [dress] would be tied with pink, or yellow with green, or pink with green. And we [also] had gloves when we were greeting the passengers and when the passengers were leaving. And [then] we had handbags and tote bags, [plus] shoes—everybody had the same shoes." Sporting a wide smile, she added, "That was what I loved about [the job]."[44]

Yet, when this stewardess matured in the job, she and her peers confronted some drastic downsides, including the extra labor involved in doing the fashion shows, bans on marrying and having children, an early policy forbidding sexual relationships between pilots and stewardesses, and, most glaringly, the airline's policy of pushing stewardesses out after five years. Even the most glamorous beauty pageant veterans looked upon this artificial expiration date with consternation. After all, being a stewardess was their livelihood, not a one-and-done beauty pageant. Such concerns took root at the same time as the election of Michael Manley in 1972, creating a political climate that was now more sympathetic to treating stewardesses, both as workers and as women, with greater dignity.

In the early 1970s, the stewardesses' National Workers Union local was able to press these concerns with Air Jamaica's management. What was not won via negotiation was pursued in two other ways: via arbitration at Jamaica's Industrial Disputes Tribunal and through women's own challenges on the job. On this latter point, one stewardess described what she termed a "classic case" of asserting herself more aggressively at work:

> I wore glasses, and [Air Jamaica management] insisted that we had to wear contact lenses. But the pilots who wore glasses could wear their glasses and carry a spare pair. . . . [So] the chief pilot at the time saw me one day, and I had been wearing my glasses for a

while. . . . [He] said to me, "Have you been flying in your glasses?" And I said, "Yes." He said, "And who gave you permission to do that?" So I said, "I do believe that the pilots are allowed to wear theirs and carry a spare pair, so I have a spare pair in my bag."[45]

Within the first five years of the new Air Jamaica, this combination of personal assertiveness, collective bargaining, and national political change brought an end to three of the major tension points: the restrictions on marriage and pregnancy were jettisoned, the policy prohibiting fraternization with pilots ended, and, most importantly, women were now permitted to stay in the job for as long as they were qualified. This same flight attendant recalls that each of these reforms happened, "relatively quickly, because it wasn't worth it" for the company to resist them. She added, "You have to understand that Air Jamaica was not a [well-]funded airline. They couldn't afford a long strike." She also described a "press" to keep Air Jamaica flying "because the only other airline [in the Caribbean] was [BWIA]," which she dismissively referred to by its nickname: "Be Waiting In Agony."

From this worker's perspective, the changes stewardesses most wanted came about with plenty of union pressure but no overt labor action: "usually, when there were negotiation times, there were things going on behind closed doors" between the union and the company, "and eventually things just changed."[46] There appears to be no available internal corporate documentation or press accounts about the end of the marriage and pregnancy bans nor about the end of forced retirement for stewardesses after five years. As such, it does seem plausible that these changes were adopted quickly and with consensus between management and the union, as this former stewardess describes.

Finding a way to end the in-flight fashion shows took longer—until the final year of Michael Manley's first tenure as prime minister in 1980. It also required a more involved intervention from the flight attendants' new labor union, the Bustamante Industrial Trade Union, which pursued the issue at the country's Industrial Disputes Tribunal (IDT). Yet, the impetus for this change was, once again, a choice by an individual flight attendant to confront her employer. On a November 1979 flight between London and Jamaica, stewardess Christa Wilson was selected to participate in the fashion show. Insisting she was too tired, Wilson refused the purser's orders. Upon landing at Montego Bay, the disagreement escalated, such that Wilson was pulled off the plane before it continued to Kingston.

In its findings, the IDT tribunal ultimately sided with Wilson and the union, ruling that Wilson's ouster from the plane "was unnecessary and unjustifiable and could only have served to humiliate and embarrass her." When a meeting between Wilson and her managers a few days later descended into cursing and door-slamming, the airline made the choice to dismiss Wilson for her intransigence. However, the IDT's decision to reinstate Wilson with all but one month's back pay (a penalty for her actions at the follow-up meeting) signaled to Air Jamaica's management that stewardesses' displeasure with the fashion shows could not be contained. Wilson's precedent could now be emulated without penalty.[47] Soon thereafter, with the same unpublicized swiftness as previous reversals on age and marriage policies, managers ended the fashion shows.

Stewardesses and the Postcolonial Turn: Confronting Racism

A majority of my interviewees from Air Jamaica's flight attendant corps shared the class status and also the light-skinned racial standing of Carol Joan Crawford and Marguerite LeWars Kirkpatrick. They grew up learning Jamaica's intricate codes tied to race and class, typically from within the country's better-off neighborhoods and schools. Then, when they traveled abroad and interacted with Americans and Europeans, they also became conversant in the United States' Jim Crow–inflected racism as well as the more subtle but equally pernicious racisms operating in Canada, the United Kingdom, and Germany. At the same time, however, attitudes on race were changing throughout the Western world, as when one of the judges of Miss World in 1963 described the light-skinned, African-descended Carol Joan Crawford as a desirable wife and daughter for any man.[48] Thus, when Air Jamaica's stewardesses started flying in 1969, it was unclear whether these beauty queen–marketed women would be treated like Crawford, or whether their mixed-race status would expose them to various forms of discriminatory treatment.

Meanwhile, at home in Jamaica, the Walter Rodney riots gave rise to a similar process whereby many Jamaicans were reexamining their attitudes on race. That said, for some lighter-skinned women growing up in more conservative families, the riots were barely noticed. One future stewardess was studying at the University of the West Indies when the protests and police actions temporarily disrupted life on campus. She, however, stayed away from the turmoil: "I was kind of one of those shy little withdrawn persons, and I remember now . . . in my history class, I remember this young lady who was very vocal and very out there. And as a matter of fact she was heavily involved in . . . the Rodney stuff." Yet, this fellow student was an outlier, in her experience: "I think all of the people that were doing political science and sociology were heavily into that, [whereas] my history focus was on European history . . . I don't know." In explaining how she was unaffected by the unrest, she surmised, "I guess I just had my head down like a little turtle or something."[49]

Further enabling the ability to ignore Jamaica's racial tensions was another common strategy detailed by another stewardess who hailed from a light-skinned, middle-class family. "Jamaica"—here, she invoked the whole nation, even though the claim pertains more to the higher social strata—"Jamaica has this false sense of, 'we're classist, not racist.' And I think that is true for the most part. We are [actually] more classist than racist."[50] However much it reflects an individual's personal experiences, this claim obscures how racism has played a central role in constituting Jamaica's social classes and in generating such strong antagonism against lower-class Black Jamaicans. It nonetheless helps clarify how some stewardesses were unmoved by the overt discussions of racism that Walter Rodney and others encouraged as Air Jamaica was taking off.

Whatever sense of race was cultivated by Jamaican flight attendants' experiences in Jamaica, they found themselves perceived differently when they traveled abroad. Some were already exposed to the Global North and its racial systems in their childhoods when their families followed the paths of previous generations of Jamaicans by migrating off-island. One stewardess recalls that "my first exposure [to racism] was when I was ten years old," in 1960, when "my parents were in Washington [DC]. My father—the government had sent him to do a course—[and] my mother was working at the World Bank." What stood out to her was that "never in my entire life [had I been] told I was Black." On a bus ride through the tony Dupont Circle neighborhood, "this little old lady, white old lady, white hair, got on the bus. So my brother got up and offered her the seat," adding that such was expected of children in Kingston. In this case, however, "she looked him up and down and . . . pushed past him. . . . And he turned to my mother and said, 'What did I do wrong?' And she said, 'I'll tell you when we get home.'"[51]

Stewardesses also encountered racism when they served the airline's American passengers. Yet, consistent with their racial and class affiliations, some of them at first failed to apprehend that this small minority of passengers was acting out of race-based animus. As one interviewee detailed, there were various moments in retrospect that she found passengers "would look at us as if we were a different species," further explaining that these passengers found Air Jamaica's stewardesses and pilots to be "curiosities—that's the word I want to use." There was quite a bit of "curiosity of seeing, 'Oh hey, these guys can really fly a plane!' or 'They had the best landing!'" She added that the racism behind such attitudes was not immediately clear. "I think what happens with Jamaicans . . . is that there are a lot of times when the racism just slides off our shoulder," she noted. "So, many times if these people were rude to us because we were Black, we would just say, 'What a facety [i.e., rude] person.' And [we would] not think that it was because of race . . . Unless they came right out and say, 'You Black-whatever'. . . we would never pick up on it and say it's because of racism."[52]

If some stewardesses were initially ill-equipped to handle American racism, some passengers were equally ill-equipped to deal with Jamaicans' diversity of skin tones. One flight attendant described the confusion of a customer flying on a 747 jumbo jet that Air Jamaica had temporarily leased. The passenger asked her, "'Can you put me upstairs, because I don't want to sit next to this Black person.' And they would actually say it just like that!" Hailing from a mixed-race background, the flight attendant wasn't perceived as Black, so "I [said], 'And [what do you think] I am?!' . . . And they wouldn't understand that I was saying that I'm Black. So, then we'd have to say, 'Look here, I am Black, I am serving your food, I'm making your drink. You're going to depend on me to get off the plane. So, at least for three and a half hours, deal with a Black man sitting beside you.'"[53]

The same chromatic confusion sometimes led passengers to misunderstand flight attendants' seniority. As a different flight attendant detailed, the fact that a handful of Air Jamaica stewardesses were white was one basis for this confusion:

> That particular day there were eight of us [stewardesses] on the airplane. I was the one in charge. I had another girl like me [mixed-race] up at the front and an Indian girl in the cabin. In the back [a white flight attendant] was down there. There was another Indian girl, there was a half-Chinese one, and then there were two other Black girls. There was a problem down in the back, [and] somebody asked to see the purser and I went down . . . [The passenger

then said] "I want to talk to the person in charge," and I said, "Well, I'm the person in charge."

She looked me up and down and she looked around her, and I think maybe if nobody had laughed. . . . But somebody else laughed. There were Jamaicans on the flight, and a Jamaican person laughed because they realized that she wasn't comfortable. . . . And [the white attendant] was going by, and she said, "How can you be in charge? I choose the white girl," whereupon the white girl turned around and looked at her and said, "No, I am not in charge here," and kept going. She [finally] demanded to speak to somebody from the cockpit, but I don't think she realized the pilots were all Black. So, that was very interesting when the second officer came.

As if providing a point of consolation, the stewardess ended her account with the claim, "I must admit, it was a rare occasion" to have passengers so outspoken.[54]

As women not used to attributing the social inequalities surrounding them to racism, some stewardesses found themselves confused, even judgmental, when working with other members of the African diaspora, in particular African Americans. Recognizing African Americans as a vital secondary tourist market, Air Jamaica marketed heavily in Black publications in the 1970s and found a very receptive audience. That said, the cultural differences and alternative experiences of racism in their respective societies created misunderstandings. One stewardess described such encounters as "another whole dynamic" than working with white Americans, as she lamented that some African Americans "didn't know how to react to us." The language differences between the two diasporas caused some disconnect: "One of them actually asked me, 'Where does that accent come from? Did you go to school in England?'"[55]

Another stewardess admitted to having negative preconceptions of African Americans due to her middle-class Jamaican upbringing. Initially she found African Americans too inclined toward confrontation: "As a matter of fact, I did ask a passenger once, I said, 'Why are you . . . Black Americans so angry?'" The way she saw the US's race problems, "everything . . . it's about race-race-race and [African Americans are] getting angry." Thanks to one particularly understanding passenger, however, her views evolved:

You know, he said to me: "Let me see if I can put it to you in one way. You're going home,"—it was on a flight going home to

Jamaica—"You're going to Jamaica, right?" I said, "Yeah." He said, "It's your country, right? You're going to be home?" I said, "Yeah, I'm going home to Jamaica." He said, "Well, imagine if the country that you thought was yours, people acted as if it wasn't yours . . . People telling us to go home and whatever." He said, "We don't know any other country. This is our country, yet it's like we have no home, and so we're . . . angry. We have this anger. We have a tree on our shoulders, not just a chip."

The stewardess was left far more empathetic: "Oh, I can see that," she responded, reflecting for the first time on how statehood and statelessness impacted Africa's diaspora in different ways.[56]

There were moments when postcolonial yearnings for racial progress jelled in some stewardesses. This woman, for example, expanded her political and social horizons and found some solidarity across the colonial-era divides between Jamaicans and the African diaspora elsewhere. Meanwhile, other colleagues subtly, and sometimes more directly, challenged the racist mentalities of various white passengers. In these ways, Air Jamaica's stewardesses sometimes asserted racial equality in impactful ways, even in the course of their mundane work activities. Despite some women's personal preferences to remain apolitical and avoid racial introspection, Air Jamaica's primarily brown stewardesses were increasingly aware of the racism all around them, both in the North Atlantic countries they visited and back home.

Even in its white, middle-class American cultural context, Jet Age feminism was deeply problematic. After all, younger middle-class women in the United States were torn between supporting aspects of Helen Gurley Brown's *Single Girl* feminism and Second Wave activists who saw this sort of sexualization as demeaning. Some such women were also deeply troubled by the classist bias of Brown's formula for women's social inclusion, as it disproportionately sexualized working-class women like stewardesses. However, when Jet Age feminism took root in Jamaica, it exposed an additional problem: the fraught ways in which colonial-era norms of racial inequality were grafted onto notions of feminine beauty. Cultural theorists from Edward Said to Ann McClintock have eloquently established that white Westerners' erotic desires were employed in colonized societies to differentiate supposedly civilized white Europeans from their allegedly more primitive—and, sexually speaking, more libidinous—non-white colonial subjects.

When imperialists' sexual gaze was cast toward tropical climates like the Caribbean, this tendency to both exoticize and eroticize women impacted Jamaicans. In the 1950s, in the dying days of colonialism, perhaps the island's most alluring image in Western popular culture was the calypso music craze that launched the careers of Jamaicans and Jamaican-Americans like Harry Belafonte. Their musical performances, in nightclubs or on the Hollywood screen, included women and men dancing to the up-tempo music in stripped-down outfits exposing their skin, gleaming with sweat. Jamaica, like the whole of the Caribbean, was an exotic land of enchantment.

This legacy complicates the history of Air Jamaica's first stewardesses. On the one hand, there was something mildly egalitarian about these non-white women who hailed from a small postcolonial nation embodying the same sort of Jet Age feminism that influenced cultures around the globe. By adorning stewardesses in bright, sexy, but still elegant leisure wear, Air Jamaica allowed them to partake in a cosmopolitan style that was very much in vogue. Of course, these women were also the first generation of Jamaicans to ever engage in this highly mobile work that included overnights in New York, Toronto, Frankfurt, Los Angeles, and London.

While still a working-class endeavor, stewardessing was quite distinguished, at least in comparison to the harsh treatment endured by other traveling working-class countrywomen. This includes women in the so-called "Windrush generation" who migrated to the United Kingdom soon after the war and found conditions so harsh—in terms of discrimination by police, landlords, and school officials—that Britain's first full-fledged race riots flared up in the West Indian neighborhood of Notting Hill, London, in 1958.[57] Rather than toil as despised migrants, these stewardesses were instead vetted for their looks and sized for Pucci-inspired uniforms. The Jet Age, it seemed, was offering progress to certain Jamaican woman, at least those who could conform to the rigors of being thin, young, curvy, well-spoken, and clear-complexioned.

At the same time, however, the airline's advertising campaigns and its uniform choices, not to mention its novel in-flight fashion shows, reflected the same fetishizing impulses inflicted on women in the Global South during the peak of colonialism. As though lubricating a sexual transactional process, the "rare tropical birds" served their American and European passengers a specialty cocktail upon boarding. They then did clothing changes, sometimes into bikinis, while promising to make passengers "feel good all over." Yet, importantly, the economic relationship undergirding this display of exotic, non-white, female skin was different than under colonialism: this was a Jamaican company, run mainly by Jamaican executives, for the sake of developing Jamaica's economy. This was an independence-era take on imperialist tropes.

Air Jamaica's Jet Age stewardesses were not completely disempowered in this process. They used their labor union and their own acts of disobedience to push back against objectification and ultimately attained more workplace protections more quickly than their peers in the United States and Western Europe. This reality made their public personae a complicated mixture of neo-imperial fantasies and postcolonial aspirations. Just as Air Jamaica's founding and growth aimed to dismantle the cartography of colonialism, stewardesses worked to undermine white supremacist erotic fantasies that dated back to the colonial era, even if their employers did not.

The various oral histories in the next chapter highlight in greater depth how these individual women negotiated this neo-imperial and yet postcolonial tension. Even as their sexualization diminished their agency and exposed them to personal harm through sexual harassment and abuse, they also experienced growing economic independence, growing (though still imperfect) racial self-awareness, and growing self-confidence won through their work and travel. These oral histories, then, add an important narrative of Jet Age feminism that further complicates the whitewashed versions coming from Mary Wells, *Cosmopolitan* magazine, and the West's stewardess corps.

CHAPTER 10

Jet Age Feminist Subversives
Firsthand Accounts from Air Jamaica and JAT Stewardesses

Innovators in the Western world like Mary Wells Lawrence introduced a Jet Age feminism that fetishized stewardesses as a group of young women who were attractive, well-traveled, working yet focused on fun, and sexually liberated. Thanks to similar cultural developments in disparate countries like Jamaica and Yugoslavia, this fetishization also found enthusiastic adherents well beyond the confines of the United States and Western Europe. With executives and marketers at Air Jamaica and, to a lesser extent, at JAT following Wells Lawrence's lead as the Jet Age took hold, this stylized version of women's liberation made inroads into all three of the Cold War era's so-called worlds.

Typical of Madison Avenue's creations, Jet Age feminism seemed to promise women that they could have it all: workplace success, a rich leisure life, a fun and fulfilling sex life, and adulation thanks to their physical beauty. Yet, this marketing fantasy created an untenable reality for women without the same financial means as Wells Lawrence. This included stewardesses, perhaps especially those who resided in parts of the world with far lower living standards than the United States. Naturally, then, the greatest stress point for JAT and Air Jamaica stewardesses was their unsteady income. Even though they personally enjoyed inarguably upper-class perks like free hotels in glamorous locales like

London, their pay was only solidly middle-class—based on either Yugoslav or Jamaican standards, not those of the United States. This meant that their families back home in Tito's Yugoslavia or Manley's Jamaica sometimes lacked access to essentials, much less to the more superficial accoutrements of the good life.

A second struggle for these stewardesses arose from the fact that they were especially vulnerable to sexual victimization at work. While a good number of them loved their designer outfits and the ability to turn heads with their looks, they also encountered the downsides of being a sex object, including dismissive treatment from pilots and managers, unwelcome come-ons, even rape and unwanted pregnancies. Finally, most stewardesses at JAT and Air Jamaica by the 1970s were starting families, which meant that they struggled to maintain their Jet Age life of work and travel while fulfilling commitments to husbands and children. After all, there was almost never a nanny at home, nor were these women part of husband-wife power couples with the financial resources to own multiple homes. Together, these three complicating factors—income, sexual threats, fragile family lives—were realities that neither Mary Wells Lawrence's "Air Strip" ads nor Helen Gurley Brown's *Cosmopolitan* columns ever seriously considered.

These three concerns often dominated stewardesses' everyday experiences. They also led to the various forms of pushback from stewardesses at JAT and Air Jamaica that have already been discussed. JAT's efforts to glamorize stewardesses via lavish and colorful uniforms had to pass muster with a Workers' Council that forced the designer to alter these outfits to suit stewardesses' more practical needs. Meanwhile, in Jamaica, even as stewardesses were drawn to a workplace filled with bold fashion, they did not endlessly tolerate the indignity of changing into skimpy beachwear in the plane's restrooms for in-flight fashion shows. Jet Age feminism had excesses that led stewardesses and their managers into protracted conflicts.

This chapter goes beyond these more public struggles to chronicle stewardesses' private acts of resistance. These acts happened quietly and often with no onlookers; they were responses to counter indignities that were conveniently airbrushed out of airlines' high-gloss marketing images of Jet Age feminism. These private acts were even more important in Yugoslavia and Jamaica, where feminist activist groups were slower to organize than in North America and Western Europe.[1] Plus, just as in the West, these stewardesses were not fully aligned with feminists, since they largely ascribed to Jet Age feminism's fetishization of feminine beauty. As such, private acts were the main way for these women to negotiate the contradictions of income, sex, and family in their non-glossy everyday reality.

Securing a Jet Age Income

While each boasted different economic systems, there were significant similarities between the Jamaican and Yugoslav economies and labor markets in the late 1960s and 1970s. The countries had similar rates of per capita GDP, and Yugoslavia was only slightly ahead in terms of industrialization.[2] Unemployment rates in Yugoslavia were considerably lower than in Jamaica, but they were also stubbornly high for a country with an ideological commitment to full employment.[3] Indeed, each country relied heavily on out-migration to address the employment shortages in their respective countries. Meanwhile, women's participation rates in the labor market in both countries were high and rising, though there was a palpable ceiling to women's advancement into the highest-paying careers. Nonetheless, by the dawn of the 1970s, both countries boasted a larger number of middle-class working women and the corresponding consumer culture that empowered female customers. Indeed, the "single girls" that Helen Gurley Brown promoted in the United States differed from Yugoslavia's and Jamaica's versions mainly in the amount of disposable income they enjoyed. This was only a difference of degree in how much they could consume their way to a Jet Age lifestyle.

Salaries and Benefits

Importantly, in both countries, the incentive to become a flight attendant was more than just an aesthetic aspiration to rival beauty queens. The job's stable salary and additional financial perks also established it as a pathway to their countries' middle class. The salaries themselves outpaced what women could earn in the agricultural or manufacturing sectors, which absorbed many other female laborers in both places. In fact, even in relation to more female-identified positions in the service economy—whether in hospitality, healthcare, or office administration—both JAT and Air Jamaica paid their flight attendants more.

In Jamaica, the politically well-connected union representing flight attendants even succeeded in basing their wage negotiations on foreign flight attendants' salaries. In later moments of austerity, especially when serious deliberations began about privatizing the airline, this practice came under attack. As a cabinet paper from November 1990 stated, "Considering the duties, type and duration of specialized training involved for flight attendants, there appears to be no reason for external (off-island) wage comparison."[4] Throughout the 1970s and '80s, however, stewardess salaries were empowering. Moreover, they were supplemented with stipends paid in US dollars for cosmetics, some clothing items for layovers, and per diems.

Pay was also quite good at JAT. One stewardess who started in 1962 noted that she was already making good money at a large Belgrade-based import-export firm. In her case, she noted that she "probably would have been better off staying in my old job" in terms of salary.[5] Nonetheless, her wages at JAT sufficed to rent her own apartment and even to purchase her own car. More typically, the young women and men who entered JAT's flight attendant corps did not have previous jobs that paid as well. One male flight attendant found that his first JAT paycheck in 1969 was considerably larger than his earnings from working the front desk of Belgrade's most glamorous hotel, the Metropol. Two years after starting, he could afford to rent his own apartment for the first time. When he opted instead to remain living with family, he was able to purchase a used BMW 1600 sedan, quite the status symbol for a young, single worker in Belgrade at the dawn of the 1970s.[6]

Meanwhile, an original stewardess at Air Jamaica also found she could enjoy the good life, though her tastes leaned toward travel: "Early in the 1970s, myself and two other flight attendants decided that we were going to go on a trip" to London, Athens, and Barcelona over a few weeks. Testifying to her newfound financial independence, she noted, "I actually had to borrow money from the bank," a feat that made her feel empowered: "Here I am, you know, I can do this!" The opulence of her travel actually made her self-conscious: "And then you come back and somebody would say . . . .'Where were you for the last couple of weeks?' And you start to say it, and then you'll be like, that kind of sounds like bragging, maybe I shouldn't say."[7]

Because these jobs provided a solid income, employers could be very selective. JAT by the 1960s instituted a six-month probationary period, during which time an employee could be terminated without cause. Thereafter, only a certain number were granted full-time contracts, while others were placed in a pool of part-time workers who typically worked only in the busier summer months and around holidays. Air Jamaica did something similar in the 1980s as part of cost-saving cuts.

One employee, who started in 1988, spent her entire five years at Air Jamaica as a so-called "temporary" employee, lacking the guarantee of a monthly salary, pension benefits, or even the scheduling seniority that came with a permanent position. For many months, she went without scheduled hours and instead was "on call," awaiting word via phone to report the next day.[8] Despite this increase in contingency, jobs at Air Jamaica remained prized. As one flight attendant recalls about the 1990s, "With the job situation in Jamaica being very limited, I mean, I heard that during one [open call] for applications . . . they wrapped around the whole building. . . . Thousands of them showed up."[9]

Once a candidate was fortunate enough to land a permanent position, their employer provided more than a base salary. Along with their contingent colleagues, Air Jamaica and JAT stewardesses both received a certain number of tailored uniforms with matching shoes and bags. Jamaican stewardesses also received—for some of them, at least—their first-ever winter coats and boots. Both airlines additionally provided stipends expressly for cosmetics. One Air Jamaica veteran recalls that in her starting year, 1987, she received several supplements in US dollars: "We got paid, because you had to wear makeup, so you got US$90 a month . . . for grooming. And then we got either $250 or $400 for shoes a year."[10] Permanent employees in both countries also enjoyed benefits mandated by their countries' labor-friendly laws: health care, maternity leave, a retirement pension, and paid time off.

Additional perks in socialist Yugoslavia were exceptionally generous. It was common under the Yugoslav system for companies to provide employees with housing and fully paid vacations.[11] The housing benefit, if they could get it, provided a worker and her family with a high-quality home for below-market rent. At JAT, top priority for corporate apartments went to managers and pilots, though interviewees reported that a fair number of flight attendants also qualified. More common, however, was that flight attendants found housing on their own or lived with parents or extended family. In all cases, flight attendants asserted that they had high-quality and affordable housing choices, even in a tight housing market like Belgrade.

JAT also excelled at subsidizing workers' vacations. It was typical in socialist Yugoslavia for companies to maintain seaside resorts on the Adriatic, with workers invited to sign up by the week for accommodation for their families. In JAT's case, the perks were even better. As a stewardess who started in the late 1960s noted, "We had at that time two months of paid holidays, one in summer and one in winter."[12] JAT employees could sign up for an all-expenses-paid winter ski trip, which allowed them access to Yugoslavia's best resorts. She recalled, "One year I went to Bled [Slovenia] on a JAT vacation with my young daughter, and at the same hotel, President Tito appeared with his wife to have doughnuts for breakfast." As she explained, "my daughter wanted to go say hello to Tito. She was three, and she looked up to Tito like he was a god. . . . And she started to cry," until a fellow JAT stewardess successfully bargained with the security detail. With their permission, "My daughter went over, tapped him on the shoulder, and Jovanka Tito placed her on her knees, and she stayed a long time."[13] Such glamorous perks were, of course, otherwise available only to Yugoslavia's most privileged.

Cashing in on Per Diems

While these forms of compensation—a good salary, extensive beauty allowances, and generous vacations—were part of one's contractual benefits, flight attendants at both airlines also found additional income support when they worked beyond their national borders. The key mechanism was per diems paid on layovers. Provided in local currency at rates based on the locale, this additional money granted Air Jamaica and JAT flight attendants even more direct access to the consumer products that were markers of Jet Age feminism's good life: Jordache jeans, high-end jewelry, and high-tech consumer goods. A JAT stewardess flying in the 1970s and '80s recounted a list of the most popular goods to bring back home, either for gifting or reselling: "TVs, VCRs, clothes, sneakers, jeans."[14]

While neither Yugoslavia nor Jamaica were closed economies from the 1960s onward, there were a few factors that limited the free circulation of such consumer goods. Fundamental, of course, was the higher degree of poverty and the overall lower per capita spending power, which thereby reduced incentives for Western companies to export to these countries. In addition, however, both the Yugoslav and Jamaican governments frequently used currency devaluations to keep the incomes of their workforce lower than in Western economies, a move that further reduced spending power for Western imports. There were also occasional currency controls and import restrictions in both countries that created artificial barriers to such importation. This tool was most prominently used in Jamaica in the 1970s during the economic reforms and debt crisis under Michael Manley, when some imports became particularly scarce. Such factors made the daily payments in US dollars for overnights in New York—or the equivalent in pounds for London—all the more enviable. A JAT stewardess who worked charters to New York in the early 1970s recalls the per diem being US$33 at the time, while a colleague who flew there in 1979 recalls the amount being between US$35-40.[15]

If used as designed, the per diem spiced up life on layovers. It meant chances to visit museums, go shopping, or partake in cultural outings. Several JAT stewardesses boasted that they were regulars at the half-price ticket booth for Broadway tickets, and they may have stood in the same queues as Air Jamaica stewardesses using their per diems to visit Madame Tussaud's in London. As one JAT veteran shared, while laughing at the good memories, "One of our stewards just loved saying in the New York crew room on the day of our return home, 'This New York! Every time I come here, I lose one day and one hundred dollars!'"[16]

When in more frugal moods, these same flight attendants became experts at saving their dollars, pounds, and Deutsche marks for the future. Since breakfasts were always included at crew hotels, only one additional meal was needed, while otherwise costly cultural outings or shopping trips could be replaced with free outings or downtime at the hotel. Also, since both Jamaicans and the various national groups that comprised Yugoslavia had large diaspora populations, it was often possible to eat one's second meal with family or friends. "The thing is," noted an Air Jamaica veteran, "every port we went, somebody had a relative there" who would be happy to host their visiting relative and a colleague or two. In addition to offering a free meal, these relatives also eased cultural transitions, "So they would tell us what is what," and "how when you go to Rome, you do as the Romans do."[17] Family members also advised them where to eat and shop cheaply, and stewardesses then shared the news with colleagues.

Once saved, per diem funds could buy items in short supply back home. For Jamaicans in the 1970s, this task was especially urgent. Being in places like Miami with extra money, as one stewardess explained, "gave you a chance to do something for people in your family and friends in the Manley years." She noted that "every single flight attendant that went to Miami owned a bag to shop, and you weren't buying clothes and shoes, you were buying food. You bought rice and sugar and things that were in short supply . . . to make sure that the family was well looked after."[18] An equivalent practice occurred on JAT flights from Zurich, where the airport boasted a high-quality pharmacy with medical supplies that were hard to find back home. Flight attendants combined lists of items that they assembled from family and friends, then one flight attendant was tasked with making a pharmacy run while armed with a collection of money from per diems and extra hard currency provided by family members.[19]

Profiting from Imports and Exports

Flight attendants, like pilots, were uniquely positioned to import desirable goods into their home countries, and this reality fostered in some a desire to profit from the practice. An Air Jamaica stewardess matter-of-factly explained, "Yeah, and some people did use [the job] as an opportunity to start a small business . . . it was just something that you did."[20] A similar observation was made by a JAT stewardess, who recalls that layovers in Singapore became a focal point for this activity. "I didn't participate in this, as I only bought what I needed or what I wanted to gift to someone," she noted, "but there were people who were smuggling . . . and earning a lot of money on it." The wealth they accrued in this manner became clear in the years after socialism: "Then they bought apartments, bought land. One steward has a winery, he makes wine, all thanks to that money."[21] That said, a vast majority of flight attendants abstained from this practice. They knew that Yugoslav customs could inspect them, and they were held to the same import limits as passengers. Plus, as several interviewees said, "We wouldn't do anything to sully the reputation of the airline."[22]

Thus, importing televisions, stereo equipment, computers, and other bulky items was not a typical endeavor. Occasionally, however, charter flights returned to Belgrade from Australia, Singapore, or North America without any passengers, but with a full retinue of pilots and flight attendants returning home. In these cases, the flight might also be assigned to land at the military base in Batajnica, located not far from Belgrade's civilian airport. The Batajnica landings happened without customs checks, meaning that pilots—who typically were notified a day or two before takeoff of their landing location—could then inform the entire crew. Crew members then had time to gather their cash, reach out to their preferred merchants, and purchase as many items (of whatever weight) as they could transport on the empty plane.

Importing on such an extensive basis required lots of savvy, the risky handling of cash, and good information on Yugoslav customs controls. The Batajnica landings were also too rare for those seeking to profit consistently off such trade. Thus, the most enterprising employees developed a strategy that arose because so many Yugoslav citizens worked abroad temporarily, whether as *Gastarbeiter* or as workers with Yugoslav engineering companies in the Middle East and Africa. One steward recounted how his preferred importation practice transpired:

> At that time, every person who worked outside the country . . . for at least four years got a list of items that he could bring back to the country without custom. And I found a Bosnian trader . . . who sold me such a blank list for 1,000 German marks. Each blank paper I bought could yield me, well, it depends. Before home computers, I could get about 5,000 to 10,000 marks per list. With computers, though, I could get up to 15,000. . . . And, of course, my expenses were very small, since we did not pay for transport.[23]

As this steward detailed, "Other flight attendants were living from their salary, from what JAT gave them." In contrast, hardcore traders comprised those "who understand the business . . . And the biggest problem is how to sell [within Yugoslavia]. Everybody could buy, but the problem really was how to sell." When he was asked by fellow flight attendants about what to buy, he responded, "I can't tell you what you to buy. But you better buy something that you can sell."[24]

The handful of JAT flight attendants who engaged in intensive importing were mostly male. Indeed, as one interviewee said, "They were mostly stewards, and they were hanging out together," comprising a somewhat isolated group less concerned with their work as attendants than their endeavors as traders. At Air Jamaica, however, even after men entered the job in 1988, much more trading took place among stewardesses. This was activity that my interviewees who flew in the 1970s identified as essential. However, even as import restrictions eased in the 1980s, certain goods were still priced lower outside the country. This disparity was an incentive to import clothes, jewelry, or household goods—anything that sold in Jamaica at a higher price.

As the financial situation at Air Jamaica deteriorated in the late 1980s—with the accompanying talk of privatizing the airline, growing attacks from the government on flight attendants' high wages, and increased hiring of "temporary" stewardesses—stewardesses increased their importing activities. Some packed multiple suitcases for the flights back to Jamaica, even in excess of the regular baggage allowance. This prompted the manager of base operations in Kingston to issue a bulletin in December 1989 stating that she had been "inundated with complaints from Station Managers regarding luggage of Flight Attendants operating as crew." The bulletin "further warned that disciplinary action would be taken against anyone found breaching the regulations regarding baggage."[25] This warning led to the dismissal of at least one stewardess, who in 1990 tried to check six suitcases for her flight to Kingston. The flight attendant's firing was upheld by Jamaica's Industrial Disputes Tribunal, who found that the company's action was consistent with its labor contract.[26]

Interviews with Air Jamaica veterans reveal a similar pattern as at JAT: many engaged only in occasional, small-scale importing for family and friends, while others made this their main focus, superseding their in-flight duties. Permanent hires were loath to risk their salaries and benefits by trading frequently, but temporary hires lacked this incentive. One temporary hire from the early 1990s reflected, "You have to realize that the airline's a very attractive place for a lot of illicit behaviors . . . So you're going to have people coming in just for that." When asked whether her mention of "illicit behaviors" included drug trafficking, the stewardess responded, "All that. Right. So you're going to have certain people that . . . that's why they came [to the job]. We heard some people say that's why they joined."[27]

By the 1980s, Jamaica was a key node for drug shipments into North America and, to a lesser extent, Europe. The airline's direct flights to both continents made it a ripe target for smugglers, who were increasingly tied to Colombia-based cartels using Jamaica as a way station for cocaine and high-quality marijuana shipments. In October 1986, the front page of the *Air Jamaica Staff Newsletter* issued a dire warning to employees under the headline, "Drugs and the U.S. Threat of Aircraft Seizure." Pointing to recent arrests of Air Jamaica employees "to rid our aircraft of the drug menace," the newsletter warned of dire consequences for employees and the entire airline if smuggling continued. It stressed that "the U.S. Drug Enforcement Agency has threatened to impose severe fines on the Airline and to seize our aircraft if the problem continues." It admonished "every employee to be alert against this cancer which could ruin the entire operations of the Company."[28]

Stewardesses were not the only, nor even the primary, means that traders used to ferry drugs further north. More suspicion was cast on baggage handlers and ground crews, who could access cargo holds with minimal supervision. Nonetheless, stewardesses knew drug smuggling could offer quick money if they accepted the risks. Those not involved in the drug trade saw colleagues profit handsomely from this enterprise. The same stewardess reported that colleagues bought themselves homes, even multiple pieces of real estate. Another colleague from the late 1980s and 1990s lamented, "I mean, I have been on flights where [flight attendants] have been busted. It just breaks your heart. Just. Literally. Breaks your heart."[29]

Another stewardess explained, "Remember that Jamaica is a Third World country." As such, "the opportunities are not as vibrant as in other First World countries. So you have to find, you have to create your job. . . . Let me tell you, the country is not investing in manufacturing, they're not investing in farming the way they should. And not creating jobs for people." It was this dearth of stability-producing opportunities that stimulated flight attendants' resourcefulness: "So Jamaicans, right now, they are known as having [higher levels of] entrepreneurship than any other Caribbean country. The entrepreneurial spirit is high here, and that's just because of the lack of opportunities."[30] While this was certainly not their employers' design, every time a stewardess took such steps toward entrepreneurship, she also seized the type of financial autonomy characteristic of the West's Jet Age feminism. In an otherwise dead-end, pink-collar profession, this was the most realistic path for advancing not only into the middle class, but higher.

Coping with the Sexual Risks of Jet Age Feminism

Beauty was the currency that purchased access to the job for stewardesses at JAT and Air Jamaica, with the subsequent payoff being a steady salary and certain perks of a Western-influenced Jet Age lifestyle. At the same time, being sexually accessible, or at least perceived as accessible, was a cost stewardesses incurred to keep their jobs. In Helen Gurley Brown's vision from *Sex and the Single Girl*, deploying one's sexual appeal could advance a woman's career. "As for sleeping with the boss to get ahead," she wrote, "you will undoubtedly make certain advances in your career if a particular boss has promised them to you."[31] Yet, for stewardesses only one promotion was possible, to purser. At both airlines, this promotion came early, in the first decade or less. As such, stewardesses at these airlines, just like in the West, endured sexual objectification only to maintain their jobs, not to advance. Helen Gurley Brown's claim that "single girls" controlled their own sexual agency was misleading for all women, but especially so for stewardesses.

Instead, these women regularly faced the dark side of Jet Age feminism's sexual libertinism: they were frequent targets of unsolicited advances from managers, pilots, and stewards who could tarnish their work reputations, as well as from drunk and horny customers. These airlines' Braniff-style ads—more pronounced at Air Jamaica than at JAT—perpetuated the Jet Age feminist lie that eroticizing the workplace was consequence-free and fun. These stewardesses then had to handle the fallout of this lie by employing under-the-radar strategies to defuse unwanted advances. All the while, they were cognizant of being at physical risk and potentially at odds with their superiors if they did not allow or artfully de-escalate these advances.

Passengers and Sexual Risk

Even as JAT transitioned to the Jet Age in 1963, a few of its under-traveled domestic routes—to small southern towns like Mostar, Žabljak, or Berane (Ivangrad)—were still serviced by the airline's World War II-era DC-3s. Then a novice stewardess, Milica Lukić recalls a practice that initially confused her, though she later looked back at it with laughter. When these flights filled up, one passenger would join her, the lone flight attendant, on the plane's front bench. It was never difficult to find a male volunteer, she noted wryly, adding, "from those days I have quite the collection of business cards."[32]

These were incidents that, while they may have been sexually charged for the customers, were easy enough to navigate. More challenging, she recalls, were the risks that accompanied flying to the Middle East in the 1960s. At layover hotels in places like Cairo, she and other stewardesses stayed alert through the night, as stories abound (though no interviewees affirmed that this happened to them) of hotel receptionists selling men access to single women's rooms. Similarly, regardless of the layover city, stewardesses avoided rooms with connecting doors: "If there was a steward on the crew and he had a normal room, I would ask to trade with him," noted Lukić.[33] Such fears highlight the sexual risks that existed for any female traveler at the onset of the Jet Age. Whether on planes or in hotels, women traveling without a companion knew these risks existed and took measures to protect themselves. Stewardesses were different than other women in two ways: they traveled more frequently and their employers marketed them as sexually available.

Passengers at Air Jamaica may have felt particularly entitled to be overt about their attractions to stewardesses. After all, they had purchased seats on "love bird" planes with the promise of ogling "rare tropical birds." One flight attendant from 1971 who competed in the Miss Jamaica pageant before joining Air Jamaica cited the fashion show as a moment of particular concern. On the whole, she supported having the fashion shows and even volunteered for media events where she served as a model. Yet, with the in-flight shows, she saw an unwelcome contrast with her pageant days: "Passengers were kind of getting out of hand . . . They would touch you."[34] Several women distinguished between unruly passengers based on nationality. One insisted that most problematic behavior came from "more the Americans, I would say, the Jamaicans and the Americans," while British and European guests were comparatively well-mannered. She added of Jamaican passengers: "They felt at home with us, sometimes too much at home." She also claimed that the lewd behavior came more often from wealthier flyers: "We used to complain about the first-class passengers all the time. It's as if they felt that they could do things or say things that they shouldn't."[35]

A stewardess who flew in the 1990s also claimed Jamaican passengers were particularly difficult to manage: "Jamaican men are very touchy; they are very verbal; they'll say things to you. You know, if you have a big butt they will comment on it, you know. Just inappropriate kind of talk." She then recalled—with laughter—an episode from when the fashion shows briefly returned to Air Jamaica in the mid-1990s under the ownership of Jamaican business magnate Gordon "Butch" Stewart. Clad in swimwear while walking the aisleway in coach, "I remember one day this man said to me, 'Stand right there and turn for me darling, turn for me!'"[36] Other flight attendants found that non-Jamaicans were equally offensive, if perhaps in a more muted way. One stewardess who started flying in the late 1980s shared her view that, "With the foreigners, it was weird. Because men would be coming here to get married, and they'd [also] be coming to hand [me] a magazine and inside [they had placed] their contact info."[37]

In response to these unwelcome advances, stewardesses developed coping strategies. One of Air Jamaica's original stewardesses resorted to being what Jamaicans call "facety" (feisty or combative) when the company again pushed the boundaries in its marketing campaigns:

> They gave us these pin buttons, big buttons, to wear that was very suggestive but not quite blatantly sexual, "Ask me almost anything!" So, this is a different moment in history, but . . . you had this marketing of your body.

My family will tell you that I need to be very careful, so that what I am thinking doesn't show on my face. I had never been in a position where I was made to feel like an object. I found that difficult to deal with. I'm what is known as a "facety Jamaican." In other words, you can only just go so far and no further. So I was not into the whole, "Look at me, look at me."

In my mind I had come here to do a job. I was required to serve drinks and a meal, make sure you were safe, to be polite but not over friendly. I'm not sure everybody realized that there should be a line drawn, but I definitely drew a line.[38]

A colleague who started a generation later in the 1980s was equally exasperated with passengers' objectification. She was particularly frustrated when they touched her: "One of my most used sayings on Air Jamaica was, 'Please don't poke me!' Because you're standing, and they're looking, and then [they poke me anyways]. 'Excuse me! I'm right here. You don't need to!' And it was not just Jamaicans. People just touch you."[39]

Sexual Risk from Pilots and Stewards

Women working for JAT and Air Jamaica experienced perhaps even more risk from their straight male coworkers, especially pilots but also their male peers working as stewards. My interviewees insisted that a vast majority of pilots were exceptionally professional and a pleasure to work with. As one JAT stewardess succinctly explained, "We [at JAT] were lucky with pilots. They were, to be honest, very talented. They were skilled, and they met very high standards . . . [and] they were also very professional. You would never ever hear, when sitting somewhere with the captain of your crew, [him] talking anything bad about his colleagues."[40] Other stewardesses married pilots and built long-term, mutually nurturing relationships with them. One Air Jamaica stewardess happily reported that she and her pilot husband have "been married for, what, 36 years?!" She then recounted that their love affair started before he became a pilot, when he worked as an Air Jamaica mechanic and she as a stewardess: "I wasn't even paying him any mind. I mean I was just going about my business, you know," she began. Her future husband, after spending time abroad, "came back to work in Jamaica as a mechanic in Montego Bay. So, he says that he used to go and check the [flight roster] to see when I was flying through, and then he job-switched with another mechanic for that shift."[41]

The flipside was a pattern of sexual aggressiveness from a handful of pilots that forced stewardesses to develop more coping strategies than those used on passengers. One JAT stewardess confirmed that unwelcome advances came "from pilots, stewards too, but mostly pilots." She added that the complaints she heard "have never really been fully clarified. But generally speaking, there would be parties with drinking and then maybe from one side there would be unwelcome contact. But, [again,] these things never were fully clarified, everything was covered up a bit, kept quiet."[42] Her emphasis on the lack of clarity regarding these issues, in her case, reflected the secondhand nature of these claims, but also the fact that the company had no mechanism—and no desire—to investigate sexual harassment and abuse.

Another JAT stewardess admitted that she was the intended victim of such behavior:

> It happened to me on a layover in Beirut that one steward who was older than me ... Well, we all had dinner together on layovers, then we all stayed a bit longer for a couple of drinks. And when I came back to my room, I found that steward in my room. You know, in the Middle East, you can get another room's key by paying a bit ...
>
> So, he was in my room waiting for me, but I opted to stay elsewhere for a while, and eventually he fell asleep ... And then I took his room key from his pocket and my small suitcase and changed rooms with him. Of course, he was drunk ...
>
> And the next morning on the flight he was still so hung over that he couldn't help with the heavy door on the Caravelle jets. So I had to call the flight engineer to help out instead.

In this particular case, the awkward and nearly comical conclusion to the story allowed the stewardess to laugh off the encounter, to continue working side by side with this colleague, and to dismiss the event as what she described "Balkan" behavior and nothing more. Of course, she also vividly remembers this event decades later.[43]

This same stewardess saw this behavior as a pattern that was especially common at JAT's layover hotel in Zagreb (the Hotel Esplanade), where the company leased a large bloc of rooms, all on the same upper floor. Here, a handful of her male colleagues would go "knocking on the doors during the night. And if you didn't open, they continued [down the hall]." This was their way of looking for sex before turning in for the night. She continued, "So, one of my colleagues said to a pilot [who was doing this], 'Stop this!' She knew he went from door to door." She then added that the pilot dismissed her concern with a simple, "So what?" and was never held accountable for his actions.[44]

This mixture of coping strategies—keeping vigilant, evading direct confrontation when possible, confronting violators when necessary, and not reporting incidents to management—was also common among Air Jamaica stewardesses. Rather than immediately expressing discomfort in a confrontational, "facety" way, the primary coping strategy for unwelcome advances was deflection. This included cases when workplace conversations became unprofessional. As one interviewee recalled, "I mean, the most lewd things were said in the cockpit, so you had to, you had to be able to deal with it. You had to let them know that it didn't bother you." In one incident, she sat in the cockpit for takeoff alongside the pilots and a visiting official from the United States Federal Aviation Administration (FAA): "And [the chief pilot] turns to the FAA guy, and says, 'Mike, you know what? . . . I'm sure everybody in here, just like that seat belt across [the stewardess's] left breast, is just wishing that they were in that position." The stewardess remained unfrazzled and played along, while shutting down the chance for escalation: "I would have to say something like, 'But that you'll never know!'"[45]

Many of my Jamaican interviewees, like those from the former Yugoslavia, were willing to explain away these behaviors as a cultural trait of their home societies where such banter was more tolerated. Another stewardess explained pilots' and stewards' risqué exchanges in this way: "How Caribbean men interact with women is, umm, friendly. And we understand certain levels of interchange, and, yes, there is a point at which you step over. But it is much more friendly than in North America, to the point where you could be charged, considered liable, for stepping over the boundary in North America for what you say in the Caribbean." In her estimation, Jamaicans have their own sense of limits on such banter that factored in other elements, including being a part of the same corporate workforce and, potentially, having familiarity with a particular man from social circles outside work. "So, how we banter between each other as a culture, as a camaraderie in a flight crew, in the same corporation, is all different levels," she began. "And if you knew the person prior to your association in the corporation, it's a different level. [This] is a whole different frame of reference to

North America." In her analysis, the freer-flowing banter had two explanations, "It's a cultural thing, and a level of familiarity."[46]

Of course, when physical predation was a risk, then Jamaican women also activated more aggressive coping strategies. The most effective countermeasure involved women looking out for each other. One stewardess flying in the 1970s spoke of how stewardesses quickly schooled each other not to host crew parties in their rooms, leaving the hosting duties to pilots: "You pretty soon learned not to have food delivered to your room [for the entire crew]. Because then they would linger. We would get together in one room, and you needed to make sure it was somebody else's room, so that when you're ready to leave you can pick up your bag and leave."[47]

Several more senior stewardesses played this protective role for newer hires. As one stewardess added:

> There were also . . . senior people, which I am also, [that were] real mother hen[s], because if I saw somebody was going in hard on a youngster, . . . I would say [to the stewardess], "Are you comfortable with this? If you're not comfortable, let me know." And I had no problem talking to the pilots any which way, you know, letting them know to quit. And if I realized that there were people who were not going to quit, then I would keep on.
>
> We normally got rooms with two double beds. And I would also say, "You, young person,"—it could be a young man or a young woman—"if you are not comfortable, I'm not usually in my room, because I'm normally not at the hotel. [So,]. . . stay in my room, where they don't have you down [on the company's room roster] and can't find you."

This same interviewee saw younger hires as particularly vulnerable to such predation: "You kind of need to protect them, the new ones, the naïve ones, because a lot of them thought—the new ones from the beauty contests—they thought that they were special. And they didn't realize that they weren't very special, they were just there to be used."[48]

Throughout these accounts, one finds an alarming dark side to the exhilarating aspects of women's sexual liberation as promoted by Helen Gurley Brown's work and Mary Wells Lawrence's application of Jet Age feminism to the airline industry. In stewardesses' actual lives, the threats of sexual predation, from passengers and coworkers alike, required a code of unwritten rules and coping strategies to deflect unwelcome advances that they faced regularly. It also required tolerating a deeply unjust reality: that airlines like JAT and Air Jamaica "covered up" and "kept quiet" on such incidents, as one stewardess described JAT's corporate response.[49]

Forming Families as Jet Age Feminists

Family was not a concept that meshed well with the "single girl" ethos. Indeed, Gurley Brown's prototype of the liberated woman was nicely embodied in key ways by the Braniff Airways stewardess of the 1960s: young and beautiful (and fired when you turned thirty-five), unmarried and thereby sexually available (and fired when you did marry), working to generate income in your own name, traveling the world, and looking to advance socioeconomically through sexual liaisons. Yet, these foundations of Jet Age feminism are strikingly incompatible with traditional forms of marriage and especially motherhood. Thus, when JAT by the 1950s and Air Jamaica by the early 1970s permitted their stewardesses to keep their jobs upon marrying and having children, they broke with this skewed version of women's liberation. In their efforts to simultaneously embody the single girl ethos at work while being devoted wives and mothers at home, these women encountered numerous tensions and developed novel coping strategies.

Stewardesses and Companionate Marriages

An exceptional challenge for the women at JAT and Air Jamaica involved not only the classic double burden faced by all working women (a full-time job plus the lion's share of household duties) but also the additional factor of frequent travel. Overnight absences were very common for stewardesses, as even those whose schedules were round trips back to their home cities were sometimes stranded by bad weather. Additionally, both airlines flew intercontinental routes that required one or more overnights overseas. JAT also had a month-long station in Singapore at which flight attendants flew between Singapore and Australia, while Air Jamaica stationed stewardesses for several months in Frankfurt who flew only as far as Newfoundland before returning to Germany.

While this sort of mobility might have worked well for a true "single girl," it was exceptionally challenging for JAT and Air Jamaica stewardesses who married and raised children. The result was that these stewardesses frequently exhibited two traits. First, a high number of my interviewees found men supportive of their career choice and willing to oversee the household for extended periods. Second, if stewardesses' husbands failed to offer such support, the women commonly opted for divorce.

One JAT stewardess who started in 1972 initially had traditional notions of marriage and family. As a single woman starting her career, she looked forward to JAT's charter flights that took her overseas for extended stays: "If you fly to America [or] Australia, it meant you would be out of Belgrade for three weeks, or ten days, certainly five days [at the] minimum. And when you came back, you might have two days off and then you're off flying again." Seeing this pattern as incompatible with marriage, she recalls, "my thoughts were [that this routine] would be fine up until I get married, and [especially] until I decide to get children and have a family." Thus, when she got engaged a couple years later, even before children came, she opted to change her schedule: "I stayed in Europe." She valued being home with her husband at night, as she knew stories from colleagues whose marriages had collapsed due to long separations. There were, she noted, "so many broken marriages, so many broken relationships," among her colleagues.[50]

Eventually, however, this particular stewardess and her husband found ways to stay together, even raising two children while she went back to flying to America and Australia. Her husband's attitude was crucial: "I had the right support from my husband," she asserted succinctly.[51] Another JAT stewardess stressed the need to find a man committed to companionate marriage, even though such men were somewhat rare in Serbian society. When asked how she and her husband stayed together and even managed to raise children, this stewardess smiled and said, "My husband did the job [of raising the children], because we were equal, right?" Her smile turned to laughter as she noted how socialist-era Yugoslavia's progressive laws on gender equality far outpaced the traditional notions of gender found among many citizens. She then explained how picky she was when dating, "I always detested these men who don't know how to shop for their own pants, how to cook, how to clean. They're worthless!" If she had married a man like that, "I have this terrible part of me, a killer awakens in me. I would kill him in the bedroom!" She returned to laughing jovially.[52]

An ocean away in Jamaica, a stewardess the same age, from the class of 1972, found a similarly collaborative man to marry and raise children with. "I had a husband who was very understanding," she said. "He knew I loved the job." Her passion was so intense that she frequently refused to take her vacation time and even pressed to return early from maternity leave: "I couldn't stay home, no no. I was just itching to go back." Her husband supported such choices: "My husband, really, he just said, 'No, you really love this thing here,'" and he agreed that she should return to work.[53] Of course, for Jamaican families in the 1970s, companionate decision-making also had practical economic benefits: by prioritizing a wife's time earning a salary and her various stipends, they could maintain a foothold in the middle class. The combination of economic deprivation from the era of colonialism, the tumult of the debt crisis, the austerity in the Manley years, and the continuing lack of job security and income growth all conspired against economic stability. Companionate marriage was one more tool that stewardesses could employ in their pursuit of economic security and personal autonomy.

The Hazards of Child-Rearing as a Jet Age Feminist

The core promoters of Jet Age feminism, Helen Gurley Brown and Mary Wells Lawrence, did not envision motherhood as an aspiration, at least not for their core market of women in their twenties. Instead, these women were encouraged to work, travel, date, spend money having fun—and use birth control. The Braniff stewardesses that Wells Lawrence refreshed for the Jet Age still were fired when they got pregnant. Stewardesses at both JAT and Air Jamaica diverged from the Jet Age feminist vision, as many of them—probably a majority at both airlines—also chose motherhood. They thereby invested their time off work raising young children and designing complex childcare support systems when the job required their absence.

While early childcare was always deemed a private responsibility of parents in the United States—minimal maternity leave, no state-sponsored day care, no state-sponsored preschool education until the late 1960s—this was not supposed to be so in states devoted to welfare capitalism like Jamaica, nor especially in socialist societies like Yugoslavia. In theory, a worker-run and state-owned company like JAT could have offered childcare for their employees. In reality, however, JAT's stewardess-mothers had no help beyond what was offered to all citizens: generous maternity leave, coupled with limited access to day care and early education.

The persistent realities of financial limitations and rigid patriarchy in Yugoslavia made childcare a challenge for many women workers, as detailed in Chiara Bonfiglioli's research into female textile workers.[54]

Many of these women resorted to locking their toddlers up alone in their homes when they worked, especially when their primary source of childcare, grandparents or neighbors, were unavailable. In fact, as Bonfiglioli points out, when the dual commitments of being both full-time workers and mothers was combined with the state's encouragement for women to become politically active, women in socialist Yugoslavia endured a "triple burden" largely unknown in the West. This reality widened the gap between the state's de jure gender equality and de facto persistent institutionalized sexism.[55]

State commitments to support working mothers in Jamaica arrived far later than in Yugoslavia. Reflecting the imperative to stimulate economic development through reducing the country's birth rate, the first state interventions into reproductive politics after independence were focused on disseminating birth control and education about its use. The neglect of women's needs beyond birth control was rectified only after Michael Manley's 1972 victory, perhaps especially due to his marriage to Beverly Anderson. Soon into Manley's tenure, the state began funding women's education centers and day care facilities, though typically only in public housing communities for poor families. Middle-class working women, including stewardesses, still had to find their own childcare. Thus, the main state benefit for such women came with the first maternity leave law passed in 1979. Stewardesses could then take paid leave for up to twelve weeks. Thereafter, however, childcare reverted to being a private expense.[56]

The most prevalent childcare option in both Jamaica and Yugoslavia had also served previous generations of parents: older women looked after children, a group that potentially included mothers' own mothers or grandmothers, aunts, retired neighbors, or family friends. One JAT stewardess from the class of 1970 began work in a way that would have been unthinkable at a Western European or North American airline: she was pregnant when hired on her first probationary six-month contract. Thereafter, she said, "I received my permanent contract, along with my entire class, as I recall. And all of us were really needed, but I immediately left on maternity leave. Immediately." When she returned to work, and with her husband busily looking for a job, they opted to part with the child: "[When she was] a small child, my mother took care of my daughter. Not in Belgrade, but in Knjaževac," a town over three hours away. This left the parents precious little time to spend with their daughter: "whenever we had a day or two, we would go out there." They finally brought the child back to Belgrade at age five, when schooling began.[57]

Thereafter, the husband and wife co-parented in a way that was unorthodox in Yugoslavia: "I decided that it was time for us to live together, especially since my husband no longer had a job . . . I basically said, if we're a family, then we need to live like a family. You'll look after her, and she can go to the kindergarten." Parental roles were reversed, with the father as the primary caregiver. However, the husband, still jobless, also found that this had advantages: "He took care of her, and he would also take her with him to the café, if that's what was needed, so he could meet up with his friends. I really don't think he was deprived of anything." She did confess that these choices were unsettling: "I [was] not exactly happy about this, but honestly it was good that way. . . . And then after a while she was big enough to take care of herself."[58]

This woman's colleague, the one who originally believed her work to be incompatible with marriage, found a similar mix of support from her husband and extended family. Child-rearing became a shared responsibility, with the husband often preparing meals, waking up the two children, and getting them off to school. Meanwhile, in summers, the couple relied on her family to give them extended breaks. "Because my parents moved to Montenegro," she said, "I could send my kids there to spend [time]. They were little, and my mom was happy to have them. Plus, they lived in a house with my brother . . . They could go to the beach and play around and enjoy themselves." When the children were away, the couple undertook adventures together: "He would come with me if I was on a long flight to, let's say, Sydney or Singapore. Or for my vacation, we would go and travel around to the places we liked, just the two of us." Over the years, this travel added up: "We flew to Rome, and then from Rome we flew to Geneva. And then we would go skiing in Switzerland, France, Austria." As part of JAT's winter vacations, the children sometimes accompanied their parents: "We got to take our children skiing at Jahorina [in Bosnia] or Kopaonik [in Serbia]. . . . It was really great."[59]

Over time, this stewardess realized that keeping her job benefited her family. "If you get your parents to help you out with the kids, and if you have the father of your children to look after them, then you can organize your life," she discovered. Coupled with JAT's perks, she said, "my husband and I had all the benefits you could get." Thus, when she pondered whether to stay at JAT, she now asked, "There are so many of my colleagues with a family, with children, and they still do the same job. Why shouldn't I?" The question was never fully resolved until her children were older. Instead, each year, she said, "You keep thinking, let's make it another year. You never said, I'm going to stop now or by the end of this year. You always thought, probably next year would be the best time to stop . . . It was always next year."[60]

Stewardesses at Air Jamaica had children just as frequently. A majority entered the job uncoupled and childless, but they tended to marry and have children over time. One stewardess from the class of 1970 remembered that her earliest years were very much aligned with Jet Age feminist norms: "At that time, I was free [and] single. I mean I had no children or anything, so I was just up and down, just trying to do . . . whatever it was to make life interesting. And, you know, flying with the airlines gave us the opportunity to do so many things," which included in her case being part of the flight attendant base in Frankfurt, where stewardesses lived for six months at a time. These adventures were curtailed sharply with the birth of the first of two daughters, when she chose to switch to a ground operations job.[61]

She was not alone in such moves. The airline by the 1980s had what one former stewardess described as "an aging flight attendant population . . . who now wanted to really have husbands, start families, have a more predictable schedule, and to really have off Christmas or New Years, or both." Staying on the job longer "create[d] a cycle of life where they want[ed] to have the husband and the children, and so they didn't want to work at times."[62] Another stewardess from the class of 1969 fit this pattern, as she finally looked to settle down after twenty years on the job. She then married a pilot and started a family, before finally quitting in 1992: "My younger daughter was two years, and I just wanted to go home . . . My husband had just made captain that year, and I said to him, 'Here's the deal: when you make captain, can I stop working?'"[63] Her husband's high salary allowed her to devote herself to their daughters, while his perks still benefited the entire family in terms of being able to travel.

A final account from an Air Jamaica stewardess details how single mothers coped with the contradictions between Jet Age feminism and motherhood. In her case, she lacked not only a husband, but also a parent or extended family member to help with the child. Yet, she found that her salary, supplements, and the additional money she made through trading sufficed for a true luxury: a live-in nanny. That said, her limited budget also limited where she could live. While she held dual citizenship as a Jamaican born in the United States, she settled with her daughter in Jamaica: "When I had my daughter, I was not going to go to the US with a young child as a single mother to put my child in day care while I go and do some little job to come home. No!"

The cost disparities between the two countries meant that Jamaica was the wiser choice: "In Jamaica you can afford to have a helper in your house. And I had a live-in helper every day from when she was born." Whereas in the United States, as she claimed, "You can't afford that nanny unless you're a movie star or very wealthy person," the reality in Jamaica was different: "In Jamaica you can have someone living in your house and paying them twenty US dollars a day." She concluded, "So, I was not willing to leave Jamaica," even though, "if I was married or had my boyfriend with me and it was just the two of us, I would probably have tried [living in the US]." Without affordable childcare, however, the prospect "was just a scary thought for me."[64]

By the 1970s flight attendants in the West had begun to catch up with their peers at JAT and Air Jamaica. The rights that JAT stewardesses had from the late 1940s to keep working regardless of age, marital status, or whether they had children—these same rights that were quickly won by stewardesses at Air Jamaica just a few years after their 1969 inaugural—slowly began to take root at American, Canadian, and Western European airlines as well. Within the European Economic Community, Sabena Airways' Gabrielle Defrenne helped dismantle such restrictions. When she won her case against Sabena at the European Court of Justice in 1976 for firing her at age forty, her victory forced changes to the hiring and firing policies of all Western European airlines.[65] Similarly in the United States, in the aftermath of the inclusion of employment protections for women in the 1964 Civil Rights Act, a series of flight attendant plaintiffs forced an end to such practices.[66] Ironically, Braniff was forced to change its policy on marriage bans in 1965, the same year that Mary Wells Lawrence launched the "Air Strip," when the airline lost an arbitration case brought by a secretly married stewardess.[67] Her precedent became a model for stewardesses at other airlines to use the Civil Rights Act in their favor.

In time, then, stewardesses from all the world's regions, whether West, East, or South, had converging workplace experiences. They also shared increasingly similar frustrations about income vulnerability, sexual harassment and abuse, and challenges with balancing work and family commitments. In this new moment in the 1970s, Western stewardesses joined the efforts of stewardesses at JAT and Air Jamaica to overcome the systemic injustices of Jet Age feminism. Of course, even before this moment the West's stewardesses also had private coping strategies to compensate for their comparatively low salaries, and they too found ways to navigate the risks of sexual abuse on the job. With the end of marriage and pregnancy bans, these stewardesses then also struggled to develop private solutions to childcare and to find more egalitarian marriages.

Thus, perhaps the only unique elements of JAT and Air Jamaica stewardesses' narratives involve their opportunity to import and trade hard-to-find goods from the West. These activities arose in economic systems of comparative deprivation, which in turn led their governments to pursue economic development programs that included more import restrictions and currency controls. Surely, some Western European stewardesses also traded in goods like designer jeans (which were always much cheaper in the United States) and some American flight attendants were also tempted to smuggle drugs into the country. But these activities did not occur with the same regularity as in Yugoslavia and Jamaica.

Ultimately, then, Jet Age feminism became not only a worldwide trend in aviation but also a worldwide scourge for stewardesses. Its vision of "liberation" via a consumption-based beauty regimen and the marketing of oneself as not only physically alluring but also sexually freethinking and available had downsides for all flight attendants. The truest allies of these working women were the West's Second Wave feminists, Yugoslavia's socialist feminists who called on the state to deepen its commitment to women's rights, and Jamaica's Third World feminists like Beverley Anderson Manley, who combined the fight for women's workplace rights with a racial reckoning for Black Jamaicans. In the end, these movements created a global flight attendant corps in which the worst of the indignities of Mary Wells Lawrence's "Air Strip" could be jettisoned by 1980. Gone were the very short skirts, the denial of flight attendants' safety roles, and the patronizing gimmickry of Air Jamaica's fashion shows.[68]

The future was not all rosy, however. Even as the 1970s saw progress against the overt sexualization of stewardesses, airlines across the world continued to ignore the rampant incidents of sexual harassment that took place on planes and on layovers. A 2018 survey commissioned by the largest labor union for flight attendants in the United States found that 68 percent of flight attendants had experienced sexual harassment while working.[69] There remains little incentive for airlines to go after passengers, pilots, or fellow flight attendants who engage in such activity. Meanwhile, another glaring failure of Jet Age feminism, income insecurity, has only worsened over time. Flight attendants at airlines in the West did see rising salaries through the 1970s, but a wave of neoliberal changes started soon thereafter, especially in concert with the United States' deregulation of the airline industry in 1978. The resulting competition has certainly lowered the cost of air tickets for passengers, but it has also led to major cuts in flight attendant salaries, such that only more senior flight attendants at higher-end legacy carriers can aspire to enter the middle class.

Neoliberalism hit both Jamaica and Yugoslavia even harder, though with a different and arguably even blunter instrument: IMF-imposed austerity programs. By the mid-1970s Jamaica and Yugoslavia had unsustainable debt burdens, and the countries' state-owned airlines were identified as austerity targets. Salaries for flight attendants on permanent contracts were reduced, though they typically remained at levels high enough to keep workers in the middle class. Both airlines now saved money by leaving more flight attendants on short-term, contingent contracts, sometimes for several years. These moves only exacerbated preexisting undesirable behaviors among such flight attendants: more importing of goods to sell on the black market, more creative use of per diems from layovers outside the country.

This evidence illustrates how flight attendants have been deeply disadvantaged by Jet Age feminism. They lacked a voice to counter their employers' rigorous beauty standards and sexualized marketing campaigns, and they suffered as a result. It was mainly through their own ingenuity and mutual support—these private acts of resistance—that many were able to persist in this career despite its risks. Yet, even as they constantly fought sexism, these women struggled to find common ground with more progressive feminists, who often saw stewardesses as willingly complicit in Jet Age feminism's beauty and sexual norms. This positioning in a sort of no-man's-land (if you will) regarding feminism was borne out in one interview with a member of JAT's class of 1969. When asked, "Do you consider yourself as a feminist?" there was a long pause and quite a bit of facial contortion. Then came laughter.

There was so much that did not make sense about the question. There was the fact that "feminists" barely existed in Yugoslavia when she started working, then had been aligned against stewardesses later in the 1970s when she was still young. There was also the fact that feminism has often been treated as a Western import that did not necessarily pertain to local realities. This sentiment is perhaps even stronger in today's post-Yugoslav Serbia, with its nationalist, largely anti-Western political climate. When she finally spoke, she first said, "I don't know how to answer that question. I need to think about it." Then, as she further pondered her struggles for dignity as a Jet Age stewardess, she did offer one addition: "But I like the place that women now have in the world. They have the right to show their own opinions, and all that is more acceptable now than before. So I think that women are going in the right direction."[70]

Conclusion

In 1943 Clare Boothe Luce introduced an idealistic and cosmopolitan yearning that, she predicted, would disrupt world politics after World War II. It was a yearning she found among young Americans: "The post-war air policy of these hundreds of thousands of young air-minded Americans is quite simple. It is: 'We want to fly everywhere. Period.'"[1] Were her views a bit less confined by her nationalism—in other words, less tied to "keeping America on wings all over the world"—she would have recognized similar yearnings happening the world over, on both sides of the Iron Curtain and both sides of the gaping North-South divide.[2] She also would have recognized that in the postwar moment more airlines than just those of Western Europe would strive to compete with American airlines.

Boothe Luce acknowledged that she had "every desire to see the British Overseas Airways Corporation shoving us so closely in many regions of the world" in a global competition for profits.[3] Yet, it did not enter her calculus that airlines from Yugoslavia in Europe's socialist East and from Jamaica in the Global South would eventually compete as well, at least in modest ways. After all, the perception, even in Belgrade and Kingston, was that the geopolitical realities of the Cold War disadvantaged smaller and poorer states. Thus, their new entrants into global aviation, JAT Airways and Air Jamaica, had a more pressing motive than profit for challenging Boothe Luce's efforts to resuscitate the cartography of colonialism. For these airlines and the states that owned them, ideological commitments to nonalignment in the Cold War or to postcolonialism in the age of decolonization turned aviation into a sphere in which they could combat America's market imperialism. As part I of this book details, each country's aspirations to forge greater political and economic sovereignty were at stake. As Clare Boothe Luce well knew, this was a world where such benefits accrued disproportionately to larger and more powerful states and their essential allies. Neither Yugoslavia nor Jamaica was destined to be either powerful or essential.

Importantly, Clare Boothe Luce's articulation of the desire to fly everywhere had its origins, though subtly obscured, in her commitment to women's liberation. Her famous articulation from 1943 was in fact a loose reiteration of a feminist sentiment she composed for her 1936 play *The Women*, in which a main character optimistically asserts how women "do all the things men do," not least of which is "fly[ing] aeroplanes across the ocean."[4] Thus, as this book traces in parts II and III, the spread of aviation after World War II corresponded with the spread of new roles for women—as workers, as travelers, as harbingers of modernity—that offered exhilarating potential for women's liberation. With the global adoption of women into the flight attendant profession after World War II, stewardesses assumed a position on this fault line of potential progress for women and potential backlash against such changes. These were, after all, the only women allowed to work aboard the planes that now crisscrossed the globe. And yet, whether in the pre-jet era or in the Jet Age itself, none of the Cold War's three worlds afforded these women an empowered experience as workers that would have put them on the same level as men. Full women's liberation was seen more as a threat than as progress, even in places like Yugoslavia where there was both a legal commitment to women's full equality and a wartime legacy in which women truly did "all the things that men do," including soldiering for the country.

If this book were to continue its investigation beyond its rough conclusion point of the late 1970s, it would chronicle far more defeats than victories, whether for the geopolitical battle against the West's cartography of colonialism or the West's iterations of pseudo-liberation for women like the ethos of Jet Age feminism from the 1960s and '70s.

In terms of part I's focus on airlines as tools for pushing back against Western dominance, neither Air Jamaica nor JAT entered the 1980s (and especially not the 1990s) with the same potential as before to disrupt the cartography of colonialism. In the example of Air Jamaica, the airline's debt burden became perilously high as the losses of the 1970s persisted. This did not, however, mean that the airline contracted its route network in the 1980s. In fact, as competitors like Pan Am also succumbed to financial pressures, Air Jamaica had even more incentive to maintain its connectivity with various cities beyond the obvious regional hubs that American market imperialists would have cited as desirable destinations. The airline became a cash-starved behemoth for Jamaican standards, a too-big-to-fail company that drained state coffers. However, even as the airline's labor unrest increased, maintenance on aircraft was deferred, and overall reliability suffered, the country's tourist resorts depended on Air Jamaica more than ever.

Air Jamaica failed to post profits as a government-run enterprise through the 1980s, then also as a private company after 1994, when hotelier Gordon "Butch" Stewart and a group of investors purchased the airline. Stewart's group lost US$674 million over ten years. The airline was back in government hands after 2004, but this change only exacerbated its problems. Its annual debt tripled under government control, with losses totaling US$900 million over the next half decade.[5] Finally, in 2011, the government acquiesced to IMF demands that it sell the airline, and Air Jamaica disappeared. The Jamaican government assumed a 16-percent share in Trinidad's Caribbean Airlines (the former BWIA) as part of the transaction, mainly to protect a few essential nonstop routes between Jamaica and North America. It also secured assurances that some Jamaicans would continue working as pilots, technicians, and flight attendants. Caribbean Airlines is still flying today and still losing money, despite reducing its long-haul Jamaica routes to just New York, Toronto, and a few Florida cities.

JAT, too, barely survived the awful decades of civil strife and eventually outright war from the mid-1980s onward. In its modest way, JAT exacerbated Yugoslavia's debt crisis, as the government was forced to cover the airline's consistent deficits that accrued through the 1970s and 1980s. Nonetheless, JAT continued to expand in these years and boasted an impressively global route network and growing passenger numbers. It reached its passenger peak in 1987, when it handled over 4.5 million passengers flying in various directions: to a large set of cities within Yugoslavia, dozens in Europe, several lucrative routes to the Middle East (especially to Iraq and Libya), and long-haul destinations stretching from Los Angeles to Sydney.[6] All the same, it too, like Air Jamaica, was increasingly fragile in terms of its financial health, accruing ever more debt as the overall Yugoslav economy was roiled in the late 1980s by IMF-imposed shocks and growing political destabilization within the federation.

In the 1990s, JAT was hobbled by the fact that it was the airline for postwar Europe's first failed state since World War II. When the Yugoslav state started to disintegrate in 1991, with particularly vicious wars flaring in now-independent Croatia and Bosnia-Herzegovina, JAT barely stayed alive. As the national carrier for Yugoslavia, JAT's raison d'etre diminished with each republic's declaration of independence. It technically remained Yugoslavia's carrier through the 1990s and early years of the twenty-first century, even as Yugoslavia at the time consisted only of Serbia and Montenegro. When Montenegro left this union in 2006, the now very awkwardly named JAT (Yugoslav Aerotransport) served as the national airline of only one republic, Serbia. It finally rebranded as Air Serbia in 2013, with a new ownership structure comprised of the Serbian government as majority shareholder and Etihad Airways of Abu Dhabi as both the minority shareholder and the airline's de facto operational manager. In 2023 the Serbian government completed its buyout from Etihad and now owns 100 percent of Air Serbia.[7]

Despite JAT's afterlife as Air Serbia, aviation in the states of the former Yugoslavia and in Jamaica roughly mirror what America's nationalist-globalists like Clare Boothe Luce envisioned back in 1943. In their view, American carriers would dominate Caribbean traffic, with routes to places like Jamaica determined by the flow of capital and people from the nearby economic hubs in North America. Likewise—especially if communism had not taken root after World War II—less economically powerful European regions like the Western Balkans would have also seen their air traffic dominated by Western European carriers linking the region to more economically prominent cities further west. Indeed, the lion's share of flights into and out of Jamaica today are on American airlines, with Canadian carriers also having a robust presence. Meanwhile, in the former Yugoslavia, foreign-owned low-cost carriers rival the airlines of the German-based Lufthansa Group (Lufthansa, Austrian, Swiss) for top market share in almost every city, with most flights heading to cities in the European Union's wealthier countries further west and north. Belgrade, as the hub of Air Serbia, and Zagreb, the hub of Croatia Airlines, are the only former Yugoslav cities where domestic capacity outstrips foreign capacity.

Just as Jamaican and socialist-era Yugoslav planners' creative responses to the cartography of colonialism have been erased, similar backsliding is evident regarding flight attendants' status. Of course, there have been some positive developments since Jet Age feminism took off in the mid-1960s. Most importantly, the worst abuses perpetuated against stewardesses in the West have been eradicated. These women can now marry, have children, weigh what they want (as long as they can pass through an emergency exit), and work until they are no longer able. The airlines' pilot corps and management teams are also more open to women than ever before, affording women more prospects than the single dead-end, lower-paying, pink-collar job of stewardessing, into which all women were formerly corralled.

But what of aspiring women—or men, for that matter—from Jamaica or from the vast swaths of the former Yugoslavia who are now without national carriers? With no local airline to offer jobs, these work-seekers follow the pathways of the neoliberal economy into far less attractive positions. Many Jamaicans working as flight attendants or pilots do so with low-cost carriers like Spirit or JetBlue based in the United States. The same option exists for citizens of the former republics of Yugoslavia, who find positions at airlines like Wizz Air, Ryanair, and EasyJet. When they do, they typically surrender the most promising benefits of the golden years at Air Jamaica or JAT. Their pay is far lower, their time off is less, generous maternity leave options may not exist (especially at American-based carriers), and other perks like JAT's all-expenses-paid vacations are gone as well.

For other Jamaicans or citizens of the Western Balkans, the pathway to a job in aviation leads them even further afield, to the Gulf States of the Arabian Peninsula. Airlines like Emirates, Etihad, and Qatar offer tax-free salaries and free living quarters at their home bases, in return for the massive sacrifice of leaving families and friends back home. Wahhabist-inspired social strictures, enforced at least partly on foreign workers, also jeopardize one's personal freedoms, especially when living as women and/or as queers in these base cities. Moreover, these airlines' oversight of flight attendants leaves employees vulnerable to Braniff-style discrimination: weight restrictions, grooming regimens, and uniform requirements are all enforced with the vigor of American carriers a half century ago.

Meanwhile, the global decline of states' safety-net benefits under neoliberalism has left all women—certainly including flight attendants—more vulnerable to concerns about income stability and caring for their families. The interviews shared in chapter 10 from Air Jamaica and JAT flight attendants coping with these pressures under Jet Age feminism revealed a crucial insight: even women living in states ostensibly committed to social welfare had to cope with these struggles privately. Income instability led many of these women to become entrepreneurial even in the 1970s, as though they were the precursors of workers in today's neoliberal gig economy. Meanwhile, obligations for childcare were similarly shouldered by stewardesses themselves, in tandem with husbands and concerned grandparents and neighbors. Neither the state nor the employer assumed responsibility for alleviating such family burdens.

As feminist scholar Nancy Fraser argues when addressing caregiving under neoliberalism, this same privatization of women's burdens transpires today.[8] Fraser presses for feminists to engage with other activist groups in order to push back against neoliberalism's attack on state-based or otherwise communal solutions for social ills like poverty, racism, and sexism. Catherine Rottenberg, in her critique of what she calls "neoliberal feminism," adds to this point, expressing alarm about "the increasing compatibility of mainstream feminism with the market values of neoliberalism. What does it mean, many longtime feminists are asking, that a movement once dedicated, however problematically at times, to women's liberation is now being framed in extremely individualistic terms."[9]

Fraser and Rottenberg are particularly critical of neoliberal feminists like former Meta COO Sheryl Sandberg. In her 2015 best-selling book *Lean In*, Sandberg affirms the long-held feminist aspiration that women will attain all the access to work and wealth that men do.[10] It is not difficult to hear the echoes of Clare Boothe Luce from 1936 in Sandberg's yearning: "These days . . . ladies do all the things men do," or at least so they should. Yet, consistent with a neoliberal framing that privatizes efforts to gain equality, Sandberg promotes a self-help credo, encouraging women to fix their own perceived inadequacies that are holding them back. At no point does she support a broader effort to root sexism out of the underlying social system.

This work on Jet Age feminism in the 1960s and '70s adds two important contributions to the field that scholars like Fraser and Rottenberg have opened. First, it globalizes their critique of feminisms that privatize women's struggles for equality. As chapter 10 details, the very same privatization of protests against Jet Age feminism that feminist scholars now see happening under neoliberalism were happening in socialist-era Yugoslavia and postindependence Jamaica as well. Yet, even more importantly, this work deepens the historical context of these feminist scholars' claims regarding neoliberalism and feminism.

While Fraser and Rottenberg trace the rise of imposter feminisms to the decades since 1990, a very similar dynamic was already at play in the 1960s. The perpetrators were women in the United States, positioned similarly to Sheryl Sandberg, who succeeded as corporate executives in fields of social influence like advertising and publishing. Helen Gurley Brown published *Sex and the Single Girl* in 1962 to stress that young women could now have it all: career work, steady income, sexual freedom, groovy fashion, and ample travel. And when Mary Wells Lawrence applied this ethos in her makeover of stewardesses in 1965, she promoted the lie that these lower-middle-class working women could have it all as well. Never did either Brown or Wells Lawrence attack the underlying sexist culture that kept women economically vulnerable and socially disempowered. Instead, books like *Sex and the Single Girl* offered a how-to manual for young women to remake themselves as Jet Age feminists.

This formula worked impressively well for Brown and Wells Lawrence, who, like Sandberg, enjoyed abundant financial resources. They could spend their way to beauty and pay a nanny to resolve the time dilemma posed by childcare demands. Yet, for stewardesses—indeed, for all non-elite women aspiring to live out the Jet Age feminist ethos promoted in *Cosmo* and at Braniff—there were too few options to circumvent the contradictions of Jet Age feminism. For these women, solutions to income instability, sexual harassment, and especially childcare were already privatized in the 1960s. When faced with the saccharine vision of women's liberation offered by Jet Age feminism, these working women had to shut up, dress the part, and smile invitingly at the next set of passengers who boarded their airlines' jets heading far away.

NOTES

Introduction

1. Clare Boothe Luce, "America in the Post-War Air World," *Congressional Record—House*, 78th Congress, February 23, 1943, 762.
2. Daniel Immerwahr, *How to Hide an Empire: A History of the Greater United States* (New York: Farrar, Straus and Giroux, 2019), 17.
3. Victoria De Grazia, *Irresistible Empire: America's Advance through Twentieth-Century Europe* (Cambridge, MA: Belknap Press of Harvard University Press, 2005), 3.
4. Boothe Luce, "America," 760.
5. Boothe Luce, "America," 761.
6. For a better understanding of global history, consult Sebastian Conrad, *What Is Global History?* (Princeton, NJ: Princeton University Press, 2017). For an example that applies global history to an investigation of aviation, see Andreas Greiner, "Aviation History and Global History: Towards a Research Agenda for the Interwar Period," *Bulletin of the German Historical Institute* 69 (Fall 2021–Spring 2022): 123–50.
7. This work is not the first to chronicle the development of civil aviation outside the West, even if the number of scholars writing such accounts is still quite modest. See, for example, Arratee Ayuttacorn and Jane Ferguson, "Air Male: Exploring Flight Attendant Masculinities in North America and Thailand," *The Asia Pacific Journal of Anthropology* 20, no. 4 (2019): 328–43; Willie Hiatt, *The Rarified Air of the Modern: Airplanes and Technological Modernity in the Andes* (New York: Oxford University Press, 2016); Elizabeth Manley, "Runway Hospitality: Air Jamaica's 'Rare Tropical Birds' and the Embodied Gender and Race Politics of Tourism, 1966-1980," *Hispanic American Historical Review* 102, no. 1 (2022): 285–319; Philip Muehlenbeck, "Czechoslovak Aviation Assistance to Africa (1960-1968)," in *Czechoslovakia in Africa, 1945–1968* (New York: Palgrave Macmillan, 2016), 125–56; Jessica Lynne Pearson, "Decolonizing the Sky: Global Air Travel at the End of Empire," *Humanity: An International Journal of Human Rights, Humanitarianism, and Development* 14, no. 1 (2023): 68–84; Peter Svik, *Civil Aviation and the Globalization of the Cold War* (Cham: Palgrave Macmillan, 2020); Jenifer Van Vleck, "An Airline at the Crossroads of the World: Ariana Afghan Airlines, Modernization, and the Global Cold War," *History and Technology* 25, no. 1 (2009): 3–24; John D. Wong, *Hong Kong Takes Flight: Commercial Aviation and the Making of a Global Hub, 1930s–1998* (Cambridge, MA: Harvard University Asia Center, 2022); and Waqar Zaidi, "Pakistani Civil Aviation and

U.S. Aid to Pakistan, 1950 to 1961," *The Journal of Research Institute for the History of Global Arms Transfer* 8 (2019): 83-97.

8. This book occasionally employs the Cold War-era terminology of three worlds since it offers a convenient shorthand for the geopolitical and social divisions of the time. Nevertheless, I recognize the problematic nature of this terminology. Thus, I more frequently refer to the First World as the North Atlantic realm or the West. I also prefer Europe's socialist East to Second World and Global South to Third World.

As shorthand, I occasionally use the term "East," and capitalize it, to refer to this Cold War-era rendering of the term. East, in this sense, refers to the area consisting of the Soviet Union and its (supposedly) loyal satellite states in Yugoslavia and elsewhere in Eastern and East-Central Europe. Thus, whereas a capitalized "East" might be more familiar to readers today as a reference to Asia, during the Cold War's tug of war "West" and "East" referenced the capitalist democracies and their communist adversaries.

On the 1952 creation of the terminology of First, Second, and Third Worlds by anticolonial advocate Albert Sauvy, see Alfred Sauvy, "Trois Mondes, Une Planete," *L'Observateur*, August 14, 1952. Also note Sauvy's contribution in Georges Balandier, ed., *Le Tiers-monde: Sous-développement et développement* (Paris: Presses universitaires de France, 1961). Discussion and critique of Sauvy's creation of the terms is found in Vijay Prashad, *The Darker Nations: A People's History of the Third World* (New York: New Press, 2007), 6-7.

9. Kosta Bojović, interview with author, Belgrade, Serbia, May 11, 2018.

10. Sharon Brandt, interview with author, Kingston, Jamaica, January 14, 2018.

11. Exceptions to BOAC's policy of hiring only flight attendants from Britain were made for stewardesses whose Asian homelands were not only culturally distinct, but also linguistically different. Thus, in 1949, BOAC hired a cadre of stewardesses from Hong Kong, soon followed by women from Pakistan and Singapore.

12. Sharon Brandt, interview with author.

13. Stef Jansen, "The Afterlives of the Yugoslav Red Passport," *Citizenship in Southeast Europe* (blog), October 24, 2012, https://www.citsee.eu/citsee-story/afterlives-yugoslav-red-passport.

14. Works chronicling Yugoslavia's uniquely liberal border policies include William Zimmerman, *Open Borders, Nonalignment, and the Political Evolution of Yugoslavia* (Princeton, NJ: Princeton University Press, 2014). On Jamaica's and Yugoslavia's migration histories, see Lara Putnam, *Radical Moves: Caribbean Migrants and the Politics of Race in the Jazz Age* (Chapel Hill: University of North Carolina Press, 2013) and Brigitte Le Normand, *Citizens without Borders: Yugoslavia and Its Migrant Workers in Western Europe* (Toronto: University of Toronto Press, 2021).

15. Regarding the West Indies Federation, British plans by the mid-1950s were to bestow independence not on Jamaica itself, since the island had fewer than two million citizens and possessed limited natural resources, but rather on a federation composed of nine of its colonies in the region. When preparations became more contentious, Jamaicans opted out in a September 1961

referendum. This was a decisive defeat for Jamaica's colonial-era premier Norman Manley at the hands of his political rival Alexander Bustamante, who campaigned strongly for a go-it-alone approach to independence. Jamaica thus became independent as a single entity.

16. Immerwahr, *How to Hide an Empire*, 312.

17. Immerwahr, *How to Hide an Empire*, 314.

18. JAT purchased six Ilyushin Il-14 planes from the Soviets in 1957, after Tito and Nikita Khrushchev temporarily normalized relations. However, these planes were deemed so fragile and expensive to repair that they were largely replaced with the planes they were supposed to retire: World War II-era American-made DC-3s. Jovo Simišić, *Bio Jedan JAT* (Belgrade: Lighthouse Studio, 2022), 20-21.

19. This quote comes from the renowned aircraft engineer Milenko Mitrović, who was commissioned by the Yugoslav state in August 1945 to assess how to rebuild Yugoslavia's aviation sector. Report from Milenko Mitrović to Privredni savet D. F. J., August 20, 1945, 1, Istorijska beleška fonda vlade FNRJ—Predsedništva vlada, fond 50, subset 85-181, Archives of Yugoslavia (Arhiv Jugoslavije), Belgrade, Serbia (hereafter AJ).

20. Orlando Patterson, *The Confounding Island: Jamaica and the Postcolonial Predicament* (Cambridge, MA: Harvard University Press, 2019), 12. Patterson credits Roland Robertson with popularizing the term glocalization: Roland Robertson, "Glocalization: Time-Space and Homogeneity-Heterogeneity," in *Global Modernities*, ed. Mike Featherstone, Scott Lash, and Roland Robertson (London: Sage, 1995), 25-44.

21. Betty Friedan, *The Feminine Mystique: Annotated Text, Contexts, Scholarship*, 50th anniversary ed. (New York: W. W. Norton, 2013). This book was originally published in 1963.

22. My work on stewardesses in the former Yugoslavia and Jamaica is aligned with the relevant literature on women's history in both societies. On the former Yugoslavia: Jelena Batinić, *Women and Yugoslav Partisans: A History of World War II Resistance* (Cambridge: Cambridge University Press, 2015); Chiara Bonfiglioli, *Women and Industry in the Balkans: The Rise and Fall of the Yugoslav Textile Sector* (London: I.B. Taurus, 2019); Neda Božinović, *Žensko pitanje u Srbiji u XIX i XX veku* (Belgrade: Dvadesetčetvrta, 1996); Ana Devic, "Redefining the Public-Private Boundary: Nationalism and Women's Activism in Former Yugoslavia," *Anthropology of East Europe Review* 15, no. 2 (1997): 45-61; Vera Gudac Dodić, *Žena u Socijalizmu: Položaj žene u Srbiju u drugoj polovini 20. veka* (Belgrade: Institut za noviju istoriju Srbije, 2006); Andreja Dugandžić and Tijana Okić, eds., *The Lost Revolution: Women's Antifascist Front between Myth and Forgetting* (Sarajevo: Association for Culture and Art CRVENA, 2018); Barbara Jancar-Webster, *Women and Revolution in Yugoslavia, 1941-1945* (Denver, CO: Arden Press, 1990); Jovanka Kecman, *Žene Jugoslavije u radničkom pokretu i ženskim organicijama 1918-1941* (Belgrade: Institut za savremenu istoriju, 1978); Julie Mostov, "Sexing the Nation/Desexing the Body: Politics of National Identity in the Former Yugoslavia," in *Gender Ironies of Nationalism: Sexing the Nation*, ed. Tamar Mayer (New York: Routledge, 2012), 89-112; Mirjana Morokvašić, "Being a Woman in Yugoslavia: Past, Present, and Institutional Equality," in

Women of the Mediterranean, ed. Monique Gadant (London: Zed Books, 1986), 120–38; Ivana Pantelić, *Partizanke kao građanke: Društvena emancipacija partizanki u Srbiji, 1945–1953* (Belgrade: Institut za savremenu istoriju, 2011); Sabrina P. Ramet, *Gender Politics in the Western Balkans: Women and Society in Yugoslavia and the Yugoslav Successor States* (College Park: Pennsylvania State University Press, 2010); Marijana Stojčić and Nađa Duhaček, "From Partisans to Housewives: Representation of Women in Yugoslav Cinema," *Časopis za povijest Zapadne Hrvatske* 11 (2016): 69–107; Susan L. Woodward, "The Rights of Women: Ideology, Policy, and Social Change in Yugoslavia," in *Women, State, and Party in Eastern Europe*, ed. Sharon L. Wolchik and Alfred G. Meyer (Durham, NC: Duke University Press, 1985), 234–56.

On Jamaica: Henrice Altink, *Destined for a Life of Service: Defining African-Jamaican Womanhood, 1865–1938* (Manchester, UK: Manchester University Press, 2011); Barbara Bailey, Bridget Brereton, and Verene Shepherd, eds., *Engendering History: Cultural and Socio-economic Realities in Africa* (New York: Palgrave Macmillan, 1995); Carolyn Cooper, "Caribbean Fashion Week: Remodeling Beauty in 'Out of Many One' Jamaica," *Fashion Theory* 14, no. 3 (September 2010): 387–404; Honor Ford-Smith, "Making White Ladies: Race, Gender, and the Production of Identities in Late Colonial Jamaica," *Resources for Feminist Research* 23, no. 4 (1994): 55–67; Rosamond S. King, *Island Bodies: Transgressive Sexualities in the Caribbean Imagination* (Gainesville: University Press of Florida, 2014); Patricia Mohammed, "'But Most of All Mi Love Me Browning': The Emergence in Eighteenth- and Nineteenth-Century Jamaica of the Mulatto Woman as the Desired," *Feminist Review* 65 (Summer 2000): 22–48; Janet Momsen, ed., *Women and Change in the Caribbean: A Pan-Caribbean Perspective* (Bloomington: Indiana University Press, 1993); Rochelle Rowe, *Imagining Caribbean Womanhood: Race, Nation and Beauty Contests, 1929–70* (Manchester, UK: Manchester University Press, 2013); Consuelo López Springfield, *Daughters of Caliban: Caribbean Women in the Twentieth Century* (Bloomington: Indiana University Press, 1997); Michelle Ann Stephens, *Black Empire: The Masculine Global Imaginary of Caribbean Intellectuals in the United States, 1914–1962* (Durham, NC: Duke University Press, 2005).

23. Diplomatic historian H. W. Brands considers Yugoslavia as a "wedge" to stress its in-between role in European and Cold War geopolitics. Henry William Brands, *The Specter of Neutralism: The United States and the Emergence of the Third World, 1947–1960* (New York: Columbia University Press, 1990), esp. 313–15. Meanwhile, the social historian Predrag Marković speaks of the city of Belgrade as being a cultural fusion that combined East and West in the Cold War years. Predrag J. Marković, *Beograd između istoka i zapada: 1948–1965* (Belgrade: Službeni list SRJ, 1996).

24. The historian Colin Palmer stresses the various ways in which Jamaica's sense of nationhood balances its legacy as a colony of Great Britain—and thereby a product of the West—and more vocal expressions of Pan-Africanism through the twentieth century. Colin Palmer, *Inward Yearnings: Jamaica's Journey to Nationhood* (Kingston: University of the West Indies Press, 2016).

1. Clare Boothe Luce

1. Jenifer Van Vleck, *Empire of the Air: Aviation and the American Ascendancy* (Cambridge, MA: Harvard University Press, 2013), 197.
2. As quoted in Marie Brenner, "Fast and Luce," *Vanity Fair*, March 1988.
3. Henry Luce, "The American Century," 1941, reprinted in *Diplomatic History* 23, no. 2 (Spring 1999), 166.
4. As quoted in Gayle Corbett Shirley, *More than Petticoats: Remarkable Montana Women* (Lanham, MD: Rowman & Littlefield, 2010), 100.
5. An important historical work on separate spheres is Linda K. Kerber, "Separate Spheres, Female Worlds, Woman's Place: The Rhetoric of Women's History," *Journal of American History* 75, no. 1 (1988): 9–39.
6. Details on Boothe Luce's political rise are found in Sylvia Jukes Morris, *Price of Fame: The Honorable Clare Boothe Luce* (New York: Random House, 2015).
7. Boothe Luce, "America," 763.
8. Boothe Luce, "America," 759.
9. Boothe Luce, "America," 762.
10. For deliberations leading up to the 1944 Chicago conference and proceedings at the conference itself, see Alan Dobson, *A History of International Civil Aviation: From Its Origins through Transformative Evolution* (London: Taylor and Francis, 2017).
11. Boothe Luce, "America," 760.
12. Boothe Luce, "America," 761.
13. Boothe Luce, "America," 762.
14. Boothe Luce, "America," 763.
15. Boothe Luce, "America," 762–63.
16. Boothe Luce, "America," 760.
17. For details on how the United States exercised strategic and commercial control over such "emporia" cities, see Irene Gendzier's account of US-Lebanese relations and the subsequent forging of Beirut into a regional hub of American activity in the early Cold War: *Notes from the Minefield: United States Intervention in Lebanon, 1945–1958* (New York: Columbia University Press, 2006).
18. Various historians have written on the Chicago conference and the resulting international aviation order. The historian who best considers the conference's creation of a binding legal and economic system is the late Alan Dobson. See especially his *History of International Civil Aviation*.
19. A copy of the original Bermuda Agreement from 1946 is available at: https://en.wikisource.org/wiki/Bermuda_Agreement.
20. Print ads from Pan Am have been consulted at the J. Walter Thompson Company Publications Collection, 1887–2005, David M. Rubenstein Rare Book and Manuscript Library, Duke University, Durham, NC (hereafter JWT).
21. Boothe Luce, "America," 762.
22. Boothe Luce, "America," 759.
23. An authoritative source on developments in the Eastern bloc, with a special emphasis on Soviet and Czechoslovak developments, is Peter Svik, *Civil Aviation and the Globalization of the Cold War* (Cham: Palgrave Macmillan, 2020), esp. 20–23.

24. Japan Air Lines inaugurated flights from Tokyo to Wake Island, Honolulu, and San Francisco in 1954, marking it as the first Asian carrier to fly to the United States. Air India, meanwhile, became the first airline from the formerly colonized Global South to fly to the United States when it acquired its first Boeing 707 in May 1960.

25. An authoritative account of American machinations regarding Yugoslavia during the Cold War is found in Lorraine Lees, *Keeping Tito Afloat: The United States, Yugoslavia, and the Cold War* (University Park: Pennsylvania State University Press, 1997).

26. There were local efforts, albeit short-lived ones, to forge a Caribbean airline before World War II. See Chandra D. Bhimull, *Empire in the Air: Airline Travel and the African Diaspora* (New York: New York University Press, 2017).

27. The composition of the Yugoslav delegation in Chicago and their failure to sign the final treaty is noted in International Civil Aviation Conference, *Proceedings of the International Civil Aviation Conference: Chicago, Illinois, November 1–December 7, 1944*, vol. 1 (Washington, DC: US Government Printing Office, 1948).

28. International Civil Aviation Organization (ICAO), *Convention on International Civil Aviation Done at Chicago on the 7th Day of December 1944*. Text of the treaty, with original signatories, is found at: https://www.icao.int/publications/documents/7300_orig.pdf.

2. The Nonaligned Airline

1. The various constituent regions of Yugoslavia experienced different forms of oversight once the country was conquered in April 1941. Slovenia was swallowed into the German Reich itself; the "Independent State of Croatia," technically an Italian protectorate until 1943, ceded its coastlands to Italy and then was ruled by a Croatian fascist movement (the Ustaša); Bosnia and Herzegovina were subsumed into the Croatian fascist state; Kosovo was directly ruled by German forces in the interest of mining the region; Macedonia was absorbed into Bulgaria; the Banat region north of Belgrade was effectively placed under the control of local German populations; Hungary was granted the rest of the territory of Vojvodina; and Serbia was occupied by German forces and governed by a collaborative regime of Serbs under General Milan Nedić.

2. An overview of economic conditions in Yugoslavia at the dawn of the post–World War II era is found in Andrei Simić, *The Peasant Urbanites: A Study of Rural-Urban Mobility in Serbia* (New York: Seminar Press, 1973).

3. Memorandum, Milton M. Turner to George V. Allen, July 29, 1952, file 968.52/7-2952, 1950–54 Central Decimal File, Record Group 59: General Records of the Department of State (hereafter RG 59), National Archives (hereafter NARA).

4. Report, from Milenko Mitrović to Privredni savet D. F. J., August 20, 1945, 1, fond 50, Istorijska beleška fonda vlade FNRJ—Predsedništva vlada, subset 85-181, Archives of Yugoslavia (Arhiv Jugoslavije), Belgrade, Serbia (hereafter AJ).

5. Report, Mitrović to Privredni savet, August 20, 1945, 4.

6. In certain years and in certain documents, this agency was also called by a shorter name: the Main Authority for Aviation Transport (Glavna uprava vazduhoplovstvog saobraćaja, or GUVS).

7. JUSTA stands for Jugoslovensko-sovjetsko akcionarsko društvo za civilno vazduhoplovstvo, or the Yugoslav-Soviet Joint Stock Company for Civil Aviation. On JUSTA's brief history, see Ilija Kukobat, *Sovjetski uticaji na jugoslovensko vazduhoplovstvo 1944–1949: Između saradnje i suprotstavljanja* (Belgrade: Institut za savremenu istoriju, 2020).

8. The use of "East" in this chapter refers only to the Cold War connotation of the term and its application to Europe: East, in this sense, refers to the Soviet Union and its influence, which included Moscow's postwar vision for establishing loyal satellite states in East-Central Europe, including Yugoslavia.

9. Most significantly, lack of membership in the Chicago convention's organizations made it impossible for airlines of non-member states to sell tickets in ICAO member states, at least in their own name. Tickets would have to be sold by an ICAO member airline, which would then require side agreements with the non-member airline to transfer the funds onward. Additionally, airlines from non-member states were not accountable for maintaining the high technical standards required by the ICAO and IATA, making them riskier choices for customers and for governments considering whether to allow them to fly into their airports.

10. The directives from Tito to Mates are not found in the Ministry of Transportation's holdings. Instead, they are quoted post facto in: report, Komisija državne kontrole vlade FNRJ, "Izveštaj o pregledu Glavne uprave civilnog vazdušnog saobraćaja i njezinih preduzeća," January 1949, 4, fond 190, Komisija državne kontrole vlade FNRJ, 1946–51, subset 160–1611, AJ.

11. Hungary's Mazsovlet lasted as a joint venture from 1946 to 1954, before the Hungarian government took control of the airline and rebranded it MALÉV (Magyar Légiközlekedési Vállalat); Romania's joint venture with the Soviets was named TARS (Transporturi Aeriene Româno-Sovietic) and lasted for the same duration as the Hungarian-Soviet airline, before rebranding as TAROM (Transporturile Aeriene Române); Bulgaria's airline was known as TABSO (Transportno-aviazionno balgaro-savetsko obschtestvo) and also existed as a joint venture until 1954; it rebranded as Balkan Bulgarian Airlines in 1968.

12. While JAT was incorporated as a new company in 1947 and the prewar Kingdom of Yugoslavia's airline, Aeroput, was liquidated, certain members of the aviation community of Serbia stress an important link between the two airlines: many of JAT's first managers, pilots, and other employees were former Aeroput personnel. Today's Air Serbia—the legal successor of JAT—thereby claims a history of more than ninety years, including the Aeroput legacy.

13. Eastern European carriers, including even Poland's LOT (Polskie Linie Lotnicze) and Czechoslovakia's ČSA (Československé aerolinie), purchased and flew Soviet-built airliners in the Cold War period. See Svik, *Civil Aviation*.

JAT secured twelve DC-3s between 1947 and 1953, a few of the first ones artfully acquired through UN auspices after being decommissioned by the US military. JAT also possessed three German Junkers Ju-52 aircraft that had been captured during the war and then were prepped for civilian use. The lone exception to JAT's preference for Western aircraft was when it purchased Soviet planes in 1957, which were calamitous for the airline. See Simišić, *Bio Jedan JAT*, 20–21.

14. For Yugoslavia's involvement in the Trieste crisis, see Federico Tenca Montini, *Trst ne damo!: Jugoslavija i Tršćansko pitanje 1945–1954* (Zagreb: Srednja Europa, 2021). For consideration of Yugoslavia's support of communist rebels in the Greek Civil War and the preponderance of Slavic Macedonians in this struggle, see James Horncastle, *The Macedonian Slavs in the Greek Civil War, 1944–1949* (Lanham, MD: Lexington Books, 2019).

15. The records of the Ministry of Transportation provide little additional information on Pudarić. They do mention that he was a member of the Communist Party and attribute his westward orientation to contacts established during his education in France and his service as a pilot on behalf of the Yugoslav Army during World War II while based in the United Kingdom. He later joined the Partisans. More details on Pudarić can be found in Simišić, *Bio Jedan JAT*, 35–38 and 41–42.

16. Report, Glavna uprava za turizam, "Zapisnik po pitanjima civilnog vazdušnog saobraćaja, održane na poziv Glavne uprave za turizam u Beogradu," December 15, 1947, 5, fond 290, Jugoslovensko-Sovjetsko akcionarsko društvo za civilno vazduhoplovstvo–JUSTA, subset 2, AJ.

17. Report, Glavna uprava za turizam, December 15, 1947, 12.

18. This figure comes from: report, Filimena Mihajlovna, "Kratak izveštaj o pregledu Glavne uprave civilnog vazdušnog saobraćaja," December 29, 1948, 2, fond 19, Komisija državne kontrole vlade FNRJ, subset 160–1611, AJ.

19. Letter from Ivan Režić, secretary of the Ministry of Transportation, to Savet za Izgradnju Beograda, June 30, 1947, fond 50, Istorijska beleška fonda vlade FNRJ–Predsedništva vlada, subset 85–181, AJ.

20. "Razvoj našeg vazduhoplovnog saobraćaja," *Politika*, October 11, 1947, 5. The full plan itself is published as: Government of Yugoslavia, *Petogodišnji plan razvitka narodne privrede FNRJ u godinima 1947–1951* (Belgrade: RAD, 1948).

21. The figure of 6,421 passengers is found in: Savezni Zavod za Statistiku, *Saobraćaj i Veze 1958*, published as part of the series *Statistički Bilten*, vol. 149, October 1959, pp. 115, 117, fond 599 F-129, AJ. This figure, along with the other figures cited here, is repeated in Simišić, *Bio Jedan JAT*, 39–40.

22. Report, Ing. Vukan Dešić, pomoćnik ministra saobraćaja, "Zbirni Finansijski Plan JUSTA-e za II. Tromesečje 1947 g.," April 30, 1947, fond 290, Jugoslovensko-Sovjetsko akcionarsko društvo za civilno vazduhoplovstvo–JUSTA, subset 3, AJ.

23. Savezni Zavod za Statistiku, *Saobraćaj i Veze 1958*, 115, 117.

24. Report, "Predmet: JUSTA," February 12, 1949, fond 19, Komisija državne kontrole vlade FNRJ, subset: 161–1613, AJ.

25. According to the protocol signed on August 31, 1949, the Yugoslavs owed the Soviets a total of 28.5 million dinars, much of which is directly attributable to expenses for JUSTA. The Yugoslavs placed the full amount into a clearinghouse and the Ministry of Foreign Trade came to an agreement with

the USSR's trade representative in Yugoslavia about what amount of goods and money would be exchanged for full repayment. Protocol, "Protokol o likvidaciji Jugoslovensko-Sovjetskog dunavskog parobrodskog akcionarskog društva JUSPAD i Jugoslovensko-Sovjetskog akcionarskog društva za civilno vazduhoplovstvo JUSTA," fond 290, Jugoslovensko-Sovjetsko akcionarsko društvo za civilno vazduhoplovstvo–JUSTA, subset 4, AJ.

The overall Five-Year Plan was left unfulfilled, in part due to the upheaval with the Soviets. The government opted never to publish the results of the plan.

26. Letter from the director, Jugoslovenski Aerotransport to Češkoslovenske Aerolinije, November 12, 1949, fond 620, Uprava za civilno vazduhoplovstvo, subset F-56, AJ.

27. Report to Ministar saobraćaja FNRJ, "Predmet: Kadrovi u Glavnoj upravi za vazdušni saobraćaj," February 28, 1949, fond 19, Komisija državne kontrole vlade FNRJ, subset 160-1911, AJ.

28. Details on Pudarić's fate are found in Simišić, *Bio Jedan JAT*, 41–42. Discussion of the other "enemy agents" is found in: report, "Predmet: Kadrovi u Glavnoj upravi," February 28, 1949, 3-4.

29. The historian Petar Dragišić describes Yugoslavia's relations with Austria from 1945 to 1949 as "a war after the war," in that economic and political activity between the two countries was limited and adversarial, with the Yugoslav press and politicians stressing the complicity of Austrians in the Nazi occupation of parts of Yugoslavia and the war crimes committed therein. Petar Dragišić, "Rat posle rata: Jugoslavija i Austrija 1945-1949," in *Odnosi Jugoslavije i Austrije 1945–1955* (Belgrade: Institut za noviju istoriju Srbije, 2013), 25-102.

30. The diplomatic correspondence is quoted in Thomas Bürgisser, *Wahlverwandtschaft zweier Sonderfälle im Kalten Krieg: Schweizerische Perspektiven auf das sozialistische Jugoslawien 1943–1991* (Bern: Diplomatische Dokumente der Schweiz, 2017), 251. The citation for the original quote, as found in the Swiss Diplomatic Documents (DDS), is: Schreiben der Deutschen Interessenvertretung des EPD in Basel (F. Kästli) an den Vorsteher des EPD (M. Petitpierre) vom 16.6.1945; DDS, bd. 16, dok. 12, dodis.ch/316.

31. Bürgisser, *Wahlverwandtschaft zweier Sonderfälle*, 255.

32. It was in this financial context that the Yugoslav Foreign Ministry authorized the Ministry of Transportation to conclude negotiations with the Swiss in March 1949. Memo from K. Badnjević (načelnik IV odeljenje) to Ministarstvo Saobraćaja (GUCVS), March 14, 1949, godina 1949, zemlja Švajcarska, fascikla 103, dosije 16, Vazdušni saobraćaj sa Švajcarskom, broj dok. 44631, Diplomatic Archives (Diplomatski Arhiv), Ministarstvo spoljnih poslova, Republic of Serbia, Belgrade, Serbia (hereafter DA).

33. Protocol, "Rešenje o potvrdi Sporazuma o vazdušnom saobraćaju između Federativne Narodne Republike Jugoslavije i Sjedinjenih Američkih Država," December 24, 1949, fond 50, Istorijska beleška fonda vlade FNRJ–Predsedništva vlada, subset 65-146, AJ.

34. To account for this relative largesse, an October 1950 State Department memo characterized this and future connections between Yugoslavia and the West to be in America's national interest: "The Embassy [in Belgrade] felt at the time that the existing transport connections were insufficient in view of

Yugoslavia's increasing economic and political orientation toward the West." Dispatch, from Belgrade to Department of State, Air Service between Belgrade and Athens or Rome, March 27, 1951, file 968.5281/3-2751, RG 59, NARA.

35. The economic aspects of American-Yugoslav relations were finalized about a year and a half before the aviation agreement, in July 1948. See Lees, *Keeping Tito Afloat*.

36. Memo from Yugoslav Embassy, Washington, DC, "Otvorena pitanja iz naših finansiskih odnosa sa SAD," September 28, 1949, godina 1949, fascikla 96, dosije 10, Naši trgovački odnosi sa S. Amerikom, broj dok. 423456, DA.

37. Dispatch from Belgrade to Department of State, "Memorandum of Conversation, Subject: Yugoslav Civil Aviation," August 9, 1950, 2, file 968.52/8-1050, RG 59, NARA.

38. The West German government was not permitted to start an airline of its own, Lufthansa, until 1955. Instead, Pan Am operated the largest number of West German domestic routes, including flights from Frankfurt and Munich into West Berlin's Tempelhof Airport (in the city's American occupation zone). Once Lufthansa incorporated, new aviation treaties between Yugoslavia and West Germany replaced the treaty from 1949. The same was true of an eventual Yugoslav-Austrian air treaty that followed Austrian independence in 1955 and the founding of Austrian Airlines in 1957.

39. Report from P. Tomić, šef trgovinske delegacije FNRJ, "Izveštaj o trgovinskim pregovorima sa Egiptom (17 juni–7 avgust 1950)," undated, 12, fond 50, Istorijska beleška fonda vlade FNRJ–Predsedništva vlada, subset 65-146, folder: Egipat, AJ.

40. Some of the latest scholarship on Yugoslavia's relationship with the Non-Aligned Movement is found in Paul Stubbs, ed., *Socialist Yugoslavia and the Non-Aligned Movement: Social, Cultural, Political, and Economic Imaginaries* (Montreal: McGill-Queen's University Press, 2023). The diplomacy leading to Yugoslavia's inclusion in NAM is found in Svetozar Rajak, *Yugoslavia and the Soviet Union in the Early Cold War: Reconciliation, Comradeship, Confrontation, 1953–1957* (New York: Routledge, 2010).

41. Edvard Kardelj, *Yugoslavia in International Relations and in the Non-Aligned Movement* (Belgrade: Socialist Thought and Practice, 1979), 234. As quoted in Konstantin Kilibarda, "Non-aligned Geographies in the Balkans: Space, Race, and Image in the Construction of New 'European' Foreign Policies," in *Security beyond the Discipline: Emerging Dialogues on Global Politics*, ed. Abhinava Kumar and Derek Maisonville (Toronto: York University Centre for International and Security Studies, 2010), 34.

42. Svetozar Rajak, "'Companions in Misfortune': From Passive Neutralism to Active Un-commitment; The Critical Role of Yugoslavia," in *Neutrality and Neutralism in the Global Cold War: Between or Within the Bloc?*, ed. Sandra Bott, Jussi Hanhimäki, Janick Marina Schaufelbuehl, and Marco Wyss (London: Routledge, 2016), 75.

43. Kilibarda, "Non-aligned Geographies in the Bakans," 39n11.

44. On load factor, see report, Savezni zavod za statistiku, "Saobraćaj i veze 1958," undated, 120, fond, Savezni sekretarijat za saobraćaj i veze, subset F-129, AJ. On profitability, see report, Uprava civilnog vazduhoplovstva,

"Razmatranje o planu vazdušnog saobraćaja za 1960 godinu," undated, 29, fond 599, Savezni sekretarijat za saobraćaj i veze, subset F-193, AJ.

45. Rajak, "'Companions in Misfortune,'" 75n17.

46. Patrick Hyder Patterson, *Bought and Sold: Living and Losing the Good Life in Socialist Yugoslavia* (Ithaca, NY: Cornell University Press, 2011), xvi.

47. Stef Jansen, "The Afterlives of the Yugoslav Red Passport," *Citizenship in Southeast Europe* (blog), October 24, 2012, https://www.citsee.eu/citsee-story/afterlives-yugoslav-red-passport.

48. Patterson, *Bought and Sold*, 2.

49. The flights to Cairo debuted on April 19, 1955. As the CV-340s were being delivered in the summer of 1954, the proposed routes and frequencies, which had been altered a bit from the actual 1955 flight plans, were included in US embassy correspondence from July 30, 1954: Dispatch from Belgrade to Department of State, "Sale of Convair Aircraft to JAT," July 10, 1954, file 968.526/7-3054, RG 59, NARA.

50. On American efforts to prop up Convair's product over the UK's Vickers, see memo from John Foster Dulles to US Embassy Belgrade, "Sale of Convair Aircraft to JAT," July 1, 1954, file 968.526/7-154, RG 59, NARA.

51. Memo, Dulles to US Embassy Belgrade, July 1, 1954, 2.

52. Boothe Luce, "America," 762.

53. Dispatch from US Embassy Belgrade to Department of State, "Yugoslav Purchase of Three Convair 340 Planes," November 4, 1952, file 968.526/11-452, RG 59, NARA.

54. Dispatch from US Embassy Belgrade to Department of State, "Possible Pan American World Airways (PAA) Participation in General Survey of Jugoslovenski Aerotransport (JAT) and Opening of an Agency in Belgrade," October 6, 1960, file 968.72/10-660, RG 59, NARA.

55. Dispatch from Belgrade to Department of State, "Sale of Convair Aircraft to JAT," July 10, 1954.

56. On the development of Adriatic tourism, see Hannes Grandits and Karin Taylor, eds., *Yugoslavia's Sunny Side: A History of Tourism in Socialism, 1950s–1980s* (Budapest: Central European University Press, 2010).

57. Dispatch, from US Embassy Belgrade to Department of State, "Yugoslav Plans for Use of DC-6's and Convairs in Expansion of Yugoslav Airline," December 10, 1958, file 968.72/12-1058, RG 59, NARA.

58. Airgram from US Embassy Belgrade to Secretary of State, November 3, 1958, file 968.72/11-358, RG 59, NARA.

59. Report, "Informacija o problematici civilnog vazduhoplovstva," undated, 4, fond 599, Savezni sekretarijat za saobraćaj i veze, subset F-193, AJ. The text itself notes that the document is composed of a presentation from the director general of civil aviation to the Savezno izvršno veće (SIV—the Federal Executive Council). The document is filed with other documents from 1956.

60. Dispatch from US Embassy Belgrade to Department of State, "Yugoslav Interest in Possible Purchase of Jet Aircraft," June 17, 1960, 1, file 968.726/6-1760, RG 59, NARA.

61. To put more precise figures on the size of the trade, 15.8 percent of Yugoslav exports in 1960 headed to the Global South. This percentage remained

consistent through the decade before dipping in 1970 to 13.2 percent. Exports to Eastern Europe were twice as numerous in the 1960s, while exports to the West about three times more numerous. See Central Intelligence Agency, "Yugoslavia," *National Intelligence Survey* 21, April 1973, 28, https://www.cia.gov/readingroom/docs/CIA-RDP01-00707R000200100032-0.pdf.

62. A timeline of these exchanges and meetings is found in Petar Žarković, "Yugoslavia and the USSR 1945–1980: The History of a Cold War Relationship," *YU historia* (blog), accessed March 29, 2023, https://yuhistorija.com/int_relations_txt01c1.html.

63. Jan Berge, *JAT Glory Days: Yugoslavia's National Airline through Communism, 1947–1987* (self-pub., 2013), 19 and 22, accessed at: https://www.academia.edu/14553153/JAT_GLORY_DAYS?auto=download.

64. Berge, *JAT Glory Days*, 18–19.

65. Report from Uprava civilnog vazduhoplovstva, "Informacija o liberalizaciji međunarodnog vazdušnog saobraćaja u Jugoslaviji," October 9, 1962, 1–2, fond 599, Savezni sekretarijat za saobraćaj i veze, subset F-195, AJ.

66. Adria Airways (Adria Aviopromet in Slovenian) was founded in August 1961 by the Slovenian republican government and various Slovene investors. Its relationship with JAT was at times antagonistic (mainly due to fears that the Yugoslav market was too small for two independent airlines), while at other moments cooperative. Since Adria did not have scheduled flights until the 1980s, it was often a counterpoint to JAT, as Adria exclusively handled cargo and charter passengers, while JAT—though still very much in the cargo and charter markets—was primarily a scheduled airline. When antagonisms between Yugoslavia's constituent nationalities flared up, rivalries also surfaced between the Slovene airline, a smaller Croatian airline (Pan Adria Airways) that was also founded in 1961 as a domestic-only carrier, and JAT, which was at times perceived as heavily Serbian.

67. Report from Adria Aviopromet, "Osnove, predlozi i analitički podaci za uspostavljanje redovne vazdušne linije između FNRJ i zemalja velikog Magreba—Tunis, Alžir, Maroko," June 1962, 6, fond 599, Savezni sekretarijat za saobraćaj i veze, subset F-195, AJ.

68. Report from Adria Aviopromet, "Osnove," June 1962, 7.

69. Report from Adria Aviopromet, "Osnove," June 1962, 2.

70. Report from Adria Aviopromet, "Osnove," June 1962, 11.

71. After ceasing their flights to Tunis in 1961, the Soviets by 1965 were flying to Algeria and on to Accra, even stopping in Belgrade for refueling. To protect Adria's market share, however, Aeroflot was not allowed to pick up passengers in Belgrade. Report from Savezni sekretarijat za saobraćaj i veze, "Informacija u vezi pisma preduzeća za aerodromske usluge aerodrom 'Beograd' u odnosu na liberalizaciju u vazdušnom saobraćaju," January 13, 1965, 4–5, fond 599, Savezni sekretarijat za saobraćaj i veze, subset F-259 343, folder 84, AJ.

72. Report from Savezni sekretarijat za saobraćaj i veze, "Informacija," January 13, 1965.

73. Details on Yugoslav investments in Libya are found in the Diplomatic Archives of the Ministry of Foreign Affairs for the Republic of Serbia. For the number of Yugoslav citizens living in Libya in 1968, see "Izveštaj o radu

konzularne službe u 1968 godini," January 28, 1969, sig. broj 45793, dosije 1. On the value of corporate contracts in Libya, see "Zabeleska o pitanju posete člana SIV-a Ali Šukrije u Libiji," February 10, 1969, sig. broj 44818, dosije 2. These items are both found in godina 1969, zemlja Libija, fascikla 219, DA.

74. Using 1956 and 1962 as sample points: In 1956, JAT's total income was 1.648 billion dinars, of which 600 million dinars (36.4 percent) was a state subsidy. Report, Milan Simović, direktor preduzeća JAT-a, to Saveznom izvršnom veću, Sekretarijat za saobraćaj i veze, "Rešenje o načinu upotrebe dotacije JAT-u," April 11, 1956, 3, fond 599, Savezni sekretarijat za saobraćaj i veze, subset F-194, AJ.

JAT's 1962 income was 5.214 billion dinars, of which 1.05 billion (20 percent) was a state subsidy. Report from Jugoslovenski Aerotransport, "JAT: Predloženi plan za 1962 godinu," undated, fond 599, Savezni sekretarijat za saobraćaj i veze, subset F-193, AJ.

75. Costs for Belgrade's new airport from 1956 to 1960 totaled 6.183 billion dinars. Meanwhile, construction of the new Dubrovnik airport and runways at five other airports were slated to cost another 8 billion dinars, starting in 1960. It should be noted that Dubrovnik's airport, like Belgrade's, experienced significant delays and cost overruns. Memorandum from Uprava civilnog vazduhoplovstva to Sekretarijatu SIV-a za saobraćaj i veze, "Predmet: Predlog za obrazovanje Direkcije aerodrome u izgradnji kao investitora za sve civilne aerodrome u Jugoslaviji," February 16, 1960, 1, fond 599, Savezni sekretarijat za saobraćaj i veze, subset F-193, AJ.

76. On unemployment, see Susan Woodward, *Socialist Unemployment: The Political Economy of Yugoslavia, 1945–1990* (Princeton, NJ: Princeton University Press, 1995), especially 383; on debt, see CIA, "Yugoslavia," 29; on trade deficits, 26.

3. G. Arthur Brown

1. Delays in implementing the final accords ultimately pushed back Jamaica's independence to August 6, 1962.

2. "Independence: Premier Hints Aug. 1," *Daily Gleaner* (Kingston, Jamaica), January 29, 1962, 2.

3. On the inaugural dates of Pan Am's jet service to both Montego Bay in 1959 and Kingston in 1962, see "Pan-Am Starts Jamaica-Miami Jet Service," *Daily Gleaner*, February 5, 1962, 2.

4. Because G. Arthur Brown did not complete his memoir before his death, information about his personal life and exact whereabouts for key moments in this narrative is incomplete. Regarding his participation in the London Independence Conference, see P. J. Patterson, "My Political Journey: Jamaica's Sixth Prime Minister, Part 6—The Federal Experiment," *Daily Gleaner*, December 9, 2018.

The list of Brown's accomplishments is assembled from a variety of published sources: "Dilemmas of Caribbean Development: An Interview with G. Arthur Brown," *Fletcher Forum* 9, no. 2 (Summer 1985): 255–68; "George Brown, 70, Former Governor of Bank of Jamaica," *New York Times*, March 5, 1993,

A20; "George Arthur Brown," *Prabook*, accessed December 28, 2021, https://prabook.com/web/george_arthur.brown/568082.

5. The Commission of Inquiry on Civil Aviation in the West Indies was created on April 4, 1961, by the cabinet of Jamaica to make recommendations on aviation policy. G. Arthur Brown chaired the first meeting on July 3 of the same year. A. G. S. Coombs, minister of communications and works, "Cabinet Submission: Commission of Inquiry on Civil Aviation in the West Indies," August 30, 1961, FCO 141/5476, Foreign and Commonwealth Office Records (FCO), The National Archives of the United Kingdom, Kew, UK (hereafter NAUK).

6. Roosevelt's assertion of American policing power is a quote from his 1904 address to Congress announcing what became known as the Roosevelt Corollary to the Monroe Doctrine. See "Theodore Roosevelt's Annual Message to Congress for 1904," December 6, 1904, HR 58A-K2, Records of the US House of Representatives, Record Group 233, Center for Legislative Archives, National Archives.

7. Key scholarly works that cover either US-Jamaican or UK-Jamaican relations in the run-up to independence include: Obika Gray, *Radicalism and Social Change in Jamaica, 1960–1972* (Knoxville: University of Tennessee Press, 1991); Spencer Mawby, *Ordering Independence: The End of Empire in the Anglophone Caribbean, 1947–1969* (New York: Palgrave Macmillan, 2012); Kenneth Morgan, *A Concise History of Jamaica* (Cambridge: Cambridge University Press, 2023); Jason C. Parker, *Brother's Keeper: The United States, Race, and Empire in the British Caribbean, 1937–1962* (New York: Oxford University Press, 2008); and Diana Paton and Matthew J. Smith, *The Jamaica Reader: History, Culture, Politics* (Durham, NC: Duke University Press, 2021).

8. Under the leadership of the Jamaican Labour Party in the 1960s, especially Prime Minister Hugh Shearer, the government developed a policy of Jamaicanization, which Obika Gray characterizes as a response to the "growing demand for a larger domestic share in the ownership of the national economy." Gray proceeds to characterize this as a "weak policy" that was half-heartedly applied until the more progressive prime ministership of Michael Manley that began in 1972. Gray, *Radicalism and Social Change*, 196–97.

9. Report, "Jamaica and the West Indies in 1961," attached to saving telegram from Governor, Jamaica to Secretary of State for the Colonies, April 10, 1961, GSO, ref. CSP, 138/S3, pp. 2–3, CO 1031/3624, Records of the Colonial Office (CO), NAUK.

10. Report, "Jamaica and the West Indies," 3.

11. Report, "Jamaica and the West Indies," 5–6. For details on the Colonial Development Corporation, see Mike Cowen, "Early Years of the Colonial Development Corporation: British State Enterprise Overseas during Late Colonialism," *African Affairs* 83, no. 330 (January 1984): 63–75.

12. The £6 million sum is cited in Ministry of Communications and Works, "Airport Development," Parliament Ministry Paper no. 43/1969, May 21, 1969, Government and United Nations Documents (GUND), University of the West Indies Library, Mona (Kingston), Jamaica (hereafter UWI). An example of a decision by the colonial government to borrow for runway improvements in

Kingston is found in: telegram from Acting Governor of Jamaica to Secretary of State for the Colonies, March 3, 1951, p. 2, CO 937/185/1, CO, NAUK.

13. According to numbers published in the Canadian press, tourist arrivals in Jamaica in 1956 totaled 161,000, with 1961 numbers rising to over 300,000. "Jamaican Visitors Boost Island as Tourist, Industrial Paradise," *Ottawa Citizen*, January 28, 1958, 17. Using a slightly different metric of foreign visitors, statistics compiled by the government of Jamaica detail the next doubling of tourist numbers from 1960 to 1970: 226,000 foreign arrivals were counted in 1960, with 415,720 arriving in 1970. P. J. Patterson, "Tourism Development," Parliament Ministry Paper no. 61/1975, December 11, 1975, 1–2, GUND, UWI. On Willis's promise to double the number of tourists, see "Pan-Am Starts Jamaica–Miami Jet Service," *Daily Gleaner*, February 5, 1962, 2.

14. G. Arthur Brown, *Patterns of Development and Attendant Choices and Consequences for Jamaica and the Caribbean* (Kingston: GraceKennedy Foundation, 1989), 4–5.

15. The number of hotel rooms in Jamaica are covered in: O. G. Balz, "Proposed Hotel—Montego Bay, Jamaica," draft, October 20, 1956, p. 4, folder 28, box 323, Intercontinental Hotels Corp. Collection, Pan American World Airways Archives, University of Miami, Miami, FL (hereafter PAWA).

Pan Am's original enticements to build the hotel at Montego Bay included a sales pitch from the head of the town's Chamber of Commerce, Walter Fletcher, to Pan Am's president Juan Trippe that focused on the 1944 Hotel Aid Law. See: letter from Walter Fletcher to Juan T. Trippe, president, Pan American World Airways, February 26, 1949, p. 2, folder 28, box 323, Intercontinental Hotels Corp. Collection, PAWA.

16. BOAC's losses in BWIA are reported in A. G. S. Coombs, minister of communication and works (Govt. of Jamaica), "Cabinet Submission: Report on the Commission of Inquiry on Civil Aviation," December 13, 1960, appendix A, 9, FCO141/5501, FCO, NAUK.

Jamaican ministers' antagonism toward BWIA is manifest in a cabinet decision from 1961: "It would be extremely disadvantageous to allow the Trinidad Government to acquire BWIA because that Government is mainly interested in the airline as an employment agency, whilst Jamaica's primary interest lies in tourism." See: Gov. of Jamaica, "Cabinet Decision," no. 54/61, August 14, 1961, 2, in FCO 141/5476, FCO, NAUK.

17. "Extract from Ministry Paper No. 98 Dated 13th December 1965," 2, attached as appendix A to "Air Jamaica," Ministry Paper no. 3, January 27, 1969, *Jamaica House of Representatives Ministry Papers*, 1969, GUND, UWI.

18. As a trade-off for limiting losses, there was also a cap on Jamaica's profits: UK£60,000 over three years. See letter from P. W. Beckwith, February 22, 1968, folder I, Air Jamaica Limited, April 14, 1966–3 October 3, 1969, file number 796/03, Air Jamaica Papers, Ministry of Finance and Planning Archives, Kingston, Jamaica (hereafter AirJ).

19. Cleve Lewis, minister of communications and works, as quoted in Jamaica Hansard, *Proceedings of the House of Representatives of Jamaica*, session 1965–66, vol. 1, no. 2, 680–81, GUND, UWI.

20. Discussion of American claims of a "paper airline" are found in: letter from C. E. Diggins, British High Commission, Kingston, to E. L. Sykes, Commonwealth Relations Office, London, October 4, 1963, in Records of the Dominions Office (DO) 200/33, NAUK.

21. Letter from Diggins to Sykes, October 4, 1963.

22. Letter from R. Le Goy to R. H. Oakeley, Commonwealth Relations Office, London, "Jamaica: USA," October 5, 1964, 2, in BT 245/1400, BT, NAUK.

23. The dynamic of Cold War proxies is detailed in Odd Arne Westad, *The Global Cold War: Third-World Interventions and the Making of Our Times* (New York: Cambridge University Press, 2005), 1–7.

24. The British diplomatic quote comes from Oakeley to Mr. Watson, file notes on document 35A, October 15, 1963, DO 200/33, DO, NAUK.

The quote from the Jamaican ambassador to the United States is found in: Neville Ashenheim to Civil Aviation Board, September 22, 1964, 4, BT 245/1400, BT, NAUK.

25. "Airline Not Only for Prestige Purposes—Sangster," *Daily Gleaner*, May 2, 1966, 2.

26. "BOAC's Separate U.S.-Jamaica Service Ends," *Daily Gleaner*, May 2, 1966, 9.

27. G. Arthur Brown, as quoted in "'Dream Come True,'" *Sunday Gleaner*, May 1, 1966, "Salute to Air Jamaica" special insert, ii.

28. Letter from O. H. Goldson, permanent secretary, Ministry of Communication and Works, to P. W. Beckwith, "Air Jamaica (1968) Ltd.," January 6, 1969, folder I: Air Jamaica Limited, April 14, 1966–October 3, 1969, file number 796/03, AirJ.

29. Letter from Goldson to Beckwith, January 6, 1969.

30. Internal correspondence from Air Jamaica managers from July 1969 notes: "It is hoped that . . . the first class of twelve [Jamaican pilots] will be ready for initial training either in late 1969 or early 1970." See "Report of Managing Director for Month of June 1969," July 24, 1969, folder I: Air Jamaica Limited, April 14, 1966–October 3, 1969, file number 796/03, AirJ.

31. The figures for the bank loan and redeemable preference shares are found in Economics Division, Ministry of Finance and Planning, "Subhead 10—Purchase of Share in Government Companies—£234,000," April 23, 1969. The allocation of funds and of stock for the DC-9 purchases is further detailed in Air Jamaica (1968) Limited, "Minutes of Third Directors' Meeting," January 9, 1969, 5–7. Notice of the need for the additional $10 million in 1974 is found in a memo from O. H. Goldson, permanent secretary, Ministry of Communication and Works, to P. M. Beckwith, "Air Jamaica (1968) Ltd.," February 1969, 1. All of these documents are found in folder I: Air Jamaica Limited, April 14, 1966–October 3, 1969, file number 796/03, AirJ.

32. Economics Division, Ministry of Finance and Planning, "Note on Cabinet Submission No. 789/MCW-69 Future of Air Jamaica," November 8, 1968, folder I: Air Jamaica Limited, April 14, 1966–October 3, 1969, file number 796/03, AirJ.

33. US Embassy Jamaica to Dept. of State, airgram A-300, July 10, 1968, file AV 6 JAM, 1967–69 Central Decimal File (CDF), RG 59, NARA.

34. US Embassy Jamaica to Dept. of State, telegram 1478, January 24, 1968, file AV 6 JAM, 1967–69 CDF, RG 59, NARA.

35. Letter from Neville Ashenheim to N. C. Lewis, minister of communications and works, September 2, 1969, 1–2, folder I: Air Jamaica Limited, April 14, 1966–October 3, 1969, file number 796/03, AirJ.

36. Letter from Ashenheim to Lewis, September 2, 1969.

37. Joseph S. Murphy, "Air Jamaica Stirs Up a Storm of Service . . . and That Spells Profit!," *Air Transport World*, October 1972, 15–16. At its furthest expanse, Air Jamaica flew to both the UK and to continental Europe (Frankfurt), as well as numerous cities in the United States and Canada—from Los Angeles in the southwest to Montreal in the northeast.

38. The 1956 figure, cited earlier, is from O. G. Balz, vice president, Intercontinental Hotels Corporation, "Proposed Hotel—Montego Bay, Jamaica" (draft), October 20, 1956, 4, folder 28, box 323, Intercontinental Hotels Corporation Collection, PAWA. Details of the terms of the "Hotel (Incentives) Act" are found in P. J. Patterson, minister of industry, tourism and foreign trade, "Tourism Development," Ministry Paper no. 61, 1975, 7, *Jamaica House of Representatives Ministry Papers*, 1975, UWI.

39. The guarantees for the Montego Bay Intercontinental and the Pegasus are detailed in P. J. Patterson, minister of tourism, "Tourism in 1974," speech to Parliament, not dated (1974), 8–10, folder "PJP 363" in P. J. Patterson Papers, Caribbean Leaders Collection, UWI.

Details on the additional Intercontinental projects in Kingston and Ocho Rios, as well as another eight convention-sized hotels owned by the UDC, are found in P. J. Patterson, minister of tourism, "UDC," speech to Parliament, not dated (1976), 6–7, folder "PJP 363" in P. J. Patterson Papers, UWI.

40. Brown, *Patterns of Development*, 7.

41. Andrew Marti, "Preliminary Findings and Recommendations, Air Jamaica Report #4," May 29, 1975, 1, folder "PJP 378," P. J. Patterson Papers, UWI.

42. Patterson, "UDC," 7–9.

43. As cited in "Annual Report—Air Jamaica (1968) Ltd.," Ministry Paper no. 37, July 13, 1975, *Jamaica House of Representatives Ministry Papers*, 1975, GUND, UWI.

44. As quoted in "Annual Report—Air Jamaica (1968) Ltd.," Ministry Paper no. 39, September 21, 1976, *Jamaica House of Representatives Ministry Papers*, 1975, GUND, UWI.

45. Coverage of Manley's initial economic program is offered by Christine Clarke and Carol Nelson, "A Clash of Ideologies: Jamaica and the International Monetary Fund," in *Contextualizing Jamaica's Relationship with the IMF* (Cham: Palgrave Macmillan, 2020), 164–216. The use of the slogan "Better Mus' Come" is covered in Nelson W. Keith and Novella Zett Keith, *The Social Origins of Democratic Socialism in Jamaica* (Philadelphia: Temple University Press, 1992).

46. This quote is reprinted on the website for "Life and Debt: A Film by Stephanie Black," January 15, 2022, http://www.lifeanddebt.org/about.html.

47. Details of Jamaica's debt status and the standoff with the IMF are from Karen DeYoung, "Manley's Rift with IMF Dominates Jamaican Economics," *Washington Post*, September 6, 1980.

48. Details of the 1974 conditions at the airline are found in "Annual Report [for 1975]—Air Jamaica (1968) Ltd.," Ministry Paper no. 39, September 21, 1976, UWI. The debt-to-equity ratio is found in "Annual Report [for 1976]—Air Jamaica Limited," Ministry Paper no. 30, July 29, 1977, 4, UWI.

49. "Annual Report [for 1976]—Air Jamaica Limited," Ministry Paper no. 30, July 29, 1977, 4, UWI.

50. Contrast my conclusions with other historians writing on aviation in the Global South as a venue for national prestige and autocratic corruption, as in Jeffrey Engel's work: "Leaders in the developing world, in particular heads of new nations decolonized at war's end, understood airpower's cachet equally as well. They saw aircraft as potential symbols of their authority at home and their legitimacy abroad, whether through the shining planes they ordered for their personal use or the (frequently unprofitable) national airlines that sprang up like wildflowers throughout the early Cold War. In either case, aircraft brought instant respectability." Jeffrey Engel, *Cold War at 30,000 Feet: The Anglo-American Fight for Aviation Supremacy* (Cambridge, MA: Harvard University Press, 2007), 6.

51. Letter from R. Le Goy to R. H. Oakeley, Commonwealth Relations Office, London, "Jamaica: USA," October 5, 1964, 2, in BT 245/1400, BT, NAUK.

4. Alix d'Unienville

1. For details on World War II's impact on hiring men and women in the United States, see Phil Tiemeyer, *Plane Queer: Labor, Sexuality, and AIDS in the History of Male Flight Attendants* (Berkeley: University of California Press, 2013), especially chapter 2, "The Cold War Gender Order."

2. In Europe, the few airlines hiring stewardesses in the 1930s included Swissair, which in 1934 hired Europe's first stewardess, Nellie Diener; the Netherlands' KLM, which hired some women for its intra-European flights in 1935; and Germany's prewar Deutsche Luft Hansa in 1938. On Swissair, see Pascale Marder, *Nelly Diener: Engel der Lüfte vom kurzen Glück der ersten Lufthostess Europas* (Zurich: Bilgerverlag, 2018). Note that KLM's intercontinental flights to its colony in Indonesia continued to be serviced only by men. See Frido Ogier, "Our First Steward and Stewardess," KLM (blog), September 6, 2019, https://blog.klm.com/our-first-steward-and-stewardess/ (site discontinued).

3. On Air France, see François Duclos, "Air France retrace l'histoire des hôtesses de l'air," *Air Journal*, March 18, 2016, https://www.air-journal.fr/2016-03-18-air-france-retrace-lhistoire-des-hotesses-de-lair-video-5159697.html.

On BOAC and its predecessor Imperial Airways, see "British Airways Uniform through the Years," accessed June 26, 2023, https://confessionsofatrolleydolly.com/2022/01/01/british-airways-uniform-through-the-years/.

On Sabena, see Vanessa D'Hooghe, "Article 119: How Stewardesses Obtained Equal Pay in the European Community (Belgium 1968–1980)," in *Institutionalizing Gender Equality: Historical and Global Perspectives*, ed. Yulia Gradskova and Sara Sanders (Lanham, MD: Lexington Press, 2015), 42.

On SAS, see Scandinavian Airlines (SAS), "Meet Nan, One of SAS Very First Stewardesses," 2016, YouTube, 5 min., 5 sec., https://www.youtube.com/watch?v=CB5Sjv4ltXU.

4. Kathleen Barry's work on flight attendants in the United States details how stewardessing embodied these characteristics of pink-collar labor, a general category designating "female-dominated clerical or service occupations which were generally cleaner and safer than blue-collar work" though with sizable disadvantages in terms of pay, benefits, and reputation because of women's social inferiority. Kathleen Barry, *Femininity in Flight: A History of Flight Attendants* (Durham, NC: Duke University Press, 2007), 9.

5. A firsthand chronicle of stewardesses' struggles is found in Georgia Panter Nielsen, *From Sky Girl to Flight Attendant: Women and the Making of a Union* (Ithaca, NY: ILR Press, 1982). Kathleen Barry's work offers a historical overview of such discrimination. Barry, *Femininity in Flight*.

6. Elaine Tyler May's *Homeward Bound* remains an authoritative text for linking the entrenchment of traditional gender roles in the United States with the country's de facto mobilization against communism in the Cold War. Elaine Tyler May, *Homeward Bound: American Families in the Cold War Era* (1988; repr., New York: Basic Books, 2008).

7. Alix d'Unienville, *En vol: Journal d'une hôtesse de l'air* (Paris: A. Michel, 1949), section "Le Bourget, 25 July."

8. D'Unienville, *En vol*, preface.

9. D'Unienville, *En vol*, section "New-York, 13 janvier."

10. Philippe Roland, "Revolution dans le ciel," *Figaro*, March 3, 1946, reprinted in Camille Lestienne, "Les premières hôtesses de l'air, une révolution dans le ciel de 1946," *Figaro*, March 4, 2016.

11. Scandinavian Airlines, "Meet Nan."

12. Roland, "Revolution dans le ciel."

13. Scandinavian Airlines, "Meet Nan."

14. These excerpts from interviews with Resistance fighters close to d'Unienville are found in Bernard O'Connor, *Agents Française: French Women Infiltrated into France during the Second World War* (Research Triangle Park, NC: Lulu Press, 2016), 414.

15. These and other details of d'Unienville's work in World War II are found at: "Alix d'Unienville, SOE agent—obituary," *Telegraph* (London, UK), November 20, 2015.

16. "Alix d'Unienville, SOE agent—obituary."

5. Dragica Pavlović

1. Report, from Milenko Mitrović to Privredni savet D. F. J., August 20, 1945, 4, fond 50, Istorijska beleška fonda vlade FNRJ—Predsedništva vlada, subset 85-181, Archives of Yugoslavia (Arhiv Jugoslavije), Belgrade, Serbia (hereafter AJ).

2. Jovo Simišić, "The Symbol of a Profession," *JAT Airways New Review*, September 2010, 47-51.

3. Predrag J. Marković, *Beograd između istoka i zapada: 1948–1965* (Belgrade: Službeni list SRJ, 1996), 14–15.

4. See, for example, Jelena Subotić and Srđan Vucetić, "Performing Solidarity: Whiteness and Status-Seeking in the Non-aligned World," *Journal of International Relations and Development* 22 (2019): 722–43.

5. Tijana Okić, "From Revolutionary to Productive Subject: An Alternative History of the Women's Antifascist Front," in *The Lost Revolution: Women's Antifascist Front between Myth and Forgetting*, ed. Andreja Dugandžić and Tijana Okić (Sarajevo: Association for Culture and Art CRVENA, 2018), 167.

6. The singular of the term for a female Partisan is *partizanka*; the plural is *partizanke*.

7. Josip Broz Tito, speech from the First National (Zemaljska) Conference of the Women's Antifascist Front, 1942. As quoted in "Žene u socijalizmu—od ubrzane emancipacije do ubrzane repatrijarhalizacije," *Buka Magazin* (Banja Luka, Bosnia-Herzegovina), March 2, 2015.

8. Okić, "From Revolutionary to Productive Subject," 171.

9. World War I had also been a stimulus, especially for urban women, to take on more public roles traditionally held by men. As Tijana Okić notes, even before World War II, 20 percent of the university population in Yugoslavia was female. Okić, "From Revolutionary to Productive Subject," 166.

10. "Žene u socijalizmu."

11. Constitution of the Federal People's Republic of Yugoslavia, implemented January 31, 1946. Available at: https://bs.wikisource.org/wiki/Ustav_Federativne_Narodne_Republike_Jugoslavije_(1946)

12. As quoted in "Zapisnik Konferencije po pitanjima civilnog vazdušnog saobraćaja," December 15, 1947, 2, fond 290, JUSTA, subset 2, AJ.

13. Z. Franješ and B. Ivković, "Plan Kadrova za 1948 godinu (razrađen na temelju odobrenog zbirnog plana)," May 14, 1948, fond 290, JUSTA, subset 3, AJ.

14. The ad itself appears in *Politika*, August 21, 1947, 8.

15. The original text, at least in its first portion, reads: "Glavnoj upravi civilnog vazdušnog saobraćaja potreban je izvestan broj drugarica-drugova za službenike letače na avionima."

16. The Serbian reads: "Prvenstveno dolaze u obzir drugarice."

17. The conditions set forth in JAT's working manual (*Radni Red*) from 1949 states that "those who wish to be employed by Yugoslav Aerotransport . . . cannot be younger than 18 nor older than 60 years." Jugoslovenski Aerotransport, *Radni Red*, July 30, 1949, 1, fond 620, Uprava za civilno vazduhoplovstvo, subset F-56, AJ. While this manual was published two years after the employment ad for flight attendants, it is unlikely that JAT's original employment manual differs significantly from this version.

18. This figure comes from an inspection of JUSTA's labor conditions conducted by the Komisija za pregled jedinica civilnog vazdušnog saobraćaja, "Zapisnik," October 16, 1947, 1, fond 290, JUSTA, subset 2, AJ.

19. Air pouch, from US Embassy Belgrade to Department of State, Subject: Special Report on Civil Aviation, February 6, 1959, 7, file 968.72/2-659, RG 59,

NARA. Note that this document states that this data is taken from: Statistical Bulletin 121 of the Yugoslav Federal Statistical Office.

20. On gender roles in Yugoslavia in these years, see Vera Gudac Dodić, *Žena u socijalizmu: Položaj žene u Srbiju u drugoj polovini 20. veka* (Belgrade: Institut za noviju istoriju Srbije, 2006). The aforementioned collection on the AFŽ also addresses these conflicting roles: Dugandžić and Okić, *Lost Revolution*.

21. Eric John Hobsbawm, *The Age of Extremes: The Short Twentieth Century, 1914–1991* (London: Abacus, 1995), 313.

22. Like in all Eastern bloc countries, the persecution of communists in Nazi Germany and their subsequent fight against the Nazis was used in Yugoslavia as a core basis of the regime's legitimacy. All official government correspondence in the 1940s and early 1950s included the salutation: "Death to fascism, freedom to the people!" (Smrt fašizmu, sloboda narodu!)

23. Joseph Frankel, "Communism and the National Question in Yugoslavia," *Journal of Central European Affairs* 15 (April 1955), 64.

24. Workers' Councils were devised by Yugoslav communists after the Tito-Stalin split to assert that there were differences between Yugoslavia and the Soviet Union when it came to the path toward socialism. By placing a workers' organ into the administrative structure of companies, Yugoslav officials could assert that the means of production were in the hands of the proletariat, even if this system of "workers' self-management" differed from the Soviet model. Note also that Workers' Councils, in practice, had an advisory role to the true leader of a company, the director, who was then assisted by an executive board. On Pavlović's election to head the Workers' Council, see Simišić, "Symbol of a Profession," 47, 50.

25. "25 Pitanja magazina 'Praktična žena' odgovora Dragica Pavlović," *Praktična žena*, November 5, 1956, 10.

26. Simišić, "Symbol of a Profession," 50.

27. Anonymous A, interview with author, July 5, 2018, Belgrade, Serbia.

28. Anonymous A interview.

29. Anonymous A interview.

30. Simišić, "Symbol of a Profession," 47.

31. JAT-Jugoslawischer Flugverkehr, *JAT* (Belgrade) 1, no. 1 (1956). This publication is part of the holdings of National Library of Serbia (Narodna biblioteka Srbije, hereafter NBS). The German-language publication titled *JAT* is the earliest of these materials. While it is marked as the first of a serial publication (volume 1, issue 1), there is no date on it and also no evidence that further issues of *JAT* were produced. Librarians at the NBS have assigned 1956 as its publication year. I find this date convincing given the nature of the photos used in publication, including Jawaharlal Nehru's arrival at Belgrade's Zemun Airport, which occurred on July 3, 1955.

32. *JAT*, 1.

33. *JAT*, 2.

34. *JAT*, 3.

35. *JAT*, 3

36. Patterson, *Bought and Sold*, 2.

37. Marković, *Beograd između istoka i zapada*, 270–71. The report from the Paris fashion show was originally covered in *Politika*, April 12, 1951.
38. "Magazin 'Praktična žena' uputiće ženu-suprugu, ženu-majku i domaćicu u mnoge korisne stvari," *Praktična žena*, no. 1, March 5, 1956, 1.
39. "Magazin 'Praktična žena,'" 1.
40. *Praktična žena*, no. 1, March 5, 1956, cover.
41. On divorce, see "Još nešto o razvodu braka," *Praktična žena*, no. 40, November 1957, 8; on legal and work issues, see Ljubomir Stamenković, "Pravna i poslovna sposobnost žene," *Praktična žena*, no. 171, March 15, 1963, 15.
42. The cited articles are contained in the following issues of *Praktična žena*: Syria, no. 32, July 5, 1957; Central Africa, no. 33, July 20, 1957; Lebanon, no. 35, August 20, 1957; China, no. 42, December 5, 1957; Liberia, no. 109, September 20, 1960.
43. "Pismo sa Bliskog Istoka," *Praktična žena*, no. 32, July 5, 1957, 18.
44. The actions of the AFŽ from 1947 onward to end the wearing of the veil by Muslim women in Yugoslavia are covered in Tea Hadžiristić, "Unveiling Muslim Women in Socialist Yugoslavia: The Body between Socialism, Secularism, and Colonialism," *Religion and Gender* 7, no. 2 (2017): 184–203.
45. "25 Pitanja," 8.
46. As quoted in "25 Pitanja," 10.
47. Anonymous A interview.
48. Anonymous A interview.
49. "25 Pitanja," 8.
50. "Dnevnik jedne stjuardese," *Praktična žena*, nos. 80–91, from July 5, 1959 to December 20, 1959 (in biweekly intervals).
51. "Dnevnik jedne stjuardese," *Praktična žena*, no. 80, July 5, 1959, 8.

6. Marguerite LeWars Kirkpatrick

1. One of the ways that Jamaican governments of the 1960s sought to conduct nation-building on the cultural front was to proclaim individuals from both the long history of the colony and the brief era of independence as "national heroes." These individuals would then be memorialized in works of art, in publications, and in school curricula. An early example of this nationalist, hagiographic literature is Sylvia Wynter, *Jamaica's National Heroes* (Kingston: Jamaica National Trust Commission, 1971).
2. "Stuffed Teddy Bears, Two Beauty Crowns," *Gleaner*, November 8, 1963, 28.
3. As quoted in "Prime Minister's Congratulations," *Gleaner*, November 9, 1963, 1.
4. The quote comes from "Hurrah!," *Gleaner*, November 8, 1963, 1. The mention of Crawford being the first West Indian winner is found in "'Miss Jamaica' Wins 'Miss World,'" *Gleaner*, November 8, 1963, 1.
5. Myrthe Swire, "Miss World Pushes Jamaica in Hamburg," *Gleaner*, November 14, 1963, 1.
6. "'Miss Jamaica' Wins 'Miss World' Title," *Gleaner*, November 8, 1963, 1.
7. "'A Break Away from Painted Dolls,'" *Gleaner*, November 10, 1963, 1.

8. Rochelle Rowe deftly chronicles how the British Caribbean's light-skinned, mixed-race brown elites had already attained such inclusion domestically by 1963, both through beauty contests and via intermarriage with local whites. Darker-skinned Black West Indians, however, still had not attained such parity by 1963. See Rochelle Rowe, *Imagining Caribbean Womanhood: Race, Nation, and Beauty Contests, 1929–70* (Manchester, UK: Manchester University Press, 2013).

9. "La corona de Miss Mundo a Miss Jamaica, morenita de pequeña estatura," *¡Hola!*, November 16, 1963.

10. As quoted in "Jamaica's Carol Gets Wide Publicity in British Press," *Gleaner*, November 9, 1963, 1. The original text is found in "The Loveliest of Them All," *Daily Express*, November 8, 1963, 7.

11. Gerri Major, "Negro Beauty Queen Wins Miss World Crown," *Jet*, November 28, 1963, 60.

12. Edward Said, *Orientalism* (New York: Vintage, 1979); Anne McClintock, *Imperial Leather: Race, Gender, and Sexuality in the Colonial Contest* (New York: Routledge, 1995).

13. The biographical facts on Marguerite LeWars are pulled from "Marguerite LeWars, 'Miss Jamaica' 1961," *Gleaner*, June 26, 1961, 18. Her actual birth date is not publicly available, but is likely to be circa 1940. Upon her crowning as Miss Jamaica in 1961 the *Gleaner* reported her age as nineteen, therefore placing her date of birth in 1941 or 1942. However, in other articles, the same publication suggests that her birth date was closer to 1940. Carol Joan Crawford was born in 1943.

14. Cedriann Martin, "Marguerite Gordon: Lady of the Manners," *Caribbean Beat*, August 2009, https://www.caribbean-beat.com/issue-98/marguerite-gordon-lady-manners#axzz7YxZY3jtx.

15. Martin, "Marguerite Gordon."

16. "Barbara LeWars of Jamaica's New Generation," *Life International*, July 20, 1959, cover.

17. Barbara LeWars Manley died at the age of twenty-nine, soon after having given birth to Sarah. See Sarah Manley, "Coppertone," *PREE: Caribbean Writing*, November 13, 2018, https://preelit.com/2018/11/13/coppertone/.

18. Manley, "Coppertone."

19. Kitty Kingston, "Personal Mention: Filming 'Miss Jamaica' Contest," *Gleaner*, June 22, 1961, 26.

20. Martin, "Marguerite Gordon."

21. Details of the Kingston premiere of *Dr. No* are found in Edward Biddulph, "Bond at 50: *Dr. No* in the Gleaner," *MI6 Confidential*, no. 68, April 26, 2012. The London premiere is covered in Zaini Majeed, "First James Bond Film Dr. No Released on This Day in 1962: All about Global James Bond Day," *Republic World*, October 5, 2020.

22. "Designs New Uniforms for Air Jamaica Girls," *Gleaner*, May 30, 1967, 5. Both Rochelle Rowe and Elizabeth Manley assert that the face in the tourist board ads belongs to Miss Jamaica 1960, Judith Willoughby. My research, however, finds that LeWars was the model for this renowned image. Beyond this minor point of disagreement, both Rowe and Manley offer insightful

discussion of the various iterations of this famous facial image. See Rowe, *Imagining Caribbean Womanhood*, and Elizabeth Manley, "Runway Hospitality: Air Jamaica's 'Rare Tropical Birds' and the Embodied Gender and Race Politics of Tourism, 1966–1980," *Hispanic American Historical Review* 102, no. 1 (2022): 285–319.

23. "Salute to Air Jamaica," *Gleaner*, May 1, 1966, xiv.

24. "When You're Six Years Old" (Air Jamaica advertisement), *Gleaner*, May 24, 1967, 9.

25. "Marguerite LeWars," 18.

26. "Designs New Uniforms."

7. Mary Wells Lawrence

1. Frank Sinatra, vocalist, Billy May, composer, Jimmy Van Heusen and Sammy Cahn, songwriters, "Come Fly with Me," Capitol Records, 1958.

2. A profile of the jet set from this era, including coverage of James Bond author Ian Fleming and ad executive Mary Wells Lawrence, is found in William Stadiem, *Jet Set: The People, the Planes, the Glamour, and the Romance in Aviation's Glory Years* (New York: Random House, 2014).

3. This quote is found in Mary Wells Lawrence, *A Big Life in Advertising* (New York: Knopf, 2002), 33.

4. Braniff International Airways, "Announcing the End of the Plain Plane," printed magazine insert, November 1965, box "MAR 00105 D-4," folder "Girard Press—01/1964–12/1965," Alexander Girard Archives, Vitra Design Museum, Weil am Rhein, Germany (hereafter Girard).

5. "Designs New Uniforms for Air Jamaica Girls," *Gleaner*, May 30, 1967.

6. An authoritative and well-researched biography of Helen Gurley Brown is Jennifer Scanlon, *Bad Girls Go Everywhere: The Life of Helen Gurley Brown, the Woman behind Cosmopolitan Magazine* (New York: Penguin, 2010).

7. Whereas *Feminine Mystique* was released in the early months of 1963, Brown's book came out toward the end of 1962. Helen Gurley Brown, *Sex and the Single Girl* (New York: Bernard Geis Associates, 1962).

8. Justin McCarty, "Beauty Checkout," *Vogue*, September 15, 1965, 62.

9. Braniff International Airways, "Emilio Pucci: Fashion Innovator," press release, July 19, 1965, box "MAR 00105 D-4," folder "Girard Press—01/1964–12/1965," Girard.

10. Scholarly works that chronicle the 1960s' two cultural fault lines most pertinent to this paper—feminism and the sexual revolution—include: David Allyn, *Make Love, Not War: The Sexual Revolution, an Unfettered History* (London: Routledge, 2016); Patricia Bradley, *Mass Media and the Shaping of American Feminism, 1963–1975* (Oxford: University Press of Mississippi, 2009); Barbara Ehrenreich, Elizabeth Hess, and Gloria Jacobs, *Re-Making Love: The Feminization of Sex* (Garden City, NY: Anchor Press/Doubleday, 1986); Joanne J. Meyerowitz, *Not June Cleaver: Women and Gender in Postwar America, 1945–1960* (Philadelphia, PA: Temple University Press, 1994); Scanlon, *Bad Girls Go Everywhere*; and Julie Willett, *The Male Chauvinist Pig: A History* (Chapel Hill: University of North Carolina Press, 2021).

11. Lawrence, *Big Life in Advertising*, 35.

12. Shirley Kennedy, *Pucci: A Renaissance in Fashion* (New York: Abbeville Press, 1991), 98.

13. Lawrence, *Big Life in Advertising*, 34.

14. As quoted in Cobey Black, "Meet America's Top Woman Exec," *Honolulu Advertiser*, March 25, 1975.

15. Lawrence, *Big Life in Advertising*, 35.

16. Helen Gurley Brown, "Foreword," in Kennedy, *Pucci*, 7.

17. Pucci's role as a jet-set celebrity, including his collaboration with Mary Wells at Braniff, is covered in Stadiem, *Jet Set*, 252–75.

18. J. Walter Thompson Company, "Preliminary Exploration of Consumer Perceptions of the 747 Plane in England, France and Germany," research report for Pan American World Airways Inc., November 1969, 18, box PA10, folder "Research Reports 1969," in "J. Walter Thompson Company Account Files, 1885–2008 and undated," JWT.

19. J. Walter Thompson Company, "Preliminary Exploration," 16.

20. The configurations of Braniff's DC-7Cs were either for sixty-two (all first-class seating) or seventy-five (a mix of first class and coach) passengers. Meanwhile, the 727 jets, which comprised the bulk of the order that Harding Lawrence placed, typically flew with an all-coach configuration of 154 passengers, though sometimes with a less-dense mix of first and coach.

21. J. Walter Thompson Company, "Preliminary Exploration," 18.

22. Friedan, *Feminine Mystique*, 57.

23. On the importance of women's inclusion in the 1964 Civil Rights Act's Title VII, which prevented basic workplace discrimination, see Katherine Turk, *Equality on Trial: Gender and Rights in the Modern American Workplace* (Philadelphia: University of Pennsylvania Press, 2016), and Tiemeyer, *Plane Queer*.

24. Braniff International Airways, "Exacting Qualifications Remain Unchanged as Braniff Hostesses Hold Silver Anniversary Party," press release, June 1962, box 26, folder 1, Braniff Collection, History of Aviation Archives, Special Collections and Archives Division, University of Texas at Dallas, Richardson, TX (hereafter Braniff).

25. Braniff International Airlines, "A Braniff International Hostess Is . . . ," press release, undated [circa 1968], box 26, folder 1, Braniff.

26. Braniff, "A Braniff International Hostess Is . . ."

27. Helen Gurley Brown, *Sex and the Office* (New York: Bernard Geis Associates, 1964), 183–86. This title was a sequel to Brown's *Sex and the Single Girl*. It reiterated her main points from the earlier book and added more detail of office life and women's potential roles—both professional and sexual—therein.

28. Bradley, *Mass Media*, 11.

29. As quoted in Kennedy, *Pucci*, 8.

30. As quoted in Kennedy, *Pucci*, 139.

31. As quoted in Kennedy, *Pucci*, 46.

32. As quoted in "Hero, Scholar, Jet-Age Renaissance Man, Italian Style-Setter: Pucci," *Life*, October 16, 1964, 70.

33. As quoted in Kennedy, *Pucci*, 154.

34. Braniff, "A Braniff International Hostess Is . . ."

35. Braniff International Airways, "Braniff International Introduces New Dresses, Long Hair and Discards Hats to Once Again Change the Look of Airline Hostesses," press release, May 28, 1968, box 27, folder 3, Braniff.

36. "World Fashion Press Acclaims Pucci-Braniff Flight Fashions," *The Braniff B-Liner*, July 1965, 4, box "MAR 00105 D-4," folder "Girard Press—01/1964–12/1965," Girard.

37. These statistics were cited by Helen Gurley Brown in 1964 in a business proposal, and are recorded in Scanlon, *Bad Girls Go Everywhere*, 144.

38. "Braniff Refuels on Razzle-Dazzle," *Business Week*, November 20, 1965, 110–11.

39. Stan Mays, "The Air Strip," *Sunday Mirror*, March 20, 1966, 21.

40. Memo from Rex Brack, senior vice president of marketing, Braniff International Airways, to all employees, re: "new look" announcement program, November 24, 1965, box 34, folder 2, Braniff.

41. Braniff International Airways, "Braniff International Presents the Air Strip," television advertisement, December 1965, YouTube, 59 sec., https://www.youtube.com/watch?v=7TZXryuhSMg (video no longer active).

42. Braniff, "Announcing the End of the Plain Plane."

43. "The Wild Hue Yonder," *Life*, December 3, 1965.

44. The statistic on passenger traffic comes from: Clarence Newman, "Color It Colorless: Black and White Gain in Fashions and Homes," *Wall Street Journal*, June 8, 1966, 1. The statistic on revenue comes from Carol Loomis, "As the World Turns—On Madison Avenue," *Fortune*, December 1968, 114.

45. Lawrence, *Big Life in Advertising*, 36.

46. For an account of the advertising world in the 1920s, when women's roles were quite limited and they were pigeonholed into copywriting jobs for female-directed ads, see Roland Marchand, *Advertising the American Dream: Making Way for Modernity, 1920–1940* (Berkeley: University of California Press, 1985). A famous, though fictional, account of the male dominance in advertising that persisted through the 1960s is found in the hit television series *Mad Men*, which ran from 2007 to 2015.

47. George Raine, "Creative Fizz/Mary Wells' Memorable Ad Campaigns for Such Clients as Braniff and Alka-Seltzer Helped Make Her the First Woman to Run a Publicly Traded Company," *San Francisco Chronicle*, May 30, 2002.

48. Bradley, *Mass Media*, 213.

49. Lawrence, *Big Life in Advertising*, 5.

50. For accounts of sexual harassment and other forms of abuse against stewardesses, see Nielsen, *From Sky Girl to Flight Attendant*, and Barry, *Femininity in Flight*. Accounts from JAT and Air Jamaica flight attendants are included in chapter 10.

51. Black, "Meet America's Top Woman Exec."

52. Lawrence, *Big Life in Advertising*, 59.

53. Loomis, "As the World Turns," 117.

54. Loomis, "As the World Turns," 194.

55. Lawrence, *Big Life in Advertising*, 101.

56. Lawrence, *Big Life in Advertising*, 59.

8. Love, Fashion, and the *Stjuardesa*

1. "Izgradnja novih aerodroma," *Građevinar* 14, no. 3 (March 1962), 95.
2. Memorandum, Milton M. Turner to George V. Allen, July 29, 1952, file 968.52/7-2952, 1950-54 Central Decimal File, Record Group 59: General Records of the Department of State (hereafter RG 59), National Archives (hereafter NARA).
3. Milica Lukić, *Zapisi stjuardese* [Recollections of a stewardess] (Belgrade: Partenon, 2000), 90-91.
4. On Yugoslav companies active in the Global South, see Ljubica Spaskovska, "Building a Better World? Construction, Labour Mobility and the Pursuit of Collective Self-Reliance in the 'Global South,' 1950-1990," *Labor History* 59, no. 3 (2018): 331-51 and Dubravka Sekulić, "Energoprojekt in Nigeria: Yugoslav Construction Companies in the Developing World," *Southeastern Europe* 41, no. 2 (2017): 200-229. On the Munich Olympics, see Zdenko Antić, "Yugoslav Construction Prospering in Foreign Countries," *Radio Free Europe Research*, October 29, 1970, 3.
5. On the development of Croatia's coast, see Grandits and Taylor, *Yugoslavia's Sunny Side*. On other airlines from the socialist East in the 1960s, see Svik, *Civil Aviation*.
6. On emigration to the West in these years, see Petar Dragišić, *Ko je pucao u Jugoslaviju? Jugoslovenska politička emigracija na zapadu, 1968-1980* (Belgrade: Institut za noviju istoriju Srbije, 2019) and Le Normand, *Citizens without Borders*.
7. On the IMF's role in Yugoslavia, see Adam Bennett, "Macroeconomic Stability and Enterprise Self-Management in Yugoslavia: An Impossible Marriage," in *The Legacy of Yugoslavia: Politics, Economics and Society in the Modern Balkans*, ed. Othon Anastasakis et al. (New York: Bloomsbury, 2020), 141-68. On the IMF and Jamaica, see Christine Clarke and Carol Nelson, *Contextualizing Jamaica's Relationship with the IMF* (Cham: Palgrave Macmillan, 2020).
8. These facts are found in Pregrag Marković's chapter, "Javnost i odnos između polova," in *Beograd između istoka i zapada*, 267-82.
9. Marković, *Beograd između istoka i zapada*, 281.
10. Marković, *Beograd između istoka i zapada*, 279.
11. *Love and Fashion* (*Ljubav i moda*), directed by Ljubomir Radičević, Avala Film (Belgrade), November 1960.
12. As quoted by R. Radosavljević, "Ljubav je opet u modi," *Večernje novosti*, July 1, 2010.
13. As quoted by Radosavljević, "Ljubav je opet u modi."
14. Sonja Ćirić, "Ružičasti talas," *Vreme*, December 20, 2000, https://old.vreme.com/arhiva_html/520/32.html.
15. Aleksandar Miletić, "Ljubica Otašević bila ljepša od Sofije Loren," *Politika*, April 11, 2013, http://www.politika.rs/scc/clanak/254593/Ljubica-Otasevic-bila-lepsa-od-Sofije-Loren.
16. "Te oci plavlje nego nebo kojim plovimo / sjajne kao sunce, oci pune sna."
17. "S njom se nikad ničeg ne bih bojao / celim putem oci bih joj gledao" and "Svuda tražim oci te / avione čekam sve."

18. Anonymous A, interview with author, July 5, 2018, Belgrade, Serbia.
19. Lukić, *Zapisi stjuardese*, 10.
20. Lukić, *Zapisi stjuardese*, 11.
21. For an account of the *Pobednik* monument's history and its importance to Belgrade, see Jovana Babovic, *Metropolitan Belgrade: Culture and Class in Interwar Yugoslavia* (Pittsburgh: University of Pittsburgh Press, 2018), 125–27.
22. Dušan Grbić, "Najlepši nebeski odred," *Ilustrovana politika*, May 1, 1973, 7, 8.
23. "Das traurige Schicksal der schönsten Frau Kroatiens," *Kosmo* (Vienna, Austria), October 31, 2017, https://www.kosmo.at/das-traurige-schicksal-der-schoensten-frau-kroatiens-video/.
24. Donald Bain (ghostwriter), Trudy Baker, and Rachel Jones, *Coffee, Tea or Me? The Uninhibited Memoirs of Two Airline Stewardesses* (New York: Bantam, 1967).
25. "Stjuardese o putnicima: Italijani svlače pogledom," *Bazar*, August 16, 1969, 6.
26. Grbić, "Najlepši nebeski odred," 8.
27. Grbić, "Najlepši nebeski odred," 8.
28. Mélanie Geelkens, "Une sacrée paire de pionnières," *Le Vif/L'Express*, July 30, 2020, 22.
29. Brigitte Hürlimann, "Die Töchter der Olympe de Gouges: Europas Frauen kämpfen bis heute um Gleichberechtigung—mit Unterstützing supranationaler Organisationen," *Neue Züricher Zeitung*, September 25, 2013, 9.
30. Grbić, "Najlepši nebeski odred," 8.
31. For an account of socialist-inspired fashion in these years, see Đurđa Bartlett, "Let Them Wear Beige: The Petit-Bourgeois World of Official Socialist Dress," *Fashion Theory* 8, no. 2 (June 2004): 127–64.

The details noted here and in ensuing paragraphs on Joksimović's career are drawn from Danijela Velimirović, *Aleksandar Joksimović: Moda i identitet* (Belgrade: Utopija, 2008).

32. "Modu čine detalji, ne linija," *Praktična žena*, no. 285, December 20, 1966, 14.
33. "Modu čine detalji," 15.
34. "Modu čine detalji," 15.
35. Karl Marx discusses the ways that people in capitalist economies ascribe wondrous properties to products they desire, using the example of a table in his work *Das Kapital* (1867): "But as soon as it emerges as a commodity, it changes into a thing which transcends sensuousness. It not only stands with its feet on the ground, but, in relation to all other commodities, it stands on its head, and evolves out of its wooden brain grotesque ideas, far more wonderful than if it were to begin dancing of its own free will." Karl Marx, *Capital: A Critique of Political Economy*, vol. 1, trans. Ben Fowkes (New York: Vintage, 1977), 163–64.
36. "Modu čine detalji," 15.
37. Daniel Delis Hill, *Peacock Revolution: American Masculine Identity and Dress in the Sixties and Seventies* (London: Bloomsbury, 2018).

38. Danijela Velimirović, "Kulturna biografija grandiozne mode: Priča o kolekciji Vitraž Aleksandra Joksimovića," *Etnoantropološki problemi* 1, no. 2 (2006): 91–104.

39. Velimirović, "Kulturna biografija grandiozne mode," 94.

40. As quoted by M. Savić, "Boja sigurnosti," *Politika—Bazar*, March 8, 1975. Accessed in the Aleksandar Joksimović Collection, Museum of Applied Arts, Belgrade, Serbia (hereafter Joks).

41. As quoted by Savić, "Boja sigurnosti."

42. Savić, "Boja sigurnosti."

43. JAT representatives also were mixed together with the general public for these events, as described in V. Bačlija, "Stjuardese u novoj uniformi," *Večernje novosti*, February 25, 1975, Joks.

44. As quoted in "Novo ruho stjuardesa," *JAT Revija*, summer 1975, 9.

45. As quoted in "Novo ruho stjuardesa," *JAT Revija*, summer 1975, 9.

46. Anonymous K, interview with author, May 30, 2018, Belgrade, Serbia.

47. Anonymous M, interview with author, July 6, 2018, Belgrade, Serbia.

48. As quoted in Kennedy, *Pucci*, 154.

49. Both the Japan Air Lines and Air India ads with such dresses are found in J. Walter Thompson Company, Competitive Advertisements, 1955–1997, series 1960, Transportation and Travel, box 1968-36 (Air India) and 1968-37 (JAL), JWT.

50. On the beginnings of a feminist movement in Yugoslavia in the 1970s and feminist priorities, see Zsófia Lóránd, *The Feminist Challenge to the Socialist State in Yugoslavia* (Cham: Springer, 2018) and Chiara Bonfiglioli, "Feminist Translations in a Socialist Context: The Case of Yugoslavia," *Gender & History* 30, no. 1 (2018): 240–54.

9. "Rare Tropical Birds"

1. On the riots at the university and Walter Rodney's role in fomenting them, see Walter Rodney, *The Groundings with My Brothers* (New York: Verso, 2019), and James Bradford, "Brother Wally and De Burnin' of Babylon: Walter Rodney's Impact on the Reawakening of Black Power, the Birth of Reggae, and Resistance to Global Imperialism," in *The Third World in the Global 1960s*, ed. Samantha Christiansen and Zachary A. Scarlett (New York: Berghahn Books, 2013), 142–58.

2. Manley's foreign policy, including its sharp contrasts with both his predecessors and his successor, Edward Seaga, is covered in R. B. Manderson-Jones, *Jamaican Foreign Policy in the Caribbean, 1962–1988* (Kingston: Caricom Publishers, 1990).

3. "Advertising Campaign," *Doctor Bird Chatter*, February 21, 1969, 2. This and subsequent editions of *Doctor Bird Chatter* are located in folder: Doctor Bird Chatter (February 13, 1969–November 25, 1970), box 1: Historical Documents, Air Jamaica Collection, Ministry of Finance and Public Service, Kingston, Jamaica (hereafter AirJ). *Doctor Bird Chatter* was an internal newsletter addressed to Air Jamaica employees. Its longtime news editor was employee John Scott.

4. "Successful U.S. Press Conferences," *Doctor Bird Chatter*, March 14, 1969, 1.

5. "Looking for Jamaican Air Hostesses," *Gleaner*, November 23, 1968, 28.

6. Minutes of the Second Directors' Meeting of Air Jamaica (1968) Limited, November 21, 1968, 3, file no. 796/03, vol. 1: Air Jamaica Limited—April 14, 1966 to October 3, 1969, AirJ.

7. "Looking for Jamaican Air Hostesses," 28.

8. "Air Jamaica Offers an Exciting Opportunity as a Flight Stewardess" (Air Jamaica advertisement), *Gleaner*, November 19, 1968, 13.

9. M. C. Robinson, secretary of Board of Directors, "Secretary's Report," December 19, 1968, 1, file no. 796/03, vol. 1: Air Jamaica Limited—April 14, 1966 to October 3, 1969, AirJ.

10. "Air Jamaica Trainee Hostesses Introduced," *Gleaner*, January 13, 1969, 18.

11. Minutes of the Second Directors' Meeting of Air Jamaica (1968) Limited, November 21, 1968, 3, AirJ.

12. "Air Jamaica Offers," 13.

13. Anonymous B, interview with author, February 6, 2018, Kingston, Jamaica.

14. "Air Jamaica Trainee Hostesses Introduced," 18.

15. Memo, "Requirements—Biggie," undated, 1, folder: "Inaugural Day—April 1, 1969," box 1: Historical Documents, AirJ.

16. "Air Jamaica Trainee Hostesses Introduced," 18.

17. "Looking for Air Jamaica Hostesses," 28.

18. "Air Jamaica's Rare Tropical 'Birds,'" *Gleaner*, April 1, 1969, Air Jamaica supplement, 8.

19. "The story of Air Jamaica," *Gleaner*, April 1, 1969, Air Jamaica supplement, 2.

20. "Air Jamaica Pulls Out All the Stops to the Islands" (Air Jamaica advertisement), *Life*, May 29, 1970, 8, folder "First Advertisement in Life Magazine," box 1: Historical Documents, AirJ.

21. "Check This Nuh?," *Sky Writings*, no. 1 (September 1972), 18. All issues of *Sky Writings* are located in Collection S679 (Sky Writings: Air Jamaica's Inflight Magazine), National Library of Jamaica, Kingston, Jamaica (herafter NLJ).

22. Barry, *Femininity in Flight*, 178.

23. Anonymous B interview.

24. Anonymous B interview.

25. Anonymous B interview.

26. Evon Blake, *The Best of Evon Blake* (Kingston: B. E. Blake, 1967), 24. Additional details of the incident provided by John Issa, the son of the hotel's owner Abe Issa, are reported in Annie Paul, "Colour and Tourism," *Gleaner*, February 20, 2018. This story has been repeated in important histories of tourism in Jamaica, including Krista A. Thompson, *An Eye for the Tropics: Tourism, Photography, and Framing the Caribbean Picturesque* (Durham, NC: Duke University Press, 2007), 204.

27. Blake's letter is reprinted in: "Congratulations," *Doctor Bird Chatter*, March 25, 1970, 2–3, folder "Doctor Bird Chatter," box 1: Historical Documents, AirJ.

28. The stamp is reproduced in "Stamps in the News: Air Jamaica Honored," *Reading Eagle* (Reading, PA), June 11, 1972, 74.

29. The lyrics of Wilson's "Better Mus' Come" and a brief analysis of the song's importance is included in: Diana Paton and Matthew J. Smith, eds., *The Jamaica Reader: History, Culture, Politics* (Durham, NC: Duke University Press, 2021), 334–35.

30. Beverley Anderson Manley has published an autobiography chronicling these and other life events: Beverley Manley, *The Manley Memoirs* (Kingston: Ian Randle, 2008).

31. Letter from G. Arthur Brown to Cleve Lewis, minister of communication and works, March 6, 1970, 1, folder "Air Jamaica Ltd., vol. II, October 3, 1969–June 8, 1972," box 796/03, AirJ.

32. P. J. Patterson (minister of industry, tourism, and foreign trade), Ministry Paper 61/75, "Tourism Development," December 11, 1975, appendix 2, "Summary of Findings of Studies Done by Professor Hines and by the Tourism Development Committee," 6, binder "Jamaica Ministry Papers 1975," Collection "Jamaica Parliament Ministry Papers, 1969–1980," University of the West Indies, Mona, Jamaica (hereafter UWI).

33. Patterson, "Tourism Development," 12.

34. Patterson, "Tourism Development," 15.

35. Patterson, "Tourism Development," 15.

36. Anonymous C, interview with author, via telephone, January 22, 2018.

37. Odette Dixon Neath, introduction to *A Tapestry of Jamaica: The Best of SkyWritings*, ed. Linda Gambrill (Kingston: Creative Communications, 2003), 9.

38. Anonymous C interview.

39. *Sky Writings*, no. 1 (September 1972), cover, NLJ.

40. John Hearne, "A View from the Mountains," *Sky Writings*, no. 1 (September 1972), 8–9, NLJ.

41. *Sky Writings*, no. 2 (Jan 1973), cover, NLJ.

42. Carlton Gordon, "Men, Proceed with Care. It's Really a Woman's World," *Sky Writings*, no. 2 (January 1973), 18, NLJ.

43. Anonymous C interview.

44. Anonymous D, interview with author, January 14, 2018, Kingston, Jamaica.

45. Anonymous E, interview with author, January 17, 2018, Kingston, Jamaica.

46. Anonymous E interview.

47. The Wilson case is officially known as Bustamante Industrial Trade Union v. Air Jamaica Ltd., no. IDT 2/80, March 3, 1980. Details of the case, including the quote above, are discussed in: "Sacked Stewardess to Be Reinstated," *Gleaner*, March 7, 1980, 2.

48. "'A Break Away from Painted Dolls,'" *Gleaner*, November 10, 1963, 1.

49. Anonymous B interview.
50. Anonymous F, interview with author, January 10, 2018, Kingston, Jamaica.
51. Anonymous E interview.
52. Anonymous B interview.
53. Anonymous F interview.
54. Anonymous E interview.
55. Anonymous E interview.
56. Anonymous B interview.
57. On the Notting Hill incidents, see Edward Pilkington, *Beyond the Mother Country: West Indians and the Notting Hill White Riots* (London: I.B. Taurus, 1988).

10. Jet Age Feminist Subversives

1. Literature on the growth of feminist groups in Yugoslavia includes: Lóránd, *Feminist Challenge*, and Bonfiglioli, "Feminist Translations." Works that cover Jamaican feminist groups include: A. Lynn Bolles, "Academics and Praxis: Caribbean Feminisms," in *Transatlantic Feminisms: Women and Gender Studies in Africa and the Diaspora*, ed. Cheryl Rene Rodriguez, Dzodzi Tsikata, and Akosua Adomako Ampofo (London: Lexington Books, 2015), 63–78; Patricia Mohammed, "Forever Indebted to Women: The Power of Caribbean Feminism," *Caribbean Review of Gender Studies*, no. 2 (2008): 1–10; and Judith Soares, "Addressing the Tensions: Reflections on Feminism in the Caribbean," *Caribbean Quarterly* 52, nos. 2–3 (2006): 187–97.

2. Per capita GDP levels in 1973, in 2024 US dollars, were US$1219 in Jamaica and US$1011 in Yugoslavia. Meanwhile, the combined mining and manufacturing sectors in both countries totaled 28 percent of GDP in Jamaica and 32.1 percent in Yugoslavia the early 1970s. On GDP per capita, see: United Nations Statistics Division, "National Accounts Estimates of Main Aggregates: Per capita GDP at Current Prices—US Dollars," *UNdata*, www.data.un.org. On mining and manufacturing, see, for Yugoslavia: Organization for Economic Co-operation and Development, *OECD Economic Surveys: Yugoslavia* (Paris: OECD Publication, 1973), 1, and for Jamaica: Bernard La Corbiniere, "Financing Economic Growth and Development in Jamaica: 1960–1992" (PhD diss., University of Kent, 1997), 20.

3. Unemployment in Jamaica was 23.2 percent in 1972. In the same year in Yugoslavia, it was 7 percent. On Jamaica, see Claremont Kirton, *Jamaica: Debt and Poverty* (London: Oxfam GB, 1992), 16. On Yugoslavia, see OECD, *OECD Economic Surveys*, 33.

4. "The Air Jamaica Situation," 7, included as part of "Cabinet Submission, Air Jamaica—Refinancing," n.d., prepared for meeting with Prime Minister Manley on November 23, 1990, box 796/03, vol. 20, AirJ.

5. Anonymous G, interview with author, May 7, 2018, Belgrade, Serbia.

6. Anonymous H, interview with author, November 16, 2014, Belgrade, Serbia.

7. Anonymous E, interview with author, January 17, 2018, Kingston, Jamaica.

8. Anonymous I, interview with author, January 13, 2018, Kingston, Jamaica.

9. Anonymous J, interview with author, January 17, 2018, Kingston, Jamaica.

10. Anonymous F, interview with author, January 10, 2018, Kingston, Jamaica.

11. An excellent description of the Yugoslav system of workers' self-management, coupled with case studies of its implementation, is found in Goran Musić, *Making and Breaking the Yugoslav Working Class: The Story of Two Self-Managed Factories* (Budapest: Central European University Press, 2021).

12. Anonymous K, interview with author, May 30, 2018, Belgrade, Serbia.

13. Anonymous K interview.

14. Anonymous K interview.

15. Anonymous K interview.

16. Anonymous L, interview with author, May 29, 2018, Belgrade, Serbia.

17. Anonymous D, interview with author, January 14, 2018, Kingston, Jamaica.

18. Anonymous E interview.

19. Anonymous G interview.

20. Anonymous E interview.

21. Anonymous M, interview with author, July 6, 2018, Belgrade, Serbia.

22. Anonymous G interview.

23. Anonymous O, interview with author, July 17, 2018, Belgrade, Serbia.

24. Anonymous O interview.

25. Molly Walton, "Bulletin," December 1989, as quoted in Industrial Disputes Tribunal, "Award in Respect of an Industrial Dispute between Air Jamaica, Limited and the Bustamante Industrial Trade Union," Case Number IDT 7/91, April 20, 1994, 2. Found in the Archives of the Industrial Disputes Tribunal, Kingston, Jamaica (hereafter IDT).

26. Details of the case are found in "Award in Respect of an Industrial Dispute."

27. Anonymous J interview.

28. "Drugs and the U.S. Threat of Aircraft Seizure," *Air Jamaica Staff Newsletter*, no. 10, October 1986, 1, box 3, Historical Documents, AirJ.

29. Anonymous F interview.

30. Anonymous J interview.

31. Brown, *Sex and the Single Girl*.

32. Lukić, *Zapisi stjuardese*, 15.

33. Lukić, *Zapisi stjuardese*, 119.

34. Anonymous D interview.

35. Anonymous B, interview with author, February 6, 2018, Kingston, Jamaica.

36. Anonymous J interview.

37. Anonymous F interview.

38. Anonymous E interview.

39. Anonymous F interview.
40. Anonymous N, interview with author, July 4, 2018, Belgrade, Serbia.
41. Anonymous E interview.
42. Anonymous M interview.
43. Anonymous K interview.
44. Anonymous K interview.
45. Anonymous F interview.
46. Anonymous I interview.
47. Anonymous E interview.
48. Anonymous F interview
49. Anonymous M interview.
50. Anonymous N interview.
51. Anonymous N interview.
52. Anonymous M interview.
53. Anonymous D interview.
54. Chiara Bonfiglioli, *Women and Industry in the Balkans: The Rise and Fall of the Yugoslav Textile Sector* (London: I.B. Taurus, 2021), 60–62.
55. Bonfiglioli, *Women and Industry*, 56.
56. The text of the Jamaica Maternity Leave Act of 1979 is found here: https://laws.moj.gov.jm/library/statute/the-maternity-leave-act.
57. Anonymous M interview.
58. Anonymous M interview.
59. Anonymous N interview.
60. Anonymous N interview.
61. Anonymous B interview.
62. Anonymous I interview.
63. Anonymous E interview.
64. Anonymous J interview.
65. Mélanie Geelkens, "Une sacrée paire de pionnières," *Le Vif/L'Express*, July 30, 2020, 22.
66. A list of some of these cases is provided in: US Equal Employment Opportunity Commission, "Waiting with Their Wings to Fight Workplace Sex Discrimination," press release, October 24, 2014, https://www.eeoc.gov/newsroom/waiting-their-wings-fight-workplace-sex-discrimination.
67. Cathleen Dooley Loucks, "Battle in the Skies: Sex Discrimination in the United States Airline Industry, 1930 to 1978" (master's thesis, University of Nevada Las Vegas, 1995), 34.
68. The fashion shows did return in the mid-1990s. This occurred at a moment when flight attendants' collective bargaining power had been weakened and many flight attendants were flying on contingent contracts.
69. Leslie Josephs, "68 Percent of Flight Attendants Say They Have Experienced Sexual Harassment on the Job," CNBC, May 10, 2018, https://www.cnbc.com/2018/05/10/sexual-harassment-of-flight-attendants-is-rampant-survey-finds.html.
70. Anonymous K interview.

Conclusion

1. Boothe Luce, "America," 761.
2. Boothe Luce, "America," 762.
3. Boothe Luce, "America," 762.
4. Clare Boothe Luce, *The Women* (1936), as quoted in Marie Brenner, "Fast and Luce," *Vanity Fair*, March 1988.
5. "Air Jamaica: End of an Era," *Jamaica Observer*, July 8, 2011.
6. On JAT's passenger numbers in 1987, see "Former Yugoslav Flag Carriers Handle over 1.1 Million Passengers in Q1," *Ex-YU Aviation News*, May 6, 2024, https://www.exyuaviation.com/2024/05/former-yugoslav-flag-carriers-handle.html.
7. "Air Serbia Now Fully State-Owned as Etihad Sells Last Remaining Shares," *Aviation Week*, November 15, 2023, https://aviationweek.com/air-transport/airlines-lessors/air-serbia-now-fully-state-owned-etihad-sells-last-remaining-shares.
8. Some of Fraser's sharpest critiques of feminism in the neoliberal age are found in Nancy Fraser, *Fortunes of Feminism: From State-Managed Capitalism to Neoliberal Crisis* (London: Verso, 2013).
9. Catherine Rottenberg, *The Rise of Neoliberal Feminism* (New York: Oxford University Press, 2018), 54.
10. Sheryl Sandberg, *Lean In: Women, Work, and the Will to Lead* (London: W. H. Allen, 2015).

Bibliography

Archives

AirJ   Air Jamaica Papers, Ministry of Finance and Planning Archives, Kingston, Jamaica.
AJ   Archives of Yugoslavia (Arhiv Jugoslavije), Belgrade, Serbia.
Braniff   Braniff Collection, History of Aviation Archives, Special Collections and Archives Division, University of Texas at Dallas, Richardson, TX.
DA   Diplomatic Archives (Diplomatski arhiv), Ministry of Foreign Affairs, Republic of Serbia, Belgrade, Serbia.
Girard   Alexander Girard Archives, Vitra Design Museum, Weil am Rhein, Germany.
IDT   Archives of the Industrial Disputes Tribunal, Kingston, Jamaica.
Joks   Aleksandar Joksimović Collection, Museum of Applied Arts, Belgrade, Serbia.
JWT   J. Walter Thompson Company Publications Collection, 1887–2005, David M. Rubenstein Rare Book and Manuscript Library, Duke University, Durham, NC.
NARA   National Archives of the United States, National Archives and Records Administration, College Park, MD.

        Record Group 59: General Records of the Department of State (RG 59)

NAUK   National Archives of the United Kingdom, Kew, UK.

        Records of the Foreign and Colonial Office (FCO)
        Records of the Colonial Office (CO)
        Records of the Board of Trade (BT)
        Records of the Dominions Office (DO)

PAWA   Pan American World Airways, Inc. Records, University of Miami Libraries Special Collections, University of Miami, Coral Gables, FL.
UWI   Special Collections, University of the West Indies Library, Mona (Kingston), Jamaica.

        Government and United Nations Documents
        P. J. Patterson Papers, Caribbean Leaders Collection

Bibliography

Published Primary Sources

Central Intelligence Agency. "Yugoslavia." *National Intelligence Survey* 21, April 1973, 28. https://www.cia.gov/readingroom/docs/CIA-RDP01-00707R0 00200100032-0.pdf.

Government of Yugoslavia. *Petogodišnji plan razvitka narodne privrede FNRJ u godinima 1947–1951* [Five-year plan for the development of the people's economy of the Federal People's Republic of Yugoslavia in the years 1947-1951]. Belgrade: RAD, 1948.

International Civil Aviation Conference. *Proceedings of the International Civil Aviation Conference: Chicago, Illinois, November 1–December 7, 1944*. Vol. 1. Washington, DC: US Government Printing Office, 1948.

International Civil Aviation Organization (ICAO). *Convention on International Civil Aviation Done at Chicago on the 7th Day of December 1944*. Text of the treaty, with original signatories, is found at: https://www.icao.int/publications/documents/7300_orig.pdf.

Luce, Clare Boothe. "America in the Post-War Air World." *Congressional Record—House*, 78th Congress, February 9, 1943, 759–64.

Other Published Sources

Alcoff, Linda Martín. "What Should White People Do?" *Hypatia* 13, no. 3 (1998): 6–26.

Allyn, David. *Make Love, Not War: The Sexual Revolution, an Unfettered History*. London: Routledge, 2016.

Altink, Henrice. *Destined for a Life of Service: Defining African-Jamaican Womanhood, 1865–1938*. Manchester, UK: Manchester University Press, 2011.

Ayuttacorn, Arratee, and Jane Ferguson. "Air Male: Exploring Flight Attendant Masculinities in North America and Thailand." *The Asia Pacific Journal of Anthropology* 20, no. 4 (2019): 328–43.

Babovic, Jovana. *Metropolitan Belgrade: Culture and Class in Interwar Yugoslavia*. Pittsburgh: University of Pittsburgh Press, 2018.

Bailey, Barbara, Bridget Brereton, and Verene Shepherd, eds. *Engendering History: Cultural and Socio-economic Realities in Africa*. New York: Palgrave Macmillan, 1995.

Bain, Donald, Trudy Baker, and Rachel Jones. *Coffee, Tea or Me?: The Uninhibited Memoirs of Two Airline Stewardesses*. New York: Bantam, 1967.

Balandier, Georges, ed. *Le Tiers-monde: Sous-développement et développement*. Paris: Presses universitaires de France, 1961.

Barry, Kathleen. *Femininity in Flight: A History of Flight Attendants*. Durham, NC: Duke University Press, 2007.

Bartlett, Đurđa. "Let Them Wear Beige: The Petit-Bourgeois World of Official Socialist Dress." *Fashion Theory* 8, no. 2 (June 2004): 127–64.

Batinić, Jelena. *Women and Yugoslav Partisans: A History of World War II Resistance*. Cambridge: Cambridge University Press, 2015.

Beauvoir, Simone de. *The Second Sex*. New York: Knopf, 1952.

Bennett, Adam. "Macroeconomic Stability and Enterprise Self-Management in Yugoslavia: An Impossible Marriage." In *The Legacy of Yugoslavia: Politics, Economics and Society in the Modern Balkans*, edited by Othon Anastasakis, Adam Bennett, David Madden, and Adis Merdzanovic, 141-68. New York: Bloomsbury, 2020.

Berge, Jan. *JAT Glory Days: Yugoslavia's National Airline through Communism, 1947-1987*. Self-published, 2013. https://www.academia.edu/14553153/JAT_GLORY_DAYS?auto=download.

Bhimull, Chandra D. *Empire in the Air: Airline Travel and the African Diaspora*. New York: New York University Press, 2017.

Blake, Evon. *The Best of Evon Blake*. Kingston: B. E. Blake, 1967.

Bolles, A. Lynn. "Academics and Praxis: Caribbean Feminisms." In *Transatlantic Feminisms: Women and Gender Studies in Africa and the Diaspora*, edited by Cheryl Rene Rodriguez, Dzodzi Tsikata, and Akosua Adomako Ampofo, 63-78. London: Lexington Books, 2015.

Bonfiglioli, Chiara. "Feminist Translations in a Socialist Context: The Case of Yugoslavia." *Gender & History* 30, no. 1 (2018): 240-54.

———. *Women and Industry in the Balkans: The Rise and Fall of the Yugoslav Textile Sector*. London: I.B. Tauris, 2021.

Božinović, Neda. *Žensko pitanje u Srbiji u XIX i XX veku*. Belgrade: Dvadesetčetvrta, 1996.

Bradford, James. "Brother Wally and De Burnin' of Babylon: Walter Rodney's Impact on the Reawakening of Black Power, the Birth of Reggae, and Resistance to Global Imperialism." In *The Third World in the Global 1960s*, edited by Samantha Christiansen and Zachary A. Scarlett, 142-58. New York: Berghahn Books, 2013.

Bradley, Patricia. *Mass Media and the Shaping of American Feminism, 1963-1975*. Oxford: University Press of Mississippi, 2003.

Brands, Henry William. *The Specter of Neutralism: The United States and the Emergence of the Third World, 1947-1960*. New York: Columbia University Press, 1989.

Brenner, Marie. "Fast and Luce." *Vanity Fair*, March 1988.

Brown, G. Arthur. *Patterns of Development and Attendant Choices and Consequences for Jamaica and the Caribbean*. Kingston: GraceKennedy Foundation, 1989.

Brown, Helen Gurley. *Sex and the Office*. New York: Bernard Geis Associates, 1964.

———. *Sex and the Single Girl*. New York: Bernard Geis Associates, 1962.

Bürgisser, Thomas. *Wahlverwandtschaft zweier Sonderfälle im Kalten Krieg: Schweizerische Perspektiven auf das sozialistische Jugoslawien 1943-1991*. Bern: Diplomatische Dokumente der Schweiz, 2017.

Cheah, Pheng, Bruce Robbins, and Social Text Collective. *Cosmopolitics: Thinking and Feeling beyond the Nation*. Minneapolis: University of Minnesota Press, 1998.

Clarke, Christine, and Carol Nelson. "A Clash of Ideologies: Jamaica and the International Monetary Fund." In Clarke and Nelson, *Contextualizing Jamaica's Relationship*, 123-66.

———. *Contextualizing Jamaica's Relationship with the IMF*. Cham: Palgrave Macmillan, 2020.
Clarke, Colin. *Decolonizing the Colonial City: Urbanization and Stratification in Kingston, Jamaica*. Oxford: Oxford University Press, 2006.
Conrad, Sebastian. *What Is Global History?* Princeton, NJ: Princeton University Press, 2017.
Cooper, Carolyn. "Caribbean Fashion Week: Remodeling Beauty in 'Out of Many One' Jamaica." *Fashion Theory* 14, no. 3 (September 2010): 387–404.
Cowen, Mike. "Early Years of the Colonial Development Corporation: British State Enterprise Overseas during Late Colonialism." *African Affairs* 83, no. 330 (January 1984): 63–75.
Darby, Phillip, and A. J. Paolini. "Bridging International Relations and Postcolonialism." *Alternatives: Global, Local, Political* 19, no. 3 (Summer 1994): 371–97.
De Grazia, Victoria. *Irresistible Empire: America's Advance through Twentieth-Century Europe*. Cambridge, MA: Belknap Press of Harvard University Press, 2005.
Devic, Ana. "Redefining the Public-Private Boundary: Nationalism and Women's Activism in Former Yugoslavia." *Anthropology of East Europe Review* 15, no. 2 (1997): 45–61.
D'Hooghe, Vanessa. "Article 119: How Stewardesses Obtained Equal Pay in the European Community (Belgium 1968-1980)." In *Institutionalizing Gender Equality: Historical and Global Perspectives*, edited by Yulia Gradskova and Sara Sanders, 39–60. Lanham, MD: Lexington Books, 2015.
Dobson, Alan. *A History of International Civil Aviation: From Its Origins through Transformative Evolution*. London: Taylor and Francis, 2017.
Dodić, Vera Gudac. *Žena u Socijalizmu: Položaj žene u Srbiju u drugoj polovini 20. veka*. Belgrade: Institut za noviju istoriju Srbije, 2006.
Dooley Loucks, Cathleen. "Battle in the Skies: Sex Discrimination in the United States Airline Industry, 1930 to 1978." Master's thesis, University of Nevada Las Vegas, 1995.
Dragišić, Petar. *Ko je pucao u Jugoslaviju? Jugoslovenska politička emigracija na zapadu, 1968–1980*. Belgrade: Institut za noviju istoriju Srbije, 2019.
———. "Rat posle rata: Jugoslavija i Austrija 1945-1949." In *Odnosi Jugoslavije i Austrije 1945–1955*, 25–102. Belgrade: Institut za noviju istoriju Srbije, 2013.
Dugandžić, Andreja, and Tijana Okić, eds. *The Lost Revolution: Women's Antifascist Front between Myth and Forgetting*. Sarajevo: Association for Culture and Art CRVENA, 2018.
D'Unienville, Alix. *En vol: Journal d'une hôtesse de l'air*. Paris: A. Michel, 1949.
Ehrenreich, Barbara, Elizabeth Hess, and Gloria Jacobs. *Re-making Love: The Feminization of Sex*. Garden City, NY: Anchor Press/Doubleday, 1986.
Ekbladh, David. *The Great American Mission: Modernization and the Construction of an American World Order*. Princeton, NJ: Princeton University Press, 2011.
Engel, Jeffrey. *Cold War at 30,000 Feet: The Anglo-American Fight for Aviation Supremacy*. Cambridge, MA: Harvard University Press, 2007.

Fanon, Frantz. *Wretched of the Earth*. New York: Grove Press, 1963.
Forbes, John D. *Jamaica: Managing Political and Economic Change*. Washington, DC: American Enterprise Institute for Public Policy Research, 1985.
Ford-Smith, Honor. "Making White Ladies: Race, Gender, and the Production of Identities in Late Colonial Jamaica." *Resources for Feminist Research* 23, no. 4 (1994): 55–67.
Frankel, Joseph. "Communism and the National Question in Yugoslavia." *Journal of Central European Affairs* 15 (April 1955): 49–65.
Fraser, Nancy. *Fortunes of Feminism: From State-Managed Capitalism to Neoliberal Crisis*. London: Verso, 2013.
Friedan, Betty. *The Feminine Mystique: Annotated Text, Contexts, Scholarship*. 50th anniversary ed. New York: W. W. Norton, 2013.
Gambrill, Linda, ed. *A Tapestry of Jamaica: The Best of Skywritings*. Kingston: Creative Communications, 2003.
Gendzier, Irene. *Notes from the Minefield: United States Intervention in Lebanon, 1945–1958*. New York: Columbia University Press, 2006.
Grandits, Hannes, and Karin Taylor, eds. *Yugoslavia's Sunny Side: A History of Tourism in Socialism, 1950s–1980s*. Budapest: Central European University Press, 2010.
Gray, Obika. *Demeaned but Empowered: The Social Power of the Urban Poor in Jamaica*. Kingston: University of the West Indies Press, 2004.
———. *Radicalism and Social Change in Jamaica, 1960–1972*. Knoxville: University of Tennessee Press, 1991.
Greiner, Andreas. "Aviation History and Global History: Towards a Research Agenda for the Interwar Period." *Bulletin of the German Historical Institute* 69 (Fall 2021–Spring 2022): 123–50.
Hadžiristić, Tea. "Unveiling Muslim Women in Socialist Yugoslavia: The Body between Socialism, Secularism, and Colonialism." *Religion and Gender* 7, no. 2 (2017): 184–203.
Helman, Gerald B., and Steven R. Ratner. "Saving Failed States." *Foreign Policy*, December 1992.
Hiatt, Willie. *The Rarified Air of the Modern: Airplanes and Technological Modernity in the Andes*. New York: Oxford University Press, 2016.
Hill, Daniel Delis. *Peacock Revolution: American Masculine Identity and Dress in the Sixties and Seventies*. London: Bloomsbury, 2018.
Hobsbawm, Eric John. *The Age of Extremes: The Short Twentieth Century, 1914–1991*. London: Abacus, 1995.
Horncastle, James. *The Macedonian Slavs in the Greek Civil War, 1944–1949*. Lanham, MD: Lexington Books, 2019.
Immerwahr, Daniel. *How to Hide an Empire: A History of the Greater United States*. New York: Farrar, Straus and Giroux, 2019.
James, Marlon. *A Brief History of Seven Killings*. New York: Riverhead Books, 2014.
Jancar-Webster, Barbara. *Women and Revolution in Yugoslavia, 1941–1945*. Denver, CO: Arden Press, 1990.
Janić, Čedomir, and Jovo Simišić. *More than Flying: Eight Decades of Aeroput and JAT*. Belgrade: JAT Airways Media Center, 2007.

Jansen, Stef. "The Afterlives of the Yugoslav Red Passport." *Citizenship in Southeast Europe* (blog), October 24, 2012. https://www.citsee.eu/citsee-story/afterlives-yugoslav-red-passport.

Kant, Immanuel. *On History*. Edited by Lewis White Beck. Indianapolis, IN: Bobbs-Merrill, 1963.

Kardelj, Edvard. *Yugoslavia in International Relations and in the Non-aligned Movement*. Belgrade: Socialist Thought and Practice, 1979.

Kecman, Jovanka. *Žene Jugoslavije u radničkom pokretu i ženskim organicijama 1918–1941*. Belgrade: Institut za savremenu istoriju, 1978.

Keith, Nelson W., and Novella Zett Keith. *The Social Origins of Democratic Socialism in Jamaica*. Philadelphia: Temple University Press, 1992.

Kendi, Ibram X. *Stamped from the Beginning: The Definitive History of Racist Ideas in America*. New York: Nation Books, 2016.

Kennedy, Shirley. *Pucci: A Renaissance in Fashion*. New York: Abbeville Press, 1991.

Kerber, Linda K. "Separate Spheres, Female Worlds, Woman's Place: The Rhetoric of Women's History." *Journal of American History* 75, no. 1 (1988): 9–39.

Kilibarda, Konstantin. "Non-aligned Geographies in the Balkans: Space, Race, and Image in the Construction of New 'European' Foreign Policies." In *Security beyond the Discipline: Emerging Dialogues on Global Politics*, edited by Abhinava Kumar and Derek Maisonville, 27–57. Toronto: York University Centre for International and Security Studies, 2010.

King, Rosamond S. *Island Bodies: Transgressive Sexualities in the Caribbean Imagination*. Gainesville: University Press of Florida, 2014.

Kukobat, Ilija. *Sovjetski uticaji na jugoslovensko vazduhoplovstvo 1944–1949: Između saradnje i suprotstavljanja*. Belgrade: Institut za savremenu istoriju, 2020.

Lawrence, Mary Wells. *A Big Life in Advertising*. New York: Knopf, 2002.

Lees, Lorraine. *Keeping Tito Afloat: The United States, Yugoslavia, and the Cold War*. University Park: Pennsylvania State University Press, 1997.

Le Normand, Brigitte. *Citizens without Borders: Yugoslavia and Its Migrant Workers in Western Europe*. Toronto: University of Toronto Press, 2021.

Loomba, Ania. *Colonialism/Postcolonialism*. 3rd ed. New York: Routledge, 2015.

Lóránd, Zsófia. *The Feminist Challenge to the Socialist State in Yugoslavia*. Cham: Springer, 2018.

Luce, Henry. "The American Century." *Diplomatic History* 23, no. 2 (Spring 1999): 159–71.

Lukić, Milica. *Zapisi stjuardese*. Belgrade: Partenon, 2000.

Manderson-Jones, R. B. *Jamaican Foreign Policy in the Caribbean, 1962–1988*. Kingston: Caricom Publishers, 1990.

Manley, Beverley. *The Manley Memoirs*. Kingston: Ian Randle, 2008.

Manley, Elizabeth. "Runway Hospitality: Air Jamaica's 'Rare Tropical Birds' and the Embodied Gender and Race Politics of Tourism, 1966–1980." *Hispanic American Historical Review* 102, no. 1 (2022): 285–319.

———. "'Wings over the Antilles': The Gendered Politics of Caribbean Air Travel during the Cold War." Paper presented at the Society of Historians of American Foreign Relations, Arlington, VA, June 2023.

Manley, Sarah. "Coppertone." *PREE: Caribbean Writing*, November 13, 2018. https://preelit.com/2018/11/13/coppertone/.
Marchand, Roland. *Advertising the American Dream: Making Way for Modernity, 1920–1940*. Berkeley: University of California Press, 1985.
Marder, Pascale. *Nelly Diener: Engel der Lüfte vom kurzen Glück der ersten Lufthostess Europas*. Zurich: Bilgerverlag, 2018.
Marković, Predrag J. *Beograd između istoka i zapada: 1948–1965*. Belgrade: Službeni list SRJ, 1996.
Martin, Cedriann J. "Marguerite Gordon: Lady of the Manners." *Caribbean Beat*, August 2009. https://www.caribbean-beat.com/issue-98/marguerite-gordon-lady-manners#axzz7YxZY3jtx.
Marx, Karl. *Capital: A Critique of Political Economy*. Translated by Ben Fowkes. Vol. 1. New York: Vintage, 1977.
Mawby, Spencer. *Ordering Independence: The End of Empire in the Anglophone Caribbean, 1947–1969*. New York: Palgrave Macmillan, 2012.
May, Elaine Tyler. *Homeward Bound: American Families in the Cold War Era*. 1988. Reprint, New York: Basic Books, 2008.
McClintock, Anne. *Imperial Leather: Race, Gender, and Sexuality in the Colonial Contest*. New York: Routledge, 1995.
Meyerowitz, Joanne J. *Not June Cleaver: Women and Gender in Postwar America, 1945–1960*. Philadelphia, PA: Temple University Press, 1994.
Mohammed, Patricia. "'But Most of All Mi Love Me Browning': The Emergence in Eighteenth- and Nineteenth-Century Jamaica of the Mulatto Woman as the Desired." *Feminist Review* 65 (Summer 2000): 22–48.
———. "Forever Indebted to Women: The Power of Caribbean Feminism." *Caribbean Review of Gender Studies*, no. 2 (2008): 1–10.
Momsen, Janet, ed. *Women and Change in the Caribbean: A Pan-Caribbean Perspective*. Bloomington: Indiana University Press, 1993.
Montini, Federico Tenca. *Trst Ne Damo!: Jugoslavija i Tršćansko pitanje 1945–1954*. Zagreb: Srednja Europa, 2021.
Morgan, Kenneth. *A Concise History of Jamaica*. Cambridge: Cambridge University Press, 2023.
Morokvašić, Mirjana. "Being a Woman in Yugoslavia: Past, Present, and Institutional Equality." In *Women of the Mediterranean*, edited by Monique Gadant, 120–38. London: Zed Books, 1986.
Morris, Sylvia Jukes. *Price of Fame: The Honorable Clare Boothe Luce*. New York: Random House, 2015.
Mostov, Julie. "Sexing the Nation/Desexing the Body: Politics of National Identity in the Former Yugoslavia." In *Gender Ironies of Nationalism: Sexing the Nation*, edited by Tamar Mayer, 89–112. New York: Routledge, 2012.
Muehlenbeck, Philip. "Czechoslovak Aviation Assistance to Africa (1960–1968)." In *Czechoslovakia in Africa, 1945–1968*, 125–56. New York: Palgrave Macmillan, 2016.
Musić, Goran. *Making and Breaking the Yugoslav Working Class: The Story of Two Self-Managed Factories*. Budapest: Central European University Press, 2021.

Nielsen, Georgia Panter. *From Sky Girl to Flight Attendant: Women and the Making of a Union*. Ithaca, NY: ILR Press, 1982.

O'Connor, Bernard. *Agents Françaises*. Research Triangle Park, NC: Lulu Press, 2016.

Okić, Tijana. "From Revolutionary to Productive Subject: An Alternative History of the Women's Antifascist Front." In Dugandžić and Okić, *The Lost Revolution*, 156–99.

Palmer, Colin. *Inward Yearnings: Jamaica's Journey to Nationhood*. Kingston: University of the West Indies Press, 2016.

Pantelić, Ivana. *Partizanke kao građanke: Društvena emancipacija partizanki u Srbiji, 1945–1953*. Belgrade: Institut za savremenu istoriju, 2011.

Parker, Jason C. *Brother's Keeper: The United States, Race, and Empire in the British Caribbean, 1937–1962*. New York: Oxford University Press, 2008.

———. *Hearts, Minds, Voices: US Cold War Public Diplomacy and the Formation of the Third World*. New York: Oxford University Press, 2016.

Paton, Diana, and Matthew J. Smith. *The Jamaica Reader: History, Culture, Politics*. Durham, NC: Duke University Press, 2021.

Patterson, Orlando. *The Confounding Island: Jamaica and the Postcolonial Predicament*. Cambridge, MA: Harvard University Press, 2019.

Patterson, Patrick Hyder. *Bought and Sold: Living and Losing the Good Life in Socialist Yugoslavia*. Ithaca, NY: Cornell University Press, 2011.

Pearson, Jessica Lynne. "Decolonizing the Sky: Global Air Travel at the End of Empire." *Humanity: An International Journal of Human Rights, Humanitarianism, and Development* 14, no. 1 (2023): 68–84.

Pilkington, Edward. *Beyond the Mother Country: West Indians and the Notting Hill White Riots*. London: I.B. Tauris, 1988.

Prashad, Vijay. *The Darker Nations: A People's History of the Third World*. New York: New Press, 2007.

Putnam, Lara. *Radical Moves: Caribbean Migrants and the Politics of Race in the Jazz Age*. Chapel Hill: University of North Carolina Press, 2013.

Rajak, Svetozar. "'Companions in Misfortune': From Passive Neutralism to Active Un-commitment; The Critical Role of Yugoslavia." In *Neutrality and Neutralism in the Global Cold War: Between or within the Blocs?*, edited by Sandra Bott, Jussi Hanhimäki, Janick Marina Schaufelbuehl, and Marco Wyss, 72–89. London: Routledge, 2016.

———. *Yugoslavia and the Soviet Union in the Early Cold War: Reconciliation, Comradeship, Confrontation, 1953–1957*. New York: Routledge, 2010.

Ramet, Sabrina P. *Gender Politics in the Western Balkans: Women and Society in Yugoslavia and the Yugoslav Successor States*. College Park: Pennsylvania State University Press, 1999.

Robertson, Roland. "Glocalization: Time-Space and Homogeneity-Heterogeneity." In *Global Modernities*, edited by Mike Featherstone, Scott Lash, and Roland Robertson, 25–44. London: Sage, 1995.

Rodney, Walter. *The Groundings with My Brothers*. New York: Verso, 2019.

Rottenberg, Catherine. *The Rise of Neoliberal Feminism*. New York: Oxford University Press, 2018.

Rowe, Rochelle. *Imagining Caribbean Womanhood: Race, Nation and Beauty Contests, 1929–70*. Manchester, UK: Manchester University Press, 2013.
Said, Edward. *Orientalism*. New York: Vintage, 1979.
Sandberg, Sheryl. *Lean In: Women, Work, and the Will to Lead*. London: W. H. Allen, 2015.
Scanlon, Jennifer. *Bad Girls Go Everywhere: The Life of Helen Gurley Brown, the Woman behind Cosmopolitan Magazine*. New York: Penguin, 2010.
Sekulić, Dubravka. "Energoprojekt in Nigeria: Yugoslav Construction Companies in the Developing World." *Southeastern Europe* 41, no. 2 (June 2017): 200–229.
Shirley, Gayle Corbett. *More than Petticoats: Remarkable Montana Women*. Lanham, MD: Rowman & Littlefield, 2010.
Simić, Andrei. *The Peasant Urbanites: A Study of Rural-Urban Mobility in Serbia*. New York: Seminar Press, 1973.
Simišić, Jovo. *Bio Jedan JAT*. Belgrade: Lighthouse Studio, 2022.
Soares, Judith. "Addressing the Tensions: Reflections on Feminism in the Caribbean." *Caribbean Quarterly* 52, nos. 2-3 (2006): 187–97.
Spaskovska, Ljubica. "Building a Better World? Construction, Labour Mobility and the Pursuit of Collective Self-Reliance in the 'Global South,' 1950–1990." *Labour History* 59, no. 3 (2018): 331–51.
Springfield, Consuelo López. *Daughters of Caliban: Caribbean Women in the Twentieth Century*. Bloomington: Indiana University Press, 1997.
Stadiem, William. *Jet Set: The People, the Planes, the Glamour, and the Romance in Aviation's Glory Years*. New York: Random House, 2014.
Stephens, Michelle Ann. *Black Empire: The Masculine Global Imaginary of Caribbean Intellectuals in the United States, 1914–1962*. Durham, NC: Duke University Press, 2005.
Stojčić, Marijana, and Nađa Duhaček. "From Partisans to Housewives: Representation of Women in Yugoslav Cinema." *Časopis za povijest Zapadne Hrvatske* 11 (2016): 69–107.
Stubbs, Paul. *Socialist Yugoslavia and the Non-Aligned Movement: Social, Cultural, Political, and Economic Imaginaries*. Montreal: McGill-Queen's University Press, 2023.
Subotić, Jelena, and Srđan Vucetić. "Performing Solidarity: Whiteness and Status-Seeking in the Non-aligned World." *Journal of International Relations and Development* 22, no. 3 (September 2019): 722–43.
Svik, Peter. *Civil Aviation and the Globalization of the Cold War*. Cham: Palgrave Macmillan, 2020.
Thompson, Krista A. *An Eye for the Tropics: Tourism, Photography, and Framing the Caribbean Picturesque*. Durham, NC: Duke University Press, 2007.
Tiemeyer, Phil. "Jet Age Feminism: Emilio Pucci, Mary Wells, and the Braniff Airways Stewardess of the 1960s." *History of Global Arms Transfer* 8 (2019): 67–82.
———. "Launching a Nonaligned Airline: JAT Yugoslav Airways between East, West, and South, 1947–1962." *Diplomatic History* 41, no. 1 (January 2017): 78–103.

———. *Plane Queer: Labor, Sexuality, and AIDS in the History of Male Flight Attendants*. Berkeley: University of California Press, 2013.

Todorova, Maria. *Imagining the Balkans*. New York: Oxford University Press, 2009.

Turk, Katherine. *Equality on Trial: Gender and Rights in the Modern American Workplace*. Philadelphia: University of Pennsylvania Press, 2016.

Van Vleck, Jenifer. "An Airline at the Crossroads of the World: Ariana Afghan Airlines, Modernization, and the Global Cold War." *History and Technology* 25, no. 1 (2009): 3–24.

———. *Empire of the Air: Aviation and the American Ascendancy*. Cambridge, MA: Harvard University Press, 2013.

Velimirović, Danijela. *Aleksandar Joksimović: Moda i identitet*. Belgrade: Utopija, 2008.

———. "Kulturna biografija grandiozne mode: Priča o kolekciji Vitraž Aleksandra Joksimovića." *Etnoantropološki problemi* 1, no. 2 (2006): 91–104.

Westad, Odd Arne. *The Global Cold War: Third-World Interventions and the Making of Our Times*. New York: Cambridge University Press, 2005.

Willett, Julie. *The Male Chauvinist Pig: A History*. Chapel Hill: University of North Carolina Press, 2021.

Wong, John D. *Hong Kong Takes Flight: Commercial Aviation and the Making of a Global Hub, 1930s–1998*. Cambridge, MA: Harvard University Asia Center, 2022.

Woodward, Susan. "The Rights of Women: Ideology, Policy, and Social Change in Yugoslavia." In *Women, State, and Party in Eastern Europe*, edited by Sharon L. Wolchik and Alfred G. Meyer, 234–56. Durham, NC: Duke University Press, 1985.

———. *Socialist Unemployment: The Political Economy of Yugoslavia, 1945–1990*. Princeton, NJ: Princeton University Press, 1995.

Wynter, Sylvia. *Jamaica's National Heroes*. Kingston: Jamaica National Trust Commission, 1971.

Zaidi, Waqar. "Pakistani Civil Aviation and U.S Aid to Pakistan, 1950 to 1961." *The Journal of Research Institute for the History of Global Arms Transfer* 8 (2019): 83–97.

Žarković, Petar. "Yugoslavia and the USSR 1945–1980: The History of a Cold War Relationship." *YU historia* (blog). Accessed March 29, 2023. https://yuhistorija.com/int_relations_txt01c1.html.

Zimmerman, William. *Open Borders, Nonalignment, and the Political Evolution of Yugoslavia*. Princeton, NJ: Princeton University Press, 2014.

Index

Adria Airways, 64–65, 268n66
Adriatic Coast, 46, 60
Aeroflot, 8, 63–64, 268n71
Aeroput, 36, 40, 263n12
Air Canada, 82–83, 88–89, 90, 200
Air France, 96, 100–104, 106, 113, 194, 195
Air India, 194, 262n24
Air Jamaica
  economic success of, before OPEC oil crisis, 84–85, 90
  economic weaknesses of, during OPEC oil crisis, 87–89, 91, 252
  financial difficulties of, 73–74, 76, 86, 87, 89–90, 91, 252
  first jets purchased by, 8, 82
  forms of hiring discrimination imposed on stewardesses by, 201–3
  founding of, 69, 70, 71, 72, 76, 77–80, 89–90, 138
  in-flight experience at, 198, 204, 205–6, 210–11, 213, 215–16, 290n68
  marketing practices eroticizing stewardesses of, 198–99
  and 1969 agreement between Jamaica and US regarding air routes, 83–84, 273n37
  ownership of, 79, 80, 88–89
  public evaluation of debuting stewardesses, 203–8
  racism experienced by stewardesses of, 216–20
  second incarnation of (Air Jamaica [1968] Ltd.), 81–85
  sexual harassment of stewardesses at, 98, 233–40
  and stamp issued to commemorate its flight attendants, 207–8
  stewardesses' income and benefits at, 225–33
  stewardess uniform for, 140, 146, 200, 208
  See also Jamaica

Air Serbia, 253, 263n12
  See also JAT Airways
"Air Strip" Braniff Airways ad campaign, 158–60, 194
air travel. *See* aviation
Algiers, 65
American Airlines, 151
American internationalism, 31–39
Anderson Manley, Beverley, 135, 136, 199, 208–9, 212–13
Andress, Ursula, 138
Antifašistička fronta žena (Women's Anti-fascist Front) (AFŽ), 110–11, 123, 126
Ashenheim, Neville, 80–81, 84
aviation
  American predominance and standard-setting in, 10–11
  Boothe Luce on, 2, 3
  Boothe Luce's impact on, 23–24
  expansion of civil, 1–4, 9–10, 28–31
  glamorization of, in *Love and Fashion*, 173–75
  hope promoted by spread of, 4
  interest and aspirations in, 4–6
  and Jamaican economic growth, 74–75
  as venue for national prestige and autocratic corruption, 274n50

Baker, Trudy, 182
Balenciaga, Carlos, 194, 195
Bandung Conference (1955), 54
Bank of Nova Scotia, 82
Batajnica Military Base, 230–31
Bazar, 182
beauty pageants, 97, 130–31, 136, 139, 145, 182, 185, 198, 200, 201, 214
Belgrade Airport, 61–65, 166–68, 193, 269n75
Belgrade Declaration (1955), 62
Berle, Adolf, 32
Bermuda Agreement (1946), 33

INDEX

Bermuda Conference (1946), 37
bilateral aviation agreements, 32–34, 38–39, 50–53, 83–84, 265n34, 273n37
Blackburne, Sir Kenneth, 73–74, 76
Blake, Evon, 206–7
Boeing 707, 181
Boeing 727, 181
Boeing 747, 89, 218
Boeing 787, 152
Boeing Air Transport, 95
Boothe Luce, Clare
   and American internationalism, 31–39
   articulation of freedom to fly, 3, 24–25, 28, 31, 106, 170
   on desire to fly, 250–51
   embrace of cartography of colonialism, 27–31
   and expansion of civil aviation, 1–3, 14
   impact on aviation, 23–24
   as new female political model, 125
   political career of, 24–27, 126
Braniff Airways, 140, 144–46, 148–54, 157–60, 162–63
British Airways. *See* British Overseas Airways Corporation (BOAC)
British Overseas Airways Corporation (BOAC)
   air routes of, 33, 76
   competitiveness of, 33, 34
   and feminization of flight attendant corps, 96
   and founding of Air Jamaica, 77–78, 79, 80
   hiring policies of, 258n11
   and hotel development in Jamaica, 85
   war-era route-miles of, 30
British West Indies Airways (BWIA)
   and feminization of flight attendant corps, 96–97
   and founding of Air Jamaica, 79, 80
   Jamaican ministers' antagonism toward, 271n16
   and LeWars Kirkpatrick, 131, 134–35
   and opportunities for women in aviation, 6
   as unprofitable, 78
   See also Caribbean Airlines
Brown, Sir George Arthur
   achievements of, 69
   on agreement between Air Jamaica and US Civil Aeronautics Board (1966), 84
   and founding of Air Jamaica, 71, 72, 77, 78–79, 81–82, 84, 89–90
   on Jamaican economic diversification, 75
   and negotiations with IMF in 1970s, 72, 87, 88
   on OPEC oil embargo of 1973–74, 85
Bustamante, Alexander, 77, 80, 129–30, 258n15
Butlin, Billy, 133

calypso music, 203, 221
Caravelle jets, 8, 60, 63, 64, 178, 180, 181
Caribbean Airlines, 252.
   See also British West Indies Airways (BWIA)
Carter Gambrill Robinson, 211
cartography of colonialism, 14, 27–31, 38, 56, 83
Castro, Fidel, 8, 67, 70, 71, 80, 199, 209
Centrotekstil, 186, 187, 189–90
Chicago convention. *See* International Civil Aviation Conference (Chicago, 1944)
Churchill, Winston, 29
Civil Aeronautics Board (CAB), 72, 79, 80–82, 90, 91
Civil Rights Act (1964), 153
Cliff, Jimmy, 208
Coffee, Tea or Me? (Bain, Baker, and Jones), 182
Colonial Development Corporation (CDC), 73
"Come Fly with Me" (Sinatra), 143
communism, 9, 35, 36, 37, 43, 45, 54, 73–74, 100, 110–11, 171
Connery, Sean, 136–37, 138
consumer products, Yugoslavia's shift to prioritizing, 121–22
Convair-340s (CV-340s), 58–59, 66, 118–19
Cosmopolitan, 147, 155
Cox, Edward, 27–28
Crawford, Carol Joan, 129–31, 132–34, 138–39, 200, 216, 279n13
Croatia, 46–47
Cuba, 70
Cubana de Aviacion, 8
Československa Statni Aerolinie (Czechoslovak Airlines) (ČSA), 8, 45, 169, 263n13

INDEX

Daily Express, 133
Davis, Marne, 144–45
DC-3, 44, 45, 46, 50, 51, 58, 234, 259n18, 263n13
DC-6, 60–61, 63, 64, 65, 173, 174
DC-7, 152, 281n20
DC-8, 81–82
DC-9, 81–82
Defrenne, Gabrielle, 184, 246
de Havilland Comet, 7
de Roulet, Vincent, 199
Deutsche Luft Hansa. *See* Lufthansa
Diener, Nellie, 274n2
Dr. No (1962), 97, 136–38, 180, 201, 203
drug smuggling, 232–33
Dulles, John Foster, 58–59
d'Unienville, Alix, 96, 99, 100–106, 116, 125–26
  See also *En vol: Journal d'une hôtesse de l'air* (*In Flight: Journal of an Air Hostess*) (d'Unienville)

Egypt, 54, 55, 109, 125, 267n49
Energoprojekt, 168
Engel, Jeffrey, 274n50
En vol: Journal d'une hôtesse de l'air (*In Flight: Journal of an Air Hostess*) (d'Unienville), 101–3, 104, 106, 127–28
European Court of Justice (ECJ), 184, 246
Export-Import Bank, 58–59

fashion
  and Air Jamaica uniforms, 140, 146, 200, 208
  and Braniff Airways uniforms, 144–46, 148–49
  emphasis on, in Yugoslavia, 121–22
  and JAT Airways uniforms, 185–93, 194–95
  and sexual allure of stewardesses, 193–94, 205–6
fashion shows, on Air Jamaica flights, 198, 205–6, 213, 215–16, 290n68
Feminine Mystique, The (Friedan), 147, 152–53
feminism
  intersection of aviation and, 23–25
  neoliberal, 255
  Second Wave, 147, 152–57, 164–65, 195, 247
  See also Jet Age feminism

Five-Year-Plan (Yugoslavia, 1948), 47–48, 49, 63, 107, 264n25
Fleming, Ian, 136, 137.
  See also *Dr. No* (1962)
Fletcher, Walter, 271n15
flight attendants
  Braniff's training of, 154
  and childcare, 242–46, 255
  difficulties maintaining families, 240–46
  earliest Yugoslav visions for, 112, 114–18, 123–24, 127
  feminization of corps after WWII, 95–100
  lack of promotion opportunities for, 162, 233 (*see also* pursers)
  and marriage, 5, 98, 116–17, 123, 160–61, 163–64, 240–42, 246
  and motherhood, 242–46, 255
  as objects of infatuation, 176–77
  and opportunities for women in aviation, 161–62
  and pink-collar labor, 98, 106, 113–14, 162, 275n4
  restrictions imposed on, 97–99, 102–4, 113, 127, 153–54, 165, 183–85, 200–201, 214–15, 246
  salaries for, 225–33, 248
  as sole niche for women in aviation, 100
  use of per diems, 228–30
  and vacation benefits, 227–28
  and Yugoslav sexual revolution, 171
  See also d'Unienville, Alix; LeWars Kirkpatrick, Marguerite; Pavlović, Dragica
Frankel, Joseph, 115
Fraser, Nancy, 255, 256
freedom to fly, 3, 24–25, 28, 31, 106, 170
Friedan, Betty, 13, 146–47, 152–53, 164, 195

Girard, Alexander, 145, 146
Glavna uprava civilnog vazdušnog saobraćaja (Main Authority for Civil Air Transport) (GUCVS), 42, 43, 47, 50, 51, 263n6
Gleaner, 69, 130, 132–34, 202–3
globalization/globalism, 15, 28–29
Global South
  importance to Yugoslav aviation, 64–65
  Yugoslav exports to, 297n61
  Yugoslavia's ties with, 53–57, 60, 109–10

glocalization, 10–13
"grandiose exotic," 187, 188, 189, 194, 195
Gurley Brown, Helen, 147, 151, 154–55, 162, 220, 233, 242, 256

Harder They Come, The (1972), 208–9
Hartvedt, Nan, 103, 104
Hearne, John, 212
Henzell, Perry, 208
Hepburn, Audrey, 156
¡*Hola!* 133
"Hostess College," 154
Hotel (Incentives) Act (Jamaica, 1968), 85
Hotel Aid Law (Jamaica, 1944), 75–76
hotel development, in Jamaica, 75–76, 78, 85, 86, 88, 271n15

Ilustrovana politika, 181–85
Immerwahr, Daniel, 2, 10–11, 30
Imperial Airways. *See* British Overseas Airways Corporation (BOAC)
Industrial Disputes Tribunal (IDT), 215–16, 232
Intercontinental Hotels. *See* Pan American Airways (Pan Am)
International Air Transport Association (IATA), 43
International Civil Aviation Conference (Chicago, 1944)
  and bilateral aviation agreements, 32–34, 38–39, 50–53, 83–84, 265n34, 273n37
  and reciprocity as principle in bilateral agreements, 33, 38–39, 44, 47
  and Treaty, 32, 34, 36–37, 43, 45, 47, 57, 59, 263n9
International Civil Aviation Organization (ICAO), 32, 43, 46, 263n9
International Monetary Fund (IMF), 52, 72, 87–88, 90, 248, 252, 253
Isaacs, Willis, 75
Issa, Abe, 78

Jack Tinker and Partners, 162
Jamaica
  and drug trade, 232–33
  early civil aviation in, 5–6
  economic conditions in 1950s and early 1960s, 73–75, 76, 288n2
  economic conditions in late 1960s and 1970s, 72–76, 225
  hotel development in, 75–76, 78, 85, 86, 88, 271n15
  IMF-imposed austerity programs for, 248
  independence of, 68–69, 72–73, 129, 258n15
  maternity and maternity leave in, 209, 227, 242, 243, 254
  national heroes and nation-building in, 129, 278n1
  1969 bilateral air agreement between US and, 83–84
  Pan Am service to, 35–36, 69, 74, 75, 76, 89, 252
  positioning in world politics, 14–15, 35, 37, 38
  poverty abatement efforts in, 73–74, 76, 91
  racial norms in, 129–40, 208–14
  riots motivated by race and economic deprivation in, 199, 216–17
  stewardesses in, 98, 99
  tourism in, 74–75, 84–89, 90, 132, 200, 209–10, 271n13
  See also Air Jamaica
Jamaicanization, 270n8
Jamaica Post Office, 207–8
Jamaica Tourist Board (JTB), 132, 200
Japan Air Lines, 194, 262n24
JAT Airways
  and adoption of Western consumer standards, 57–61
  Adria Airways' relationship with, 268n66
  aircraft employed by, 263n13
  Belgrade and Adriatic Coast as hubs for, 61–65
  connectedness to the Western aviation system, 11
  employment policies affecting stewardesses, 114–15, 183–85, 224, 225–33
  expansion of, 9
  financial difficulties of, 58–59, 252–53, 269n74
  first jets purchased by, 8, 60, 63, 64, 178, 180, 181, 259n18
  flight attendants as public relations tools for, 118–21, 127
  founding of, 42, 44–45
  hiring criteria for first flight attendants, 96, 112–13, 181–83, 184
  hiring policies of, 276n17
  housing benefits for employees of, 227
  link between Aeroput and, 263n12

INDEX 307

link between JUSTA and, 45, 48–50, 113
new uniforms for flight attendants of, 115, 146, 168, 185–93, 194–95
rebranded as Air Serbia, 253
recruitment of flight attendants for, 111–14, 181–83, 184
sexualization of stewardesses in 1960s and 1970s, 176–85
stewardess cameos in *Love and Fashion*, 173, 174–75
stewardesses' negotiation of glocalization, 13
and stewardesses' sexual risks of Jet Age feminism, 233–40
stewardess roles as akin to *domaćica* (housewife/hostess), 114, 116, 117, 124
ties to Global South, 9, 56, 58, 61, 63, 120, 125, 267
and Tito-Stalin split, 48–51, 107–8
Western orientation of, 45–46, 48, 50, 53
and Yugoslav sexual revolution, 171
See also Pavlović, Dragica; Yugoslavia
Jet Age feminism
and "Air Strip" marketing ploy, 157–60
as articulated by Gurley Brown and *Sex and the Single Girl*, 147, 154–55, 162, 233
and changes to stewardess uniforms, 115, 140, 146, 148–49, 168, 185–93, 194–95, 200, 208
as contrasted with Second Wave feminism, 152–57
defined, 13, 18–20, 144–47
as influenced by social class, 160–64, 223–24
as influenced by the aesthetics of Emilio Pucci and Alexander Girard, 149–52
stewardesses' sexual harassment and abuse as a consequence of, 233–40
stewardesses' struggles regarding, 223–24
Joksimović, Aleksandar, 146, 185–93, 194–95
Jugoslovensko-sovjetsko akcionarsko društvo za civilno vazduhoplovstvo (Yugoslav-Soviet Joint Stock Company for Civil Aviation) (JUSTA), 42–44, 45, 48–50, 113, 263n7, 264n25
Junkers Ju-52, 263n13

Kapo, 211–12
Kardelj, Edvard, 49, 55
Ketchum, MacLeod, and Grove, 198, 200, 203–4, 211
Khrushchev, Nikita, 62, 259n18
Koninklijke Luchtvaart Maatschappij voor Nederland en Koloniën (Royal Dutch Airlines) (KLM), 31, 36, 46–47, 63, 96, 274n2

Lawrence, Harding, 145, 149–50, 157, 159, 160–61, 163
LeWars, Barbara, 134–35
LeWars, Gloria, 135–36
LeWars Kirkpatrick, Marguerite
 background of, 134
 birthdate of, 279n13
 career of, 96–97, 131, 139–40
 comparison between Crawford and, 138–39
 and design of Air Jamaica's stewardess uniforms (1969), 146
 as "Face of Jamaica," 200
 and hiring of Air Jamaica stewardesses, 201
 Ketchum's work with, 203–4
 promoted to head stewardess, 197–98
 role as actress in *Dr. No*, 136–38
 and training of Air Jamaica stewardesses, 6
Lewis, Cleve, 81, 201–2
Libya, 55, 65, 169, 252
Lindbergh, Charles, 7, 35
Lončar, Beba, 172–73, 196
Love and Fashion (1960), 172–75, 176, 177, 196
Luce, Henry, 25–26, 27, 160
Lufthansa, 266n38
Lukić, Milica, 177, 234

Machado, Guillermo, 202
Maghreb, 64–65
Main Authority for Civil Air Transport. *See* Glavna uprava civilnog vazdušnog saobraćaja (Main Authority for Civil Air Transport) (GUCVS)
Manley, Beverley Anderson, 135, 136, 199
Manley, Michael, 71, 86, 87–88, 135, 199, 208, 209, 243
Manley, Norman, 68–69, 72–73, 74, 76, 77, 129, 258n15
Manley, Sarah, 135–36
Marjanović, Đorđe, 175–76

INDEX

Marković, Predrag, 109, 121–22, 171, 260n23
Marx, Karl, 284n35
Mitrović, Milenko, 41–42, 107, 259n19

Nasser, Gamal Abdel, 54, 62, 125, 128
National Liberation Front (Yugoslavia), 110, 125–26
National Organization for Women (NOW), 153, 164
Nehru, Jawaharlal, 54, 120, 127
neoliberalism, 248, 254–56
Non-Aligned Movement (NAM), 54–55, 60
Novak, Gabi, 174

OPEC oil embargo (1973–74), 84–89, 90
Otašević, Ljubica, 175, 196

Palisadoes Airport, 76
Pan American Airways (Pan Am)
 air routes of, 7, 76
 and development of Intercontinental Hotels in Jamaica, 75–76, 85, 271n15
 expansion of, 31
 and feminization of flight attendant corps, 95
 hiring policies of, 6
 marketing of, 34
 on OPEC oil embargo of 1973–74, 89
 and opposition to launch of Air Jamaica, 77–78, 79–80, 90, 91
 pre-World War II route coverage of, 30
 role in bilateral aviation agreements, 32–33, 52–53
 service to Jamaica, 35–36, 69, 74, 75, 76, 89, 252
 West German routes of, 266n38
Partisans, 110, 115
partizanke (female Partisans), 99, 110, 114, 115, 124, 125–26
Patterson, P. J., 86–87
Pavlović, Dragica, 107–10, 114–18, 123–24, 127, 185
Pegasus Hotel, 85
Petar II, King of Yugoslavia, 40
Petrović, Miodrag, 174
pink-collar labor, 98, 106, 113–14, 162, 275n4
pointillist empire, 30, 35
post colonialism, 208–14

Praktična žena (Practical woman), 122–25, 127–28, 171, 186
protectionism, 32, 71, 91
Pucci, Emilio, 140, 145, 148–49, 151, 155–57, 186, 188, 192
Pudarić, Zdravko, 46–47, 50, 63, 111–12, 264n15
pursers, 96, 98, 206, 233

race
 and controversy in Jamaican beauty contests, 130, 131, 136, 182, 198, 200, 201, 279n8
 and controversy involving hiring of Air Jamaica's first flight attendants, 201–3
 and Crawford's winning of Miss World, 130, 131, 133
 and its corresponding complications faced by Air Jamaica flight attendants, 129–40, 216–20
 and LeWars Kirkpatrick's role in *Dr. No* and as "Face of Jamaica," 136–38, 200
 and restrictions on types of aviation work undertaken, 134–35
 and riots in Jamaica, 199, 216–17
Rankin, Jeannette, 26
Reagan, Ronald, 71
reciprocity rights in bilateral aviation treaties, 33, 38–39, 44, 47
reproductive care and rights, 171, 243
Rodney, Walter, 199, 216–17
Roosevelt, Franklin D., 32
Roosevelt, Theodore, 70, 270n6
Rosie the Riveter, 125, 126
Rowe, Rochelle, 279n8, 279n22

Sabena Airways, 184, 246
Sandberg, Sheryl, 255, 256
Sangster, Donald, 81
Scandinavian Airlines System (SAS), 98, 103, 104
Second Wave feminism, 147, 152–57, 164–65, 195, 247
Sex and the Single Girl (Brown), 147, 154–55, 162, 233
sexism (gender-based discrimination) in the workplace
 faced by Air Jamaica stewardesses on the job, 214–16, 224
 faced by JAT stewardesses on the job, 117–18

and hiring restrictions imposed on stewardesses, 97–99, 102–4, 113, 127, 153–54
and limited career opportunities for women in aviation, 161–62
and Second Wave feminists' early activism, 164–65
and Wells Lawrence's work for Braniff, 164
sexual harassment, 98, 161–62, 206, 222, 233–40, 247–48
Shearer, Hugh, 83, 85, 88, 270n8
Sinatra, Frank, 143
"single girl," 147, 155, 158.
See also *Sex and the Single Girl* (Brown)
SkyWritings, 211–14
slavery, 68
Stalin, Joseph, 43–44, 48–51, 55–56, 107–8
Steinem, Gloria, 161
stewardesses. See flight attendants
Stewardesses for Women's Rights (SFWR), 164
stewards. See flight attendants
Stewart, Gordon "Butch," 252
"Stjuardesa" (Marjanović), 175–76
Subotom uveče (*Saturday Evening*) (1957), 171
Swissair, 51, 96, 274n2
Switzerland, 35, 51–52, 53, 56, 59, 118, 169, 244
Syria, 123

Tito, Josip Broz
 ascent to power in 1945, 40–41
 at Belgrade Airport ribbon cutting (1963), 167
 and early post–World War II cooperation with Soviets, 43
 economic and political developments under, 168
 in JAT Airways brochure, 120, 121
 and Non-Aligned Movement, 9, 54
 on *partizanke* and gender equality, 110
 relationships with Nehru and Nasser, 54
 and relations with USSR, 62
 split with Stalin (1948), 48–51, 55–56, 107–8
 vision for civil aviation before 1948, 43–44, 45, 48
 and Yugoslavia's economic ties with Global South, 55–56, 60, 109–10

Tito, Jovanka Broz, 228
tourism
 decline in Jamaican, 209–10
 and Jamaican economic growth, 74–75, 271n13
 OPEC oil embargo and Jamaican, 84–89, 90
 promotion of Jamaican, 200
 and Pudarić's plan to tie Yugoslavia to West, 46–47
transatlantic route competitions, 34–35
Trans World Airlines (TWA), 31, 83, 163
treaties. See bilateral aviation agreements; International Civil Aviation Conference (Chicago, 1944), and Treaty
Trippe, Juan, 25, 271n15
Truman, Harry, 32
Tupolev-114, 63–64
Turner, Melvin, 41, 50

uniforms
 for Air Jamaica's flight attendants, 140, 146, 198, 200, 208
 and "Air Strip," 157–60
 for Braniff Airways flight attendants, 144–46, 148–49
 designs for Western legacy carriers, 194
 for JAT Airways flight attendants, 115, 168, 188–93, 194–95
United Airlines. See Boeing Air Transport
United States
 Caribbean states' foreign policy alignment with, 70–71
 d'Unienville on treatment of women in, 102
 and failure of Air Jamaica, 91
 and feminization of flight attendant corps, 95–96
 leading role of, in aviation's cartography of colonialism, 1–3, 10–11, 14, 27–39
 1969 bilateral agreement between Jamaica and, 83–84
 as point of origin for Jet Age feminism, 13, 143–47
 and poverty abatement in Jamaica, 73–74, 76
 and Yugoslav connections to West, 265n34
 Yugoslavia opens bilateral air negotiations with, 51, 52–53
 Yugoslavia purchases CV-340s from, 58–59

U Nu, 120, 127
Urban Development Corporation (UDC), 85, 86
USSR, Yugoslav relations with, 35, 42–46, 48–51, 56, 62–63, 259n18

Wallace, Henry, 28–29, 31–32
Wells Lawrence, Mary, 140, 145–46, 149–50, 152, 158–64, 242, 256
Wells Rich Greene, 162, 163
West Germany, 52, 266n38
West Indies Federation, 77, 258n15
Wideroe, Turi, 98
Wilson, Christa, 215–16
"Windrush generation," 221
Wirtschaftswunder (economic miracle), 97
Women, The (film, 1939), 24–25
Women, The (play, Boothe Luce), 24
Women's Anti-fascist Front. *See* Antifašistička fronta žena (Women's Anti-fascist Front) (AFŽ)
Workers' Council(s), 115–16, 188, 195, 224, 277n24
World War II
 and Boothe Luce's political career, 25–27
 d'Unienville's espionage activities during, 104–5, 106, 126
 impact on Yugoslavia, 40–41
 role in helping expansion of civil aviation, 28–31
 Yugoslav women's contributions in, 110

Yugoslav Communist Party, 50
"Yugoslav dream," 57–61, 66
Yugoslavia
 bilateral negotiations with Western states (1948–50), 50–53, 265n34
 change in production goals in mid-1950s, 121
 childcare in, 242–44
 cultural tensions facing women in 1950s, 114–18
 dependence on West, 45–46, 48, 50, 53, 169
 development of modern aviation system in, 65–67
 disintegration of, 253
 economy of, 59–60, 168–70, 288n2
 evolution of foreign affairs and aviation sector, 120
 exports to Global South, 297n61
 Five-Year-Plan of 1948, 47–48, 49, 63, 107, 264n25
 forges economic ties with decolonizing states in Global South, 53–57, 60, 109–10
 formula for economic development in 1940s and early 1950s, 53–54
 gender equality in, 110–11, 126, 241
 IMF-imposed austerity programs for, 248
 infrastructural shortcomings in aviation systems of, 41, 48
 as "in-between" state in Cold War, 14–15, 260n23
 opposition to West's cartography of colonialism, 38
 oversight of regions of, 262n1
 prewar international aviation service to, 36
 sexual revolution in, 170–76
 Soviet relations with, 35, 42–46, 48–51, 56, 62–63, 259n18
 World War II's impact on, 40–41
 See also JAT Airways

Zapisi stjuardese (Recollections of a Stewardess) (Lukić), 177
Žarković, Petar, 62

www.ingramcontent.com/pod-product-compliance
Lightning Source LLC
Chambersburg PA
CBHW030522230426
43665CB00010B/730